ROOTS of the NE

ROOTS OF THE NEW ARAB FILM

Roy Armes

Indiana University Press

This book is a publication of

Indiana University Press
Office of Scholarly Publishing
Herman B Wells Library 350
1320 East 10th Street
Bloomington, Indiana 47405 USA

iupress.indiana.edu

The paper used in this publication meets the minimum
requirements of the American National Standard for Information
Sciences—Permanence of Paper for Printed Library Materials, ANSI
Z39.48-1992.

Manufactured in the United States of America

Library of Congress Cataloging-in-Publication Data

Names: Armes, Roy, author.
Title: Roots of the new Arab film / Roy Armes.
Description: Bloomington, Indiana, USA : Indiana University Press,
    2018. | Includes bibliographical references and index.
Identifiers: LCCN 2017046670| ISBN 9780253034182 (cloth :
    alk. paper) | ISBN 9780253031723 (pbk. : alk. paper)
Subjects: LCSH: Motion picture producers and directors—Arab
    countries. | Motion pictures—Arab countries. | Motion pictures,
    Arab—France.
Classification: LCC PN1993.5.A65 A77 2018 | DDC 791.430917/4927—
    dc23 LC record available at https://lccn.loc.gov/2017046670

1 2 3 4 5   23 22 21 20 19 18

To Annie

Genres—such as the novel, the short story, drama and framed painting—emerged in Arabic culture in the twentieth century as a result of a comprehensive process of change and cultural modernisation that occupied most of the nineteenth century. . . . As soon as the process of modernity took root in the culture and started to yield its fruits, most of the Arab countries fell under the yoke of colonialism and the struggle for independence became inseparable from the quest for national identity. The literary and artistic elaboration of this identity was a vital element in the process of national transition.

—Sabry Hafez

Contents

Acknowledgments

I GUESS I OWE a lot to my sister. Thanks to her, I saw my first film in 1943, when I was just six and she fourteen. Somehow she managed to sneak me into a back-street cinema in Norwich for the rerun of Alexander Korda's imperial epic, *The Four Feathers*. The significance of the plot, Harry Faversham redeeming himself by "doing the right thing," was beyond me, but the colors were wonderful and the Sudanese landscape was like nothing I'd ever imagined. But when it came to the scene where a gallant British officer is blinded by vicious Arab "fuzzy wuzz-ies" (as they are called in the film) who hold a red-hot sword in front of his eyes, I apparently screamed inconsolably and had to be carried, kicking and struggling, out of the cinema. Life being what it is, I suppose it was inevitable that, from that moment on, I would be fascinated by film, spend my entire adult career working as a film historian, and find myself, at the age of eighty, publishing a three-volume study of contemporary Arab filmmaking. Proving, as always, the superiority of novelists over mere critics, Michael Ondaatje reveals that, as a child, he too saw the same film and also had to be dragged from the cinema. But in his case, it was only after the ending credits—he wanted more.[1]

On a more serious note, many people have helped me with the compilation of this book, and I thank those, among them festival organizers and film distributors, who have guided me to new sources of material: Masoud Amralla Al Ali of the Gulf Film Festival, Catherine Arnaud, Marie-Claude Behna of the Association de Cinéma Arabe, Stéphanie Boring of Les Films d'ici, Mona Deeley of Zenith Films, Nick Denes of the Palestinian Film Foundation, Christian Eid of Abbout Productions, Alberto Elena of the Carlos III University in Madrid, Haithem El-Zabri of the Palestine Online Store, Yael Friedman, May Hossam of Misr International Films, Yara Jäkel of Dschoint Ventschr, Tarik Khalami of the Centre Cinématographique Marocain, Thierry Lenouvel of Ciné-Sud Promotion, Nicole Mackey of Fortissimo Films, Diran Mardirian of Video Chico in Beirut, Egil Odegard of the Norwegian Film Institute, Lucy Parker, Anne-Cécile Pavaux of 3B Productions, Eliane Raheb of the Beirut Film Festival, Michel Riachi of Nadilekolnass in Beirut, John Sinno of Typecast Films in Seattle, Annabel Thomas, and Abdellah Zerguine of Regard Sud.

I am especially grateful to those filmmakers who helped provide access to DVD copies of their own films: Daoud Aoulad-Syad, Asma El Bakry, Jean-Claude Codsi, Najri Hajjaj, Nizar Hassan, Kassem Hawal, Abdelkader Lagtaâ, Moez Kamoun, Mohamad Malas, Najwa Najjar, Yousry Nasrallah, Ghassan Salhab, Samir, Moumen Smihi, Heiny Srour, and Mohamed Zran.

I must thank most warmly Dee Mortensen, my editor at Indiana University Press, for commissioning this, the sixth successive book of the series on African and Arab cinemas, and all the staff at the press for the care with which they have produced this volume.

Last, but by no means least, I must thank the Leverhulme Trust for the further emeritus fellowship, which has helped fund the research for this volume and its predecessor.

Note

1. Anthony Minghella, *The English Patient* (London: Methuen, 1997), vii.

Abbreviations

ACCT	Agence de Coopération Culturelle et Technique (France)
AFAC	Arab Fund for Arts and Culture
AIF	Agence Intergouvernementale de la Francophonie (France)
ALBA	Académie Libanaise des Beaux Arts (Lebanon)
ALN	Armée de Libération Nationale / National Liberation Army (Algeria)
ANAF	Agence Nationale des Actualités Filmées (Algeria)
CAAIC	Centre Algérien pour l'Art et Industrie Cinématographiques (Algeria)
CAV	Centre Audio-Visuel (Algeria)
CBA	Centre Bruxellois de l'Audiovisuel (Belgium)
CCM	Centre Cinématographique Marocain (Morocco)
CNC	Centre National Cinématographique (France)
CNCA	Centre National du Cinéma Algérien (Algeria)
CNSAD	Conservatoire National Supérieur d'Art Dramatique
DAMS	Départment d'Art, de Musique et du Spectacle (part of the University of Bologna, Italy)
ENADEC	Entreprise Nationale de Distribution et d'Exploitation Cinématographiques (Algeria)
ENAPROC	Entreprise Nationale de Production Cinématographique (Algeria)
ENPA	Entreprise Nationale de Productions Audiovisuelles (Algeria)
ESAD	École Supérieure d'Art Dramatique (part of the University of Geneva, Switzerland)
ESEC	École Supérieure des Études Cinématographiques
FAMU	Filmov Akademie Múzickych Umeni (Czechoslovakia)
FAS	Fonds d'Action Sociale (France)
FED	Fonds Européen de Développement (Brussels, Belgium)
FEMIS	Fondation Européenne des Métiers de l'Image et du Son (France)

FEPACI	Fédération Panafricain des Cinéastes (Burkina Faso)
FESPACO	Festival Panafricain du Cinéma de Ougadougou (Burkina Faso)
FNL	Front National de Libération / National Liberation Front (Algeria)
FTCA	Fédération Tunisiennes des Cinéastes Amateurs (Tunisia)
GPRA	Algerian Republican Provisional Government (Algeria)
IDHEC	Institut des Hautes Études Cinématographiques (France)
IESAV	Institut d'Etudes Scéniques et Audiovisuelles (part of the Université Saint-Joseph in Beirut, Lebanaon)
IFC	Institut Français du Cinéma
IKON	Interkerkelijke Omroep Nederland (Netherlands)
INC	Institut National du Cinéma d'Algers (Algeria)
INSAS	Institut National des Arts et du Spectacle et Techniques de Diffusion (Belgium)
JCC	Journées Cinématographiques de Carthage (Tunisia)
MAF	Ministry of Foreign Affairs
OAA	Office des Actualités Algériennes (Algeria)
OIF	Organisation Internationale de la Francophonie (France)
ONCIC	Office National du Commerce et de l'Industrie Cinématographiques (Algeria)
ONPS	National Office for Social Protection
RTA	Radiodiffusion Télévision Algérienne (Algeria)
RTBF	Radio-Télévision Belge de la Communauté Française (Belgium)
RTM	Radio Télévision Marocaine (Morocco)
SATPEC	Société Anonyme Tunisienne de Production et d'Expansion Cinématographiques (Tunisia)
USJ	Université Saint Joseph (Beirut, Lebanon)
ZDF	Zweites Deutsches Fernsehen (Germany)
ZSP	Zone de Solidarité Prioritaire (France)

Introduction

THIS BOOK IS a personal journey through aspects of contemporary Arab film-making that deal with feature-length documentary films and fictional features, with a particular focus on those filmmakers who emerged in the 1980s and 1990s. It avoids the newcomers to Arab filmmaking in the 2000s, who have been dealt with in a separate study.[1] It also ignores the continuing commercial force of the Egyptian film industry, which still operates, with great success, in traditional ways. Only a couple of Egyptian filmmakers who have turned away from the mainstream and funded their work largely from sources abroad—particularly from the various French government support programmes—are considered here. Egyptian cinema as a whole calls for (and has received) quite separate studies.

The main focus here was intended to be on contemporary filmmaking in seven other leading filmmaking countries of the Arab world, three in the Maghreb—Algeria, Morocco, and Tunisia—and four in the Middle East—Lebanon, Palestine, Iraq, and Syria—alongside the work of the handful of Egyptian independents and the filmmakers of the *beur* community based in France. In any event, it has proved impossible to access enough Syrian film productions for me personally to assess the films produced there, apart from the work of Mohamad Malas and Omar Amiralay. The sheer quantity of films produced by filmmakers of Maghrebian origin working in France means that their work is merely touched on here. There are other significant gaps, too, so I have included—where possible—brief outlines of developments, largely names and dates, together with quotations from filmmakers and those who have been able to survey these fascinating (and unique) aspects of contemporary Arab filmmaking.

I am not an Arabic speaker, so the films dealt with in detail here are, by necessity, those that have been subtitled for possible international festival screenings and eventual foreign distribution or DVD sale. They are, that is to say, aimed at an audience located at least in part outside the immediate Arab world, and this book is a response to that situation. Though my insights have been deepened by visits to various film festivals, the bulk of my research has been carried out by viewing subtitled VHS and DVD copies of those films made available—either through commercial distribution or by the filmmakers themselves—in these formats.

This limitation in fact defines precisely the body of work that I wish to examine here: Arab films with an international definition in terms of both their total or partial funding and their intended audience. In effect, what we are concerned with here is, to a large extent, a kind of art house Arab cinema, designed to please international festivalgoers and foreign audiences, as well as European funding organizations and (for documentaries) global television corporations and NGOs, as much as local Arab viewers, whose potential access to these films through conventional Arab distribution circuits will most likely be very limited.

My assumption is that most readers of this book will view the films as DVDs under similar limitations: watched privately at home or projected, often in digital format, at an Arab film festival or in a college classroom. This leaves me with two questions, posed by Brian T. Edwards, to which I have no immediate reply. What is a feature film when "those who will view feature film length films in the darkened social space of the cinema, with its implications on creating a public, must be counted in the minority"? And are we "watching a film," when we view it "on YouTube, or on digitally pirated copies purchased off the street, or on a laptop computer in a train, on a plane, or lying in bed"?[2]

To track the development of cinema in the Arab world is, in many ways, to trace Arab confrontation with Western modernity in the twentieth century and beyond. As Samir Kassir remarks: "Of all the arts, the cinema best illustrates the Arabs' embrace of modernity. Once again, Egypt was the driving force, accounting for three-quarters—maybe more—of Arab film production. Its success, and the demand for its films throughout the Arab world, made it a transnational Arab phenomenon."[3] Though this study traces the careers of its chosen filmmakers up to and after the Arab Spring, it leaves out the developments after 2000 initiated by the generation born post-1960, whose work constitutes a further, quite distinct phase (which I have considered elsewhere).[4] This volume deals with two of four overlapping prior stages of development.

The first stage is the introduction of cinema to the Arab world, long before independence, at a time when Arabs in North Africa lived under European colonial rule, when Egypt's independence was largely notional, and when Arabs in the Middle East were subjects of the still-unified Ottoman Empire. In the silent era, a key contribution to film production was made by members of the expatriate community in Egypt. But there are also highly personal efforts by a handful of other Arab pioneers whose work will be considered briefly here.

The second stage is the immediate postindependence era, during which the roots of contemporary Arab cinema can be found. Here, all the key elements have initially, but in very distinctive ways, a national dimension. This stage was heralded by the increasing importance, from the 1930s onward, of the Egyptian commercial film industry, which, as Viola Shafik notes, "developed alongside and in correlation with the nation's endeavours to achieve independence, and was involved in crucial social, political, and economic changes and challenges."[5] The Egyptian option was subsequently, if only briefly followed by several Middle Eastern countries, most notably Lebanon. Much later, in other parts of the Arab world (particularly in Algeria and Palestine), film found a different and contrasting definition, playing its part in the national liberation struggle.

A further and quite distinct way in which film became involved in the notion of the national after independence was with the creation, in the 1950s and 1960s, of state organizations set up to develop film production, usually deriving funding from taxes on admissions to cinemas (where the programming consisted largely of imported films). These organizations had very different functions. In the Maghreb, which, like many parts of sub-Saharan West Africa, continued to bear the marks and influence of French colonization, the model adopted was that of the CNC (Centre National Cinématographie) in Paris. In Morocco and Tunisia in the late 1950s, the impulse behind government involvement in filmmaking was largely cultural, even if the state structured the market and provided some funding. Very different was the creation of a state film monopoly in Algeria, which occurred two years after the military coup carried out by Houari Boumedienne on June 19, 1965. Bizarrely, this political action coincided with the location filming in the capital of *The Battle of Algiers*, and, as Benjamin Stora notes, many passersby imagined they were watching the shooting of Gillo Pontecorvo's film, which won the Golden Lion at the Venice Film Festival the following year.[6] From the start, the new Algerian film organization had clear state propaganda aims and objectives.

A few years earlier, in Egypt, the creation of the General Organisation of Egyptian Cinema had reflected, though less directly, President Gamal Nasser's distinctive socialist program for the whole Egyptian economy. In Iraq and Syria, the setting up of state film organizations in the mid-1960s followed directly from military coups organized by the Ba'ath Party, which established the long-lasting dictatorships of Saddam Hussein and Hafiz al-Assad. In both Iraq and Syria, the propaganda functions for cinema were much less precisely defined than in either Algeria or Egypt, but there were considerable censorship restraints.

The third stage in this historical development—the one with which we are mainly concerned here—is the creation of new, contemporary Arab cinemas from the 1970s and 1980s onward. These cinemas have a different and more distant relationship with the state. As a result, there is a discernible shift in the style and subject matter of Arab films from the state productions of the 1970s to the independently funded works that began to emerge in this period. Some of the older generation successfully negotiated the change from state-funded production to independent filmmaking, but a new generation of filmmakers emerged, as well. These men and women were mostly born in the 1940s and 1950s and had lived through the transition from colonialism to independence, either as children or as adolescents. Their work can therefore be characterized as postcolonial, and much of it is initially concerned with issues related to the shaping of the newly independent nation. Thanks to their access to foreign funding, their approach to their subjects is marked by a freedom impossible to obtain within a state-controlled production system.

Television's expansion throughout the Arab world has also had an important role to play. The role of the Egyptian film industry as the traditional prime purveyor of fantasy and fictional tales to Arab audiences has been undermined by the intrusion of Hollywood, bringing quite different realities and imaginings. But this shift has not seriously challenged Cairo's preeminence, as Viola Shafik notes: "Despite increasing competition in the Arab market and an evident diversification of products and services in the Arab media industry—Syria excelling in high-quality television serials and Lebanon in producing music clips and advertisements, and Dubai running an up-to-date, efficient, and unbureaucratic media city—Egypt still hosts the major entertainment industry in the Middle East."[7]

Kai Hafez has shown that the mass media in the Arab world and the Middle East have undergone further profound changes since the beginning of the 1990s: "The introduction and spread of new technologies such as satellite television and the Internet have extended media spaces beyond the local, national, and regional realm."[8] He argues, too, that "the media from outside the Middle East are not as appealing to the consumers and societies of the Middle East or as socially mobilizing as one might suppose" and doubts whether "the old and the new media of the Middle East will be as politically and culturally liberalizing in the age of globalized media spaces."[9] At the time of writing, this negative view is being challenged, as we contemplate the ambiguous aftermath of the upheavals associated with the Arab Spring that have swept through virtually the whole Arab world.

In one sense, the freedom from direct state intervention and access to overseas funding made the filmmakers of the 1980s and 1990s subject to new international pressures. The impact of global television's insatiable demand for programming has been crucial. Much of the momentum for the move toward internationalization in Arab cinema stems from the growing willingness of European television channels from the late 1970s onward to fund, first, documentary filmmaking and, later, feature film production in the Arab world. Western sponsors allowed the establishment of an Arab documentary tradition and gave filmmakers a freedom often denied them by their own autocratic regimes. But, in return, these Arab filmmakers had to shape their material to a greater or lesser extent to meet the demands of the foreign television channels and their European or US audiences. This process led to some very productive creative tensions. As this study shows conclusively, filmmakers have been able to bring an intelligence shaped partly by foreign education and training to bear on the problems of their countries of origin and to offer real and original insights based on their unique insider/outsider statuses.

As far as feature film production is concerned, the 1980s also saw the development of a whole range of new European funding structures, organized by both governments and charitable foundations, to support filmmaking in less developed countries across the world—"films from the South," in the conventional terminology. The most relevant of these schemes, as far as Arab filmmaking in the 1980s and 1990s was concerned, was the French Fonds Sud Cinéma, which, since its inception in 1984, has contributed to the funding of perhaps two hundred films by 150 or more Arab filmmakers. Indeed, an absolutely crucial role in the shifting definition of what constitutes "an Arab film'" has been played by French government policies. In France itself, the indigenous film aid program encouraged low-budget feature film production, and the mid-1980s saw the emergence of a distinctive body of films dealing with issues within the immigrant community made by resident filmmakers in France but who were of Algerian origin (the so-called *beurs*). Similarly, France's overseas aid programs offered new possibilities of production funding for feature filmmaking in all parts of the world. In particular, they offered to Arab filmmakers key support with regard to the costs involved in distribution and festival screenings and, much later, the transfer of digitally shot material to 35mm.

Notes

1. Roy Armes, *New Voices in Arab Cinema* (Bloomington: Indiana University Press, 2015).
2. Brian T. Edwards, "*Marock* in Morocco: Reading Moroccan Films in the Age of Circulation," in *North African Cinema in a Global Context*, edited by Andrea Khalil (New York: Routledge, 2008), 16.
3. Samir Kassir, *Being Arab* (London: Verso, 2006), 60.
4. See Armes, *New Voices in Arab Cinema*.
5. Viola Shafik, *Popular Egyptian Cinema: Gender, Class and Nation* (Cairo: American University of Cairo Press, 2007), 4.
6. Bernard Stora, *Histoire de l'Algérie depuis l'indépendance* (Paris: Éditions La Découverte, 1994), 27.
7. Shafik, *Popular Egyptian Cinema*, 4.
8. Kai Hafez, "Mass Media in the Middle East: Patterns of Social and Political Change," in *Arab Society and Culture,* edited by Samir Khalf and Roeanne Saad Khalf (London: Saqi, 2009), 452.
9. Ibid., 453.

ROOTS OF THE NEW ARAB FILM

1 The International Era

Across the Maghreb and Mashreq, the past few decades have seen major transformations, ably detailed by Ami Elad-Bouskila: "In the spheres of politics—the decline of pan-Arabism and Nasserism; economics—increased industrialization at the expense of agriculture, open-door policies; and society—increased urbanization, social and religious polarization, urban Westernization which parallels growing Islamicism, a faster pace of living, and the alienation of the individual—especially city-dwellers."[1]

One of the consequences of these changes has been that, since the 1960s, "literature is less in the service of ideology and has a more personal orientation," a shift that, Elad-Bouskila argues, has made possible, among other things, the development of a "woman's literature."[2] A similar movement away from film-making at the service of the state can be traced a decade or two later in cinema, but here the real breakthrough of women's creativity has had to wait largely until the 2000s.

As far as Arab filmmaking outside Egypt is concerned, Andrea Khalil's specific comments on North African cinema, in her introduction to *North African Cinema in a Global Context*, have equal resonance for Arab filmmaking throughout the Middle East. Whereas once the national was defined in relation to the former colonizing power, now the "outside" is increasingly "a more expansive, globalising and hegemonic cultural political force that both frees and restricts the production of North African cinema." This outside is "manifested as both imaginary, in geographical flights as well as flights of fantasy, and very material."[3]

Whereas once filmmakers were embedded in their national communities, even on occasion working as salaried state employees, now they are more likely to be foreign educated and trained and often resident in Europe. They travel between Europe and the Arab world, looking "at each shore of the globe's waters with the other shore already imprinted on their film of vision."[4] As Hamid Naficy observes, "Thanks to globalization of travel, media, and capital, exile appears to have become the post-modern condition. But exile must not be thought of as a generalized condition of alienation and difference."[5] Indeed, as we shall see, there are almost always very specific factors at play that shape the careers of the individual filmmakers with whom we are concerned here.

Foreign Influences

For many contemporary Arab filmmakers, one of their first tastes of Western culture was the films screened at the film clubs and cultural institutes that the French established throughout their former colonies in Africa and their mandated territories in the Middle East. This is perhaps one reason why the models these filmmakers refer to in interviews tend to be European *auteurs* or Hollywood filmmakers. Ferid Boughedir, for example, recalls his early film viewings at the Lycée Carnot film club in Tunis on Sunday mornings, noting that all their favorite filmmakers were Westerners: Ingmar Bergman, Luis Buñuel, Roberto Rossellini, Alfred Hitchcock, Elia Kazan. "For us at that time," he adds, "film masterpieces could only come from abroad."[6] The film society movement—as well as an accompanying and ongoing tradition of amateur filmmaking—was particularly strong in Tunisia. Nouri Bouzid describes himself as "a child of the Louis Lumière film club in Sfax. It's there I first learned to read images, thanks particularly to Tahar Cheriaa."[7] For Néjia Ben Mabrouk, too, the Saturday film club was "a precious transition from the cinema of my childhood—mass audience films, mostly Indian and American—to a more demanding form of cinema."[8] Like Boughedir, she mentions Youssef Chahine, seeing him and Chadi Abdel Salam as the two filmmakers who opened her eyes to the possibilities of a new kind of Arab cinema. The foreign experiences of most future Maghrebian filmmakers of this generation have been largely limited to Europe, but at least one Lebanese director actually managed to work for his Hollywood hero: Maroun Bagdadi, who trained under Francis Ford Coppola in Hollywood.

Another way in which many of the filmmakers who pioneered Arab cinema from the mid-1970s onward were influenced by the West was through the film training they received in Europe. For those pioneers seeking professional training in western Europe, the choice at the time was largely between the Institut des Hautes Études Cinématographiques (IDHEC) in Paris and the Institut National des Arts et du Spectacle et Techniques de Diffusion (INSAS) in Brussels. Moumen Smihi, who trained at IDHEC and made his first feature, *El Chergui*, in Morocco in 1975, notes, "The IDHEC courses were very bookish at the time, and it can't be said there was great openness to what is called the Third Cinema. No one was really interested in that, except for Georges Sadoul. Then, the cinema was only really considered from two angles: the Hollywood angle and the angle of French cinema, old or new wave. In fact the teaching was essentially technicist, and kept to that."[9]

The approach to teaching at INSAS was somewhat different. Tunisian Lotfi Thabet, who cowrote and codirected the feature-length documentary *It Is Not Enough for God to Be on the Side of the Poor* with a fellow INSAS graduate, Borhan Alawiya from Lebanon, in 1976, observes, "We didn't really learn to make cinema

as it was: comedy, thrillers, musicals. We only learned only how to express ourselves, in the way Belgian cinema allowed. As a result, one of the strong links
between Tunisian and Belgian cinemas is the production of an *auteur* cinema."[10]
In Thabet's view, Belgian training corresponded to Tunisian needs at the time:
"An *auteur* cinema bringing to bear a subjective look at both people's personal
and collective problems."[11]

This is a point also made with slightly different emphasis by Rebecca Hillauer: "The returnees from European film school brought with them the idea
of making films that deal with current social and political problems facing the
country."[12] This is backed up, again from a Tunisian viewpoint, by Néjia Ben
Mabrouk (another INSAS graduate), who has said of her own work that it "was
less a reference to an Arab history of film, than it was what we had been taught in
European film schools. . . . For many of us, our film 'education' was based on the
critical documentary film. We wanted our films to reach Tunisian audiences, to
show them their own problems in order to make changes."[13]

The third of the shaping factors is that, because of the history of French and
English colonization and the current Western involvement in Middle Eastern
affairs, there has been a continued European public interest in what has happened (and, more especially, what is happening now) in Palestine and Lebanon.
As a result, there has been a potential audience for television documentaries that
deal with issues arising in the Middle East. A major initial source of funding
for foreign-based or exiled Arab filmmakers has been the network of European
and US television stations. Naficy lists just a few of the more prominent of these:
"Channel 4 (in the United Kingdom), ZDF (in Germany), Canal Plus (in France),
Arte (in Germany and France), and PBS, Bravo (including its Independent Film
Channel), Sundance Independent Channel, and Arts and Entertainment (in the
United States)."[14]

A good example of the extent of this funding is offered by the work of the
man who established Palestinian cinema on the international map, Michel
Khleifi. Nurith Gertz and George Khleifi offer a listing of his 1980s documentary works, with their sources of funding: *Fertile Memory* (1980), "which was pre-
financed by the German television channel ZDF, and the Dutch networks IKON
and NOVIB; *The An-Naim Route* (1981), which was produced by the Belgian network RTBF; *Ma'aloul Celebrates Its Destruction* (1984), mainly financed by the
Brussels foundation for the Audio Visual Arts, CBA."[15] The full funding credits for Khleifi's first fictional feature, *Wedding in Galilee* (1987), include Khleifi's
own production company, Marisa Film, in Brussels; QA Production in London;
the German television network ZDF; the Ministry for the French Community in
Belgium; the French production company LPA (Société Les Productions Audiovisuelles) in Paris; a French coproducing company, Avidia Films; the French
television organization Canal Plus; the French distributor Lasa Films; and the

French Ministry of Culture (through the Centre National Cinématographique prefinancing scheme—the *avance sur recettes*).[16]

Throughout the Arab world in the 1980s and 1990s, and continuing into the 2000s, major documentaries and feature films have been partially or wholly financed by European television organizations and through various European (especially French) government funding agencies. Filmmakers are very aware of the issues this funding has raised. Soudade Kaadan sums up the Syrian (and other Arab) filmmaker's problem precisely as one of audience: though the intended viewer is Arabic, Arabs do not watch documentaries, whereas Europeans do. Kaadan's aspiration is clear: "I don't want to fall into a European vision. I'm not trying to make a film for a European festival. I don't want to make any compromise. I make documentaries for an Arab public . . . that's the hard part. As Arab directors we run the great risk of falling into a European vision."[17]

An additional foreign influence on contemporary Arab filmmaking—often one chosen by the filmmakers themselves—is the use of foreign production crews. Michel Khleifi, who lives in Brussels, has often used Belgian crews. The use of French technicians in key roles is common among Maghrebian filmmakers and in certain Middle East countries, such as Lebanon. In addition, Samir Habchi used a Russian crew for *The Tornado* and Maroun Bagdadi an American one for *Little Wars*.

In part, the problem of foreign influence for documentary filmmakers has been answered from within the Arab world by the rise of the Al-Jazeera television channel, which increasingly commissions Arab documentaries (though, obviously, it imposes its own constraints on independent-minded filmmakers). More recently Gulf funding has also extended to feature filmmaking, with the Doha Film Institute cofunding not only Jean-Jacques Annaud's superproduction *Black Gold* but also a number of independent productions by Arab filmmakers, including Ghassan Salhab's totally personal film, *The Mountain*.

It would be wrong, however, to see this response to the potential of European training, aid, and technical assistance as somehow constituting a diminution of Arab identity. In absorbing European and American influences in their work, filmmakers are doing no more than following the general pattern established in modern Arabic literature from the 1960s. As Ami Elad-Bouskila notes, contemporary writers have focused on "the individual rather than the community at large": "The individual at the centre is engrossed in problems of alienation, loneliness and estrangement, especially in urban existence—together with questions of tradition, style of life, customs and religion, especially in rural areas."[18] These are definitions that apply equally to the majority of contemporary filmmakers, and certainly those at work since the 1980s.

As far as the specific filmmakers are concerned, while it is true that exile brings a new international perspective, it does not inevitably cut off links to one's place of origin. As Hamid Naficy rightly observes, "Exile is inexorably tied to homeland and to the possibility of return."[19] On a wider level, the shared experiences of filmmakers—authoritarian governments at home and a precarious existence abroad, alternations of exile and return—form part of a wider development in Arab culture, captured by Samir Kassir when he talks of "the growth of a homogenous and, at the same time, plural field of Arab culture": "Despite the fragmentation of states and hence the market, and despite the cultural borders patrolled by national censors, this field of Arab culture is in many ways the most definitive expression of a cohesive Arabness at a time when all other attempts at integration—economical, political, pan-Arab and sub-regional—are deadlocked."[20]

The Role of Television

The challenges of documenting the realities of Palestine and Lebanon, exploring the issues raised, and constructing appropriate narratives have provided a stimulus for the establishment of a documentary tradition in Middle Eastern Arab filmmaking. The struggle of the Palestinian people and the impact of the fifteen-year Lebanese Civil War, which broke out in 1975, have given a real impetus to documentary production in Palestine (much of it by filmmakers of Palestinian descent) and in Lebanon. In both areas, the work of major figures has been supplemented by dozens of short films by committed newcomers. A key format is the fifty-minute documentary of the kind favored by most European television channels. Such works herald the beginning of the new international era of Arab filmmaking. The documentaries produced bear many of the marks of exile—recording devastation, chronicling expulsion, sharing the anguish of blocked return to a shattered land. But, unlike so many of the films dealt with by Hamid Naficy in his studies of exilic and diasporic cinema, they are public statements, works addressing a known audience, inevitably shaped in part by the market for which they have been produced. Even a personal story, such as Mohamed Bakri's *Zahara*, which explores the filmmaker's own family history, is fashioned in this way. Since the mid-1970s onward, there have been half a dozen or so Middle Eastern Arab documentary filmmakers who have stood out for their efforts to create accessible, but at the same time personal, family-orientated films.

Feature Film Funding Mechanisms

As Martin Dale notes, "France has the highest level of state subsidy and regulation in Europe."[21] State support for filmmaking in France has a long history, the chief component being automatic funding for any film that meets the basic criteria for being considered "French" (i.e., use of the French language, French actors and technicians, and so on). State support increased with the founding of the Centre National Cinématographique in 1946, though this organization did not begin to operate fully until 1959, when it came under the auspices of the newly formed Ministry of Cultural Affairs. It was in 1959 that a new and additional system of support for film production—in terms of an advance against box office takings (*avance sur recettes*), funded by an additional tax on the box office receipts of all films (including foreign imports)—came into being. The new funding was reserved for "films shot in French as the original language, which represent a cinema, whose independence and audacity with respect to the norms of the market make public aid necessary for the establishment of financial equilibrium, so favouring a creative renewal and the production of works with a clear cultural ambition."[22] Dale, who is no advocate of the state support system, argues forcefully that though the system—in theory, at least—frees the filmmaker from dependence on the market, it in effect makes the filmmaker "wholly dependent on the state, which is no greater a freedom than being dependent on a capitalist corporation."[23]

The French state commitment to film strengthened after Jack Lang became minister of culture in 1981 and advanced his arguments in favor of the concept of "cultural exception," which achieved prominence at the 1993 GATT negotiations: "Cultural exceptionalism positioned the concept of discrimination as both the positive act of being intellectually discriminating and a response to discriminatory global market forces dominated by the Hollywood culture industry."[24] The aim was both "to accentuate a distinctive vision of Frenchness" and to provide "the distinctive patina of enlightened cultural policies with international ambitions."[25] In addition, as Dale notes, "subsidies are granted to those projects with the greatest 'cultural merit' and funds are allocated directly to the director or scriptwriter." This gives the *auteur* "a significant bargaining tool in negotiating with producers and distributors."[26]

Peter J. Bloom argues that the French Social Action Fund (Fonds d'Action Sociale [FAS])—which was charged with the affairs of the members of the immigrant community in France, mostly of Algerian origin and known generally as *beurs*—used this context to develop a cinema that would reflect immigrant concerns: "Within this context, *beur* cinema became linked to new sources of public financing that empowered FAS to serve as an intermediary for small-scale productions through the French National Film Centre."[27] Bloom makes an explicit comparison with the funding accorded, originally under the Cultural and Technical Cooperation Agency, the Agence de Coopération Culturelle et Technique (ACCT), to filmmakers from the former French colonies in West Africa, in that both schemes produced films that "never made it beyond the circuit of theatres in the Quartier Latin or the international French cultural affairs circuit."[28]

Whether this kind of ghettoization was intended, *beur* cinema, like Cinema South of the Sahara, blossomed after its circumscribed and low-funded beginnings in the 1970s as its filmmakers grew in assurance and widened their cultural horizons.

Francophonie

For many years now, in a world dominated by US political power and media output and marked by the increasing spread of the English language, successive French governments have sought to create a distinctive space for France and the French language. One key to these efforts has been the concept of *Francophonie*. This term, as Dennis Ager has pointed out, has three distinct, if related, meanings. First, it denotes the geographical areas where French is spoken as a national or administrative language. Second, it denotes the official governmental organization (akin to the British Commonwealth) formally linking the states where French is spoken. Finally, it has a cultural meaning: "An attitude, a belief in a spirit, an ideology and a way of doing things, inspired by French history, language and culture, but not necessarily using French, aware of and responsive to the nature of the modern world."[29]

It is *Francophonie* in this third sense that underlies France's attitude toward world cinema, and it is not by chance that the mid-1960s saw both the birth of *Francophonie* as an organization linking French-speaking states and also the beginning of the first aid program for filmmakers from the former French colonies in West Africa by the Bureau du Cinéma de la Coopération, itself part of the ACCT (now restructured as the Agence Intergouvernementale de la Francophonie [AIF]).[30] With the roles of Louis Lumière, Charles Pathé, and Léon Gaumont so crucial in the development of early cinema (and the French film industry providing 90 percent of the films shown worldwide in 1914),[31] France has always seen itself as a player in world cinema. Today, finding screens in France, like those in most of the rest of Europe, dominated by Hollywood, the French government has responded by setting up an alternative worldwide network of "cultural" film production for which Paris is the focal point. There is a strong argument, advanced by Raphaël Millet, that "it is less a case of a French aid policy serving the cinemas of the South, than of the latter being used to assist French cultural policy."[32]

Whatever the case, there has been a proliferation of shifting French official funding sources for the cinemas of the South in the past three decades (each, inevitably, with its own acronym): the Ministry of Foreign Affairs (MAF), either directly or through the Centre National Cinématographique (CNC); the Fonds francophone de production audiovisuelle du Sud (supervised by AIF); the Fonds d'Action Sociale (FAS), instrumental in promoting *beur* cinema; the ADCSud, which was replaced by the now discontinued Fonds Images Afrique (FIA); and, above all, the Fonds Sud Cinéma, created by three ministries (Culture, Cooperation, and Foreign Affairs) in 1984 and is still in operation today. Aid is available not only for production and postproduction but also for training, scriptwriting schemes, and the costs involved in the transfer from digital to 35mm film, distribution, and festival screenings. There are also numerous French regional organizations that aid film production, and there is the aid from the European Development Fund (FED), which the French government has persuaded to become involved in film production. There are also a number of private European foundations (such as the Hubert Bals Foundation, Montecinema Vérité, and the Gans Foundation for the Cinema), as well as powerful television organizations, such as Arte and Canal Plus. What is particularly important here is that, in this French context, backing from one organization does not preclude funding from another; rather, it strengthens the case for additional support.

In an observation that has considerable relevance for Arab cinema, David Pryce-Jones begins his book *Betrayal: France, the Arabs, and the Jews* with the observation that he has "long been struck by the way that French rulers and intellectuals have habitually described France as a Muslim power." This was not, in any sense, an anticipation of the fact that the increasing millions of Muslim immigrants and their descendants in France might, one day, come to have a decisive influence on French domestic politics, but rather, it implied that "France was well placed to take advantage of Muslims either under direct rule in what were once colonies and protectorates, or otherwise within the French sphere of influence in more recent years, when Muslim countries had gained independence."[33] Certainly this notion of a legitimate "French sphere of influence" is very apparent when we look at French policy toward Arab filmmaking. The Fonds Sud Cinéma has—from its inception in 1984—cofunded well over one hundred feature films made by Arab directors, with well over a dozen each from Algeria, Morocco, Tunisia, and Lebanon, as well as a handful from Iraq, Palestine, Syria, and Egypt. Many of the key filmmakers from the last thirty years of Arab filmmaking have profited from this support.

Aid to the Cinemas of the South

French government involvement with African film began in 1963, with a modest scheme set up by the Ministry of Cooperation to assist filmmakers from the francophone area of sub-Saharan Africa. Preproduction funding for 16mm short and feature-length films was given through the advance purchase of the non-commercial rights to the eventual film to enable it to be screened in schools and colleges in France and in French cultural centers abroad. The scheme required a French producer to be appointed (to control the budget) and for postproduction activities to be undertaken solely at the facilities set up by the Ministry in Paris (a clear example of aid money being returned to the donor and the prevention of infrastructural development in the recipient filmmaker's own country).

However well intentioned, the scheme had a number of drawbacks. Since commercial distribution in Africa, as in other parts of the world, was exclusively in the 35mm format, the commercial distribution rights to their 16mm films given to the filmmakers had no value whatsoever. Work of real distinction was made, however, by filmmakers such as Oumarou Ganda and Mustapha Alassane in the 1960s and early 1970s. These works, some of which won prizes at the first African film festivals, form an integral part of the history of African cinema. But the filmmakers rightly saw their work as being forced into a noncommercial ghetto and wanted to make (more expensive) 35mm films that could, potentially at least, reach African audiences. Initially, in the days of 16mm production, the ministry could give money to all who applied, but as the number of applicants grew and the costs rose, it became clear that decisions about which films to fund would have to be made. Alongside the African filmmakers, others who objected to the scheme were French distributors serving the noncommercial (largely educational) market in France, who complained of the unfair competition. This stemmed from the free distribution of the ministry films, which were all properly cataloged, preserved, and made available from the ministry's archives. From the perspective of French administrators, the scheme was a great advance on the situation in the mid-1950s, when the Senegalese pioneer Paulin Soumanou Vieyra graduated from film school in Paris only to find that, as an African, he was legally banned from shooting a film in Africa under a law established in 1934. But, from a more modern perspective, the cooperation scheme can be seen as a telling example of neocolonialism: the French producing "African" films, for which they constitute the targeted audience.[34]

When the French began their schemes to aid the cinemas of the South in the 1980s, a new model was needed. This was furnished by the prefunding scheme (the *avance sur recettes*), introduced by the Ministry of Culture under André Malraux, which was designed to aid all francophone filmmaking and which had already served to support productions by directors from the *beur* community in France. As René Prédal explains, this was "a new kind of aid before production designed to encourage producers to agree to produce difficult projects, that is to say, *films d'auteur*, which ran the risk of not paying their costs in a market dominated more and more exclusively by violence, the star system, and sex." Under French law, the director of a film is recognized as its author (*auteur*), and the new funding arrangement was focused on him or her. To quote Prédal once more, "To obtain this advance against future receipts, the *auteur*, that is the writer-director, has to submit a fully worked-out dossier, with a shooting script, a provisional budget, a statement of intent and all the documentation which will support the request, such as press reviews of previous films, or short films in the case of a first feature." This *auteur* cinema has therefore a precise definition: "It is a film with deliberate artistic ambitions, written by the person intending to direct it, the nature, interest, form and content of which can be well presented in the writing of a long statement elaborated by the filmmaker him- or herself."[35]

What is striking about this definition is that it totally neglects any question of potential box office receipts or audiences. There is a tacit assumption the institutions most likely to screen such works will be international film festivals and art house cinema outlets. The commercial release of the film in the filmmaker's own country is more of a bonus than a requirement. But availability in a 35mm format is normally required, and if the film is (as is increasingly the case) digitally produced, then funding will be included for transfer to film, as well as for subtitling to meet the needs of foreign audiences. Thus, though the Arab feature films with which we are concerned here are often products of exile or diaspora, they are not the private, self-funded, alternatively produced, totally personal works that concern Hamid Naficy in his studies of "accented" cinema.[36] From the 1980s onward, much Arab cinema produced outside Egypt has been addressed to an international audience as well as to an audience, perhaps only hoped for, in the filmmaker's country of origin.

Notes

1. Ami Elad-Bouskila, *Modern Palestinian Literature and Culture* (London: Frank Cass, 1999), 5.

2. Ibid.

3. Andrea Khalil, introduction to *North African Cinema in a Global Context: Through the lens of Diaspora* (London: Routledge, 2008), ix.

4. Ibid.

5. Hamid Naficy, ed., *Home, Exile, Homeland: Film Media and the Politics of Place* (New York: Routledge, 1999), 4.

6. Ferid Boughedir, "Youssef Chahine: A Lesson in Freedom," epilogue to *Youssef Chahine: Fire and Word*, ed. Alberto Elena (Andalucia: Consejería de Cultura, 2007), 325.

7. Nouri Bouzid, in *Parcours de Cinéma*, ed. Daniel Soil (Tunis: Cérès Éditions, 2010), 13.

8. Néjia Ben Mabrouk, in Soil, *Parcours de Cinéma*, 38.

9. Moumen Smihi, "Moroccan Cinema as Mythology," in *Film and Politics in the Third World*, ed. John D. H. Downing (New York: Praeger, 1986), 78.

10. Lotfi Thabet, in Soil, *Parcours de Cinéma*, 23.

11. Ibid.

12. Rebecca Hillauer, *Encyclopedia of Arab Women Filmmakers*, translated by Allison Brown, Deborah Cohen, and Nancy Joyce (Cairo: American University in Cairo Press, 2005), originally published as *Freiräume—Lebensträume, Arabische Filmemacherinnen* (Unkel am Rhein: Arte-Edition, 2001), 362.

13. Ibid., 362–63.

14. Naficy, *Home, Exile, Homeland*, 135.

15. Nurith Gertz and George Khleifi, *Palestinian Cinema: Landscape, Trauma and Memory* (Edinburgh: Edinburgh University Press, 2008), 56.

16. Michel Kleifi, *Noce en Galilé* (Paris: L'Avant-Scène Cinéma, 1988), 19.

17. Soudade Kaadan, interview, www.eurodmedcafe.org, June 21, 2009.

18. Elad-Bouskila, *Modern Palestinian Literature and Culture*, 4.

19. Naficy, *Home, Exile, Homeland*, 3.

20. Samir Kassir, *Being Arab* (London: Verso, 2006), 87–88.

21. Martin Dale, *The Movie Game: The Film Business in Britain, Europe and America* (London: Cassell, 1997), 186.

22. *État et culture: le cinéma* (Paris: La Documentation Française, 1992), 69.

23. Dale, *Movie Game*, 201.

24. Peter J. Bloom, "The State of French Cultural Exceptionalism: The 2005 Uprisings and the Politics of Visibility" in *Frenchness and the African Diaspora*, ed. Charles Tshimanga, Didier Gondala, and Peter J. Bloom (Bloomington: Indiana University Press, 2009), 244.

25. Ibid.

26. Dale, *Movie Game*, 187.

27. Ibid.

28. Ibid.

29. Dennis Ager, *"Francophonie" in the 1990s: Problems and Opportunities* (Clevedon: Multilingual Matters, 1996), 1.

30. For a discussion of French aid to filmmakers in Africa, see Roy Armes, *African Filmmaking: North and South of the Sahara* (Edinburgh: Edinburgh University Press, 2006), 53–58.

31. Stephen Crofts, "Reconceptualising National Cinema/s," in *Theorising National Cinema*, edited by Valentina Vitali and Paul Willemen (London: BFI Publishing, 2006), 44.

32. Raphaël Millet, "(In)dépendance des cinémas du Sud &/vs France" (Paris: *Théorème 5*, 1998), 163.

33. David Pryce-Jones, *Betrayal: France, the Arabs, and the Jews* (New York: Encounter Books, 2006), ix.

34. See Millet, "(In)dépendance des cinémas du Sud &/vs France."

35. All quotations in this paragraph taken from René Prédal, *Le cinéma d'auteur, une vieille lune?* (Paris: Éditions du Cerf, 2001), 85.

36. See especially Hamid Naficy, *An Accented Cinema: Exilic and Diasporic Filmmaking* (Princeton: Princeton University Press, 2001).

2   A New Independence

The complex issue of the impact of colonialism on the Arab world has been excellently defined by Albert Memmi in *The Colonizer and the Colonized*: "We have no idea what the colonized world would have been without colonization, but we certainly see what has happened as a result of it. To subdue and exploit, the colonizer pushed the colonized out of the historical and social, cultural and technical current. What is real and verifiable is that the colonized culture, society and technology are seriously damaged."[1]

The challenge for all artists, including filmmakers, has been excellently formulated by Edward Said: "After the colonial parenthesis, it is our task now to research what might constitute the African being, the Arab being, their imaginary, their culture."[2] The specific task for filmmakers involved a rethinking of both narrative structure and the role of the protagonist. Expressing his discontent with the structures of traditional Arab (that is to say, Egyptian) melodrama, Nouri Bouzid wrote: "We must show that the cinema is capable of saying everything and must break down the old forms to invent a new Arab cinema."[3] Equally, there was the need to create a new protagonist who is unable to change the world by an imposition of will or even to develop his or her own potentialities to the full as the Western hero does.

Throughout the Arab world, particularly from the late 1970s onward, small, often loosely linked groups of new filmmakers emerged who were prepared to take up this challenge. This was not an easy choice. Certainly in the 1970s, working outside the state funding system was not easy. As Moumen Smihi has said of the making of *El Chergui* (1979): "The technicians were badly paid or not paid at all. The camera crew worked on barely half the normal wage. Leila Shenna (who played Aïcha) was nice enough to accept a ridiculously low fee. I got absolutely nothing at all. Everyone worked on the basis of sharing the eventual receipts."[4]

In the 1980s, with the emergence of a new generation of independent specialized producers who succeeded in obtaining funding from abroad (of whom the best known is Ahmed Attia in Tunisia[5]), things became easier. But even when these independents were dependent on foreign (usually French) support, they maintained strong national and local community links and focused their films on the current issues facing their respective societies.

There were the film projects within the *beur* community in France, pioneered by Abdelkrim Bahloul, Rachid Bouchareb, and Mehdi Charef. Similar groups emerged across the Maghreb. Within Algeria, new voices asserted themselves as the state-ordered structures collapsed. Algerians who were driven abroad to France, such as Merzak Allouache, added their insider/ousider perspectives. The Berber language was heard for the first time in mainstream productions, and Mohamed Choukri broke free from earlier constraints. In Tunisia, the emergence of a new breed of independent film producers, such as Ahmed Attia and Hassan Daldoul, led to a fresh group of filmmakers, including Nouri Bouzid, Ferid Boughedir, and Moufida Tlatli, achieving international reputations. In addition, the idiosyncratic style of Nacer Khemir became apparent for the first time. In Morocco, three female filmmakers, all in some way outsiders, gave documentary filmmaking a new impetus, while a new social realist vein of filmmaking was explored by a trio of feature filmmakers—Jillali Ferhati, Mohamed Abderrahman Tazi, and Hakim Noury—to be joined in the early 1990s by Abdelkader Lagtaâ and, a few years later, Daoud Aoulad-Syad.

In Egypt, two of Youssef Chahine's former assistants—Yousry Nasrallah and Asma El Bakry—followed his example of independent filmmaking, aided, like many other filmmakers of this generation, by funding from the Fonds Sud Cinéma. In addition, in Lebanon, three independent-minded filmmakers—Heiny Srour, Borhan Alawiya, and Jacqueline Saab—eased the transitions from the 1970s to the 1980s and from documentary to fiction. Lebanese documentary filmmaking flourished with the truly impressive output from Maï Masri and her partner, Jean Chamoun, backed up in the late 1990s by the more personal style of Mohamed Souheid. Fictional production was given a new stimulus by Maroun Bagdadi, while Ghassan Salhab expressed his fascinating personal vision of Lebanese society. Palestinian film production, both documentary and fiction, was dominated by Michel Khleifi, but other distinctive voices—Mohamed Bakri, Samir Abdallah, and Ali Nassar—also made themselves heard. Documentarists based abroad—Kassim Abid, Maysoon Pachachi, Samir and Saad Salman—predominated in Iraq's output. Syrian documentary filmmaking was marked especially by the work, in exile, of Omar Amiralay. But there was also the emergence of a "second generation" of locally based feature filmmakers—Samir Zikra, Mohamed Malas, Oussama Mohammad, and Abdellatif Abdelhamid. These filmmakers achieved international success despite being constrained to work within a state-dominated production system.

*

The figure who towers over the new Arab film and serves in some ways as its role model is **Youssef Chahine** (1926–2008), a complex and controversial figure throughout his lifetime. Though born in Alexandria, he was the son of a Lebanese Christian father and a Greek mother. Brought up Catholic, he was sent to the exclusive Victoria College in Alexandria, where the language of tuition was

English. At the age of twenty, he persuaded his family to allow him to study drama for two years at the Pasadena Playhouse near Los Angeles. His cosmopolitan background made him fluent in half a dozen languages and, as David Murphy and Patrick Williams observe, "Chahine's Egyptian identity is, on the face of it, not absolutely straight-forward—though for Chahine himself it is simply not a problem."[6] He always defined himself—nationally and religiously—as an Egyptian.

Even as a child, he was fascinated by the cinema and organized film shows for his family and friends. On his return from his studies in the United States, he abandoned the theater for filmmaking. Despite his lack of formal training and without having made any short films or having had to follow the normal practice of working for several years as an assistant director, he managed to make his first feature, *Baba Amin*, at the age of just twenty-four. The year was 1950, two years before the overthrow of King Farouk.

Chahine's stylistic range is extraordinarily wide. Much of his early work fits in with the demands and constraints of Egyptian commercial cinema, with its concentration on musicals and melodramas. When the base of Egyptian cinema shifted to Lebanon in the mid-1960s, he moved there, too, and made two features, one of which is the highly regarded and hugely popular musical *The Ring Seller / Bayya' al-khawatim* (1965). But Chahine was always willing to experiment and take on challenging subjects. Among the dozen or so films he made in the 1950s, despite the social and political upheavals of the times, is the work that is generally recognized to be the best of his early films, the uncompromisingly social realist drama *Cairo Station / Bab al-hadid* (1958). He has admitted his debt to Vittorio De Sica and Cesare Zavattini for the inspiration behind this film, and, like so many of the neorealist masterpieces, it proved unpopular with audiences expecting undemanding entertainment. Chahine was to return to this realist style ten years later in his adaptation of Abderrahmane Sharkawi's novel *The Land / Al-ard* (1969), dealing with agrarian issues.

But Chahine was equally at home directing a complex allegory, such as *The Choice / Al-ikhiar* (1970), or a patriotic nationalist epic, such as *Saladin / Al-nasir Salah al Din* (1963), which reflected his original enthusiasm for the Nasserite vision of the Arab world. His relationship with the authorities was always difficult, but he proved to be totally independent. His tribute to a heroine of the Algerian liberation struggle, *Jamila the Algerian / Jamila al-jaza'iriyya* (1958), was not shown at the time in Algeria, and his masterwork, *The Sparrow*, was banned for two years by the Anwar Sadat's government. His study of past religious intolerance in *The Emigrant / Al-muhair* (1994) led to a prosecution for blasphemy, to which his response was to make another film with a similar subject, *Destiny / Al-masir* (1997), dealing with the persecution by the state of the twelfth-century philosopher Averroes.

Chahine's principal strength, throughout his career, was his ability to combine his interest in every aspect of his characters (their loves and enthusiasms, as well as their doubts and traumas) with a probing insight into the interaction of the individual and society. These concerns are perhaps best expressed in *The Sparrow / Al-usfur* (1973), which deals with the Egyptian response to defeat in the Six Day War. It deals not just with the politics but also with a range of characters, central to whom is an ordinary working woman, Bahiyya. The closing sequence of the film, which depicts her rushing through the streets shouting, "No! We shall fight!" and being joined by hundreds of other ordinary Egyptian citizens, is one of the most memorable in all Arab cinema.

The immense respect in which Chahine's work is held is very apparent in Nouri Bouzid's 1988 essay, "New Realism in Arab Cinema." Looking at the debt that his generation—born in the 1940s, brought up on Nasserite slogans, and subsequently faced with the undeniable reality of Arab defeat—owes to its Arab predecessors, Bouzid picks out three Egyptian "mentors," all of whom "found themselves rejected by the private sector producers after the General Institution of Cinema was dissolved, forcing them to turn to funding sources outside the establishment."[7] The three Bouzid singles out are Chadi Abdel Salam (*The Mummy*), Tewfik Saleh (*The Duped*), and Youssef Chahine. He writes of *The Sparrow*: "It is the ultimate in Arabic cinema. Its idea was novel, by global as well as local standards (the presentation of a political incidence of great import through the portrayal of the complexity of everyday life), and its form was also new and sophisticated, with several intertwined story lines and numerous main characters, some of whom exist only offscreen. *The Sparrow* is considered the only film to probe, as it were, into the hidden causes and roots of defeat; exploring and exposing not just in its military aspect, but all its social ramifications."[8]

Chahine's contribution to the new Arab film did not end there. For the young filmmakers in the wider Arab world setting out in the 1980s, he also offered a fresh incitement to draw on their own personal lives and experiences. Autobiography was hitherto rare in Arab cinema, as in Arab literature. Above all, Chahine offered a unique example of the power that could be achieved by combining personal experience with social commitment and political insight; this is especially evident in his masterly Alexandria Quartet, which mixed his own personal experience and longing with wider fictional elements and social concerns. The four films—*Alexandria . . . Why? / Alexandrie . . . pourquoi / Iskandariyah . . . lih?* (1978), *An Egyptian Tale / La mémoire / Hadduta misriya* (1982), and *Alexandria Again and Again / Alexandrie encore et toujours / Iskandriyah kaman wa kaman* (1989), supplemented by *Alexandria–New York / Alexandrie–New York / Iskandariyah–New York* in 2004—form a unique sequence of films in Arab or, indeed, international cinema that could only provoke a creative response from those seeking to renew Arab cinema.[9]

*

Beginning in the late 1970s, a new Arab cinema came into view that was to offer fresh insights and stylistic models in works of real distinction. These, in turn, helped shape the output of a new generation emerging in the 2000s. The filmmakers making their debuts in the late 1970s and after were almost all born in the 1940s or 1950s. A determining feature of their growth to maturity was the June 1967 Arab defeat. As Nouri Bouzid has noted, it was tantamount to an alarm bell that aroused the domant Arab consciousness from its long slumber; it awakened the Arabs from their dreaming, shaking their faith in all the nationalistic slogans and bringing into question the ability of the military regimes to to fulfill the duties they had taken on and had so loftily and widely declared.[10]

Two-thirds of all the newcomers of this period have formal film school training. Mostly, this training took place in western Europe. Filmmakers from a wide range of countries studied at Institut National des Arts et du Spectacle et Techniques de Diffusion (INSAS) in Belgium: the Palestinian Michel Khleifi, the Tunisian Nouri Bouzid, the Algerians Brahim Tsaki and Belkacem Hadjadj, and the Lebanese Jean-Claude Codsi and Randa Chahal-Sabbag. Those trained in France were mostly Maghrebians—Merzak Allouache, Hassan Benjelloun, Taïeb Louhichi, Daoud Aoulad-Syad, Abderrahmane Bouguermouh, Moufida Tlatli, and Farida Benlyazid—but also included the pioneering Lebanese filmmakers Maroun Bagdadi and Heiny Srour. In addition, the Tunisian Fadhel Jaïbi and a pair of Moroccans (Jillali Ferhati and Hakim Noury) studied drama in Paris.

Other emergent Arab filmmakers were scattered singly across Europe: in Sweden (the Lebanese Leila Assaf) or Poland (the Moroccan Abdelkader Lagtaâ). Soviet film schools, especially the VGIK in Moscow, also played a very important role. Most of the Syrians (Samir Zikra, Mohamed Malas, Oussama Mohammad, and Abdellatif Abdelhamid among them) studied there, as did the Palestinian Ali Nassar. Two other Syrians (Raymond Boutros and Ghassan Shmeit) graduated from Kiev University. Significantly, only the Egyptian Yousry Nasrallah is a graduate of the Cairo Higher Film Institute, and he, like the rest of the group, makes no attempt to adopt the model of Egyptian popular commercial filmmaking.

The mid-1960s, when most of these future filmmakers were undertaking their studies abroad, were a crucial period in world cinema, what Nouri Bouzid has called "the Golden Age of Cinema": "That was the era of the best Fellinis, Bergmans, Godards, Resnais, the best Japanese, Czech, Polish, Hungarian, Swedish, Canadian and Indian films. It was also an auspicious era for the American cinema in New York, 'free cinema' in England, 'cinema novo' in Brazil and the Latin American cinema."[11] Encountering this mass of new approaches to film narrative (all breaking with the conventional Hollywood model of film storytelling) could hardly fail to have had a profound effect on a group who were themselves intent on turning away from the Egyptian model of Arab cinema.

A small proportion of the 1980s and 1990s filmmakers live in permanent voluntary exile, but many move constantly to and from Europe. Virtually all—including the Moroccans, whose state-funded system continues to operate—have to look to foreign sources for at least some production support. Indeed as far as the filmmakers considered here are concerned, about two-thirds have received French government Fonds Sud Cinéma support for at least one film. Some have received such support on a regular basis: Nouri Bouzid for five films and Asma El Bakry, Yousry Nasrallah, and Nacer Khemir for three each.

During the 1980s and 1990s, French funding sources allowed a small number of female filmmakers to make their debuts: the French-based Zaïda Ghorab-Volta, Farida Benlyazid from Morocco, Moufida Tlatli and Kaltoum Bornaz in Tunisia, Asma El Bakry in Egypt, and Leila Assaf and Randa Chahal-Sabbag in Lebanon. The French-based Rachida Krim worked within conventional funding and production structures in France, while a few others others made their breakthrough without French support: Jocelyne Saab in Lebanon and Hafsa Zinaï-Koudil in Algeria, for example. But the fact remains that none of these female filmmakers was able to make more than a film or two in a period of two decades, though some were able to continue into the 2000s. Overall, as in earlier periods of Arab cinema (apart from the pioneering days of Egyptian expatriate filmmaking), the effect of female filmmakers on Arab film production was limited during the 1980s and 1990s. Their time was to come in the following decade.

It is difficult to generalize about the films of this generation, as the filmmakers worked in a wide variety of styles and from a diversity of standpoints. But the work of a number of filmmakers does stand out. Some of these filmmakers of the 1980s worked in isolation, with distinctive voices not acquired in a film school but expressing a totally personal vision that had no precedent in their respective national cinemas or, indeed, within Arab cinema as a whole. Among these lone figures are half a dozen filmmakers with totally original styles of filmmaking: the Algerian Mohamed Chouikh, the Tunisian Nacer Khemir, the Egyptian Asma El Bakry, and two Lebanese filmmakers, Ghassan Salhab and Heiny Srour. Yousry Nasrallah occupies a place apart in relation to Egyptian cinema, though he did have the conventional Egyptian film school training and began his career in the customary way by working as an assistant director. Rachid Bouchareb, who acquired his skills by working initially in French television, likewise stands out among the French-based filmmakers (the *beurs*) for the breadth of his international concerns. Hafsa Zinaï-Koudil received backing from the Algerian national television production organization, but only for a single film (like Assia Djebar in the earlier generation). But others of equal stature were trained at film schools abroad while remaining intimately caught up in developments within their own national filmmaking contexts. Here one thinks of Michel Khleifi's decisive contributions to the founding of Palestinian cinema, the role of Nouri Bouzid and Moufida Tlatli in creating a new, internationally acclaimed Tunisian cinema, Daoud Aoulad-Syad's achievements in breaking with the dominant realist approach in Morocco, and Mohamed Malas's involvement in the development of a distinctive Syrian cinematic style.

An apparent paradox arises when we discuss the work of these filmmakers and that of their slightly older contemporaries. We are considering a new form of Arab cinema, distinct from the previous state-controlled production (even if, on occasion, using those same structures) but still recognizably linked to the filmmaker's country of origin. But these films have been created at a time when, as Hamid Dabashi has pointed out, "national cinemas are losing their distinct visual vocabularies to a vacuous globalization that manufactures aesthetic consent with the same rapidity that it dismantles it."[12] International funding becomes virtually the norm, and it is increasingly difficult to specify the corpus of what might constitute any single specific Arab "national cinema" in the 1980s and 1990s, as one can with Egyptian cinema in its "golden years" (say, the mid-1930s to the mid-1960s) or the Algerian state cinema of the 1970s.

The key Arab filmmakers maintained close relationships with their home countries, even if they were wholly or partly based abroad. For those still at home, one factor of significance was, and is, the diversity of dialect in the Arabic language, which often means that (subtitled) distribution through European festivals is more likely than commercial screenings in a neighboring Arab state. Apart from Nacer Khemir, virtually all the Arab filmmakers of the 1980s and 1990s viewed the wider problems and issues of Arab life through a specific national lens, even if their funding came from elsewhere and they were located abroad. This applies as much to those who adopted allegorical patterns (such as Mohamed Chouikh) as to those who saw their task as probing and analyzing Arab life in a more realistic mode (such as Nouri Bouzid or Rachid Boudjedra).

Over the two decades of the 1980s and 1990s, there was a tendency for social realist approaches to take on a sharper political edge, for formerly taboo subjects to be tackled a little more readily (particularly those relating to sexuality), and for filmmakers to adopt a greater freedom of language. There was a new focus on the individual protagonist and, in some cases, such as that of Nouri Bouzid, even a move toward autobiography (a form comparatively rare in Arab literature and culture), following the path opened up by Youssef Chahine with his Alexandria Quartet. What is perhaps most crucial is that across the Arab world, despite pressures of autocratic regimes and the impact of wars, social upheavals, and political disasters, striking films were made by a number of courageous and tenacious individuals, true film *auteurs*. But the opportunities have been limited and, of the filmmakers singled out above, only Allouache has made made a dozen features, while Bouzid, Bouchareb, and Nasrallah have had the possibility of making only half a dozen or so features in twenty years.

Beur Filmmaking in France

Filmmaking by members of the Algerian immigrant community in France— generally known as *beurs*—falls outside the scope of this volume. It requires and has received a separate consideration. These filmmakers began to make an impact in France and abroad from the mid-1980s onward. There is no meaningful way of separating those filmmakers who had arrived as children from those who were born in France, since all the new filmmakers began their careers with studies of individual immigrant lives and experiences. Subsequently many of them have diversified their approaches and gone on to make films with much wider subject matter. In particular, in the 1990s and 2000s, most key *beur* directors turned toward Algerian subjects and locations.[13]

Much of this work is of high quality, but, as I have noted elsewhere,[14] the attribution of any precise national definition to the work of any members of this group—the separation of it from mainstream French cinema, on the one hand, or the establishment of its relationship to work from the wider Arab world, on the other—is becoming increasingly problematic. The actual nationality of the filmmakers is also of little help. Of the three pioneers, Abdelkrim Bahloul retained his Algerian identity, while Rachid Bouchareb and Mehdi Charef are French citizens. Okacha Touita retains his Algerian nationality, but all his films are classified as French. Though the Fonds Sud funding is intended "to bring support to filmmakers in countries *whose filmmaking situation is fragile*, to support their creativity,"[15] this aid has been given to a number of *beur* filmmakers securely located in France, among them Abdelkrim Bahloul, Mehdi Charef, and Amor Hakkar. The decisions of Arab film festivals show a similar confusion, with the Journées Cinématographiques de Carthage (JCC) in Tunis accepting as "Maghrebian" features films that, by virtually any criterion, are mainstream European productions.

*

An initial trio of French-based *beur* filmmakers, all born in the 1950s, made their international reputations in the mid-1980s. All three began with studies of the immigrant community before moving on to look at some of the issues facing contemporary Algeria.

Abdelkrim Bahloul, who was born in Algeria in 1950, arrived in France at the age of twenty. He studied drama in Algiers and Paris and then followed a master's degree in modern languages with formal film study at the Institut des Hautes Études Cinématographiques (IDHEC). He worked in French television for several years before making his feature film debut with *Mint Tea / Le thé à la menthe* (1984), a study of the immigrant community that was screened in the French Film Perspectives category of the Cannes film festival. After a tongue-in-cheek vampire comedy, *A Vampire in Paradise / Un vampire au paradis*, Bahloul returned to his original subject matter with two more realistic studies of immigrant life, *The Hamlet Sisters / Les soeurs Hamlet* (1996) and *The Night of Destiny / La nuit du destin* (1997). In the 2000s, he worked extensively as an actor and also made two features set in Algeria. The first, *The Murdered Sun / Le soleil assassiné* (2004), is a study of the French poet Jean Sénac, who remained in Algeria after independence, attracting not only a following of young people inspired by his advocacy of freedom but also the wrath of the authorities. This was followed by *Journey to Algiers / Le voyage à Alger* (2010), a more conventional tale of a widow who travels to Algiers to protest to the president of the newly independent republic about the treatment she has received since the death of her husband.

Mehdi Charef was born at Maghnia in Algeria in 1952 and arrived in France at age ten. He received no formal film training and used his own semiautobiographical first novel, about growing up in Paris, as the basis for his debut feature, *Tea at Archimedes' Harem / Le thé au harem d'Archimède* (1985). He has continued his literary career alongside his filmmaking, publishing three more novels: *Le harki de Meriem* (1989), *La maison d'Alexina* (1999), and *À bras le cœur* (2006).

After *Tea at Archimedes' Harem*, Charef made two more major studies of the immigrant community, narrated from very different perspectives. *Miss Mona* (1987)[16] traces the doomed relationship between a young Maghrebian and an aging French transvestite (the "Miss Mona" of the title). By contrast, *Marie-Line* (2000) has as its chief protagonist a woman who has joined the National Front. Between these two features, Charef made a number of téléfilms while continuing his feature film career with *Camomile /Camoumile* (1988) and *In the Land of the Juliets / Au pays des Juliets* (1992). In 2002, he initiated a narrative form that would become an obligatory film for this generation of *beur* filmmakers. *Keltoum's Daughter / La fille de Keltoum* (2002) traces its nineteen-year-old heroine's "return" to her roots in Algeria, the unknown land of her parents. This was followed by a more substantial work, *Summer of '62 / Cartouches gauloises* (2007), that reflects on Charef's own departure from Algeria at the age of ten. Eight years later, he made another feature, *Graziella* (2015).

Rachid Bouchareb is the only one of the trio to be born in France. He was born in Paris in 1959 to Algerian parents and has French nationality. He learned his craft working in French television, and, as his career has unfolded, he has come more and more to favor strong narrative lines destined to grip a wide audience. His work has a wider scope than that of any of his contemporaries. He has filmed on locations across the world, worked on occasion on studio-based movies, and covered a whole range of subjects and genres.

Bouchareb began with typical *beur* subject matter but with a distinctive twist. *Bâton Rouge* (1985) deals with three young immigrants who try to find a new life in Louisitania, and *Cheb* (1990) is the story of an illegal immigrant who makes his way from Algeria to France, traveling through Morocco and Spain. Bouchareb went on to film a drama set in postrevolutionary Algeria, *Shattered Years / Des années déchirées* (1992). This was followed by a study of Vietnam orphans, *Life Dust / Poussières de vie* (1994), shot in Malaysia. He then returned to the subject of the immigrant community in France with *My Family's Honour / L'honneur de ma famille* (1997). Always attracted by exotic subject matter, Bouchareb made *Little Senegal* (2001), which looks at relationships between black Americans and Senegalese immigrants in the United States.

In 2005, he made the first of two big-budget epic films. *Days of Glory / Indigènes* (2005) deals with an overlooked subject—the role of troops from North Africa in the liberation of France during World War II. This film is an excellent example of the confusion of national identity. It was selected, as an Algerian film, to open the JCC in 2006 but is in fact a coproduction among Tessalit Productions and Kissfilms Productions (France), Taza Productions (Morocco), Tassili Films (Algeria), and Versus Productions and Scope Invest (Belgium), with further support from a wide range of French and foreign television companies, French national and regional support organizations, and other Belgian and Moroccan financial sources.

In 2010, in the same vein and working with the same scriptwriter Olivier Lorelle, he looked at controversial aspects of Franco-Algerian relations in *Outside the Law / Hors-la-loi* (2010). The film deals with three Algerian brothers drawn, in their very different ways, into the Front National de Libération (FNL) struggles for Algerian independence in Paris in the 1950s. Whereas *Days of Glory*, which was shot in Europe, relied on location for much of its impact, *Outside the Law* is a studio movie, with the infamous Sétif massacre in Algeria and the Pigalle streets of 1950s Paris both reconstructed in Tarak Ben Ammar's studios in Tunisia. Between these two huge films, Bouchareb made a touching, downbeat and sensitive film, *London River* (2009). Set in London, it deals with just two disparate people, a woman from Guernsey and an African who has lived fifteen years in France, who are thrown together by the common search for their children in the aftermath of the London bombing of July 7, 2007.

Though it is a French-language film, *London River* heralds a new interest in the English-speaking world. Bouchareb's first US production, starring Sienna Miller, was *Just Like a Woman* (2012), a road movie in the vein of *Thelma and Louise*. He has since made two more features: *Two Men in Town / La voie de l'ennemi* (2014), with Forest Whitaker, and *Road to Instanbul / La route d'Instanbul* (2016).

*

Other directors born before 1960 also emerged fom the immigrant community but failed to make the same international impact. Among these are four men—Okacha Touita, Amor Hakkar, Ahmed Bouchaâla, and Karim Traïda—and one woman, Rachida Krim.

Okacha Touita, who was born in 1943 in Algeria, studied at the Institut Français du Cinéma (IFC) in Paris and worked for a time as an assistant director. Technically he belongs to the 1980s group, since he made his first feature in 1982, but it took him far longer to establish his reputation. His four features—*The Sacrificed / Les sacrifiés* (1982), *The Survivior / Le rescapé* (1986), *The Cry of Men / Le cri des hommes* (1990), and *Morituri* (2007)—deal with the violent tensions within Muslim resistance and terrorist groups and with their bloody conflicts with the police.

Amor Hakkar, born in 1958 in Algeria but brought up in Besançon, made *Bad Weather for a Crook / Sale temps pour un voyou* (1992), which received little critical attention. Sixteen years later, he made a second feature, this time well received, *The Yellow House / La maison jaune* (2008). This was followed by *A Few Days of Respite / Quelques jours de répit* (2011) and *The Proof / La preuve* (2013). He has also been active as a writer with the prize-winning *La cité des fausses notes*, published in 2000.

Ahmed Bouchaâla was born in 1956 in Algeria and has lived in France since the age of six. After work as an assistant director and the directing of a few short films, he turned to feature filmmaking, working with his Lille-born wife, Zakia. She coscripted his first feature, *Krim* (1995), and codirected his second, *Control of Origin / Origine contrôlée* (2001). Together the pair also scripted Abdelhaï Laraki's Moroccan debut feature, *Mona Saber*. Bouchaâla also coproduced his wife's solo debut, made under her maiden name, Tahiri. *Number One* was shot in Morocco in 2008 and remains one of the country's most popular comedy films.[17]

Karim Traïda, born in 1949 in Constantine, then part of France but now, of course, Algeria. He studied sociology in Paris and then moved to the Netherlands in 1979. There he studied at the Netherlands Film and Television Academy, worked in television, and made his first feature, *The Polish Bride / De Poolse Bruid* (1998). Subsequently, in France, he made his second feature, *The Truth Tellers / Les diseurs de vérité* (2000), about the Algerian struggle.

Rachida Krim was born in 1955 at Alès in France and studied painting before making a first short film in in 1990. She made an impressive feature debut with *Under Women's Feet / Sous les pieds des femmes* (1996), dealing with FNL involvement within the immigrant community in France, which was followed by a short film, *The Unveiled Woman / La femme dévoilée* (1998), an amusing exposé of male sexual harassment. She has made two features in the 2000s: *Permission to Love / Permis d'aimer* (2005) and *Not That Simple / Pas si simple* (2008).

Also active as early as the late 1990s were three younger filmmakers, all born after 1960: Malek Chibane, Bourlem Guerdjou, and Zaïda Ghorab-Volta. Their films are among those discussed in Will Higbee's book *Post-Beur Cinema* (2014).[18]

Algeria

The restructuring of the state's involvement with filmmaking in Algeria happened constantly during the 1980s, with the Office National du Commerce et de l'Industrie Cinématographiques (ONCIC) first being split in two in 1984 and then reconstituted to create the Centre Algérien pour l'Art et Industrie Cinématographiques (CAAIC) in 1987. Television production was similarly reorganized to form the Entreprise Nationale de Productions Audiovisuelles (ENPA) that same year. The previous sharp divide between film and television became blurred as the two new organizations collaborated to produce a less tightly controlled program of features in the period leading up to the complete withdrawal of all state support for filmmaking in 1993. New freedoms and constraints for filmmakers appeared as the old patterns of tight control over style and subject matter gradually disappeared. The patriotic rhetoric found in the earlier work of Mohamed Lakhdar Hamina and Ahmed Rachedi largely disappeared from view, though the two directors continued to dominate much of Algerian filmmaking through their various administrative roles.

On the margins of the state industries, there were a number of fascinating films made across the Maghreb in the 1970s that look forward to the new styles of the mid-1980s. In Algeria, perhaps the most innovative film produced by ONCIC was Merzak Allouache's debut film, *Omar Gatlato* (1976). The film even gave its name to a book about 1970s Algerian cinema by Wassyla Tamzali, *En attendant Omar Gatlato*: "We wondered what we were waiting for, as we marched up and down in front of the film insitute or wandered about at foreign film festivals. The longer we waited, the more cinema seemed to slip through our fingers. Now we know. We were waiting for *Omar Gatlato*."[19]

*

Three other feature films made in the 1970s outside the state production organization also deserve more than just a mention for their precocious elements of form: playing with narrative structures, mixing fiction and documentary, and creating striking interactions of image and sound. These are the sole feature films of Mohamed Zinet, Assia Djebar, and Farouk Beloufa.

Mohamed Zinet, who was born in Algiers in 1932 and died in France in 1995, is an important figure in Algerian theater and the creator of a single unique feature film. He has described himself as a globe-trotter and while still young made visits to Paris and Cairo. A fervent nationalist, he fought with the Armée de Libération Nationale (ALN) and, when wounded, was sent to Tunis, where he worked on the project for the creation of a national theater. He subsequently studied drama at Humboldt University in East Berlin and at Karl Marx University in Leipzig. He then began work as an actor on stage and gained experience as an assistant director in Algiers, most notably at Casbah Films, where he worked on Gillo Pontecorvo's *Battle of Algiers* (1966). He also collaborated as an actor and assistant on two early shorts by René Vautier. In the 1970s, he appeared in films shot in France, Tunisia, and Algeria. The most significant of these was the Tunisian feature *Aziza*, shot in 1979 by Abdellatif Ben Ammar.

Zinet's *Tahya ya didou /Alger insolite* (the title means literally "Long Live Didou") was made in 1971, a film produced on the margins, funded by the Algiers Municipal Council. It offers quite a unique view of postwar Algiers and the heritage of its French colonization, which was totally rejected by its sponsors. As Zinet records, it was given a single showing in Algiers on February 1, 1971, and immediately was withdrawn. Zinet has claimed that the film, as it now exists, is still not finished: "Quite simply because they did not allow me to finish it in the way I had first conceived it."[20]

Tahya ya didou mixes documentary and fiction, with the action punctuated with songs by the Algiers poet Himoud Brahimi, generally known as Momo, who introduces the film with an extreme close-up statement. Lizbeth Malkmus offers an excellent definition of his role in the unfolding narrative. Momo, who is naked to the waist, does not move from his cross-legged position on an Algiers pier, but his vision seems to extend over time; he sees all, at least about Algiers, and comments both on events just presented in the film and on those that will follow. Not only does this produce a kind of authorial prescience rare in Arab films, but he constantly emphasizes the effect of his words by further commentary in poetry.[21]

At the end of the film, his role is taken over by a small child who mimics his tone and gestures.

The film opens at the Algiers airport and, with characteristically quirky Zinet humor, we are shown, throughout the lengthy precredit sequence, the problems of an oddly dressed Swiss who has arrived without a visa. He reappears a couple of times but plays no part in the film's subsequent narrative. The people we do not see arriving are the two tourists who will form the dramatic focus of the film. After the airport, the film switches to become an observational documentary on the diversity of Algiers (it was initially planned as a short documentary), following the activities of children, delivery men, and traders and recording the first of a number of patriotic demonstrations. The initial shots of children are developed into a series of lightly staged scenes, where they annoy and then outrun a fat policeman. Here, and throughout the film, the music is inventive and often unexpected.

Initially the tone is lighthearted, with plenty of humor, comic chases, and some good jokes ("What's capitalism?" "The exploitation of man by man" "Then what's socialism?" "The opposite"). A visiting French couple enters, initially innocuously, from the crowd, uttering the usual tourist banalities. The mood darkens, however, when it emerges that the husband, Simon, was previously involved in the torture of Algerian patriots, and the film comes to a climax in a restaurant. There Simon has to flee from the seemingly relentless gaze of a man he once tortured. This sparks a long flashback sequence in which the ruthless treatment of prisoners by the French is graphically depicted, and this is followed by a formal documentary depiction of the French invasion of Algeria using contemporary paintings and drawings. But, in fact, Simon need not have worried. The gaze was not implacable recognition, since the victim (played by Zinet) is actually blind as a result of his mistreatment in prison.

The shooting of *Tahya ya didou* was difficult. There seems not to have been a fully worked-out script—no more than a fairly vague synopsis—as the director of photography, Bruno Muel, revealed when asked how Zinet worked as a director: "It was fairly crazy. I have to say there was some improvisation, which was sometimes inspired, but in which we very often did not know where he was going. . . . I was a little uncertain. . . . But when I saw the film I was surprised. Everything was fine. Zinet's vision was right."[22]

The film's initial difficulties continue to be echoed in the present. Though virtually all studies of Algerian cinema refer to *Tahya ya didou* as remarkable or striking, these are judgments made in passing, and there has been no in-depth analysis of the film in either French or English. There is no commercial DVD of the film available and the version on YouTube has no subtitles. True, it is a difficult film to sum up. Perhaps the most apposite comments are those of Nacer Khemir: "Zinet didn't make a film for the pleasure of making one. He made it to say that he loves everything that he shows in it: the city, the people, the walls, the sea, this land which he is prepared to defend by any means, by trickery, through his intelligence, with his body. . . . What interests him is everything he brings to life. And that is an act of rare generosity."[23]

The French-language novelist (and future member of the Académie Française) Assia Djeba, who was born in 1936, produced the second Algerian experimental film of the 1970s, *La Nouba / La nouba des femmes du mont Chenoa* (1978). This is the first and only feature to be completed by an Algerian female filmmaker during the decade. A 16mm film produced by Algerian television, *La Nouba* is both the simple story of a woman, Lila, returning home and a deeply autobiographical work in which Djebar explores the mountains of Cherchell, where she was born.

La Nouba is complex work that begins as a formalized interior drama and ends as a celebratory song. In tackling its subject matter, it adopts a variety of stylistic approaches: formal fictional drama, conventional documentary shooting and interviewing, enacted reconstructions, and voice-over commentaries. Throughout there is interplay with words and sounds. This occurs within the sound track itself, which uses silence to powerful effect. It also juxtaposes natural and distorted newsreel sounds, direct-to-camera speech and a questioning voice-over commentary. The sound track also brings together Arab song and dance and Western musical forms. In addition—and equally important—there is a constant interplay between this sound track and the image track, and here discordance rather than synchronization is the rule. The audio-visual texture is thus dense and complex and, as Mireille Calle-Gruber has noted, shows the same concern with a musical structure that Djebar's novels reveal.[24]

Though the basic narrative structure—a personal journey to explore the past—is straightforward, the film juggles four separate time levels: the present of the filmed exploration, the immediate past as remembered by female witnesses, the distant past evoked by the grandmother, and the retrospective meditation on the images by the narrator (Lila and, by extension, Assia Djebar herself). The story emerges only gradually, through delicate touches, added details, and embroidered variants, which together give the film its slow rhythm and lyrical quality. Always, we are left with only part of the story: the film draws us in to fill its gaps and omissions. Indeed, the film moves steadily away from the tight dramatic narrative of the opening so that it—like the protagonist Lila herself—is free to roam in search of a past accessible only in fragmentary form from the film's elderly female participants. *La Nouba* is an outstanding formal feminist experiment in film narrative that is far removed from the prevailing male-oriented and male-dominated realistic conformities of 1970s and 1980s Algerian cinema.[25]

Farouk Beloufa, who was born in Oued Fodda in 1947, began his career alongside Merzak Allouache in the 1960s (there is a fascinating joint interview by Samir Ardjoum in which they recall their past that appeared in 2012).[26] Both Beloufa and Allouache attended the short-lived Algerian film school Institut National de Cinéma d'Algers (INC) and then went on to continue their studies at IDHEC in Paris. Allouache even appeared in one of Beloufa's short films. Both were profoundly influenced by the range of great European films that they could see in France at that time, and both had a well-received first feature edited by the future director Moufia Tlatli. But there the comparison ends. In Paris, Beloufa also followed the courses given by Roland Barthes at the École Pratique des Hautes Études and worked as assistant to Youssef Chahine. Subsequently, while Allouache went on to become the most prolific of all independent Arab

filmmakers, Beloufa made just one compilation film about the liberation struggle, *Insurrectionary / Insurectionelle* (1973)—it was censored, totally reedited, and
released unsigned—as well as a single fictional feature, *Nahla* (1979). None of his
further projects came to fruition.

Nahla, which was produced by Radiodiffusion Télévision Algérienne (RTA)
for cinema release, is one of the few Maghrebian films to look at events abroad in
the Arab world, in this case the situation in Lebanon in 1975. Cowritten with the
novelist Rachid Boudjedra and the film critic Mouny Berrah, the film is stylistically innovative, combining live action, songs, dancing, newsreel material, and
radio broadcasts into a perceptive and flowing narrative. The central figure is the
twenty-year-old singer Nahla, already a star and the focus of popular attention.
Her face in close-up, as she is being made up for a television performance, opens
the film's credit sequence, and the early part of the film contains frequent shots of
her in rehearsal. These scenes are totally realistic (as is all the detail in the film),
as her musical coach is played by Ziad Rahbani, who not only wrote the film's
musical score but also went on to occupy the same role of coach in real life, in his
work with the great Lebanese singer and star Fairouz. Nahla's voice is also used
to link the diverse opening sequences of this multilayered film. The personal climax of the film comes when she dries up on stage during a major performance at
Beirut's Piccadilly Theatre. She is initially plunged into total despair, but toward
the end of the film, she announces that she intends to revive her career in the Gulf
and is last seen being driven off in the limousine of a wealthy arms dealer.

Key figures in the group around her are her two female friends, the journalist Maha and a young Palestinian activist Hind. The social interrelationships of
the three women are complex, and all have tortured emotional problems at some
point. Maha, for example, has to cope with the end of her six-year marriage to
her handsome, estranged Egyptian husband, Nabil. Also drawn to Nahla and
forming a fourth member of the central group is the Algerian journalist Larbi.
His experiences as an outsider in Beirut form a key element of the film, but he is
basically an ineffectual and indecisive individual whose main occupation seems
to be constantly getting in the way of the more forceful female characters.

The film is set in 1975, beginning after the defeat of Kfar Chouba. Throughout, the interactions of the leading characters are interspersed with press conferences, radio reports, and newsreel clips all dealing directly with immediate
political events that year in Lebanon. At first, the violence is far away, a series
of disasters to be watched on television. But as the attention moves away from
Nahla after her personal disaster, the film's focus shifts to the wider perspective.
An increasingly violent civil war comes to Beirut. Characters are displaced and
secure spaces are increasingly invaded by explosions and armed men. Particularly striking is the documentary-style image of up-market Beirut at night, when
violence is just below the surface—one character, armed with a gun, expresses

the need to go out and kill someone "on the other side." There is also a brilliantly shot and edited sequence in which Larbi, foolishly ignoring all warnings, finds himself on the frontline between the two factions, threatened by crossfire and ruthless sniping.

Nahla is a remarkable, confident first feature, inventively interweaving its complex mix of elements. It offers an insightful vision of Lebanon slowly slipping toward civil war. It is full of realistic detail but also has a hallucinatory aspect (particularly in the way that, despite all the shooting, no one is killed or seriously wounded). It is easy to relate the two dramatic threads of the film, to see Nahla's personal failure as prefiguring the fate of the once-confident Lebanon as a whole. The film's relationship to situations in Algeria is more complex to define, as Beloufa's comments on Larbi, made in an interview thirty years later, make clear: "The fact that we do not see him arrive or depart suggests that the Beirut shown here derives more from interiority, from the imagination. . . . The character Larbi could have imagined this whole story, without ever having left Algiers. It could have been call 'Larbi the Schizophrenic' or more precisely 'The Schizophrenic Arab,' since from the beginning he is caught between two cultures."[27]

But, surely, if these were to be Larbi's imaginings, he would have given himself a more sympathetic and dynamic role?

*

The same spirit of independence is shown by a number of filmmakers who began their careers in the 1980s. The ways in which the changes in production organization worked out in the 1980s and early 1990s are particularly apparent if we compare the contrasting careers of three additional filmmakers who were all born in Algeria in the 1940s and followed formal programs of film study abroad, in Paris or Brussels: Brahim Tsaki, Mohamed Rachid Benhadj, and Mahmoud Zemmouri. The restrained and more lyrical approaches offered by Tsaki and Benhadj in their first works strike a fresh note, as does the comic, at times derisive, attitude toward the liberation struggle and the postwar Algerian situation adopted by Zemmouri. The paths they have chosen could hardly be more divergent.

Brahim Tsaki, who was born in Sidi Bel Abbes in 1946, studied at INSAS in Belgium and worked initially in the documentary section of the state organization ONCIC. All Tsaki's films are studies of children. His first feature, *Children of the Wind / Les enfants du vent* (1981), remains his favorite, because, he says, it was made "in total freedom. It's a film made without constraints, with very little money, in Algeria."[28] Originally it was shot as three separate short films of about twenty minutes each that were brought together for release to make a single three-part fiction.

The first story, *Boiled Eggs*, deals with a little boy who, to survive, sells eggs in a bar. Much of the episode has a documentary feel, with the boy looking directly at the camera in key moments. The focus of his despair and disillusionment is a drunk who frequents the bar. The drunk is played by Boualem Bennani (the lead player in Merzak Allouache's *Omar Gatlato*), and he is openly presented to us as an actor—we see him being made up. But the boy's anguish is real, as the frozen image of his weeping face at the very end powerfully conveys. Again in the second story, *Djamel in the World of Images*, very little happens. We simply see another small boy living in anguish, alone with his father in a desolate urban landscape. The boy is caught up, confused, and above all alone. The backdrop to his world comprises media sounds—dialogue from the cinema next door and noises from the domestic television—but we see none of the related images, a fact that emphasizes the bleakness of his situation. *The Box in the Desert* is more positive. The boys here may live against a background of agricultural equipment (tractors, harvesters, trucks of various kinds), but they themselves are creatively engaged, making fantastic toys with wire from barbed-wire fences and scraps of junk. Again the episode ends with the close-up of a boy's face, this time accompanied by a French song, "Tomorrow, tomorrow, what shall I become?" the words of which appear on the screen before the end credits.

Children of the Wind set the pattern for Tsaki's work, with all four of his features dealing with the world of children. There is no dialogue here (though there is a limited amount in the subsequent films) and no linear narrative as such. The wind of the title has a double significance for the director: "You believe it's nothing, that it leaves no traces, and yet it flattens and hollows out mountains. Children of today live such a situation." Tsaki's approach demands that the spectator look attentively at every detail of the image and background, because nothing is explained: "Everyone is free—but completely—to compose their own text. I offer the spectator a freedom which is certainly channelled, but which authorises a wide range of readings."[29]

Tsaki's second feature, *Story of an Encounter / Histoire d'une rencontre* (1983), is one of the last films produced by ONCIC. It is a tale of two fourteen-year-old deaf-mutes who meet and find communication and friendship despite their very different backgrounds. He is a local working-class boy; she is the American daughter of an engineer employed on a nearby petrochemical installation. They achieve a real connection—unlike anything either of them has previously experienced—but the gifts they offer each other to affirm their friendship serve to emphasize the social gulf between them. Seemingly inevitably, the demands of the girl's father's job intervene to separate them. He has to move to a new site, making the end of their relationship inevitable. Again, Tsaki's empathy with his young protagonists is total, making this—a feature-length film in which very little happens—a very moving and absorbing experience for the spectator.

The Neon Children / Les enfants des néons (1990) reflects Tsaki's disillusionment after several years of living in Paris. Though he had some support from the

French Ministry of Culture (the CNC) and the television company Canal Plus, he had a very limited budget and hence a very tight shooting schedule, meaning that he was no longer able to work with the same freedom he had enjoyed in Algeria. Once more, the story concerns the relationship between young people separated by their backgrounds. Djamel and his deaf-mute friend Karim are both from the *beur* community in Paris. Djamel's love for a young French student, Claude, is real but destroyed by the cultural differences that separate them. He later dies, the victim of a racist assault.

Once Upon a Time / Il était une fois / Ayrouwen, the director's fourth film, made seventeen years later, in 2007, is a third tale of a failed relationship between two young people from very different backgrounds. Amayas, a Tuareg, and Claude, who comes from a European city, meet in the Djanet desert in Algeria. In Tsaki's words: "This is an imagined story, not a true one. A story of impossible love . . . in a desert, beautiful, full of mystery, and riches. . . . Imagining a story, making a film, means trying to feel the unforeseeable. The unforeseeable must be mastered in everyday life, so as to avoid tragedies in the future."[30]

Tsaki's studies of young people are united by the director's very personal vision of childhood and adolescence, as well as by the stylistic pattern of his work, which consistently uses a minimum of dialogue and eschews voice-over comment and the demands of conventional dramatic development. Hesitant relationship are born and flourish, only to be destroyed by forces outside the characters' control. Tsaki denies that his vision is pessimistic, but in none of his films do the characters have the possibility of controlling their own destinies. Tsaki's delicate realization of this very personal vision, in Algeria and France over more than twenty-five years, is a tribute to his tenacity and sense of purpose in the face of real commercial and financial difficulties.

Mohamed Rachid Benhadj, who was born in Algiers in 1949, is an artist as well as a filmmaker who studied architecture in Paris before turning to filmmaking at the Université de Paris. He, too, made his debut in the last years of ONCIC's existence, but his career has since taken a very different direction to that followed by Tsaki.

Benhadj began excellently in a low-key style that parallels that of Tsaki, with *Louss / Rose des sables* (1989), which begins with a fable about how poverty and disease entered the world and contains other such tales as it unfolds. The film is, in itself, a fable, telling the story of a crippled young orphan, Moussa, living with his beautiful sister, Zeinab, in a remote oasis situated in the timeless desert, hundreds of kilometres from Algiers. Despite having no arms, Moussa, accepted unconditionally by his neighbors, is helped to live as full a life as possible within the community. But the balance is precarious. He copes with the prospect of his sister getting married to Rachid, his closest friend and ally. But when his sister is taken to the hospital and the woman he desperately loves, Meriem, leaves to marry a rich suitor, he momentarily succumbs to despair. But Moussa is never patronized at any point in the film. Depicted as intelligent and with a good sense of humor from the beginning, he shows, in a totally affirmative ending, that he can cope even while living alone. Using his one good foot, he demonstrates that he can cook, shave, tend his beloved plant out in the desert, and pass a written examination. Throughout, the film has a touchingly poetic sense of innocence, and the delicacy with which Benhadj handles his players, the precision of his camerawork, and the beauty of his visual style make the film a success with a wide range of audiences. Though coproduced by the state organization CAAIC, *Louss*'s focus on a lone protagonist living outside the social forces of modernity captures one of the key aspects of the new mood of the 1980s, far removed from the state propaganda of the 1970s.

Benhadj's second feature, *Touchia* (1992), reveals a new political awareness in its depiction of the rising Islamist threat, but it is a difficult film to come to terms with. The film's end title talks of revolt growing to give birth to hope and dreams, but what we have just seen enacted in the narrative is rape, disillusionment, and the shattering of all aspiration. The film's subtitle is "Canticle of the Women of Algiers," but this is, in truth, the customary tale of the female victim, helpless in the wider world.

On a day when she is due to go to the television studios to give an interview, a woman, Fella, is trapped in her apartment by fundamentalist demonstrators on the streets outside, who are shouting, "Down with democracy!" The stress brings back memories of her childhood, beginning in 1958 with her father's imprisonment while battle raged on the street, the personal humiliation of bed-wetting at the age of eleven, her first period, the joy of her friendship with Anissa, and their dreams of going together to see the sea. The two girls share the joy of all Algerians on Independence Day in 1962 and feel themselves to be finally free: this will be the best day of their lives. They leave the shelter of home to roam out in the countryside. The result is catastrophic: Anissa is murdered and Fella gang-raped by four men. Despite these recollections, Fella does summon up the courage to go to the studios, and only then do we learn the deeper cause of her stress. She is to be interviewed about the anniversary of Algeria's independence. The interviewer's innocuously intended opening question, "Tell us about your experience . . ." renders her literally speechless—she can only utter a piercing and prolonged scream.

The transitions in time are smoothly handled in *Touchia*, and the performances of the cast are well realized. But the excesses and contrivances of the plot (how could Fella have possibly agreed to a television interview on that specific day?) are in no way helped by the overlayering of highly orchestrated, emotive Andalousian music at every moment of dramatic tension.

Subsequently Benhadj has lived in exile in Italy, where much of his work falls outside the scope of this study. He has made two Italian films, *The Last Supper*

/ *L'ultima cena* (1995) and *The Tree of Suspended Fates* / *L'albero dei destini sospesi* (1997), followed by an unashamedly commercial movie, the international blockbuster *Mirka* (2000), in which the talents of Vanessa Redgrave and Gérard Depardieu and the cinematographic skills of Vittorio Storaro are expended on a rather slight if well-meaning tale of a small boy bullied because he is the outcome of a brutal rape during ethnic cleansing in the Balkans.

More recently, Benhadj last turned his attachment back to the Maghreb. *For Bread Alone* / *Le pain nu* / *El-khobz el-hafi* (2006) is an adaptation of the celebrated 1952 autobiographical novel by the Moroccan author Mohamed Choukri. The stature of the novel can be judged by the quality of its translators: an English version by Paul Bowles was brought out in 1974, while the French translation is by Tahar Benjelloun. Though Choukri died in 2003, work on the film was already under way, and prior to the author's death, Benhadj had persuaded him to make a brief appearance before the camera. *For Bread Alone* tells the story of Choukri, growing up in poverty and terrorized by his alcoholic father. He eventually turns to drink and petty crime. It is only when, as an adult, he has been arrested and thrown into prison that he has the chance to learn to read and write. Since this time, Benhadj has completed a another feature, *Perfumes of Algiers* / *Parfums d'Alger* (2012), which tells the story of the return to Algiers of a Paris-based photogragrapher, Karima, to care for her dying father, whose attitudes had driven her to seek exile in France twenty years before. The visit allows her to come to terms with her own past and her native city.

Mahmoud Zemmouri was born in Boufarik in 1946 but did not return to work in Algeria after completing his studies at IDHEC in Paris. Instead, he worked, first as an actor and then as an assistant director in the French production context. He does not form part of the *beur* group of filmmakers, as from the start his films were particularly concerned with developments in Algeria rather than with the immigrant situation in France. His insider / outsider status undoubtedly helps him bring a fresh, satiric eye to the country of his birth.

Under the presidency of Valéry Giscard d'Estaing, the Stoléru Law was enacted, which offered immigrants ten thousand francs to go "home." This forms the basis of Zemmouri's first feature, *Take a Thousand Quid and Get Lost* / *Prends dix mille balles et casse-toi* (1981). The Ghani family decides to take up this offer, though their two children, who are at senior school level, have grown up in Paris and do not speak Arabic. The parents can reintegrate into the village where they grew up—sometimes with difficulty—but the children find themselves in an unimagined world in which they do not fit. But other families have made the same journey, and Mustapha (whose nickname is Travolta) finds an immediate friend in Fifi (aka Red Lips), who is in the same situation. The gulf between the two communities is apparent from the very beginning, when

Mustapha, exploring the village for the first time, asks to "visit" the mosque, only to be angrily expelled: "A mosque is for praying, not for visiting."

Zemmouri, who displays an admirable lightness of touch as well as an ease in handling the action, draws out all the humor that can arise from this clash of cultures. On the villagers' side, there is basic hostility from the older generation to anything outside their traditional culture, though a few of the younger villagers, who have been to Paris briefly, spin tall stories. Djelloul, who spent three weeks there, claims, for example, to have shared a flat with Elvis Presley. Other younger villagers are attracted to the newcomers' appearances, attitudes, and lifestyles, particularly Aïssa, previously a model young man in the eyes of his now scandalized parents. The differences give rise to numerous clashes and moments of mutual incomprehension, and Zemmouri, while keeping totally to the truth of the situation, emphasizes its comic absurdity. Zemmouri's feeling and sympathy for all of his characters is constantly apparent.

The Crazy Years of the Twist / Les folles années du twist (1983) is a far more ambitious challenge. Not only did Zemmouri satirize the Algerian War of Independence, but he also persuaded the state corporation, ONCIC, to coproduce the film. *The Crazy Years of the Twist* opens with a serious credit that gives little hint of the approach Zemmouri will adopt: "The real subject of the film is the [Algerian] people and its daily survival, its heroism, its cowardice, sometimes even its opportunism or its indifference to the conflict."

The narrative follows the exact chronology of events from January 1960 (after the Battle of Algiers) to July 3, 1962 (Independence Day), with titles locating us exactly, but the film treats this period in a way no other previous Algerian film up to that time had done. The two protagonists, Boualem and Salah, are not heroic resistance figures (though they pretend to be) but layabouts and petty thieves. Their choice of clothing—patched jeans and check shirts open to the waist—says it all. It is a time when chaos rules. French jeeps control the streets, but there are also seemingly sinister FNL men at large; everybody is nervous. When a beggar touches the back of the French commandant, the latter immediately raises his hands in a gesture of surrender. A running joke through the film is the series of explosions in the market that make everybody run. One of the shooting incidents is serious, but another is precipitated by a car backfiring and the third instigated by Boualem and Salah, using a firecracker to enable some petty pilfering.

The troops of the Tenth Parachute Brigade are instructed to adopt new tactics in he run-up to the referendum. At a Christmas party, Father Christmas appears, but all his presents are stolen before he can distribute them. There is a singing competition with the prize of an appearance on television. Boualem wins it, but only because he is the only person to come forward (his performance is booed by the spectators). In a popular demonstration, Salah gets a scratched finger but is hailed as a wounded hero. The French generals' putsch comes and goes, and independence is imminent. New security forces are needed, and only at that time does Boualem join up and prove himself to be an arrogant bully—even stopping Salah to demand his papers. The old people are also recruited to protect their homes and instructed how to use Molotov cocktails. The first fails to go off, but the second blows up Boualem's car. Meanwhile, Boualem's father has turned to selling Algerian flags to celebrate independence, but unfortunately, these show a four-pointed star as the national emblem instead of the correct five-pointed one. The film concludes with a modest celebration of independence: a parade of schoolgirls in their uniforms. An end title tells us that, a few years later, Boualem is still trying to prove he fought in the resistance, while Salah has changed his choice of music from the twist to Algerian *chaabi*.

From Hollywood to Tamanrasset / De Hollywood à Tamanrasset (1990) was a difficult film, taking two years to make, with three fires on the set and threats from Islamic extremists. But none of this is apparent in the film, in which Zemmouri shows himself again able to create comic, even absurd, situations, while not diminishing our genuine involvement with his characters. The film, which is set in one of the remoter districts of Algiers, takes a satiric look at the impact of satellite television on an otherwise traditionally organized community. Part of the humor comes from the failings of the popular traditional healer / soothsayer, who has a highly modern appointments system and an approach that makes very explicit demands ("You understand that is cure [*sic*] / outcome will only be achieved if you show yourself to be a generous person . . .").

But most of the humor comes from the locals' obsession with the newly available television programs, with some men watching television through their legs during prayer. There is one man who watches Egyption television on his handmade set of reception dishes, but the rest are obsessed with American popular television, with one woman even prepared to sell her family jewels to obtain a properly functioning satellite dish. This obsession comes to dominate their private lives, as many of them give themselves the names of their favorite characters—J. R. and Sue Ellen, Kojak, Columbo, Rambo, and Clint Eastwood, for example—and expect to be addressed accordingly. Part of the humor comes from the physical disparity between them and the on-screen figures whose names they have taken, but most stems from the extremes to which their identification drives them. A market seller claims to have Madonna's underwear for sale—for a price. The grocer J. R. avidly seeks ways of disposing of his twenty-stone Sue Ellen, while the bricklayer Clint Eastwood imagines his trowel gives him the same authority as the on-screen Clint's revolver, and the imagined detectives (Colombo, Kojak, and company) think they can outdo the police. The chaos even involves Rambo disguising himself as a woman, and the cross-dressing causes Rambo identity problems that are enhanced by the abrupt appearance of a kilted Scotsman. Eventually, the exasperated commissioner for police has to put them all behind bars. Zemmouri's comic inventiveness is sustained throughout the film and is aided by an imaginative (and often parodic) musical score.

The Honour of the Tribe / L'honneur du tribu (1993), adapted from a novel by Rachid Mimouni, is the bleakest of Zemmouri's films to date. Though it contains moments of humor, it is also littered with gratuitous sexual incidents, obviously included to provoke or titillate an Arab audience. More significantly, it expresses Zemmouri's total disillusionment with the Algerian independence struggle: "Islamic fundamentalism doesn't date from 1988; it was born on 1st November 1954, with the outbreak of the Algerian revolution. . . . What I show in my film is just that, the fear of the peasants on whom a baseless modernisation is imposed, where villages are destroyed with nothing put in their place, and FLN officers are installed who are neither educated nor competent."[31]

He was aware that the film would get little cinema distribution in Algeria but comforted by the thought that millions of Algerians watch French television and that the film would be shown on French Canal Plus.

Despite the film's title, no one emerges with honor from this tale. Traditional Arab culture is disposed within the film's prologue. When a bear tamer arrives to make his annual visit to the isolated little community of Zitouna and challenges one of the villagers to step forward to defend the honor of the tribe by confronting his bear, only an outsider takes up the challenge. He is defeated and killed in the subsequent struggle, but no one from the community then steps forward to take care of his orphaned children, Omar and Ourida, who are left to grow up in poverty and neglect.

Twenty years later, French troops patrol the village, but the villagers put up no opposition—they hardly seem to notice. Even when a political prisoner from Algiers, Ali Ben Saad, arrives, there is no hint of dissent. Because he wears a suit and is treated respectfully by his French captors, they assume he is French. More of concern to the villagers is Omar, to whom we are initially drawn because of his background, but he emerges as a domineering bully, cheat, and thief who is able to cow the villagers with a mere swing of his stick. Instead of supporting his ostracized sister, Ourida, he rapes her, and she later dies in childbirth. Omar goes on to become a member of the Algerian resistance, but only because he is on the run after killing a French officer during a fight in a brothel.

Again time passes. Algeria has gained its independence, and a new local governor arrives. It is Omar, complete with a miniskirted French wife whom the traditionally minded villagers regard as a she-devil. Like Boualem in *The Crazy Years of the Twist*, Omar is totally corrupted by his newfound power. He systematically destroys normal life in the village, even uprooting the tree that is the traditional center of community life. There is no sense of a progressive new Algeria here. The village postman gets a motorbike to replace his donkey, but, of course, he cannot ride it. Omar's modernization project ends in farce and darkness, when the lights installed by his Russian engineers blow one after the other, plunging the village (and the film) into total darkness.

Earlier, three of the village elders had traveled to Algiers to appeal to Ali Ben Saad, now the new minister of justice. But they were ignored, locked in a waiting room, and then prosecuted and imprisoned for breaking out. We seemed to have a positive hero at last in Djamel, the young lawyer who defends them and who is, it transpires, Omar's incestuous son. But Zemmouri's end title to the film rids us of our illusions: "Since the events at Zitouna, the lawyer Djamel and his Islamic friends have finally shown their true face. Everyday, intolerance kills people in Algeria."

After the muted reception of *The Honour of the Tribe*, Zemmouri predictably changed his focus. In *100% Arabica* (1997), the director, for the first time, set a film in a poverty-stricken immigrant community of the Parisian suburbs, nicknamed "100% Arabica" by the local population. This is a simple film, and there is no real plot as such. The outcome of the battle between the bigoted imam—who views music as being non-Islamic and is backed up by hypocritical followers—and the two *raï* stars, Khaled and Cheb Mami, who entrance the populace, is never in doubt. Equally inevitable is the film's climax, when the two stars—previously depicted as rivals—come together to wow the people in a final concert and to repel a club-wielding team from the mosque. Throughout the film, the action, which has no real narrative force, constantly comes to a halt to let the audience hear yet more *raï* music. A lesser sound leitmotiv is constituted by repeated sirens of the vans driven by the police, who are consistently shown as totally ineffective. As always in Zemmouri's films, there are plenty of moments of humor, but these are often more than a little clichéd: a family of black Africans called Diop all use the same ID card (all black Africans look alike?), and the imam is finally made to flee in a van clearly labeled "pork meat" (hardly an effective final gag).

Zemmouri's next feature, *Arab, White, Red / Beur, blanc, rouge* (2004), retains this focus on the immigrant community, particularly the younger generation, born in France and legally French citizens. It has the characteristic Zemmouri combination of humor and barely developed narrative. The film was inspired by a football match between France and Algiers in 2001 in which the French anthem, "La Marseillaise," was booed by a portion of the crowd. The game ended in chaos, as spectators, mostly Algerian supporters, stormed the pitch when France scored its fourth goal, forcing the game to be abandoned.

The film's focus is on the personal confusions of a range of young Parisians, particularly young men who have grown up in France but have a dream image of the Algeria in which their parents grew up, though they have never set foot there and do not speak Arabic. Their confusions are enhanced by the fact that their parents' generation holds on to the values of the rural Algeria in which its members grew up, while the present generation are young French-educated citizens with the values and expectations of all French young people, though a trip from the *banlieue* to the Left Bank is a trip into a foreign country. Particularly poignant is the situation of Wassila, who has to break with her family because of her demand for the basic freedoms—to an education, in particular—basic to any French girl of her generation. Brahim, the film's protagonist, is caught up in the cultural confusions and takes part in the pitch invasion. He finds his face on the front page of newspapers with reports of the football incident. Arrested and subject to a fine he has no possible way of paying, Brahim and his parents decide to return "home" to Algeria. They sail through customs as they leave France, but—in a typical Zemmouri touch—they are refused entry to Algeria, because they are French citizens traveling without visas.

Certified Halal / Certifiqué halal (2015) is largely set in remote southern Algeria, where traditional social customs remain unchanged. As Alexandra Guellil tells us, the heroine, Kenza, is a revolutionary (in the eyes of her brother at least), because at the University in Seine-Saint-Denis she preaches equality between men and women and attacks traditional notions of marriage, such as the dowry and the certificate of virginity. To avoid what he sees as family dishonor, her brother decides to kidnap her, drug her, and force her into marriage in Algeria. This could obviously be told as a conventional tale of suffering womanhood. But as Guellil makes clear, Zemmouri adopts a typically distinctive comic approach.

The script of *Certified Halal* was born from an observation made by the director. In Algeria, the wedding season (which generally coincides with the summer months) is usually celebrated with great pomp: family processions, feasting, celebrations at the mausoleum of the local *marabout*, and so on. Watching these actual scenes, the director asked himself what would happen if two marriage processions delivered the bride to the wrong destination.[32]

Mahmoud Zemmouri has been a distinctive voice in Algerian cinema for the past thirty-five years. Though himself part of the French immigrant community, he is less concerned with this group's immediate problems than with Algeria itself, which dominates their imaginations, whether as an idyllically remembered past or as an unknown land crying out to be explored. Many of his films are sparked by observations of actual events, but he is able to generate situations that bring out in their full absurdity the contradictions between modern France and traditional Algeria and the impossibility of living in both worlds. He is always respectful of his characters but that does not prevent him from being ruthless in depicting the comedy inherent in their life styles.

*

The filmmaker who has best managed the transition from Algeria to France (and back again, at least for shooting purposes) is Merzak Allouache, who is also the most prolific of all contemporary Arab filmmakers outside Egypt. He was born in

Algiers in 1944 and studied filmmaking first at the short-lived Institut National du Cinéma d'Algers (INC) and then in Paris at IDHEC. He subsequently worked for a variety of media institutions in Algeria and France, made a number of short films from the mid-1960s onward, and served as assistant on a feature film directed by Mohamed Slim Riad. At the start of his career, he described his ambition: "To make films that are popular, accessible to a big audience and relaxed. I love humour and irony, not gratuitously, but to give cause for reflection."[33] His debut feature for ONCIC, *Omar Gatlato* (1976), is generally regarded as one of the organization's most innovative works. The film brought a fresh and penetrating look both at urban youth in general and at the effect—particularly on young males—of social segregation in Algerian society.

Omar, who lives in Bab el Oued in Algiers, is a young official in the fraud office. Starting at home and continuing as he goes about his daily live, Omar introduces us (partly in direct-to-camera narration and partly in voice-over) to his family, his neighbors, and his work colleagues. We constantly see him with his male friends—he is "one of the boys." His great passion is music and his prize possession is his mini-cassette recorder, with which he spends all his spare time recording local *chaabi* singers and, when he goes to the cinema, songs from Hindi movies. He has a secure, uneventful life, until he is mugged one evening and his precious recorder is stolen. His friend Moh procures him a replacement, complete with a supposedly blank tape. But, in fact, the tape contains the recording of the voice of a young woman, Selma, and Omar becomes obsessed with who she is. He pesters Moh for more and more information—her name and workplace, for example. Eventually he phones Selma and she agrees to meet up, but at the last minute, Omar's nerve fails: he cannot cross the road to greet her.

Though the film is structured as a comedy, it has comparatively few gags, the best of which comes when the film breaks in a cinema and the projectionist refuses to restart it until the audience stops shouting at him. He sits impassive in front of the blank screen, immobile as the audience continues to hurl abuse. Most of the film's humor comes from the ever-widening gap between Omar's self-perception (as revealed in his narration) and how we see him actually behave. This structural pattern simultaneously involves us with Omar and distances us, so he becomes a comic character while in no way ceasing to engage us. At the beginning, he masters life through his recorder, but at the end, he is its slave, obsessively listening to Selma's voice. Allouache maintains a lightness of touch throughout, and the film became a great commercial, as well as critical, success.[34]

Allouache's second film, *The Adventures of a Hero / Les aventures d'un héros / Mughamarat batal* (1978), is totally different, though again the director adopts a distinctively experimental approach. As he has said, "Cinema has existed for more than a century and has acquired codes, which tend to become universal today. We have an oral tradition which is still alive and vibrant. My ambition was to deal with the osmosis of these two languages, which wasn't something easy to do."[35]

The film begins with the birth of Mehdi in a peasant community where he is acclaimed as a "son of the tribe" who has a great mission to accomplish. Twenty years later, after training with a very dubious master, he sets out on a motor-scooter to devote his life to bringing justice, in the manner of the legendary Che Guevara. But, in truth, he has no real taste for the demands of his mission. He is ill-tempered and sometimes violent. As he continues his incoherent travels, he ends up—totally unexpectedly—in the postrevolutionary political world of contemporary Algeria, at a debate on the new National Charter. Just as Mehdi's journey follows no direct line and is full of gaps and detours, so, too, is the film's narrative—fragmented and constantly digressing, using devices from the world of fairy tales, such as stories within stories and illogical jumps in time and space.

Whereas *Omar Gatlato* played with words and dealt with their power in a realistically defined Algerian context, *The Adventures of a Hero* is a fable in which the normal rules of everyday life no longer apply. As Allouache points out, there is a double discourse here: "Political, since it questions revolutionary roman-ticism, and cultural, since it is constructed in the discursive manner of Arab storytelling. . . . Throughout the film, I've tried to show the predominance of words serves as a confusion, not as a form of enlightenment. It happens that peo-ple talk in order to say nothing."[36]

Allouache continued his Algerian career, again in quite a new direction, with a curious but affecting tale of a man's plunge into madness and murder. As in *Omar Gatlato*, the setting of *The Man Who Looked at Windows / L'homme qui regardait les fenêtres / Rajulun wa nawafidh* (1982) is the world of bureaucracy, but the tone is markedly more bleak and harsh. Monsieur Rachid, a librarian in this fifties, has been demoted (in a typical Allouache humorous touch) to work in the film section of the state library. Where Omar could sometimes enjoy some liberty in his job (letting off, instead of arresting, an old woman who was clearly guilty), Monsieur Rachid has no such pleasure. Instead he broods on the whole range of problems that afflict him, in the office, at home, with his family, and with his car. His sense of oppression increases as he recalls the tragic death of a colleague, and he resolves to take the drastic but, from his point-of-view, totally necessary act of killing the boss who demoted him.

A Love Affair in Paris / Un amour à Paris / Hubbun fi Baris (1986) is a minor work that was shot in France and with French dialogue but nevertheless antici-pates much of Allouache's later output. Marie is a Jew from Algiers, newly arrived in Paris with ambitions to become a top model, and Ali is a *beur* brought up in Clichy who has just emerged from three years in prison (though there is nothing in his behavior to indicate that he is a criminal). They could hardly be more dif-ferent, but they fall in love at first sight. Their affair, conducted in his tiny room in a run-down hotel, is totally idyllic and makes her give up her own ambitions. Instead, she comes to support him in his crazy dream of becoming an astronaut in Houston.

The affair is too brief to generate any of the dramatically interesting tensions that their divergent social backgrounds must inevitably create. It is also too intense for them to notice that Ali is followed and spied on everywhere by the police, who are, we eventually learn, hoping that he will lead him to his former accomplice, Albert, who is still on the run. When Ali does visit Albert to collect his share of the proceeds from their last robbery to finance the trip to Houston, he brings the police with him. He is killed, along with Albert and several policemen, in the shoot-out that ensues. By this point, the trite gangster movie plot elements have become the real substance of the film. It may have been a release for Allouache to depict female nudity and intimate sexual behavior after what has been described as "the degree zero of depicted or spoken sex" in *Omar Gatlato*.[37] But the rather embarrassing appearance of Daniel Cohn-Bendit as Benoît, a friend of Marie's father, who acts out his own real involvement in the 1968 student protests, serves only as a painful reminder of just how far removed *A Love Affair in Paris* is from the social and political reality of the lives of young immigrants in Paris in the 1980s. The film ends, as it began, with Marie alone in the airport.

Following the muted success of *A Love Affair in Paris*, Allouache had to wait eight years before he could make another feature. During this time, he made a series of documentaries on Algerian issues, and when he did return to feature filmmaking, it was with a film set in, and focused directly on, Algeria and its problems. *Bab el Oued City* (1994) is one of the finest of all Algerian cinema's studies of the rise of Islamist violence.

The film also marks the director's return to the district of Algiers that formed the setting of *Omar Gatlato* but that, at the time of filming, was being progressively transformed by the force of Islamic fundamentalism. The film's action is set in motion by Boualem, who is driven crazy by the mosque loudspeaker situated on his balcony. He tears it down and throws it into the sea but immediately regrets what he has done. His action allows Saïd, the domineering brother of Yamina, the woman he loves, to set out to bring "order" to the neighborhood through a reign of violence, on the grounds that Boualem's act has served to muffle the voice of Allah.

The subsequent action depicts some unemployed young men finding a new sense of direction in the new rigid Islamic attitudes and demands, while young women suffer from the way their lives are stifled in this changed environment. Mixing humor with serious social insights and making good use of popular music (with a final *raï* lament for a lost city as its conclusion), *Bab el Oued City* paints a vivid picture of everyday life in the overcrowded neighborhood and the growing oppression under which the inhabitants have to live. The characters could not be more varied. In addition to Boualem, there is Saïd, a hero in 1988 but in the film's present just a bully who aims to become imam. He puts on mascara before strutting out with his gang of followers to bring his version of justice to the people. Mabrouk, Boualem's friend at the bakery, dabbles in stolen goods and ends up beaten by the gang and made to betray Boualem. Ouardya is a former student activist who was once imprisoned and loves speaking French, as well as drinking wine. Her open behavior is an affront to Saïd, who scares her with the gun his "controllers" have given him and warns her to leave within a week. Messaoud spends the film convincing no one with his claims to be French but finally and unexpectedly receives a replacement for his lost passport. In the background are the sequestered young women, including Yamina, who seek escape and romance from cheap novels and movies on television, while some of their male colleagues dabble in drugs. As a leitmotif throughout the film, there is Paolo, a former European settler, who takes his blind elderly aunt on a tour of the present run-down Algiers, pretending all the time that nothing has changed since the colonial days and that everything looks, and is, perfect.

The mood gradually darkens as the film proceeds, with Saïd and his small band of bearded, black-jacketed supporters bringing increased violence and intimidation. Behind Saïd, and seemingly controlling him, are shadowy, unnamed figures who make half a dozen appearances and who are presumably responsible for his death when he has served their purposes. Certainly his death solves nothing. The moderate imam resigns, and Boualem, who has also been beaten up by the gang, decides to emigrate.

The film ends, as it began, with the sufferings of a woman. At the outset, Yamina has waited three years for news from Boualem, the man she still loves, though she has had no contact from him. We return to her at the end of the film, remembering their single stolen kiss and forced to mourn his exile as a kind of death, writing letters to him that she cannot post. The film was partly shot clandestinely, and at times, the first take was the only one possible. It is dedicated to all the young people of Algeria.

Bab el Oued City is striking in its realistic view of Algiers. Allouache adopted a very different approach in his next feature, *Hello Cousin! / Salut cousin!* (1996). Though by this time permanently a resident in France, the director admitted that he had no intimate knowledge of the problems faced by immigrant communities. As a result, the new film is structured as a fable, with a number of explicit references to La Fontaine's fable "The Town Mouse and the Country Mouse." Alilo arrives from Algiers for his first trip to Paris to be greeted by his friendly and hospitable cousin Mok, very much a Parisian citizen. But Alilo has a problem: he has lost the address of the tailor from whom he has been sent to collect a suitcase full of (presumably fake) designer clothes. This means that he has to stay several days in Paris, much of the time being organized by Mok.

As the days unfold, Alilo is confused and dazzled by Paris, but he also comes to see how false Mok's assertions are. The members of their joint family, from which Mok says he has "divorced" himself because of their failure, prove to be content and totally integrated. Similarly Mok's claims to have succeeded in his own chosen career are undermined by what Alilo experiences directly. Mok is booed off stage when he attempts to present himself as a rap star (a love of La Fontaine takes one only so far). His certainty about the outcome of a boxing match is delusional, and he loses a great deal of borrowed money. His earnings as the fake groom in a sumptuous wedding arranged to allow the bride to get around passport restrictions are dubious at best. The narrative, which mixes comedy and surprise, finds a neat and unexpected ending. Alilo, who has always seen himself as a resident of Algiers, is tempted to stay on in Paris, thanks to his blossoming relationship with Mok's attractive Guinean neighbor, Fatouma. Mok, meanwhile, a second-generation immigrant who sees himself as 100 percent Parisian, is arrested for a past offense and expelled to Algeria, a country he has never set foot in and whose language he does not speak. Once again, as in *Omar Gatlato*, Allouache uses humor and a self-deluding protagonist to offer both an entertaining fiction and meaningful insights into complex situations.

Allouache's next work was a feature-length television film, *Algiers-Beirut— A Memory / Alger-Beyrouth—pour mémoire* (1998), that, for once, had a French protagonist (though one with deep Lebanese connections). Laurence, a journalist, returns to Beirut for the first time since 1975 to visit her father's grave and is shown around Beirut by Samir, an old family friend. By chance, she meets up with an Algerian journalist in exile, Rachid, whom she is sure she encountered years before in Algiers. He denies this, but they embark on an affair. The film is well constructed, with a double pattern of development. Laurence's persistence leads to the truth about the murder seen in the film's precredit sequence, but she also inadvertently drives Rachid to his own death, as he has to face up to his responsibility for the death of his closest friend.

The Other World / L'autre monde (2001) follows a narrative pattern also favored by several *beur* filmmakers born or brought up as children in France: the "return" of a protagonist born in France to Algeria, a country he or she does not know and with an alien, unknown language. In this case it is Yasmine, who sets out to track down her fiancé, Rachid, who has been missing for six months. She gets help from Hakim, a former terrorist who has learned French from watching television, and discovers that, after being conscripted, Rachid was kidnapped by Islamic fundamentalists. She continues her search, suffering hostility and humiliation and discovering a society in collapse, full of senseless violence and inhabited by people who long for peace but do not want to come to terms with the immediate past. Though she finds the traumatized Rachid, this is a doomed journey, resulting in death. Though the various massacres are well handled and the sex is explicit, the film's contrived plotline fails to generate emotion or engagement and shows little real sense of discovery.

After one of his least successful works, Allouache returned to the world of Paris, which by that time was his own, to make what would be his most popular commercial success. *Chouchou* (2003) again mixes insight and humor and is based on a sketch by Gad Elmahleh (who played Alilo in *Hello Cousin!*) developed for his one-man show. From the moment Chouchou enters the film, clad in ornate Latin American peasant garb and claiming to be a Chilean political refugee, we know we are again in the world of fable, which will avoid any real involvement with actual immigrant life in Paris in the early 2000s. Though he is openly a gay transvestite, Chouchou is warmly welcomed everywhere—first, by a Catholic priest, Father Léon, who finds him his lodgings, and subsequently by a psychiatrist, Dr. Nicole Milovavich, who is happy for him to work as her assistant dressed as a woman. In part, this is due to the manner in which Gad Elmahleh exhibits his comic flair and presents Chouchou as an essentially open, loveable, lively, and untroubled character. In these respects, he differs totally from the young priest with whom he shares his lodging, Father Jean, a drug user haunted by visions of the Virgin Mary.

The plot, as such, is inconsequential. Chouchou is ostensibly in Paris in search of his nephew. He finds him, starring as the singer "Vanessa," in a gay nightclub, the Apocalypse, where Chouchou also finds work, as a waitress. The nightclub is also the place where Chouchou can meet the man of his life, Stanislas de la Tour-Maubourg, with whom he falls instantly in love. The relationship is idyllic (even Stanislas's elderly parents approve), but a little frenetic drama is introduced when one of Dr. Milanovavich's patients (a troubled police inspector) takes a violent dislike to Chouchou. But all is well, and Chouchou can make a final appearance as striking as his initial entry into the action, this time dressed in a red wig and and long white wedding dress.

Allouache succeeds totally in creating a world where there are no problems (not even any questions) despite the outrageous and potentially shocking actions depicted. His lightness of touch is assured, as he effortlessly maintains the humorous mood, mixing subtle comedy and broadly farcical elements. As a box office venture, the film benefits from blending strong performances by rising Maghrebian actors Gad Elmahleh and Roschdy Zem (as Father Jean), with cameo appearances by veteran French stars Claude Brasseur and Micheline Presle. The film was a total commercial success, with a reputed three million admissions in France alone.

The ease with which Allouache handles a theme—transvestism—that would be taboo in the Arab world shows the extent to which he has become, over the years, essentially a French filmmaker. This is borne out by his next feature, *Bab el Web* (2005), which marks his return to the Bab el Oued district of Algiers, twenty-eight years after *Omar Gatlato*. While this is a big-budget French-language film shot in 35mm CinemaScope, it is essentially an intimate comedy. Allouache has recorded that the idea of the film came to him when he saw the actual Bab el Web cyber café when he was in Algiers to present *Chouchou*.

Certainly this film presents a very different view of Bab el Oued, now in the age of the internet. Problems still exist, but they are in many ways the opposite of those that shaped Algerian life in the past. The menace in the background of this plot is not Islamic fundamentalism but a set of caricatured villains—the local mafia—whose behavior seems to be based on viewing too many Hollywood B movies. Similarly the two brothers, Bouzid and Kamel, at the heart of the action are not young Algerians longing for escape to a dream France but *immigris*, brought up in France and transposed as children to Algiers when their father decided to return "home" (a plot justification for the use of French throughout the film). Bouzid, the younger of the brothers, spends his life on the internet, inviting any woman he contacts to visit him in Algiers. The plot gets under way when one of them, Laurence, decides to accept his offer.

The brothers make frantic preparations, getting rid of their family (urged to go on holiday) and redecorating the flat and their hired car in the very worse possible taste. But nothing goes to plan, Laurence falls for Kamel, not Bouzid, and though Bouzid has planned a whole tourist program, she has her own agenda. This is to look for the father who deserted her and her mother when she was a child. There is plenty of humor and some nice gags: the sight of the newly redecorated flat, Laurence suddenly emerging as a talented karate fighter, and Gad Elmaleh (in a cameo appearance) performing as a would-be amateur comedian who cannot tell a joke. But the film glosses over all the real issues of contemporary Algeria and also shies swiftly away from the aftermath of any of the potentially serious personal issues that the loosely constructed plot raises (such as the relationship of Kamel and Laurence after they have ended up in bed together or that between Laurence and her father after their initial wordless confrontation). At the end, in the plot's most outrageous device, Laurence's father, briefly glimpsed earlier as a crippled old man who cannot control his dog, turns out to be the boss of bosses who spares Kamel (who has defied the gang) when he recognizes his daughter. Nothing is resolved in *Bab el Web*, and the plot could easily begin all over again when, in the final shots, Laurence mails "salut" from France, where she has retreated.

Bab el Web did not achieve the same commercial success as *ChouChou*, and five years elapsed before Allouache made a new film for cinema release, though he did make a television feature, *Tamanrasset*, in 2008. *Harragas / Les brûleurs* (2009) opens a new phase in the director's work, the first of a trio of Arab-language films that leave comedy behind to focus on immediate Algerian social issues. The title, derived from the Arabic word meaning "to burn," is the name given in Algeria to those who attempt to immigrate clandestinely to Europe. They burn with a passion to leave their native country and also, quite literally, burn all their papers and passports, in the hope that they cannot be identified and made to return. As the narrator Rachid puts it at the outset of the film, "to burn" is "to take exile, leave, disappear from this country, erase the past."

The film starts with lengthy preparations in Mostaganem, an Algerian port two hundred kilometers from the Spanish coast and a favorite place for such departures to Europe. Though the characters describe the city as a prison and Algeria as a land of poverty and misfortune, there is nothing that we see that could create this almost suicidal desperation to leave. *Harragas* does not probe the characters' motivations; Allouache is concerned primarily with the physical journey, its preparations and outcome. The film's opening is ominous. One of a trio of local friends who had planned to leave, Omar, has already made three failed attempts. On the eve of departure, he commits suicide, leaving a note that reads, "If I leave, I die. If I do not leave, I die. So I leave without leaving, and I die. It's simpler." Rachid, the film's narrator from outside the narrative, as well as its protagonist, introduces us to those planning to depart, with Omar's sister, Imène, choosing to replace him. We also meet the organizer of the project, an old sailor named Hassan, whom Rachid describes as "a real bastard" and whom, we see, is quite indifferent to the safety of the boat he offers them. The three locals are joined by a second group coming from the South. The waiting is long and tedious, but on the very eve of departure, drama erupts as the project is hijacked by an armed stranger who kills Hassan and takes over the organization of the group's departure.

Finally, would-be immigrants are under way as darkness falls. If all goes well, this is a twelve-hour crossing, but, of course, all does not go well: the motor breaks down and the compass ceases to function mid-trip. With nine men and one woman crammed onto the tiny boat, tensions soon rise. The gunman, who turns out to be a corrupt policeman on the run, comes to blows with Hakim, the solitary Islamist (whose motives for making this journey to Europe are totally unclear). Both fall from the boat and drown. Allouache has said that he wanted "to show the contradictions and tensions present within Algerian society through the conflicts which arise between the travellers,"[38] and certainly there is little contact or understanding between the three well-educated city dwellers and the five peasants from the South. Eventually, the two groups separate, with the three from Mostaganem swimming ashore, leaving behind those from the southern desert who, of course, cannot swim.

We do not know the final outcome for the group of peasants, four of whom are picked up (the fifth had gone crazy and jumped into the sea). But, as one imagined from Omar's suicide at the start, the effort has been futile. Rachid and another city-dweller, Nassar, are imprisoned (along with three hundred others from across Africa), and Imène is repatriated within two days. The action is filmed with Allouache's usual fluency and a concern to maintain an almost documentary-style realism, with minimal musical accompaniment. But Rachid's commentary is sometimes intrusive—explaining things we can see on the screen and also telling us things he cannot, logically, know. Allouache's sincerity is never in doubt, but the attempt to use the journey to explain wider issues concerening Algeria has only a muted result.

The screening of *Harragas* in Algeria met with censorship problems, and when Allouache began his next film, *Normal!* In 2009, the context was the Second Pan-African Cultural Festival. The film "started with the idea of shedding light on cultural corruption." Not surprisingly, the Algerian Ministry of Culture refused to back the film, and the project was abandoned after a month or so of shooting. Allouache returned to France to make a television comedy, *Tata bakhta*, but then received funding from the Doha Film Festival, which allowed him to reassemble the cast. But the context had now changed, thanks to the Arab Spring, and the film became instead "a dressing down of tyranny and censorship." Reflecting on the situation he now faced in Algeria, Allouache stated: "I am from a generation that grew up in the years that followed the war of liberation. Like many others I was patient and idealistic. I attached great hopes to the country's independence, tomorrow looked promising, the nation was being rebuilt. Today we need to reconsider everything, tear it all down, and rebuild from scratch."[39] The sense of continuity between *Haraggas* and *Normal!* is strong and is emphasized in the end titles of the second film: "This film is a fiction, but it comes from the bitter reality of the young in Algeria." *Normal* is the term used by young Algerians when they cannot find the proper answer to a question, and it defines the film's subject perfectly. This revised film *Normal!* (2011) is a fiction based closely on Allouache's personal experience. The theme is set out in the opening sequence. In the changed circumstances of 2011, a young director, Fouzi, wants to update the film he worked on two years before that is still unfinished. His scriptwriter wife, Amina, thinks they ought instead to be out demonstrating on the streets, joining the crowds they see on television. While he summons his actors, she paints a poster: "Algeria Democratic and Free." This, the film's final titles tell us, is "more than a slogan written on a banner. It is the aspiration of all those young people who, in spite of their anguish and feeling of helplessness, believe that a true change can be brought about."

The group of actors gradually assembles, as Fouzi begins to show his compilation of the rushes. What started as the film version of a play rejected by the censors, and containing some (presumably authentic) footage of the Pan-African Cultural Festival, has become, under Fouzi's direction, something very different, a drama veering toward passion and melodrama (a typical Allouache humorous approach). These rushes allow Allouache to exhibit his gift for rich imagery (an actress swimming sensuously in the sea) and to poke fun at Algerian attitudes toward sex (a male actor refusing to continue with a kissing sequence because his French costar insists on pushing her tongue into his mouth).

But at the core of the film and the source of its immediacy are the discussions among the director, his actors, and the writers. They find Fouzi's film incoherent and not what they expected, and none of them can see how he can integrate freshly shot scenes of the contemporary demonstrations on the streets of Algiers. More important, they differ as to how each responds to the demonstrations on the streets and the authorities' response (the action is interspersed with images and sounds of government helicopters overhead). They appreciate that the key developments are happening elsewhere, in Tunisia and Egypt. What, they ask, is the role of filmmaking here in Algeria when the key images are shot on mobile phones and entering the country via Facebook and Youtube? The film finds no answer, as Fouzi makes clear in his second direct-to-camera, statement: "In truth, I want to say things, which I don't know how to say. I want to write, and I don't know what to write. I try to think about what I am feeling, and I can't. I don't know why."

If *Normal!* is a film full of hectic discussions and real verbal disagreements (no one is shown actually demonstrating on the streets), Allouache's next feature, *The Repentant / Le repenti /El taaib* (2012), is about gaps and silences. We are denied the content of key conversations and telephone calls until much later in the narrative, and the killings in the film occur either in almost complete darkness or offscreen. Only at the very end of the film do we realize the full meaning and significance of the events we have seen unfold on screen.

The 1990s were a time of civil war in Algeria, with perhaps as many as 200,000 people killed. The film, which is fictional but based on an incident Allouache read about in a newspaper article in 1999, looks at the unspoken and unexpected consequences of the law that brought the fighting to an end. The law of "Civil Concord," inaugurated by the new president, Abdelaziz Bouteflika, in 2000, promised to every Islamic militant who repented, gave up his weapons, and solemnly asserted that he had killed no one the right to be reintegrated into Algerian society. It did nothing to help or reassure the hundreds of thousands who were victims of the war and had lost their loved ones. The law brought at least a partial cessation of hostilities but created a situation of what has been termed "national amnesia." In Algeria, the truth of the past decade's horrors had to be put aside, never discussed, forgotten.

The film opens with Rachid running through the snow and ice in a mountainous district in southern Algeria. He is a "repentant," returning from the battle zone to his native village, and the setting is appropriate, as this is the bleakest of all Allouache's major films. At first, Rachid appears a sympathetic figure, young and seemingly vulnerable, loved by his family. He protests his innocence of any killings but faces the open hostility of the men of the village. The local head of the gendarmerie reintegrates him into society and even finds him a job away from his village, but only in return for a "deal," the terms of which we do not know. We assume Rachid's confrontations with the local pharmacist Lakhdar are part of this deal, but, in fact, he is acting on his own behalf. Lakhdar's shop is smart and bright, but his personal life is a shambles. Faced with Rachid's threat (still unknown to us), he summons his ex-wife, Djamila. When the two of them meet up with Rashid and drive up through the mountains (now ironically bathed in spring sunshine), the truth emerges. During the civil war, Lakhdar helped the Islamists with medicine but not enough, in their view. As a punishment, his daughter, Selma, was abducted. What Rachid is offering—in return for a large sum of money—is to take the pair to where their daughter's body is buried. Still protesting his personal innocence, Rachid unwittingly leads them to their deaths. Though he assures them that his former colleagues have all left the area, this is not the case. Islamist fighters emerge from the trees, and all three are gunned down at the graveside.

As Allouache has said, his choice from the start with regard to Rachid was "not to present him as the cliché figure of the archetypal terrorist, but as a human being, coming from that generation without hope or education, often caught despite themselves in the storm of tragedy which Algeria has endured."[40] He recognizes that Rachid's aim is abject and that he acts only for himself. There is nothing in the film (apart from his own protestations) to indicate that Rachid has not been a killer and torturer. Certainly there is no sign of genuine repentance. But even so, Allouache cannot bring himself to condemn his protagonist. Despite the extent to which seemingly vital information is deliberately withheld and the ambiguities surrounding the protagonist, *The Repentant* is a well-paced film that constantly holds the spectator's attention and offers a satisfyingly unexpected dramatic resolution.

Allouache has made a number of fictional features for French television, but only one of them, *The Bay of Algiers / La baie d'Alger* (2014), is commercially available on DVD. This is a surprising work, given the very real commitment to probe some of Algeria's major problems in his three previous Arab-language features for cinema release. The new film is in French and was shot, it seems, at Sète in southern France.[41] As a result, there is little sense of the real city of Algiers and, though the work is largely set in 1955, little period sense. The film, scripted by Allouache as always, is based on an autobiographical novel by the *pied-noir* (French settler) novelist Louis Gardel, who offers a nostalgic portrait of the country where he was born, depicting a world inhabited almost exclusively by wealthy French settlers (Arabs feature only as servants and fishermen).

The protagonist is the fifteen-year-old Louis, who is staying with his grandmother Zoe and experiencing his first childhood passion, his discovery of French literature and his awe at meeting Albert Camus in the local bookshop. The principal difficulty with the film is that it is told from the level of Louis's sheltered existence, in which the Arabs and their cause hardly exist. He is most interested in girls, particularly the beautiful blonde Michèle. Though he gradually becomes aware of changes in the country, as the violence gets steadily nearer, politics is not a real concern for him, even after the old Arab fisherman, with whom he regularly goes out to sea, is shot by French troops. The issues for the settlers, as the movement for liberation grows in strength, are not shown in enacted sequences but merely debated rhetorically over the dining table, either at Zoe's house or at the mansion of her friend Didi, the leader of the settler community. By the end of the film, as the settler community splinters, Louis becomes aware that the French Algeria in which he has grown up has been lost forever. But even his mature awareness, as expressed in his voice-over commentary from his new home in Paris fifty years later, is essentially limited to personal reminiscences, offering little real insight into the wider issues dividing Algeria and France.

The Terraces / Les terrasses / Es-stouh (2014), Allouache's subsequent film, was shot from terraces overlooking five districts of Algiers: Bab el Oued, Notre Dame d'Afrique, Télémy, Belcourt, and the Casbah. Allouache has explained the film's origin: "The idea came to me while I was researching locations for my daughter's first film. I noticed that there was an incredible life on these terraces. And as it has become complicated to shoot in the streets of Algiers, because of the crowds and the traffic, I thought that to shoot on the terraces would allow things to be peaceful, while being in an 'exterior / interior' situation."[42] The action unrolls to the rhythm of the five daily Muslim calls to prayer.

The almost forty-year feature film career of Merzak Allouache is unique in contemporary Arab cinema. He has made twice as many feature-length films for cinema or television release as any of his eminent contemporaries. While the films for cinema release include some of the major works of contemporary Arab cinema, there has been little praise for his work for French television (most of which is unavailable to outsiders). A simple listing of the subjects he has successively treated reads like the output of a contract director at the height of the Hollywood system: dramas and comedies, films of great insight alongside escapist fiction, French films skirting over the truths of immigrant life in France and Arab-language films probing crucial issues concerning Algerian society. But, of course, Allouache has personally selected and written all of these films. The twists and turns of his career are his personal choice, a constant reinvention of self.

Allouache always eschews complex or convoluted dramatic structures. The narrative line is invariably straightforward, sometimes seemingly willfully underdeveloped. The social situations depicted are often problematic, but they remain in the background of the action. The focus is always on the protagonist, whether this is a young man unable to approach the girl he loves, a man who unthinkingly creates havoc in his community because we wants a good night's sleep, a woman desperately searching for her missing lover, a gay transvestite untroubled by issues of identity, a well-educated woman seeking clandestine emigration on the spur of the moment, or a "repentant" whose behavior shows little sign of repentance. Everybody has their reasons. The attraction of Allouache's films is that these protagonists are invariably personally engaging. The simple narratives are shaped to be constantly engaging for the spectator. They are conducted at the level of these characters' aims, activities, and ambitions but usually touch—if only lightly—on real social issues.

*

Though Ahmed Rachedi's masterly compilation film, *Dawn of the Damned / L'aube des damnés* (1965), is one of the founding films of Algerian cinema, there has been little impetus in the Maghreb itself for documentary production since the end of the Algerian war. There was little significant output in the 1980s and virtually all of this was the work of directors working for television and dependent on the funding and distribution opportunities offered by European companies. As a result, there is again little that is specifically experimental in terms of approach or structure. The strengths of this work lie in the choice of articulate witnesses who can tell their stories to the camera in an unaffected way. The filmmaker rarely appears, but a discrete presence can be felt in the voice-overs, which are often very personal in tone and help shape the straightforward narrative lines. Many talented documentary filmmakers actively examining the Algerian scene—Yamina Benguigui and Djamila Sahraoui, as well as Kamal Dehane and Malek Bensmaïl—are European residents and had to wait until after 2000 to complete a film of full feature length. The work of these four filmmakers has been discussed elsewhere.[43]

Some of the most significant Algerian documentary work of the 1990s has come from filmmakers for whom a shift abroad has led to a totally different kind of filmmaking. Jean-Pierre Lledo and Ahmed Lallem were both born in the 1940s and worked for the Algerian state production system making feature films before being driven into exile, where they have made exclusively documentary films.

Jean-Pierre Lledo, who was born in 1947 in Tlemcen, is a graduate of the VGIK in Moscow. He made his first reputation with two idiosyncratic features about filmmaking dreams and aspirations—*The Empire of Dreams / L'empire des rêves* (1982) and *Lights / Lumières* (1992)—before being forced into exile in Paris in the mid-1990s after Islamist threats. Lledo is a union-activist with a Jewish background, and when he resumed filmmaking in France, he began a series of documentary portraits of some of Algeria's "outsiders": *L'oasis de la belle de mai* (1996), about the painter Denis Martinez, who is of Spanish origin; *Lisette Vincent, une* *femme algérienne* (1997), about an Algiers-born Frenchwoman living in exile; and *Jean Pelegri, alias Yehia el Hadj* (2001), about the *pied-noir* novelist. Lledo then compiled a number of feature-length works (some over two hours long), the first of which was *Algeria, My Ghosts / Algérie, mes fantômes* (2003), a journey into his own past via a trip across France to meet other exiles like himself. His interest continues to be in those who, like him, could not form part of the Algeria that emerged from the years of liberation struggle.

An Algerian Dream / Un rêve algérien (2004) traced the return of Henri Alleg to Algeria after forty years. Alleg is the former editor of *Alger Républicain* who fought for Algerian freedom but was captured by the French. He subsequently denounced torture (of which he had himself been a victim) in a book that found a worldwide readership, *The Question* (2006). For Lledo, Alleg represents not just the denunciation of torture but also "the proof that one could fight for Algerian liberation without being Arab or Muslim."[44]

Lledo accompanies the articulate Alleg on his return, after forty years of absence, to Algiers and the offices of his newspaper, and on to Constantine, Chechell, and Oran. Much of the film is narrated by Alleg, who, along the way, recalls his experiences of the liberation movement (including torture and three years' imprisonment), meets survivors from those days, and visits the graves of those who died in the struggle. Alleg is also a Jewish outsider who arrived in Algiers in 1939 to avoid conscription in France. He shares with Lledo a regret that the multiethnic Algeria ("the Algerian dream" of the title)—embracing Arabs, Jews, and *pieds-noirs*—for which he fought and for which Lledo longed as a child did not emerge with independence, when Algerian nationalism took quite a different path.

Algeria: Unspoken Stories / Algérie, histoires à ne pas dire (2007) sets out once again to probe what Lledo regards as one of the unexplored issues in the emergence of post-independence Algeria: the flight to France of some 900,000 Algerian settlers and Jews at the point of independence in 1962. Why, Lledo asks, did this occur? Was it the result of panic, a response to violence, or simply the logic of events? Was there no possibility for Lledo's dream of a multicultural Algeria where Arabs, Jews, and settlers would live side by side as a single community? The answers given are only partially satisfactory. There is no overall historical or cultural analysis—just (largely unedited) interview material. While the effect of ordinary Algerians looking back on events fifty years before produces some interesting statements, it also creates a mass of contradictions. Many of those interviewed share Lledo's recollection of a multiethnic society, but none can give a convincing reason for its disintegration. The film's scope is impossibly wide: witnesses from four separate cities or regions (Skikda, Algiers, Constantine, and Oran) discussing different issues with people they meet on their way. The structure, moreover, is flawed by the withdrawal of the Constantine representative after the first screening (his face and that of his small son had to be masked out, and the sequence has, it seems, been reduced by half). Overall the film, which runs to two hours, forty minutes, is self-indulgent and ill-focused. What it finally makes clear is that the situation of the non-Arab communities prior to the moment of independence matches in complexity and contradiction that of the power play within the FLN in the period prior to the military *coup d'état* by Houari Boumediene in 1965.

Ahmed Lallem, who was born in 1940 in Sétif, studied briefly at IDHEC in Paris and then completed his studies at Lodz in Poland. He made his sole feature, *Barriers / Barrières*, in 1977 but is better known for the series of short documentaries he has made since the 1960s. His most fascinating project is the fifty-two-minute *Algerian Women, Thirty Years On / Algériennes, trente ans après* (1996), in which he reinterviewed some of the women who had been featured as schoolgirls in his documentary *Women / Elles* in 1966 to discover their personal stories and what had happened to their youthful dreams. None of them found their dreams confirmed. Those who stayed in Algeria and came to terms with their narrowed horizons and restricted possibilities seem to have fared better. For those who chose exile, emancipation proved more fraught, because of the difficulty of sustaining a life lived across two parallel worlds. This is again a story of women "put back in their place" after a brief moment of freedom, with the 1984 family law giving them the right to choose the president but not a husband, offering them rights at work but not at home. In law, divorce is always the woman's fault, so she and her children can be thrown out onto the street. Perhaps the most chilling aspect of life for these women who were given the possibility of education as girls is that their educated adult sons are among those who now demand that they again become veiled.

*

A key feature of mid-1990s Algerian filmmaking—and a political event in its own right—was the making of a trio of films not only set in the Atlas Mountains but also using the Berber language, Tamazight. Until the 1990s—despite the existence of five million Algerians who speak only that language[45]—this had been expressly forbidden by the government, which wanted to proclaim Algeria as one nation with one language and one religion. The three pioneering films of the mid-1990s (two backed by Fonds Sud funding) are Belkacem Hadjadj's *Once Upon a Time*, Abderrahmane Bouguermouh's *The Forgotten Hillside*, and Azzedine Meddour's *Baya's Mountain*. The filmmakers vary widely in age (having been born in 1950, 1938, and 1947, respectively) but all trained abroad—Hadjadj at INSAS in Brussels, Bouguermouh at IDHEC in Paris, and Meddour at VGIK in Moscow. They all also established themselves securely outside the feature film world with short films, documentaries, and work for television. Their films, too, had much in common: their tiny budgets, their respect for Berber culture, and the very real dangers that accompanied the shooting, since this was a time of civil unrest and ruthless violence by Islamic fundamentalists.

Belkacem Hadjadj's *Once Upon a Time / Machaho* (1995) has a sense of tranquility in the handling of scenes involving traditional Berber language, values, costumes, and rituals, which is remarkable given the upheavals occurring everywhere at the time of its filming. Hadjadj explained his decision to plunge into Berber history in an interview at the time of the film's release: "It is no doubt necessary for cinema to be harnessed to immediate reality, but faced with a whole oppressed generation, there's a need to look at the new models which have been forced upon it, and which have not worked. After 132 years of a process of depersonalisation, first attempting to impose a colonial model in the period up to independence, and now the importing of a Western model, you have only to look at the results."[46]

Set in an unspecified period and avoiding the slightest trace of immediate crises within the community, the film is a simple peasant drama. It examines the traditional codes of honor in Berber society, telling of a father who kills the man who seduces his daughter, only to discover that he had come back to marry her. Hadjadj himself played the leading role of the father. Hadjadj's second film, *El manara* (2004), is by contrast explicitly set at the time of the October 1988 uprisings and traces the impact of these upheavals on three young people.

Bouguermouh's *The Forgotten Hillside / La colline oubliée* (1996) is the adaptation of a novel by Mouloud Mammeri, who, like many Berber writers of the postwar independence era, chose to publish in French rather than Arabic because he saw the attempted arabization of Berber culture as constituting as much of a threat as the colonial intrusion of the French. It was a project that Bouguermouh had wanted to make for over twenty years and that he had discussed at length with the author. When the new attitude of the government in the mid-1990s allowed him to get the project under way, he still had to face the constraints imposed by Islamic violence in and around the Atlas Mountains. For Bouguermouh, the film is rooted in Mammeri's thought and on "an undeniable anthropological, social etc. truth." His sole concern was "to show Kabylie as it is, dress having a part to play in this, just as much as the language, which was the condition *sine qua non* for me to make the film." In casting his nonprofessional players, Bouguermouh was concerned not just to match them physically to the characters depicted in the novel but also to hear them speak in a genuine *kabyle* accent ("not people educated in town and only speaking the language to talk to their grandparents").[47]

Azzedine Meddour's *Baya's Mountain / La montagne de Baya* (1997) took some eighteen months to complete, the shooting being constantly interrupted because of very real security concerns (some members of the crew were killed in one explosion). The film is set in 1939, during the time of French colonization, but the conflicts are essentially internal to the Berber community, between the mass of the peasants and their traditional leader, the Bach-agha, who had become a key collaborator with the French. The struggles of the peasants, constantly driven from their homes while struggling to rebuild their community, even on the bare slopes of a mountain, form the background to the film's main narrative. This involves two legendary figures: the warrior Djendel, who comes down from his mountain stronghold to fight and die with the villagers, and Baya, revered in her community as the daughter of a saint. Baya refuses to accept the blood money due to her from the Bach-agha, whose son has killed her husband. To accept would be to lose her honor and also the chance of ever avenging his death. This sets her apart from the peasants, who would have used the money to pay off their taxes and reestablish their village. The film's heroine, Baya, is a fictional character, but Meddour is anxious to assert that she is "inspired and nourished by historical figures and by women who still struggle today."[48] He also accepts that Baya can be seen as a sort of metaphor for the artist: "It's certainly extraordinary the extent to which the script and the history of the shooting suffered the same fate: we began to live what Baya lived through. She struggled from certain values. So did we."[49]

Meddour published a novel based on the film shortly before his death in 2000.

*

Female filmmakers continued to be virtually nonexistent in Algerian cinema during the 1990s. Just as Assia Djebar was marginalized in the 1970s, so too was her only successor in the 1990s, the novelist-turned-filmmaker Hafsa Zinaï-Koudil. Zinaï-Koudil, who was born in 1951, had written three novels in Algeria before the shooting and published a fourth in Paris, where she eventually settled, in 1997. Like Djebar, she had no formal film school training, but she had worked as a scriptwriter and as an assistant on three features before she began to make her sole 16mm feature for RTA.

Woman as the Devil / Le démon au féminin (1993) is a film that was shot and set at a time of threat from radical Islamists for all intellectuals and that confronts contemporary problems faced head-on. It is fascinating that, though the film was based on real events that dominated the headlines in Algiers for months, the form that Zinaï-Koudil chose was that of the Hollywood melodrama. Safy Boutella's powerful music therefore plays a key role in shaping what is, in essence, a tragic melodrama with a very muted happy ending.

Salima, a teacher, and her architect husband, Ali, both lead busy lives. They have three children: two girls who are still at school, Amel and Faiza, and an eldest son, Habib, who causes some distress by giving up work in order to read the Koran and go constantly to the mosque. In fact, he has been radicalized there, and, increasingly, he criticizes his family's supposed bad practices, demanding that Salima give up her work and her Western-style clothing. When Ali, who is overworked and (unknown to his wife) had suicidal tendencies in his twenties, suffers a mental breakdown, family life collapses. One can feel a novelist's power in the narrative depiction of the gradual shift of power from Ali to Habib. Stylistically the film owes much to the horror movie genre, as we hear the voices as experienced by the deluded Ali and see his crazed visions. With Habib as the dominant force within the family, the fundamentalists from the mosque can intervene. They see the problem as deriving not from Ali's illness but from the demonic possession of Salima. As a result, with Ali's consent, she is subjected to a violent exorcism that leaves her mute and paralyzed.

Up to this point, the film's dramatic logic works totally, exposing the lunacy of the fundamentalist Islamic thinking, which places all the responsibility for the world's ills on the actions of contemporary liberated women, who lead independent lives, go out to work, and wear Western clothes and makeup ("going about naked," as the Islamist preacher proclaims). It is unfortunate, from a dramatic point of view, that Zinaï-Koudil tries to tie up all the loose ends of the narrative, perhaps because she was dealing with actual events, known to the public. The film loses momentum when Salima's brother intervenes to bring the ignorant radicals to court. An unseen voice of power orders the judges to acquit them, and so they go free. The still delusional Ali kills himself. The trial, however, brings Habib to his senses, and Salima, now mobile in a wheelchair and able to speak, can comfort him and offer him reconciliation at the very end of the film. As a woman, Zinaï-Koudil had great difficulty in being accepted as a film director: "I was the object of a general outcry; a veritable wall rose up in front of me."[50] *Woman as the Devil* is a brave and powerful work dealing directly with the gravest problem facing Algeria in the early 1990s in a manner virtually unique in Arab cinema. There seems an inevitability about the fact that the director did not make her planned second feature and, indeed, that she felt the need to seek exile in France after her protracted battles with her producers and distributors.

*

As we have seen earlier in the chapter, Algerian state cinema struggled through a decade of unsatisfactory reorganizations before finally expiring in 1997, and the resultant careers of most of those who began within these structures in the 1970s but were subsequently forced abroad have already been touched on. Within the state-controlled context, making a film independently, outside the existing structures, was a counterrevolutionary act that just did not happen. It was impossible to get permission to shoot or even to obtain film stock outside the state sector. Though there was a certain security (in that filmmakers were paid by the month, whether they were actually filming or not), their position was far from ideal. As Mohamed Chouikh observes, the state organization's function was generally limited to acting as "a letterbox, because you had to do everything—collect the support and financing—and hand the management over to this organisation, which paid you a derisory salary. Nevertheless it had the power of life or death over the production of the film."[51]

Mohamed Chouikh, who made his debut at the beginning of the 1980s, is the one director to maintain his independence within the state organization and go on to work independently while not leaving Algeria. Chouikh was born in 1943 in Mostaganem and began his career as an actor, playing the lead in one of Algeria's first features, Mohamed Lakhdar Hamina's *Wind from the Aurès*. He also appeared in Tewfik Farès's *The Outlaws* and Sid Ali Mazif's *The Nomads*. His method—shared with many other filmmakers worldwide working under authoritarian regimes—has been, as we shall see, to use metaphor and symbolism in order to get his ideas across to the public. Chouikh was nineteen at the time of independence and has described the key change in his life as "going swiftly from a system of 'colonial' oppression to an East-European-style state 'social' structure, in which mere slogans served as expressions of 'culture.'"[52] Though he was later to become one of the most articulate critics of the Algerian state system, Chouikh was initially very much a part of it, involved in the making of Ahmed Rachedi's pioneering *Dawn of the Damned* and starring in several of the key early features of Mohamed Lakhdar Hamina and Tewfik Farès. He also directed two téléfilms for Algerian state television.

But when he began to make films for cinema release from the late 1980s, he proved himself to be one of the few Algerian filmmakers able to develop a truly distinctive style within that state system. In terms of its originality and stylistic innovation, his work ranks with that of his independently produced contemporaries in, say, Tunisia. He was also the sole major director to remain and continue to work in Algeria throughout the civil war that tore the country apart in the 1990s. Chouikh's reputation rests on a remarkable trio of films—*The Citadel, Youssef: The Legend of the Seventh Sleeper*, and *The Desert Ark*—in which he turns his back on realism to explore the possibilities of parable and allegory. In this way, as Denise Brahimi notes, "he constructs revealing situations and invents images with a strong symbolic charge."[53]

The Citadel / La citadelle /Al-qala (1988) presents itself as a fable, not precisely located in time and space but offering a very recognizable world where power is in the hands of the elders, whose role is validated by tradition but who care only for themselves. Women are sequestered in polygamous marriages and allowed absolutely no freedom. The two innocents who flout the system are the shoemaker's flirtatious wife and the young man who falls in love with her, Kaddour, a dreamer isolated from his fellow villagers. His innocent love is seen as an offense that threatens the order of the village, so his father, one of the self-indulgent elders, devises a cruel punishment. He arranges his son's marriage, and, as is customary, Kaddour is not allowed to see his bride until after the wedding ceremony has taken place. Then, in front of the whole village, the cruel trick is revealed. Kaddour has been married to a tailor's dummy. Deeply humiliated and jeered at by the villagers, he throws himself to his death from a cliff top.

The Citadel works well as a neatly constructed narrative, and the tailor's dummy is a telling symbol of the situation of a woman in this society: deprived of life, choice, and even a voice and handed as a veiled object from one family to another. Kaddour stands equally for deluded Algerian youth, plunged into despair when deceit is revealed. More telling still is the parallel between the hollow authority of the village elders with that claimed at this period by the sole political party in Algeria, the National Liberation Front (the FNL). But by the late 1980s, the FNL had, in fact, lost the historical legitimacy it had claimed from the war of independence and had long been discredited because of its growing bureaucracy and corruption. The people had gradually come to see that the glorious myth of a people totally united behind "its" army (to which Algerian cinema had contributed so much) and the claims of the FNL as sole founder and guarantor of the country were both mere myths. The riots in Algiers in October 1988 and the sudden rise of popular support for Islamic fundamentalism merely underlined this state of affairs.

The status of Chouikh's next film as a fable is underlined by its full title, *Youssef: The Legend of the Seventh Sleeper/ Youcef, la légende du septième dormant / Youcef kesat dekra sabera* (1993), which refers to an Arab legend about seven warriors who slept for three centuries and awoke in a very changed world. The hero of the film is a traditional figure in Arab narrative, the holy fool who sees the truth everyone else denies or overlooks. Youssef is, in fact, a wounded former FNL combatant who has been held in an asylum in the south of Algeria for thirty years, since the end of the fighting. Having lost his memory because of his wounds, Youssef thinks he is still in the 1960s and in an Algeria still colonized by the French. Nothing he sees makes him doubt this. Nowhere does he find the independent Algeria that he and his comrades had fought and sometimes died for. His journey across Algeria makes a complex story, full of twists and surprising revelations, leading almost inevitably to his own death (ironically shot down at the FNL's official celebration of his return—"an independence day for a comrade who arrived late"). *Youssef* offers remarkable insight into the complex and contradictory situation in Algeria at this period, and though the script was originally written in 1988 and submitted to the authorities in 1990, it contains chilling parallels with the assassination of the Algerian president Mohamed Boudiaf, which occurred during the shooting of the film.

Youssef is by no means a seamless work, veering, as it proceeds, from black farce (with some really broad gags—as when Youssef, disguised as a woman, is accosted by an unwitting man) to tender emotional scenes (with the women in Youssef's life and with his nephew, Ali). There are also episodes of real horror (such as the burning to death of an illegitimate child). The film's plot twists and turns, and the narrative is always full of surprising revelations. Chouikh's choice of Ali, forced to live in fear as a transvestite (and seeming at home in the role), as a symbol for Algerian youth, crippled by thirty years of FNL rule and a society based on the total segregation of the sexes, is just one of Chouikh's daring symbolic innovations. There is rich irony, too, in the fact that the film images that his former comrades show Youssef (in a cave of all places) to convince him that liberation really did occur come from a fictional film, Gillo Pontecorvo's *The Battle of Algiers*. Chouikh denies any desire to bring solutions or to make definitive judgements, but what emerges with total clarity is the failure of the FNL over thirty years. Chouikh's chosen device of showing events through the eyes of a man who assumes that the country is still colonized is totally effective. The contradictions of a country where the old FNL fighters now live in the ex-colonizers' villas and have adopted their attitudes while the ordinary people queue endlessly for bread are vividly brought to the fore. As is so often the case in parables, the madness in *Youssef* lies within the society, not in the apparent madman.

The Desert Arc/ L'arche du désert (1997) is another parable, this time about meaningless violence between two communities, triggered, as in *Romeo and Juliet*, by the innocent love of two young people. The film is not explicitly set in contemporary Algeria but in a timeless Saharan village where a boat is mysteriously stranded in the dunes. Chouikh's view is straightforward: "We are on the earth, as if in an oasis, where we are obliged to share everything in order to survive: water, pasture, work. If we do not manage to tolerate each other within the limitations of the possible and to unite against the hostility of the desert, then everything is finished."[54] Here the observer (and judge) of the action is not a simpleminded youth or a holy fool but a small boy who sets off at the end to find a land where children are not slaughtered senselessly.

Chouikh's return to filmmaking in 2005, *Hamlet of Women / Douar des femmes / Douar al-nissa*, took the surprising form of a comedy based on role reversal, as the women of a remote village threatened by outsiders take up arms to protect themselves while their men are away working in a local factory.[55]

The fact that Chouikh's work is novel in form and questions simple notions of cultural identity and social realism does not mean that it is any less concerned with the realities and contradictions of postcolonial Algeria. Indeed, as Richard Porton has noted, "Since allegory depicts, and indeed revels in, the 'brokenness' of the world, it is a genre that is well suited to the requirements of contemporary African directors."[56] Chouikh's work, with its mixture of tenderness and grotesquerie, tragedy and farce, is a powerful answer to mainstream Algerian cinema's crippling lack of originality of form and conformity of message.

Morocco

A program for the renewal of Moroccan cinema was set out by Moumen Smihi in an interview with Guy Hennebelle recorded after the completion of his first feature: "There's a general problem here. Cinema is the product of western bourgeois society. It is therefore the production of this society's imagery of this society, that is to say, it is integrated into a novelistic, theatrical, dramatic tradition. From the moment when the same means of expression, the cinema, is manipulated in another cultural atmosphere, it is necessary, even if only to escape servile imitation, to interrogate the forms and cultural traditions of this different atmosphere."[57]

Key to Smihi's vision is a different notion of film structure: "It is true that it is hard to destroy narrative in cinema. However, you can think of forms which would function precisely to translate another way of living and thinking, another culture, other social options than those put forward up to now by the West."[58] This new plot structure, in turn, will have its roots in the national culture, insofar as this can be recovered. In the case of Morocco, in Smihi's view, "the particular character of Moroccan colonization, under the Protectorate structure, allowed the country to preserve its social core in a deeply authentic form, despite the viciousness of the aggression from outside."[59]

In attempting to create this new Moroccan cinema, Smihi found support from two other young filmmakers, Hamid Benani and Ahmed Bouanani. The trio, all born in the 1930s or early 1940s, had studied filmmaking at IDHEC in Paris in the 1960s and made their marks with debut films in the 1970s. All three were highly experimental films, no doubt influenced by the wave of innovative European filmmaking that they would have enjoyed during their stay in Paris. These were the first Moroccan films to have an international impact. As a result of the hiatus in Moroccan state-produced feature films between 1970 and 1977, the first two of these three features were independently produced.

The first pioneer is Hamid Benani, born in Meknes in 1942, who released *Traces / Wechma* in 1970. Five years later, he was followed by Moumen Smihi, who was born in Tangiers in 1945 and made *El Chergui* in 1975. The third of these pioneering features was *Mirage*, released in 1979 and made by Ahmed Bouanani, who was born in 1938 and died in a village a hundred kilometers from Casablanca, Ait Oumghar, in 2011. Bouanani was able to get full state funding for his debut film, as the Centre Cinématographique Marocain (CCM) had by then resumed its support for feature filmmaking. All three films treat contemporary subject matter and mix realistic images of contemporary society with symbolic images to create disjointed and often enigmatic narratives that provoked wide critical interest. The three form a coherent group, collaborating on each other's films. Despite the international attention and screenings these debut films received, none of the three filmmakers was subsequently able to establish a fully satisfying filmmaking career.

Before his IDHEC studies, Benani had completed a degree in law in Rabat and while in Paris followed the seminars led by Roland Barthes and Paul Ricoeur. During and immediately after these studies, he worked as a film critic, publishing in particular an article on ambiguity in the work of Luis Buñuel. He also directed a few shorts for Moroccan television. To produce *Wechma*, he set up a collective company, Sigma 3, together with Ahmed Bouanani, who edited the film; his fellow IDHEC graduate (and future director) Mohamed Abderrahman Tazi, who supervised the cinematography; and Mohamed Sekkat, who served as director of production.

Wechma is structured in two parts, the first dealing in masterly fashion with the protagonist, Messaoud's childhood. His initial adoption from an orphanage seems promising. His new father, Meki, is not unsympathetic and his adoptive mother open and loving. But Meki proves to be an authoritarian and dominating parent, and Messaoud cannot even begin to integrate himself into his new environment. He responds to Meki's harsh treatment by retreating into a private world ornamented (like a shrine) with small pilfered objects and stolen fruit. His sense of alienation is clear from a succession of lingering close-ups, underlined by brief snatches of music. There is no attempt to create a sequential narrative. Messaoud's encounters are random and disconnected, typified by his encounter with a group of youths who have captured and proceed to torture an owl. The tone is set in Messaoud's first (highly symbolic) experience of his new country environment: being shown a donkey laboring to drive a grindstone. The final scenes of part one comprise a succession of snapshots rather than a logical narrative succession: Messaoud runs away, is caught, and, as punishment, is branded by his father, who promptly and totally unexpectedly dies, tended by Hatari, a traditional healer. Messaoud's response is to use the funeral as a cover to steal his father's revolver and set out on a life of his own.

The second part of *Wechma* shows Messaoud's subsequent drifting progress as a young adult through a series of petty crimes, carried out by the gang of layabouts to which he has come to belong. The discontinuity is even more apparent in this part of the film, which is shot through with symbolic imagery and enigmatic events. The identification with Messaoud's subjective experience is enhanced, underlined again by the musical score, so that we are never quite sure whether the incidents we see are real or imagined. There are a number of moments that would be seen as "continuity errors" in a conventional narrative. For example, Messaoud is seen throwing away the gun he had stolen during his father's funeral when it fails to fire, but it is subsequently still in his possession. He again tries it, and again it does not fire. When he fires it at El Bashir, his employer, at the end of the film, there is once more no explosive sound—the gun merely clicks—but El Bashir falls dead at his feet.

The director's concern is less with constructing a conventional story line than with patterning narrative motifs: the repeated references to owls, for example, or the role played by motorcycles in Messaoud's life. At the beginning of part two, he is working in a fairground, totally captivated by the wall of death performer. At the end, he dies in an accident on a stolen motorcycle. Messaoud is an outsider even within the gang to which he belongs. He does not participate in the film's strangest event—the gang rape of a woman found wearing an owl mask who seems to enjoy the experience. When the gang leader organizes the torture of the youngest member of the group, Messaoud intervenes and drives the others away with his revolver. He is now on his own and gets work looking after the sheep belonging to El Bashir, who keeps owls as a hobby. But this, too, does not last, and the film ends with an unnecessary death and a pointless accident. Hatari (married to Messaoud's adoptive mother) is there to give Messaoud the last rites: "It is God's will."

Benani has said of his film, "I've tried to describe a form of social alienation due to a patriarchal society, to tradition, and so on, but denounced from within. . . . Messaoud, the foundling, father and mother unknown, is illegitimacy personified according to traditional society. He represents a radical challenge to this society. I chose a marginal character with no hope of salvation because the type of morality that tries . . . to save him excludes him at the same time."[60] The film was well received at its international screenings and by Moroccan critics and ciné-clubs, though its commercial distribution seems to have been largely blocked. But, as Fouad Souiba and Fatma Zahra El Alaoui write: "*Wechma* was a true revolution in Maghrebian cinema. For the first time, a filmmaker has thought deeply about the film language which he is going to use, shot by shot. He has sought and found an original form of expression, which distinguishes itself totally from the clichés of Western art or commercial cinema and has gone directly back to the sources of the Moroccan imaginary."[61]

Benani made just two more features—*A Prayer for the Absent / La prière de l'absent* (1995) and *The Child Sheikh / L'enfant cheikh / Atefl achäkh* (2013)—in the next forty-five years, neither of which attracted the same attention and acclaim.

A Prayer for the Absent is the adaptation of a novel by one of Morocco's leading novelists, Tahar Benjelloun. Again it is structured in two parts. The opening sequence of black-and-white newsreel footage, featuring the patriotic riots and subsequent French repression after the exiling of Mohamed V, firmly locates the action in October 1953. The subsequent fictional action alternates violent action on the street and complex domestic dramas in the shuttered-off houses. Mokhtar and his friend Jamal study incessantly, endlessly reciting religious texts, and are bound by a highly intense friendship that would seem to exclude women. But Jamal has seduced Mokhtar's schoolgirl sister, Laila, and Mokhtar has had a sexual relationship with the maid, Yasma. Both girls have their virginity tested by anxious older women. Laila is able to bribe the maid who carries out the inspection, but Yasma is denounced, humiliated, and expelled from the house. Meanwhile, Mokhtar's behavior is becoming increasingly erratic, and when Jamal vanishes, he experiences a breakdown, suffering from amnesia (he now gives his name as Sindbad). He is condemned to an asylum, which provides the film with a memorable image with which to conclude this part of the film: inmates are compelled to "fill" an empty swimming pool with imaginary water carried in bottomless buckets.

Seven years later, a bearded Mokhtar emerges from the asylum, though his problems remain essentially the same. His first encounter is with Boby, who claims to be an old friend but who is in a worse mental state than he is. Boby thinks he is a dog—barks like one, even pees like one—and will eventually drown attempting to dog-paddle in a sacred lake. At the moment when Mokhtar finds him, he lives in a cemetery, which is the site of the first of many dream images and memory flashbacks in this part of the film. Mokhtar resolves to travel south to meet up with the *marabout*, Moulay Bouchaïb. On the journey, there are many encounters with figures from his past, beginning with Yasma, who now has a small child and whom he does not initially recognize. The other encounters are all abortive. Laila is there but does not want to meet them; she is completing her university thesis. Mokhtar meets Jamal, but they no longer have anything in common, as Jamal is now a political activist. The *marabout* promises Mokhtar spiritual insight but almost immediately dies in his arms. Mokhtar formally marries Yasma and recognizes her son as his own. But there is no celebration. Mokhtar is resolved to live alone, and in our last view of him, dressed all in white, he is striding into the sea.

A Prayer for the Absent, perhaps because it is adapted from a novel, is in some ways an overly complex film. Once again, Benani shows his disregard for the structures of conventional narrative and the role of the positive, ultimately successful protagonist. The first part has a complex array of characters, and Mokhtar's problems tend to be drowned out by what emerges as the central theme here: the treatment of women in traditional society. Mokhtar is central to the second part of the film, but he sleepwalks through much of it because of his memory loss. He redeems himself with his formal recognition of Yasma and his son, but there is no warmth here, and, as in *Wechma*, there can be no satisfactory resolution.

The Child Sheikh, Benani's third feature, is his first to receive support from the CCM and the first to adopt a conventional narrative pattern. It is ostensibly told by the aged, blind Saïd to his grandson, though it contains love scenes and violent deaths that would not normally be part of a grandfather's storytelling to the young. We hear Saïd's voice at the outset and occasional comments from him throughout the action, but we actually see the two of them together—grandfather and child— only at the end of the film. Saïd remains the archetypal passive Benani hero:

attractive but unable to fit into or command his milieu (even though he becomes a tribal leader), unlike the film's active protagonist, his friend and the rebel resistance leader Ameur. Tellingly, it is Zahra, once the mother-figure who bathed him and put him to bed as a child, who seduces Saïd, not vice versa.

This, as the opening title tells us, is "a Berber epic from the time of the resistance" and it incorporates several sequences of black-and-white newsreel footage depicting the armed might of the French. There is the customary set of tangled domestic involvements and rivalries: the passionate love between Saïd and the beautiful Zahra and the hostility of Tuscha, the daughter of Sidi's first wife, toward her stepmother and her adopted brother. These entanglements fit well into the broader pattern, since they are largely shaped and motivated by the increasing conflict. The film's title comes from a fabled episode of the resistance involving a group of women who have lost their husbands. They decide to take up arms themselves and choose as their sheik a five-year-old child, Yidir, Zahra's son. Benani made clear during the shooting of *The Child Sheikh* his intention for the film: "I think that artists in general should celebrate their history and interrogate it in such a way as to create an artistic work and a cultural reference point, as well as seeking out the role of the imaginary in the real."[62]

His success in blending newsreel and fictional footage reflects his ability to bring together historical accounts (mostly written by the colonizers) and local tribal legends, transmitted orally from generation to generation. Benani is a true film *auteur*, who, though given few opportunities to display his talents, remained true to his artistic beliefs and formal concerns for over forty years.

Moumen Smihi was the second of this initial trio to make his mark, and he, like Benani, accompanied his film studies in Paris with attendance at Roland Barthes's seminars at the École Supérieure des Hautes Études Sociales. Smihi made his structural concerns very clear in the interview with Guy Hennebelle that has already been cited. His approach "consisted of proceeding by successive departures or entries from [the] film's main theme (the story of a Moroccan woman) but also in opposition to a linear narrative, which by this fact became disarticulated, or articulated in other ways."[63] "Inevitably, the progression of the protagonist was a 'descent into Hell.'"[64]

El Chergui / El chergui ou le silence violent, also known as *The East Wind* (1975), is set in Tangier in the early 1950s (on the eve of Moroccan independence), though this background is sketched in only lightly.[65] The central focus throughout is on the experiences of Arab inhabitants of the city. Unlike the other two 1970s pioneering debut films, *El Chergui* does have a clear central narrative: the story of Aïcha, whose world falls apart when she learns that, though they already have a son, her husband is planning to take a younger second wife.

Overall, Aïcha's story, as she makes offerings and follows the advice of a *marabout*, is coherent and seems to progress inevitably toward death, which comes at last when she, putting up no resistance, drowns following a mishap during a purification ritual. There is no attempt to dramatize her predicament, and her story is very understated. For much of the time, she is an observer of the world around her. She and her husband never exchange so much as a word during the whole course of the film, making the French subtitle for the film, *ou le silence violent* ("The Violent Silence"), very apposite. Aïcha's story is constantly tangled with and interrupted by those of her husband and son and by a number of potential narratives that threaten to emerge.

Even on repeated viewing, parts of the film remain quite enigmatic, and Smihi's own comments do little to help. But despite, or perhaps because of, these enigmas, *El Chergui*—like *Wechma* and *Mirage*—continues to be held in high regard as a major innovative force in Moroccan filmmaking. On the eve of the film's release in Paris, Nourreddine Ghali wrote that "in the context of Moroccan cinema it is a landmark film. . . . Its author shows here a stylistic mastery and the temperament of an authentic *cinéaste*."[66] Its reputation has not diminished in the present era, as three evaluations from the 1990s show. *El Chergui* is, for Moulay Driss Jaïdi, one of the 1970s films that "have as their project the affirmation of that freedom of expression ceaselessly demanded by Moroccan producer-directors."[67] For Fouad Souiba and Fatma Zahra El Alaoui, the power of the work's thematic "lies in its constant oscillation between Moroccan reality and mythology."[68] For Ahmed Araib and Eric de Hullessen, "Moumen Smihi ratchets up the level of Moroccan cinema," and his film belongs to "an experimental cinema inseparable from its social and philosophic environment."[69]

Despite its critical success, there was a ten-year gap after the release of *El Chergui* and Smihi's next film. But since 1985, Smihi has been able to make a number of documentaries and another half dozen features. *Forty-Four or Tales of the Night / 44 ou les récits de la nuit / 44 aw oustourat al layl* (1985) traces the progress of two families, a wealthy one in Fez headed by a university professor and a poor family in Chaouen, through the period 1912–56. These are the years leading from the imposition of the French protectorate in Fez and the parallel onset of Spanish rule in Chaouen to the eventual achievement of Moroccan independence under King Mohamed V. The character who links the two families is Moussa, who grows up in Chaouen, goes to Fez to pursue his studies (and to become one of the professor's most respected students), and later returns home to share in the deprivation of Chaouen.

As the official synopsis makes clear, Smihi's intention is not to act as a historian, and the opening credits describe the film as "a hypothesis." Though there are occasional scraps of radio commentary to clarify wider events, Smihi ignores the possibilities offered by the newsreel footage from the period. His concern is with the impact of the protectorate on the lives of ordinary people and the ways in which it forces them to reexamine their fundamental Muslim identity and values. The personal experiences of the settlers, whose formal European dress sets them apart from the Moroccan populace, are completely ignored. Stress is placed instead on the attempts of young Moroccans to come to terms with European culture, vividly illustrated by an all-male student production of Shakespeare's *Othello*, in which Moussa participates and Desdemona is depicted by an actor sporting a moustache.

In the film, we do not have a central character who grows to political awareness and becomes a rebel, nor do we see the actual bloody confrontations between Arab independence fighters and the opposing colonial forces. Instead, we witness the effect of startling events—the defeat of the rebels in the mountains, the efforts of the French to separate Berbers and Arabs, the removal of the king—as they are transmitted via oral reports and rumors to ordinary people cut off from wider events. There is not even a full-scale celebration of the return of Mohamed V, which seals Moroccan independence. Instead, Smihi lays his emphasis on traditional events—marriages, circumcision ceremonies, funerals—that shape people's everyday lives. The violence of the independence struggle occurs off-screen. This approach is paralleled by Smihi's stylistic choices. There is no central narrative growing to a climax, just a mosaic of tiny, juxtaposed events that are themselves often abruptly cut off before they reach their climax. The director has drawn his inspiration, predictably perhaps, from the *Thousand and One Nights* but also, as the film's opening title tells us, from the structural patterning of James Joyce's *Ulysses*.

Caftan of Love / Caftan d'amour / Qaftan al-hubb (1988), by contrast, is the very personal tale of a beautiful dream that turns into a nightmare. The film was adapted from a story, *The Big Mirror*, by the Tangier-based American novelist Paul Bowles and his Arab companion, Mohamed M'rabet. Khalil, a young boy growing up in Tangier, wants to get married and even sees his ideal girl in his dreams. By chance, he catches sight of her, in person, in the medina. He promptly asks for her hand and marries her. But Rachida, while exceptionally beautiful, turns out to be quite different from the girl he had imagined. She spends all the time looking at her own reflection in the mirror.

The Lady from Cairo / La dame du Caire / Sayyidat al-qâhira (1991) differs from Smihi's other films in that it was shot in Egypt, where he also made a documentary study of Egyptian cinema. The film is sometimes described as a musical, but it is, in fact, a melodrama with musical inserts. It begins somewhat hesitantly, as Yussra seems less confident as Amina, a simple peasant girl, than she does in later scenes, when she has become a star and socialite. At home, Amina's closest relationship is with her brother, Yahia, who shares her desire to go to Cairo but leaves without taking her with him.

Undeterred, she sets off alone to Cairo, following the trajectory Yahia had established, by visiting their two aunts, who are already living in the city. Neither is particularly sympathetic toward Amina, but one agrees to take her on as a servant—to replace the girl who has run off with Yahia. The film does not draw on the full dramatic possibilities offered by the situation of an attractive young woman alone in the big city. Amina's rise to fame and wealth is effortless. Her rich, well-connected middle-age patron agrees to marry her before they sleep together (and later agrees to separate bedrooms). Her closest ally and confidant, the journalist Omar, is in love with her but agrees to remain just a friend. She emerges unscathed from a relationship with an Egyptian football star. The various performances that set her on the path to singing stardom, as Gouhara, are all well received.

The action, which takes several years, is set against scraps of information from radio and television, alluding to the wider international events of the period, which include the Suez invasion, Nasser's resignation, and Sadat's peace efforts and his assassination. But the film is almost totally focused on personal relationships. The most striking dramatic elements involve Amina's relationship with the troubled Yahia, who is active on the fringes of these wider events. She is convinced she sees him as a soldier in scenes depicted on television, but even Abdessatar, for all his connections, cannot confirm whether he is enlisted in the army. In fact, he has joined a group of rebels working against the government. He comes to one of her performances but afterward rejects her as a disgrace for appearing on stage. Later, he summons her, but their meeting becomes an angry confrontation. He slaps her and calls her a whore, but she still gives him money and her jewelry. Unfortunately for Yahia, this is not enough for the other members of his group. They take the money but then beat him to death. Smihi does not indulge in spectacular endings, so we do not get what might be expected at this point: a performance bringing together Amina's artistry and her inner grief. Instead, we last see Amina alone on a plane to an unknown destination. She is in meditative mood, concerned about the difficulties that her new freedom brings with it. It is fascinating to see a filmmaker from outside Egypt confront the genre requirements of the film industry there. But Smihi, one feels, is much more at home with the series of small-scale local dramas, based increasingly on his own upbringing, on which he has since embarked.

Moroccan Chronicles / Chroniques marocaines / Waqa'i maghribia (1999) is a transitional work. Smihi describes his intentions as follows: "I need to analyse and understand what is happening today in our countries, like the Algerian tragedy, and I want to do that concretely, that is to say, from and on my territory, the cinema, writing with images and sounds. I would so much like to say and film everything I have in my heart about France, about us Arabs and about colonisation."[70] The film was originally shot in 16mm in 1993, but its 35mm release was held back for six years. It eventually emerged thanks to French financial support. Set in Fez, it features a mother—abandoned by her husband, who has gone to Europe—who arranges a belated circumcision, necessarily without the father and the customary ceremonies, for her adolescent son, Amine. To calm and comfort him afterward, she tells him three stories, each set in a different city and each beginning, "Once upon a time." She pauses after each one for his response (always a rejection) but does not intrude with any voice-over comment as the stories unfold.

The first is set in the famous Jama el Fna Square in Marrakesh and offers glimpses of the variety of entertainers who perform there: acrobats, a snake charmer, a storyteller, musicians, and dancers. The story concerns three boys who torment and jeer at another of the performers, a monkey tamer with his beloved monkey, Zahia. Eventually, they break into his courtyard and kill the monkey. The tamer demands justice from a sharia court, and the boys are ordered to replace the monkey. We return to Jama el Fna Square, to see the first of the boys perform and show himself sadly inferior to both the monkey and a real child acrobat performing nearby.

The second story is set on the ramparts of Essaouira, where Orson Welles did the location shooting for his version of *Othello*. Chams, a flirtatious young girl who has just left school, sees at a distance her friend Tewfik, who has just returned from the United States. They converse partly in Arabic, partly in French and English. He wants them to meet up, but she sets him a task. She will come veiled and dressed from head to toe in traditional white garb, and his job is to recognize her straightaway. He does not do this too well—there are dozens of white-clad women in Essaouira. But the third time—in Orson Welles Square—there is recognition. But she immediately slips off for a moment, and when she reappears, she is totally Westernized, wearing a little black cocktail dress. They kiss, and all seems well. But voice-over quotes, in her voice and in English, from a scene between Othello and Iago in the Shakespeare play, do not augur well.

The third and slightest of the stories, set in Tangier, concerns an old fisherman who retains his lifelong dream that one day he will encounter a gigantic whale carrying treasure in its belly. He is mocked by his fellow fishermen, but he remains firm: he will find the whale. One day, out in his tiny fishing boat, he sees what he thinks is the whale on the horizon and steers resolutely toward it. But it is, in fact, a huge vessel, and he is invisible to those on board. Inevitably, his boat is swamped, and he is drowned.

Amine is not impressed by any of these—he is too busy reading about the "great white chief," Tarzan. Mother and son go out together and, while they look out over Fez, the mother weeps. This seems to be the end of the narrative. But Smihi adds a coda. In the final sequence Amine runs away, to his mother's despair. The film ends as we hear his voice-over letter to her. He is going to Tangier and then on to France to join his father. He will send her money.

These three stories, little more than anecdotes, show a lighter side of Smihi's filming, but he is able to bring in all his favorite themes, from the treatment of women in Moroccan society to the lure of exile and the clash of cultures. Perhaps the most intriguing aspect of the film is its depiction of traditional society—mosques, chants, traditional garb—being invaded from outside by alien voices, particularly the radio news broadcasts. Amine reads his Tarzan book; Chams looks good in her Western dress. Young people switch easily between French and Arabic, and the old people sitting by the port accuse the aged fisherman of watching too much science fiction on television, describing him as a cross between Sindbad and Commander Cousteau. The great white whale turns out to be a bulk carrier—totally unlike the fishermen's boats—bringing huge German-made lorries into Morocco. The same mixture of cultures is to be found on Smihi's sound track, which combines unaccompanied Bach violin pieces with traditional Arab songs. Above all, *Moroccan Chronicles* is filmed with extreme simplicity so that the imagery has a documentary feel to it—bringing the cityscapes to the foreground and offering a vivid picture of three contrasting Moroccan cities, all experiencing rapid change.

Since *Moroccan Chronicles*, Smihi's more recent films have been noticeably autobiographical, constituting a loose trilogy. *The Boy from Tangier / Le gosse de Tanger / El ayel* (2005), also known as *A Muslim Childhood*, recounts the story of Larbi Salmi, a boy obsessed with the cinema, which even his devoutly religious father admits is not a sin. Larbi's first words in the film are to ask for money to go to see a film, arguing that the subtitles will help him with his French studies. Larbi's mother is an angry, frustrated woman. Married as a child bride, she had given birth to him when she herself was just sixteen. The dominant figure in Larbi's early life is his father, Sidi Ahmed, who spends most of his time praying and reading religious texts. His erudition allows him to find a suitable citation from the Koran for any domestic or social problem, always arguing for moderation and respect. He is a mild man, averse to violence, but he is the real authority at home, shaping the lives of Larbi and his younger brother, Khalil.

Sidi Ahmad combines his Muslim faith with a belief in the importance of knowledge, and therefore, he sends both his sons to the French lycée while requiring them to attend a Koranic school in the summer months to ensure their knowledge of the holy text. Being brought up with two sets of cultural values does not trouble Larbi too much at this stage of his life. He is more concerned with the usual preoccupations of a child: exploring Tangier and spying on its varied districts, particularly the disreputable ones. Most of his time is spent playing and squabbling with his friends, being bullied himself and in turn bullying his younger brother, and—of course—dreaming about the cinema.

There are surprising moments in the narrative—such as the arrival of his aging grandmother, who has been repudiated by her husband, and the abrupt emergence of his mentally ill uncle Allal, who has been sheltered in an upstairs room for years—but neither of these is developed into a real, forceful dramatic scene. Even the consequences of Larbi's seriously wounding his brother by hitting him over the head are underplayed. His father says that Larbi must be punished, but we know, as does his mother, that he will not be beaten. *A Muslim Childhood* is a film that is as much narrated as enacted. It is Smihi's voice on the sound track that clarifies the unique status of Tangier in the 1950s, explains the situation of the members of the family when we first meet them, and, later, smooths over the transitions in the narrative.

The title of the second episode in the trilogy, *Girls and Swallows / Les hiron-delles: Les cris de jeunes filles des hirondelles* (2008), refers, we are told, to a popular Moroccan belief that a hand that throws stones at swallows will be paralyzed. The new film follows the same stylistic pattern as its predecessor: it largely comprises long-held static interior shots of small family or community groups in conversation about the issues of the day. The characters' responses are largely passive, and these vignettes do not build together to create any dramatic tension. They each capture a single moment, and they are separated by exterior images of doors, windows and empty alleyways, accompanied again by (here un-credited) snatches of Schubert.

If anything, this second film is even more austere than the first: it lacks Smihi's voice-over commentary and the action sequences are even more sparse. We get discussion of, and personal reactions to, the current wider events—the Moroccan popular uprising and the return of Mohamed V—but most of the focus is on domestic issues within the family, with individuals facing up to new challenges. There is mention of Tahar Hussein, justly described as the founder of modern Arab thought, but, apart from a single student rally, we see virtually no active participation in outside events by any of the characters. This is a time of change for Morocco as a whole, with women in particular questioning their current situation and seeking out a new role for themselves. It is against this background that Larbi enters his adolescence, experiencing his first tentative stirrings of romance with Rabea and failing abjectly in an attempt to seduce an older, flirtatious female neighbor, Aouicha.

Tanjawi: The Sorrows of a Young Tangerian / Tanjaoui: peines de coeur et tourments du jeune Tanjaoui Larbi Salmi (2012) continues the tales of Larbi Salmi in the 1960s. Smihi has said that he is interested in "characters who interrogate themselves, who feel ill-at-ease with their heritage, and who question reality—but always without violence."[71] Larbi fits this category perfectly—as the title indicates, he is a passive hero along the lines of Goethe's Young Werther (to which the film refers) rather than a conventionally active movie hero. The sole film we see him watch is Jean Renoir's *Le caporal épinglé*, a significant choice, since the film consists largely of the protagonist's six failed attempts to escape from a German wartime prison (though he does finally succeed at his seventh attempt).

Larbi participates in a stage production of *Scheherazade*, a play by one of his heroes, Tewfik al Hakim, a suitably static production, where the novelty is, it seems, a woman daring to appear on stage. Larbi has some tentative relations with his classmates, but he is much more attracted, intellectually as well as emotionally, to the older French female teachers at his college, all respectfully addressed as "Mademoiselle." For him, love is not a physical experience but "a supreme ideal." While his father makes his peace with the new regime, becoming a sharia judge, Larbi keeps his distance. Like most of his fellow students, he is full of rhetoric about the need for revolutionary change and the abolition of poverty. He even attends a student rally, thereby appearing on the police list of political activists. He proclaims himself an atheist to his horrified father, who orders him out of the house, though they are later reconciled. It is Sidi Ahmad who helps him make the escape from Morocco that becomes Larbi's driving obsession, as his friends are arrested or disappear. Against the odds, Larbi succeeds—an occurrence that his father, who has prayed constantly for it, no doubt regards as the answer to his prayers, if not a divine intervention.

Smihi has set out his thoughts on cinema in a number of books published in Arabic and one in French, *Écrire sur le cinema*,[72] but for many years, he was unable to recapture fully the critical success and international reputation that he achieved with his first feature. As Azzedine Mabrouki notes, "Moumen Smihi's films are practically never shown in commercial cinemas, and when it does happen, the poster is quickly replaced by that of a commercial film."[73] Sandra Carter reveals (after an undated interview) that Smihi is not concerned that his films have little or no distribution in Morocco because he makes films as a personal, not a public, endeavour (though ironically his private production company is called Imago Film International). His films are his art, which would necessarily appeal to only a few viewers and would not be expected to generate much income. He is not concerned about making films for the Moroccan public and has stated that he is actually much more in tune with the urban elites of France and Europe than with the majority of Moroccans.[74] Several of Smihi's later films initially failed to receive any commercial distribution at all in Morocco and none is currently commercially available in subtitled DVD format on the world market, though a program of his films set up by Peter Limbrick has recently been very well received at international festival screenings.

The third pioneer of Moroccan 1970s cinema, whose reputation also remains high, is Ahmed Bouanani, who died in 2011. *Mirage*, which is set in 1947, under the protectorate, opens in realistic mode. As the titles unfold, the film's theme is set out for us: "The old people were right. All that's left for us now is silence, a silence to make you blush with shame." As a peasant living in poverty, Mohamed Ben Mohamed has to rely on the regular sacks of flour delivered by the authorities, who do not lose the opportunity to humiliate him and his colleagues, dismissing them as an idle lot. But on this particular day, the sack contains bundles of bank notes—a fortune beyond his wildest dreams. He rushes off to fetch his wife, Hachmaia, who works as maid for a French colonial family, and showers her with the bank notes. The only problem is that the money has to be changed in a bank, which means going to Rabat. Both have other reasons for wishing to go there—Hachmaia to see her sister and Mohamed to try to find his son, with whom he has lost contact. Together they board the bus, joined at the last minute by a flamboyant holy man, Sidi Rahal.

Rabat proves to be a place of unimaginable sights and encounters. Sidi Rahal strides through it, shouting and admonishing the people, and soon gathers an entourage. Hachmaia gets sidetracked by consulting a fortune-teller and eventually becomes one of Sidi Rahal's followers, indulging in his rituals; by the time Mohamed comes to fetch her, she has fallen into a trance. For Mohamed, the dream of riches soon fades: he does not even catch sight of a bank. Instead, he encounters the actor-visionary Ali Ben Ali, first seen doing his Charlie Chaplin imitation and then holding forth to a nonexistent audience from the top of the old city walls, He leads Mohamed on a series of flawed trajectories around the city that bring him face to face with doubt, perplexity, and fear. The mythical city has become a nightmarish labyrinth. The film has no resolution in the traditional dramatic sense: the couple are last seen, in long shot, walking hand in hand out of frame. The film fully reflects Bouanani's key concerns—reality and dreams: "As for me, I never stop asking myself about poetry in cinema. Why is is [sic] born in totally empty boulevard, when we are only used to seeing a boulevard full of vehicles and passers-by? Can it be that it is to be perceived only in an expurgated reality? Can it be that it only proceeds by expulsion?"[75]

Mirage is a film that retains its reputation. For Fouad Souiba and Fatma Zahra el Alaoui, *Mirage* is "a key moment in the evolution of the national film language,"[76] while Ahmed Araib and Eric de Hullessen describe *Mirage* as "a film which has made its mark on the national filmography. Everything contributes to the success of this film. From the script to the dialogue, from the photography to the design, from the music to the editing, as well as the performances, each element contributes to building an edifice which finishes by attaining a visual splendour hardly ever equalled."[77] After Bouanan's death in 2011, Noureddine Mhakkak wrote of "a film masterpiece which will resist the passing of time. Because in this film you can see over and over again real cinema, the cinema which makes the characters live and through them touches the spectators' emotions."[78]

Mirage was Bouanani's sole feature film. Though he was the only one of the three initial pioneers to receive CCM funding, it seems that he was subsequently banned by the state censors. The CCM branded him a communist and denied him the right to continue his feature filmmaking career, though, as his daughter reports, he never belonged to any political party.[79] After completing *Mirage*, he worked as a feature film editor (for Hamid Benani, Mohamed Osfour, Nabyl

Lahlou, and Mohamed Abbazi). He also made a number of short films and published two collections of poems in the 1980s: *Les persiennes* (1980) and *Photogrammes* (1989). An additional collection of poems, *Terriroires de l'instant* (2000), was accompanied by still photographs taken by the filmmaker Daoud Alouad-Syad, whose first two feature films Bouanani coscripted. His novel, *L'hôpital*, was first published in Morocco in a limited edition in 1990 and republished in Paris in 2012 after his death. He provides his own epitaph in *Les persiennes*:

> Once
> in memory of poets
> they erected golden statues
> Here
> through Muslim charity
> they smash in their tombs
> and our poets
> their mouths full of soil
> continue to cry out.[80]

Two other filmmakers adopting a similar narrative stance, whose work shows clearly the extreme difficulties of making a first feature film at this period, are Mustafa Derkaoui and Mohamed Reggab. Both studied extensively abroad before beginning their directing careers. On their return to Morocco, the pair both participated (along with Mohamed Abdelkrim, Nour Eddine Gounajjar, Saâd Chraïbi, and Abdellatif Lagtaâ) in the collective that made the fictional feature *Cinders of the Vineyard / Les cendres du clos*, released in 1997. All six young men from the collective went on the direct at least one solo feature.

Mustafa Derkaoui, who was born in 1944 in Oujda, followed drama studies in Rabat with a brief spell at IDHEC in Paris and a seven-year formal film training at Lodz Academy in Poland, alongside his brother, Mohamed Abdelkrim (who was to become one of Morocco's leading cinematographers).

By the time he participated in *Cinders in the Vineyard*, Derkaoui had already attempted to bring out his debut feature, *About Some Meaningless Events / De quelques événements sans signification / Anba'dh al-ahdâth biduni ma'nia*, in 1974. According to the official synopsis: "During the shooting of a film, a young director is, by chance, a witness to an involuntary crime in a café, committed by a port employee against his immediate superior. He decides to undertake his own personal investigation into the motives behind the crime. This awakens in him a bad conscience, because of the intellectual compromises he makes, and pushes him to reflect in particular on his conception of cinema, more generally on art itself and on the role of the artist in an underdeveloped country."

Apparently, during the editing, which he carried out himself, Derkaoui was visited by an official from the Ministry of Information. When asked about the film's content, Derkaoui replied "unemployment." It would seem that, as a result of this conversation, the film was banned and never received the visa that would have allowed its distribution. The few people who have seen the film are reported to have very different evaluations of it.[81]

Derkaoui has always been a prolific filmmaker. Early on, he made a number of short films in Poland and documentaries for UNESCO and worked for Moroccan television; later, he made a contribution of one episode to the Tunisian-produced collective film *After the Gulf / La guerre du Golfe . . . et après?* (1992). In all, Derkaoui has directed ten feature films in some thirty years He was not put off by the banning of his first feature or—like Smihi—by the smaller and smaller audiences attracted by his early work. Instead, he continued in the same experimental vein with two more features in the early 1980s: *The Beautiful Days of Sheherazade / Les beaux jours de Chahrazade / AyyIam chahrazad al-hilwâ* (1982) and *Provisional Title / Titre provisoire / 'Unwânun mu'aqqat* (1984). Derkaoui's first three films are generally regarded as forming a loose trilogy, not because of a continuing narrative line, but because they explore much the same issues: new ways of mixing fiction and documentary, the recurring motif of the film within a film, a constant reflection of the role of the creative artist—and more specifically the filmmaker—in contemporary Morocco.

After another eight-year gap, Derkaoui began a new series of four features: *First Fiction / Fiction Première / Riwâya'Iula* (1992), *(G)ame in the Past / Je(u) au passé* (1994), *The Seven Gates of the Night / Les sept portes de la nuit* (1994), and *The Great Allegory / La grande allégorie* (1995). The difficulty of summing up any Derkaoui film meaningfully in terms of an unfolding story is very apparent in the quite meaningless, single paragraph "narrative summaries" of these four works, published in the CCM's *Panorama du cinéma marocain* in 2004. Derkaoui himself has said of his work through the 1980s and 1990s: "I never wanted to . . . tell a story, 'make fiction' since the beginning, but I wanted to invest the cinema with the means that would enable me to better know its operations, and to the extent possible, to make its workings / machinery to the public itself."[82] Sandra Carter's own analysis backs this up. His earlier films, she writes, "are quite unique and remarkable for their intricate and difficult aesthetics. His films reflect semiotic and aesthetic preoccupations, questions about the nature of cinema itself and the metaphysics of cinema and creativity.[83] At this period, Derkaoui became, as Ahmed Ferhat notes, "the most prolific Moroccan filmmaker and paradoxically the one least seen by the public,"[84] with three successive films in the 1990s getting no Moroccan public screening.

Then, in 2001, came a development no one could have predicted. Derkaoui, after another six-year break, achieved one of the major Moroccan commercial successes of the new century with his eighth film (and first comedy), *The Loves of Hadj Mokhtar Soldi / Les amours de Hadj Mokhtar Soldi* (2001). He then turned to more sombre dramatic stories for his next two films, *Casablanca by Night* (2003) and *Casablanca Daylight* (2004).

Mohamed Reggab, who was born in 1942 in Safi and died, at just forty-eight, in 1990, traveled even more widely than Derkaoui, pursuing his film studies in France (at the École Supérieure Louis Lumière in Paris) and in the Soviet Union (at VGIK—the All-Union State Cinema Institute—in Moscow). He subsequently studied psychology at the Université Libre in Brussels and audio-visual studies in Germany. He faced even greater problems than Derkaoui with his first, and only, feature film, *The Barber of the Poor Quarter / Le coiffeur du quartier des pauvres / Hallaq darb al-fouqara*, which was eventually released in 1983. The complexity of Reggab's difficulties, which "matches the confusion of the filmmaking system in Morocco," is explained in great detail by Sandra Carter.[85] The CCM agreed to back Reggab but insisted the film be shot in 35mm, not in the cheaper 16mm format that Reggab had planned. Moreover the money was to be paid after completion of the film, not in advance. Reggab had to take out a personal loan, which the CCM refused to guarantee. The contract also stipulated that Reggab use CCM facilities, which were, at the time, totally inadequate: he had access to a 35mm editing suite one night out of three. Obviously, completion was delayed, and Reggab's debts accumulated—he was eventually prosecuted and his household belongings confiscated. Worse was to come. The CCM never paid the promised funding yet claimed all rights to the film (including future earnings), kept the negative in its possession, and hindered all Reggab's attempts to arrange showings at home or at festivals abroad. It is a tribute to Reggab's resilience that, at the time of his early death, he was planning a second feature, *Memories of Exile / Mémoires d'exil*.

Adapted from a play by Youssef Fadil, *The Barber of the Poor Quarter* looks at the lives of half a dozen characters who frequent the barbershop run by Miloud in a poor district of Casablanca. Miloud and his wife, Mahjouba, are honest people, but Miloud's cousin Hmida, just released from prison, is a thief; this gets Miloud into trouble with the authorities and forces him eventually to leave the district. One of the customers is Houmane, who is tricked into believing his wife, Zohra, is deceiving him and is driven to kill her. Presiding over the whole area is Jelloul, a rich man who owns half the district and whose ambition is to enslave the men and possess their wives (it is he who spreads the rumors about Zohra after she rejects him). Trusting no one, he even dispenses with his right-hand man and collaborator, Si Allal. Like so many of his contemporaries, Reggab was fascinated by the effect of the newly installed television systems, which bring world news (in this case the Palestinian-Israeli conflict) into the lives of people whose concerns had previously been limited and local. Reggab said of his film, "It's the audience which creates the story it wants out of the elements dispersed and projected within the film. The film doesn't aggress, it imposes nothing, It suggests ideas and it's up to the spectators to deal with them and draw their own conclusions."[86]

Though the film is currently unavailable, *The Barber of the Poor Quarter* has generally been very well received. Judging that Reggab, in 1995, was considered a person to be relied on not just in Moroccan cinema but also across the wider audio-visual field, Fouad Souiba and Fatma Zahra El Alaoui note that his film has featured on at least one list of "the best Arab films of all times."[87] Writing in 1999, Ahmed Araib and Eric de Hullessen describe it as "an accomplished film with a story and style revealing the sober and anxious character of the author." They also note that the film was very well received at foreign festivals.[88] For Ahmed Ferhati, looking back from 2004, it is quite simply "a unique and mythical film by the no less mythical Mohamed Reggab."[89]

*

There were similar limited opportunities for the two female feature filmmakers, Farida Bourquia and Farida Benlyazid, who were active in the 1980s and 1990s.

Farida Bourquia, who was born in Casablanca in 1948, has the distinction of being the first Moroccan woman to direct a feature film, in parallel with Selma Baccar (*Fatma 75*, 1978) in Tunisia and Assia Djebbar (*La Nouba*, 1978) in Algeria. At the end of the 1960s, she set off to study drama at the Iounatcharsky Institute (a state drama institute) in Moscow, where she remained for five years. On her return to Morocco in 1974, she taught drama at the Conservatoire in Casablanca and then joined Radiodiffusion Télévision Marocaine (RTM), working for many years as a director, first in Rabat and then at the Aïn Chok studios in Casablanca. She worked widely across a variety of genres, making children's programs, social documentaries, téléfilms, and television serials.

Her pioneering feature, *The Embers / La braise / Al-jamra* (also known as *Nights of Fire*) (1982), is "a dramatization of a traditional folk tale, set and shot in a primitive mountain village on the edge of the Sahara Desert. Michael Webb of the American Film Institute writes, 'in her first feature, Farida Bouquia demonstrates a mastery and narrative and character development that is heightened by a poetic sense of rural tradition.'" The drama involves three "adolescents [and] their story, full of mysterious occurrences, has been elaborated over time and incorporated into village lore. Director Farida Bourquia weaves this sense of intrigue and obscurity into her telling of the tale."[90] This was a project that, like Reggab's *The Barber of the Poor Quarter*, left the director deeply in debt.

After this pioneering effort, Bourquia had to wait twenty-five years to complete a second feature, continuing her television work in the interim. *Two Women on the Road / Deux femmes sur la route* (2007) adopts the familiar form of the road movie (Valery K. Orlando describes it as a Moroccan *Thelma and Louise*). Two very disparate characters are thrown together as they each make a very personal journey. One unusual aspect is that this time, the route is from the South of Morocco to the North. Amina, who is in her thirties, is traveling to join up with her husband, who is in prison after becoming involved with a drug-related affair. When her car breaks down, she meets up with Lalla Rahma, an elderly woman who is traveling in the same direction to make sure that her son, who has attempted an illegal crossing, is still alive. Orlando gives a clear indication of Bourquia's stance: "In general, Bourquia offers audiences a pessimistic depiction of contemporary women's lives, no matter their class, education, or social standing. Whether they are rural or urban, educated or illiterate, rich or poor, women all face a particular kind of feminine misery that can be caused only by men. However, the film also instructs audiences that in contemporary Morocco women can also persevere and survive on their own."[91]

Over thirty years after her debut, Bourquia completed her third feature, *Zineb, the Rose of Aghmat / Zineb, rose d'Aghmat* (2014). This is a new departure, a patriotic epic set in the eleventh century, at the time of the Almoravides, who sought to unite what is now Morocco from their base in the Sahara. At the heart of the tale is the beautiful and talented Zineb, who lives quietly with her father but is accused of witchcraft and chased out of the community by those alarmed by her hostility to corruption and her struggle for freedom and justice. The most beautiful girl in the city, she is married off, as a bribe for political advantage, to an aged sheikh. From then on, "from harem to harem, at the mercy of wars and conquerors, begins her fabulous story which leads her to the very summit."[92] Eventually, she becomes wife and adviser of the area's most powerful ruler, Emir Youssef Ibn Tachefine.

Farida Benlyazid, Bourquia's exact contemporary, was born in Tangier in 1948. Like so many other Maghrebian filmmakers, she studied filmmaking in Paris, in her case at the École Supérieure des Études Cinématographiques (ESEC), paying her fees by working in a bank. After film school, she had just one ambition: "Once I completed my studies, I returned to Morocco. I wanted to create a Moroccan cinema." There is a touching autobiographical note in the same piece, reprinted in Aherifa Zuhur's aptly named anthology, *Images of Enchantment*: "How could it be that a girl from a good family who was considered beautiful—which means she could make a good match—why would an educated woman who could aim for important positions and climb the rungs of a career ladder launch herself instead onto a tortuous path that could only ruin her? I do not know. Perhaps it is because I discovered the cinema before knowing anything about life, even before knowing how to read or write."[93]

Benlyazid began her film career writing scripts for others, and she went on to become one of the Maghreb's few professional screenwriters. She has described her involvement in the writing and production of Jillali Ferhati's first feature, *A Hole in the Wall* (1977), as her greatest experience, and she went on to adapt her own novel, *Aisha*, to form the basis of Ferhati's best-known early work, *Reed Dolls* (1981). She also scripted two of Mohamed Abderrahman Tazi's most successful works, *Badis* (1990) and *Looking for My Wife's Husband* (1993). In addition, she made a number of shorts and contributed an episode to the collective film *Five Films for a Hundred Years* (1995).

Benlyazid's first feature, *A Door to the Sky / La porte au ciel / Bab al-sama maftouh* (1987), is a complex, if slow-moving, work, in essence the story of a woman' spiritual quest.[94] Benlyazid has said of her approach: "I wanted to explore the world of women that has been hidden for so long and laden with stereotypes and ignorance. In my films I speak about the world and culture of women. In Morocco I live in a society with strict codes: there is a female world and a male world. My world and cultural identity is that of women."[95] The protagonist is Nadia, a woman who had previously been living, at ease it would seem, in France with a French photo-journalist lover, Jean-Philippe. She returns to the family mansion in Fez to be at her dying father's bedside as a seemingly self-assured woman. But her father's death shatters her certainties, and she suffers a breakdown. She is troubled by the paintings left by her mother, who died when she was still a child, and by memories of the past, which subsequently turn into visions. Apart from a couple of short bursts of Bach, the sound track is constantly filled with Islamic chants, prayers, and music. At one point, Nadia participates in a Sufi dance ceremony, where she falls into a trance. Benlyazid explains: "In my film trance dancing enables Nadia to open herself completely to a dimension she did not know existed. This enables her to transcend human reason and comprehend cosmic principles that are beyond human comprehension."[96]

From the beginning of her breakdown, Nadia is helped in her recovery by Kirana, the devout and active Muslim woman who conducted the women's prayers at Nadia's father's funeral ceremony. Gradually, she is reintroduced to her faith and, thanks to one vision, is able to recover jewels buried in the garden. With her new wealth, she is able to thwart her brother's ambition to sell the mansion and, instead, turns it into a *zawyia*. This is a form of sanctuary or refuge traditionally set up by wealthy Islamic women to help shelter other poor, sick, and oppressed women. At first, the combined efforts of Nadia and Kirana make the *zawyia* a total success, and Nadia discovers that she has a gift of healing. Then two incidents, which can seemingly be easily resolved, lead to a totally unexpected dénouement. The women in the *zawyia* understandably object to the presence of Rahia, a Muslim brought up in France who does not speak Arabic, wears jeans, smokes constantly, and has a swig of whiskey for breakfast. The second crisis comes when Nadia introduces into this all-female sanctuary a young man, Abdelkrim, whom she is treating. The two confrontations with other women lead Nadia to abandon the *zawyia* and to set off with Abdelkrim, whom she clearly loves, away from the refuge and, indeed, from Fez itself.

This ending is surprising in several ways. Early on in the film, when there had been a discussion of whether it was better to live a French lifestyle or a

Moroccan one, Nadia had proclaimed direct to the camera in extreme close-up, "I want it all." Throughout the film, the focus is on Nadia's successful recovery of her Muslim spiritual identity, and the whole thrust of the narrative shows how women can make their own lives, without the intrusion of men. Benlyazid's chosen ending is indeed perplexing.

Women's Wiles / Ruses de femmes / Keid Ensa (1999) is a leisurely filmic retelling of a fairy tale about Lalla Aicha once told to Benlyazid by her stepmother. As she says in one of her interviews, "Even back then the story deeply impressed me: how the heroine asserted herself against the arrogant and powerful prince."[97] In the film, it is told by a Moroccan mother to console her daughter, who has just been bullied by her elder brother. The key question in the tale is whether women can be as intelligent as men, reformulated, as the film proceeds, as whether a woman's guile (*ruses* in French) can be greater than that of a man. The tale is set in a brutal world in which male dominance is unquestioned, where women are bought and sold or offered as presents, and where the prince, when offered a gift of two beautiful virgins, responds simply by saying, "Prepare one for tonight, and save the other for tomorrow."

The film opens lightly and with simple narrative logic. Aicha is the daughter of a rich merchant whose house adjoins the prince's palace. The prince spies on Aicha as she tends her basil plants on the terrace, and the two flirt and then play tricks on each other. He dresses up as a Jewish fish merchant to get a kiss from her, and she disguises herself as a Sudanese slave, to drug him, smother his face in makeup, and shave off his beard. This is too much for the prince, who uses the power at his command. He demands, and receives, her hand in marriage and promptly locks her in a cellar until she will admit that men are more intelligent than women.

Here the logical implausibility and awkward time scales of the fairy tale world come into play for a film audience, if not for a child, who loves the surprises and repetitions when hearing the tale at its mother's knee. Using her father's resources, Aicha arranges for a tunnel to be built between her cell and her old home next door. This enables her to come and go as she pleases when the prince is away. On three occasions—by the sea, in a wood, and in a desert—she arranges an encounter during which she seduces him (while disguised of course), each time demanding a prize memento (his Koran, his dagger, his ring). When he announces he is taking a new wife, Aicha responds by sending him her three children, each the outcome of one of their clandestine encounters, each named after the place of the encounter where he or she was conceived, and each bearing the revelent memento. In the fairy tale happy ending, all is forgiven, she is recognized as the true wife, and our last glimpse of the pair is of them smilingly blissfully in the marital bed. They agree in line with the judgement of the Koran: "Man has the strength, but woman has the guile."

It is fascinating that Benlyzaid, who worked so skillfully in shaping basic, conventional film narratives for her male contemporaries, Ferhati and Tazi in particular, has chosen other, much more difficult narrative challenges—a spiritual quest, where inner developments, not physical actions, are what count, and a fairy tale, with all its inherent implausibilities and non sequiturs—for her own first directing challenges.

Benlyazid has adopted a very different narrative strategy in the two feature films she has made in the 2000s, both of which are adapted from novels. *Casablanca Casablanca* (2003) is a low-budget production for Morrocan television (RTM) adapted from a novel, *Les puissants de Casablanca*, by Rids Lamrini. It has a double focus: on Aïcha, who has gone missing and whose best friend and last known contact, Lamia, has been found dead at the bottom of a well, and on Aïcha's boss, Amine, who has returned from Canada to set up a business in Casablanca but finds himself prosecuted by the authorities. The film is shaped as a crime story, with investigations led by Inspector Bachir. As Olivier Barlet notes: "The aim here is to denounce corruption and injustice ('Without justice there can be no democracy') in the kingdom where the young king [Mohamed VI] has changed less than had been hoped. The vibrant clarion call at the end of the film to understand that 'injustice is everywhere: our duty is to remain' and to combat flight abroad in a responsible way is a theme that recurs in the cinemas of North Africa which are bled by emigration."[98]

Juanita from Tangier / Juanita de Tanger (2005), also known as *The Wretched Life of Juanita Narboni*, is a Spanish coproduction based on a novel of the same name by the Spanish writer Ángel Vázquez. The official synopsis informs us:

> Juanita, who has an English father and an Andalusian mother tells of her own troubles and those of the women around her. Her sister Helena who studied at the French lycée is obsessed with freedom. Esther, her Moroccan Jewish friend who is completely caught up in an impossible love affair with a young Moroccan Muslim. And finally, Hamruch, the faithful servant, who is all the family she has when the others are away. In the background: the story of Tangier at the time of the Spanish Civil War, with the entry of Franco's troops, then the period of the Second World War, with the arrival of refugees from all over Europe.[99]

The work of these two female directors has perhaps not been given the full appreciation it deserves in Morocco. As Farida Benlyazid stated in an interview in 1994, "We have no market for films here, and it is difficult to get financing. Every time I apply for a project, I receive less money than the men do."[100] Her first feature was produced with the aid of Hassan Daldoul, who, along with Ahmed Attia, was one of the new generation of producers reshaping Tunisian cinema. Both Bourquia and Benlyazid give a feminine slant on a subject frequently treated by male directors, namely, the problems faced by women in Muslim society. But in general, they are more positive in their approach than their male colleagues, seeing opportunities as well as difficulties for women in the Islamic context.

*

There is one area of filmmaking where women could, and did, dominate. There had been no real tradition of documentary filmmaking in Morocco, despite the fact that the state organization, the CCM, was originally set up in the 1940s by the French to make tourist and informational short films. All three major documentary filmmakers of Moroccan origin active from the 1980s onward are women. They are all outsiders who presently live abroad in Europe and have had no formal production connection with the CCM. The three are Simone Bitton, Izza Genini, and Fatima Jebli Ouazzani.

Simone Bitton is an unclassifiable figure. She was born in 1955 in Rabat, daughter of a Jewish jeweler. At home, the family spoke Arabic, but she was educated in a French school. When she immigrated with her family to Jerusalem at the age of twelve, she quickly learned Hebrew but "continued to read in French and sing in Arabic."[101] She has both French and Israeli citizenship but describes herself as "an Arab Jew who hates walls and frontiers." Though she did her military service in Israel, she has been a political activist since her teens and her anti-Zionist attitudes have led her to align herself with the Palestinian cause. After studying filmmaking at IDHEC, where she made her first documentary, she settled permanently in Paris. The Sabra and Shatila massacre in 1982 strengthened her political involvement, and, since the late 1990s, she has made a series of politically engaged feature-length documentaries, two specifically for cinema release.

Bitton's documentaries reflect her own background and offer fresh insights into the complexities of all notions of identity in North Africa and the Middle East. For example, *Mahmoud Darwish / Mahmoud Darwich: et la terre comme la comme la langue* (1999), made for French television, is less an exploration of the poet's work (though we see and hear many of his own public presentations) than an investigation of the complex trajectory of his life. The documentary begins, significantly for what is to follow, with Darwish in the mountains of Jordan in 1997, looking across into the Palestinian Territories and almost seeing the land of his birth. The filmmaker can visit the site of the actual village, now removed from the map (if not from memory) by Israeli tanks. We can hear from his uncle Abou Souheil and witness two children reading his poems in the place of his birth—but Darwish himself is banned from entry: a lifelong exile.

Initially this exile was internal. He was taken by his parents into Israel so that he grew up—and made his initial reputation as a poet—in Haifa, surrounded by Jews as well as Palestinians, with a Jewish lover whom he celebrates in some of his poems. The path he has subsequently chosen is complex and even contradictory, relating to both language and personal identity. First he went to Cairo, to live for the first time in a city where everyone spoke his language, Arabic, and to experience the sight of the Nile. Then, he moved to Beirut, to show his solidarity with Palestinian refugees and their cause; next, to Paris, where, paradoxically, he felt at home because he could not speak the language. Subsequently, there was Tunis, where the contradictions of his plight are graphically illustrated by a very emotional poetry reading. He is, as always, totally at one with his audience, but here overlooked by the inevitable, ubiquitous image of the Tunisian dictator, Ben Ali. In 1997, thirty years after the poet's period in Haifa, Palestine was allowed a limited autonomy and Darwish was permitted a brief, five-day return to those members of his family who still lived within Israeli borders. The film ends with him back in exile and with a final reading from his poetry.

The subject of Simone Bitton's second 1998 documentary, *Ben Barka: The Moroccan Equation / Ben Barka, l'équation marocaine*, is a man whose career tells much about the complexities of Arab progress toward national liberation. The film begins, where it must inevitably end, with scenes at the Brasserie Lipp on the Boulevard St. Germain in Paris, where Ben Barka was abducted with the complicity of the French secret services, in October 1965. With the aid of testimony from his three sisters, friends, and colleagues, together with newsreel footage, the film tells Ben Barka's story, which reveals much about the history of Morocco in the twentieth century, particularly its transition from French protectorate to an independent state.

Though born into a poor family in Rabat, Ben Barka was a brilliant young scholar and received the French education normally reserved for the children of the rich in the colonies and protectorates controlled by the French. This education had the paradoxical effect often found among those given such an elite education: he not only developed his skills as a mathematician but also acquired a passion for politics, shaped by the French ideals of liberty, equality, and fraternity. In his twenties, he became one of the leading figures in the Moroccan nationalist movement, Istiqlal, which led an increasingly violent campaign against the French. As a result, Ben Barka suffered both imprisonment and internal exile and was released only when he was needed to take part in the formal negotiations for independence in the mid-1950s. By this time, the Moroccan ruler, Mohamed V, who had sided with the nationalist cause, had been exiled with his family to Madagascar. The king's release became a key demand of the Istiqlal, one that the French, more concerned with holding on to their settler colony in neighboring Algeria, were ready to grant.

But the constitution was not changed, and Mohamed V was restored with the full traditional powers of an absolutist feudal monarch. A gap gradually opened up between the king and those nationalists seeking real democracy in an independent Morocco, and, as a result, Istiqlal became divided. Initially, Ben

Barka had been chosen by the king to head the national assembly, which had no actual power. Later he became more radical, separating himself from the monarchy and making demands for popular freedoms. The full effects of the monarch's absolute power became clear when Hassan II (one of whose tutors Ben Barka had been) succeeded his father and inaugurated a period of tyrannical rule, generally known as the Years of Lead (*les années de plomb*) and marked by widespead executions and imprisonments. Increasingly, Ben Barka had devoted himself to the cause of Third World development, meeting world leaders like Gamal Abdel Nasser, Fidel Castro, and Mao Tse Tung and being instrumental in the convening of the Tricontinental Conference to be held in 1965. His relations with Morocco remained ambiguous. Though still condemned to death by the Moroccan authorities, he was invited back by the king to take a leading role in government. Then the king changed his mind and ordered his abduction and execution in France, a country that ostensibly supported the aims of the Tricontinental Conference.

One of Bitton's first childhood memories is of watching the funeral cortège of Mohamed V from the terrace of her home with other members of her family. As she explains, *Ben Barka: The Morrocan Equation* is in one sense a return to that terrace, her contribution to "the work of remembering that Moroccan society has embarked upon."[102] It is also a lucid exposition of the life and ideals of a man who was, at the time the film was made, effectively written out of the history of his homeland.

Bitton's first documentary for cinema distribution (though still shot, of necessity, on video and with a French crew), *Wall / Mur* (2004), deals with a subject about which the director feels deeply: "The very idea of a wall erected between Israelis and Palestinians tore me apart. . . . I was really distressed. I had the feeling that I was being cut in half, that who I am was being denied: an Arab Jew whose entire being is the site of a permanent dialogue."[103] The resultant film is a thoughtful, largely visual statement, mostly shaped in long static takes or slow tracking shots, designed to allow viewers to draw their own conclusions, as the act of construction of the wall steadily blots out the existing landscape and divides the residents from each other. The film's opening is comparatively lighthearted: the wall is seen from the Israeli side, decorated with Matisse-style dancers and commented on by two Jewish children. This sets the overall style of the film, where Bitton as narrator and most of those interviewed remain unseen. The exception is the head of the Israeli Ministry of Defense, Amos Yaron, who gives the official justification for the wall (costing $2 million per kilometer), direct to camera in a very formal, posed interview: "Right now we are the rulers. . . . It's all the Palestinians' fault."

Much of the film records the actual building of the wall. Events are described largely from the Palestinian side—chronicling both the experiences of Palestinian farmers cut off from their land and also those of Arabs who can find work only by helping build the wall. But the voices of ordinary Israelis are also heard, one, a kibbutz member, describing what he calls "the mad love" that compels the Jews to cut off and destroy the land they are so passionate about. Bitton deliberately avoids specifying precise locations (even which side of the wall is being filmed) by means of maps and graphics or differentiating in the subtitles the language—Hebrew or Arabic—spoken by those being heard. But the division of people and communities is constant, even though individuals are continually struggling to find a way through. Toward the end of the film, in a video conversation with a psychiatrist in Gaza (whom she is prevented from meeting in person), Bitton questions her own sanity, confronted with the enormity of the Israeli undertaking. She sees this as a willfully divided land, and *Wall* as a whole reflects powerfully her own impassioned view: "The wall is not only a slap in the face of those of us who want peace, not only a crime against one of the most beautiful and historically meaningful landscapes in the world. For Palestinians it is a mechanism of ongoing dispossession and expulsion."[104]

Bitton's second film for cinema distribution is *Rachel* (2008), based on three years of research in the United States, United Kingdom, and Israel and shot under considerable difficulties—she was not allowed into Rafah and had to direct all the material shot there by her crew via telephone calls from Tel Aviv. Rachel Corrie was a twenty-three-year-old American peace activist, who—with other members of her international group, the International Solidarity Movement (ISM)—tried to protect Palestinian lives and properties as the Israeli authorities destroyed houses bordering the wall in Gaza. On March 16, 2003, she was killed by an Israeli bulldozer in Rafah. Bitton is able to draw on a wide range of material. Rachel's own diaries and e-mails (read by her friends and parents) form a constant thread through the film. This is backed up by video and still photographs shot by members of the activist group. Their testimony in direct-to-camera interviews recorded a few years later, the words of Palestinian witnesses, and even those of a Jewish conscript who took part in the clearance operation are also included As with her earlier film, Bitton's style is slow and meditative, allowing long-held images to place the action (emphasizing, for example, the huge gulf between Rafah and Rachel's small-town US background). Again her approach to uncovering the truth is meticulous.

Bitton has managed to uncover a whole range of documents and interviews backing up the official account, presented by the Israeli spokesperson, Major Avital Leibovitch. There are transcripts of the formal statements by the Israeli soldiers involved, as well as an interview with the investigator who compiled the report and openly admits the limitations placed on his inquiries and the formal report of the commander in chief of the Gaza area, who praises his soldiers' restraint and blames the protesters for the death. There is even TV footage of the bulldozer operatives, shot for Israeli television. The doctor who attempted to resuscitate Rachel and the medical officer who carried out the postmortem (to which the US embassy declined to send an observer, despite the request of Rachel's parents) are also incuded. Both give the cause of death as suffication but assert that there is no physical evidence of the bulldozer's involvement.

The tone of this Israeli evidence is in total contrast to the appreciative accounts of Rachel by her teachers at Evergreen State College; by Ghassan Andoni, who set up ISM; and by Rachel's companions, who retrace in great detail the events of March 16 and make clear their own involvement in them. One theme that emerges strongly from Bitton's film is her admiration for the young people she met while researching it. These include Yonatan Polak, the Israeli peace activist who hosted members of the ISM in Tel Aviv; he gives a forceful account of his own views: "It is possible to resist without hope. But also without despair." This admiration is presumably why we hear the rap song about Rachel by Joe Carr (another of the ISM members) over the end credits. But what emerges most strongly thoughout the film is the character of Rachel Corrie herself, shown by her own words as maturing constantly through her contact with the Palestinians and their cause. Most poignant are her words in a letter dated February 27: "Coming here is one of the better things I have ever done."

Izza Genini was born in 1942 in Casablanca and is self-taught as a filmmaker. She, too, is from the Moroccan Jewish community. She studied at the Sorbonne and the École Nationale des Langues Orientales in Paris, where she has lived since 1960. She formed her own production and distribution company, Sogeav, to produce and distribute her own documentaries and also to coproduce feature films made in Morocco by filmmakers such as Ahmed el-Maanouni, Mohamed Aboulouakar, and Tayeb Saddiki. Genini is best known for her short films (mostly around twenty-six minutes in length) documenting aspects of traditional Moroccan life, such as the twelve-part series of studies of Moroccan popular music, *Morocco: Bodies and Souls / Maroc: corps et âmes* (1987–92).

The fifty-minute *Finding Oulad Moumen Again / Retrouver Oulad Moumen* (1993), which falls within the scope of this study, is an early example of autobiographical video documentary. It tells the story of her own family and their progress from rural Morocco at the beginning of the twentieth century to international dispersal at its end. Against a lightly sketched background of world events, Izza Genini's mother traces the successive movements that led them from the Jewish community of Oulad Moumen (where the first three children were born) and on to Casablanca, birthplace of Izza, the youngest of nine children. After Moroccan independence, the children (eight of them girls) gradually dispersed and, with marriage, moved on to Paris, Italy, Mexico, and the United States. For Izza Genini, her studies of Moroccan music were a means of recovering her roots, and the film ends with a family reunion where it all began, in the now almost obliterated village of Oulad Moumen. Maghrebian cinema, like that of the Middle East, is full of stories of exile and family dispersal, but here for once the journey is joyous and fulfilling for a family who keeps their ties of affection across decades and continents.

Fatima Jebli Ouazzani is another special case. Despite the lack of a locally based documentary tradition, there seems to have been a conscious effort on the part of the Moroccan film authorities to promote one, with support going even to films chronicling uneasy truths. This was the case with Fatima Jebli Ouazzani's *In My Father's House / Dans la maison de mon père / In het Huis van mijn Vader* (1997), which was surprisingly awarded the top prize at the National Film Festival in 1998. Fatima Jebli Ouazzani was born in Meknes in 1959 but has lived in the Netherlands since the age of eleven and has worked for some years for Dutch television. The award is even more striking considering that the film's subject matter—female sexuality—precludes it from ever receiving a commercial screening in Morocco.

In My Father's House, a sixty-seven-minute work made for Dutch television, has a complex formal pattern that weaves together autobiography, fictionalized scenes, and documentary sequences in a manner that anticipates many aspects of the personal video documentary, which became much more common in the 2000s. The film questions the whole structure of the traditional Moroccan approach to marriage, with its stress on virginity, and is totally frank and open in its treatment of the taboo subject of female sexuality. The film is totally personal, with the filmmaker herself providing the voice-over narration and offering insight into her own personal situation, after fleeing the marriage about to be forced on her as a teenager. It opens and closes with restaged images of the filmmaker as a little girl. Her memories of her own childhood—longing for her father's love, remembering her embarrassment at the growth of her breasts, witnessing the pursuit and beating of a girl who did not bleed on her wedding night—are spread throughout the film.

Equally crucial are the filmmaker's painful observational scenes of her bickering grandparents in old age and her interviews with them. Both her grandmother and her mother were forced to marry at fourteen. Neither marriage was a success. There is a visit to her mother's grave. She died young, after being divorced by Ouazzani's father, who at the age of fifty-six, married a virgin of seventeen and started a second family. Earlier, her grandmother had divorced her husband (by beating herself black and blue and accusing him of attacking her) but later bowed to family pressure to return to a loveless and embittered remarriage. Her grandfather is a virtual parody of the tyrannical Arab patriarch, fundamentally despising women (a deflowered woman is "like yesterday's couscous"). Jebli Ouazzani's own story is intercut with that of a young Amsterdam-born Moroccan, Naïma, who returns to rural Morocco for a traditional wedding, though her new Arab husband is a thoroughly modern divorced Dutch resident. We witness the elaborate costumes, the singing and dancing, and indeed all the traditional rituals, including the flaunting of the bloodied sheet, as the filmmaker (herself still unmarried) participates in the celebrations.

In addition, there are comments by a gynecologist and a Casablancan female sociologist (who has two daughters of her own), offering lessons on the structure of the hymen and on traditional ways for a wife to fake virginity. Jebli Ouazzani's discussions with a group of students show how little change in attitude has occurred, even in the 1990s. The filmmaker's longing for her father, whom she has not seen for sixteen years and who disowns her, is a powerful emotional thread running through the film. At the end of the film, Jebli Ouazzani is shown phoning him and apparently getting the loving response she has always longed for. But the fact that these words of love and real communication are placed over images of the lonely little girl in a deserted Moroccan street, dissolving into the sunlight, shows that this is an imagined connection, not a real one.

*

One important feature in Arab cultural life was the growing status of Morocco in Arab literature from the 1970s and 1980s onward. Ami Elad-Bouskila argues that "from the 1970s two different and important cultural centres evolved in the Arab world." One was Paris; the other—following the swallowing up of Beirut in civil war and the increasing oppression in Damascus and Baghdad—was Casablanca. In terms of literature, the principal reasons for this were that "the quantity of writing by Arab writers—in Arabic especially—has increased since the late 1970s, and the quality of this writing in comparison with Arabic literature from the Mashreq is noteworthy."[105]

These developments find their echo in cinema. From the late 1970s, French involvement in funding the "cinemas of the South" grew year by year, and Paris became a focal point for Arab filmmakers seeking a fresh impendence from government constraints and limited resources. During this same period, the CCM acquired better resources and improved its organizational structure while loosening, to some extent, its censorship grip. In other words, it moved away from the Algerian notion of tight state control and more toward the Tunisian pattern of culturally assessed state aid. In quantitative terms, Moroccan film output grew steadily throughout the period and beyond, eventually matching Algeria in terms of overall output by the end of the 1990s and overtaking it by far in the 2000s.

These positive developments were enhanced by the emergence of a new group of four filmmakers, who, unlike their introverted forebears in the 1970s, were motivated to make films with strong narrative lines that would emotionally involve audiences in Morocco and elsewhere. All received French funding through the Fonds Sud, as well as the backing of the CCM.

Political comment was banned in Moroccan cinema until the 2000s, but realist filmmaking, which examined some of Morocco's major social problems, was permitted. The new filmmakers emerging in the 1980s and early 1990s had very different backgrounds. Two key figures had studied drama in Paris, while the other two received formal film training. But all four seized the opportunities that came their way and obtained international, as well as national, recognition. The four filmmakers were Jillali Ferhati, Hakim Noury, Mohamed Abderrahman Tazi, and Abdelkader Lagtaâ.

Jillali Ferhati, who was born in 1948 in Khemisset, studied literature, sociology, and drama in Paris, where he lived for ten years, and then made his debut with the little-shown feature *A Hole in the Wall / Une brèche dans le mur / Charkhun fi-l ha'it* in 1977. Ferhati has since made six more feature films spread out over twenty years. His first two films—*Reed Dolls / Poupées de roseau / Arais min kassab* (1981) and *The Beach of Lost Children / La plage aux enfants perdus / Shatiu al-atfal al-mafoudin* (1991)—have simple narrative lines and focus on a female victim. In the uncomprehending and unforgiving patriarchal societies featured in the films, both women are left isolated and abandoned after abuse at the hands of men.

When we first see Aïcha in the opening shots of *Reed Dolls*, she is still very much a child, skipping and playing in the street with other children. But she is already betrothed to her cousin Mohamed—the wedding will take place as soon as she begins menstruating. Here, as in the rest of the film, the narrative approach, based on Farida Benlyazid's script, is straightforward (there are no flashbacks or dream sequences) and the tone resolutely realistic. As the action unfolds, it becomes clear that the older women are totally in accord with the male-imposed conditions of life in Morocco, scornful indeed of the more open lives led by their Spanish colonizers. They are happy, for example, that Aïcha is marrying her cousin, rather than "an unknown man from Casablanca." Aïcha's role is to produce a child within a year.

In fact, she eventually has three children, but when Mohamed suddenly dies, she is totally unprepared for life outside the domestic sphere. She has to go out to earn her living (as a cleaning woman) and is easy prey for her handsome and well-educated employer. In a society where contraception is out of the question, she inevitably falls pregnant. For abortion, the women rely on folktales—Aïcha's aunt advises a regular diet of pomegranate seeds. Aïcha faces the hostility of her brother-in-law, Ali, who contemplates marrying her as his second wife when she is widowed, but he instead takes her to court to deprive her of her children when he learns she is pregnant. After a miscarriage, Aïcha is forced to go out to work again as a servant but has to quit that job, too, when her employer's son makes advances. She is now an isolated figure, and we last see her sitting by the grave of her dead husband.

Reed Dolls is an unrelenting portrayal of a society where women are totally complicit in the patriarchal rules imposed on them by fathers, brothers, and husbands. There are just two moments of hope in the film. Aïcha finds the courage to resist her second would-be seducer (though at the expense of her job), and at another point in the narrative, an adolescent girl speaks up to assert her need to go to school, though this is totally opposed by her family. The lesson of the film is clear: without access to education for women, there is no hope for change.

The Beach of Lost Children, which was both scripted and directed by Ferhati, deals with a character very much like Aïcha. Mina still has the mental age of a child, and we first see her happily playing with much younger children on the beach. She is doomed from the beginning, when her taxicab-driver lover, much older than she is, tells her bluntly he has no intention of marrying her. Frantic as he turns away, she picks up a branch and hits him with all the force summoned up by his rejection. He falls dead, and she immediately regrets what she has done. But she is aware enough to hide the body in one of the salt piles that line the beach. This is a failing fishing village, and there are repeated shots of the women waiting on shore for the boats to return. Since the piles of salt are regularly dug into by men, who take it to market, there is a genuine tension generated here.

But the film takes a different turn. Learning that Mina is pregnant, the family hide her away in the holiday home, where she has been working as a servant and which has just been vacated by the owners, a couple from the city. Though she is never seen by outsiders, Mina's lonely nighttime screams persuade the locals that the house is haunted. The family have had a difficult composition since the death of Mina's mother. Father and grandmother are conventional figures (though he is more sympathetic toward his daughter than many fathers would be), but the second wife, Zineb, is a more complex character. Barely older than Mina, she knows that she herself cannot have children. Hoping to profit from Mina's problem, she feigns pregnancy herself, aiming to take over Mina's child when it is born. Though her plan is uncovered by both her husband and Mina, Zineb manages to fool the villagers. In addition to focusing on Mina's story, *The Beach of Lost Children* is about a village society. From the start, events are commented on by a couple of aged, bearded men who spend their time lounging by the beach. They are constantly questioning what is going on and provide the film with a measure of light relief.

Time passes and Mina gives birth. Zineb takes over the child and proudly presents it as her own to the neighbours. Mina can now reappear in public, ostensibly back from working for the holiday couple in town. But Mina cannot bear to be separated from her child. Though she has nowhere to take her child, she picks it up and runs away. Her family and the villagers follow her at a distance, as she heads toward the sea. When she plunges into the shallows, no one, not even her father, tries to catch up with her. The film ends with a freeze frame of Mina and the child: her fate—and that of the child—is left in suspense. *The Beach of Lost Children* confirms both Ferhati's taste for exploring the detail of his realist narratives and his aversion to conclusive endings. He leaves it to us, the spectators, to determine how Mina's story will be resolved.

Ferhati's fourth film, *Make-Believe Horses / Chevaux de fortune / Kuius al-has* (1995), has a wider focus, chronicling the stories of a disparate group of Moroccans gathered in Tangiers who all desperately want to make the crossing to Europe. The central figure is Mohamed, whose dream arrival in France we see before the film moves on to the reality of an actual attempt at illegal emigration. The group members have varied reasons for wishing to leave Tangier. For Mohamed, who is clearly sleepwalking toward defeat, fantasizing that he is already in France, the motive is simply to bet on a live horse race. He has already lost everything he owns by gambling and has to resort to robbery to pay his passage. Ali, who is blind, wants to get to France to have the eye operation his son has promised him. Fatima wants to rejoin her mother in Gibraltar, since her father has renounced her. Elizabeth, a *pied-noir* born in Morocco, is keen to get away from her father, who is determined to die in Morocco, where he was born and where his wife is buried. They, and the rest, all have their dreams and their personal problems. Nothing is easy to resolve, and the man organizing their travel (at huge cost) is eventually killed in a dispute with his disgruntled clients.

Make-Believe Horses is a well-organized piece in which the characters come together and part, making connections that may or may not come to fruition. A departure is finally made—in a beach pedal boat—though all are well aware of the dangers. The next day, a scattering of their belongings is found on the beach.

Threads / Tresses / Safa'ar (2000) is another complex drama about the abuse of women, this time focused on a rape. The victim is Saïda; her younger brother, Amine, and older sister, Kenza, know the identity of the rapist. It is Hicham, the spoiled son of a prominent lawyer, Hamid Boussif. For the first time, Ferhati, who originated the idea for the script, confronts the reality of Moroccan politics. Elections are due, and Boussif is a man with political ambitions who does not want his chances damaged by any scandal concerning his son, particularly as his campaign slogan is "Save Our Youth." The matter is even more complicated on a personal level, because Kenza is one of his servants. When Boussif brings pressure on her, the young Amine is driven to attempt to kill Hicham. As always in Ferhati's work, there is a real concern for the film's imagery, with carefully composed views of settings. The writing is sharp, and the acting is, as usual, well controlled. But perhaps because of a valid assessment of the reality of the situation in Morocco, the film cannot be brought to an emotionally satisfactory climax. It is impossible to put the family together again, and Hicham remains unpunished.

In the early 2000s, Ferhati—alongside Abdelkader Lagtaâ and two younger filmmakers, Abdelhaï Laraki and Faouzi Bensaidi—was one of the first Moroccan directors to take advantage of the liberalization of censorship and deal with the dark aspects of Morocco's recent past. *Prison Memories / Mémoire en detention / Dakira moatakala* (2004) looks at the problems of young people released from long prison sentences and tormented by what they have suffered behind bars. These prisoners are the results of the so-called Years of Lead (*années de plomb*) of the 1970s, when political opponents were arbitrarily thrown into prison and often executed without trial. Olivier Barlet describes how Ferhati's film, which deals with two main protagonists, unfolds. Mokhtar has lost his memory and only his body bears witness to his past sufferings, whereas Zoubeir, who is deeply troubled by the broken memory of a murdered father, visits the different scenes of his past in an attempt to recover the broken thread. Zoubeir cannot reconstitute his past, and Mokhtar comes to be tormented by doubts about whether he was a resistance fighter or someone who betrayed his colleagues, including Zoubeir's father. As Barlet concludes: "Ferhati, in accord with the subtlety of this magnificent and necessary film, evokes arrest and torture only though fleeting flashbacks, which are deliberately fragmented and fragmentary. Memory does not involve replaying the past, but letting its traces speak in the present."[106] Ferhati's most recent work is *Since Dawn / Dès l'aube* (2010).

Realism is integral to Ferhati's work; for him, "the imaginary isn't something fabulous. It is based on the real." His filmmaking also entails conveying meaning visually, resulting in sparse dialogue in his films: "Good cinema is the image and therefore silence." The spectator is "to be invited to uncover the meaning, to work at the reading of the film."[107] Ferhati explores every situation in great detail and invariably shows great sympathy for his powerless and tormented protagonists, all of whom are unwittingly sleepwalking toward or thrust by circumstances into death, disaster, or isolation. As M'barek Housni explains: "The society he talks about doesn't correlate with major social events. You can feel that one event or another designates the country at a given moment without totally explaining it.... For the director, the human being is the main consideration, the human being seen inside an individual, where everyone can recognise and find himself."[108]

Hakim Noury, the youngest of the group, was born in 1952 in Casablanca. Like Ferhati, he came to the cinema from a drama background and has continued his acting career into the present. Noury concentrated his studies on drama at the Conservatoire National Supérieur d'Art Dramatique (CNSAD) in Paris, before working as an assistant film director (most notably with Souheil Benbarka) and in television. Noury made his first feature, *The Postman / Le facteur / Sâi al-barîd*, in 1980 but then had to wait ten years before he could complete his second, though he did work extensively in television during the intervening years. In the 1990s, when he was, for five years, president of the Moroccan Film Technicians Association, he made five features in quick succession, becoming one of the most prolific Moroccan directors of the decade: *The Hammer and the*

Anvil / Le marteau et l'enclume / Al-mîtroga wa aik-sindân (1990), *Stolen Child-hood / L'enfance volée / Atoufoula al-mortasaba* (1993), *The Dream Thief / Le voleur de rêves* (1995), *A Simple News Item / Un simple fait-divers* (1997), and *A Woman's Fate / Destin de femme* (1998). After a series of works for television, he continued his feature film career in a similar vein with *Love Story* in 2005.

Noury made major contributions to Moroccan realist cinema in the 1990s. *Stolen Childhood* is a film showing the stages by which a child is driven to prostitution. The film opens with the ten-year-old Rkia being sold by her parents into servitude as a maid to an upper-class family in Casablanca. The richest segment of the film is that showing the feisty ten-year-old's response to Casablanca and the world of unimaginable wealth accessible to the family's daughter, Nawal, but denied to Rkia. The slightest sign of independence on her part is punished, but she still has her dreams. There is an awkward jump to Rkia eight years or so later. She is now still dependent on the human trafficker for a factory job, which is initially successful. She also embarks on a relationship with Jamal, who initially seems an ideal match, but he abandons her when she becomes pregnant. The trafficker "helps" her by finding a couple abroad who will adopt the child. Our last view of Rkia shows her working—in flamboyant pink—as a prostitute on the streets of Casablanca. But the film does not end there. The final shots show the trafficker returning to Rkia's village to arrange a deal for her younger sister. *Stolen Childhood* is a well-crafted film, with many striking compositions and telling transitions. Despite the difficulties caused by the eight-year gap in the narrative, the final sequences bring the film's spectators face to face with the everyday reality of the trafficking of children in Morocco.

A Simple News Item, like so many Maghrebian social and sociopolitical exposés, is set in the past, in the 1970s. At regular intervals throughout the film, the events are told and commented on by a narrator in the present, an aging journalist, Omar, who talks directly to the camera. In the 1970s, Omar worked in the same newspaper office as Salim, a committed but naïve young journalist, along with a fresh young apprentice, Ali. Salim, who is unmarried but has family commitments, lives alone with a pet caged bird. When he receives anonymous indications of corruption by a senior official, he personally confronts the man concerned, Mohamed Jamali, director general of the National Office for Social Protection (ONPS). He seems not to anticipate what will ensue. In fact, his life is investigated, he is offered a substantial bribe (which he refuses), and then he is threatened on the phone and pursued in the street. Undeterred, Salim publishes a general denunciation of corruption that persuades his anonymous informant to provide the proof that will allow him to expose Jamali. We are convinced of his courage but immediately confronted by his naïveté, as he allows Jamali's mistress, Karima (masquerading as Habiba), to seduce him. He even promises her first sight of his article on Jamali. Only when Omar reveals to him Habiba's true identity does Salim realize the danger he is in; he passes on the incriminating documents to Ali for safekeeping. But it is now too late. Jamali acts ruthlessly. Karima is eliminated and Samir murdered in his flat in what the official press describes as "a killing in the course of a burglary"—the "simple news item" of the film's title.

A Simple News Item is a very effective denunciation of state corruption, with obvious relevance to the 1990s as well as to the 1970s. It has a direct narrative line, following the protagonist's actions step by step. We are engaged by his passionate drive to establish the truth, despite being aware of his personal weaknesses. A sort of "happy ending" (largely narrated rather than shown on screen), whereby Ali publishes the denunciation of corruption and Jamali (according the official reports) commits suicide, does not make good the loss of Salim. Like so many Maghrebian film protagonists, he is not able to both carry out his mission and survive.

A Woman's Fate / Destin de femme (1998) turns its attention to contemporary Morocco to offer an acute portrayal of the position and status of women. Saida is an attractive and intelligent woman who has studied for her degree in France and is now the respected head of human resources in a big Moroccan company. She meets up with Hamid, who is a personable, Belgian-educated computer scientist who says all the right things. He is looking, he says, for a woman with personality who is modern and intelligent. The pair are both ambitious: she has political aspirations, and he wants to set up his own company. The courtship goes well— he even agrees to give up smoking—and they seem to be an ideal couple. But the film's title has already warned us to expect anything but an idyllic future.

They marry and Saida continues with her job, even after she becomes pregnant. But things start to go wrong when the child turns out to be a girl, not the boy Hamid wanted "to continue the family name." He has absolutely no time for his daughter, and, when Saida's father dies, he assumes her inheritance will be handed over to him to help him start his own business. He is anything but the modern, liberal-minded man he proclaimed himself to be before they were married. He does not want the money invested in a family home: "A house I didn't pay for would never be mine." While she continues to thrive in her workplace, he proves timid about his own career, afraid even to take out a business loan. His negative attitude toward his wife and women in general is supported by the two men with whom he drinks regularly in the evenings, and he becomes more and more abusive toward Saida. When he proceeds to beat her, she asks for a divorce, to which he replies, "Do you think we live in Sweden?"

Things get progressively worse, and Saida learns the sad truth: in Morocco, divorce is for men, not women. After another drunken evening with his friends, Hamid beats Saida savagely and tries to rape her. Though her doctor arranges for her to take twenty-five days off work because of the severity of her injuries, a judge will not listen to her plea for a divorce. He accepts Hamid's denials and says that Saida needs witnesses to the assault (which took place in the couple's bedroom!). Perhaps more troubling than the misogyny is the attitude taken by all the women around Saida. Her mother will happily look after the child, but involving the authorities in a domestic dispute or seeking a divorce are both unthinkable to her. Hamid's mother and sister side with him totally. They even move into Saida's home, and, when she refuses to give them housekeeping money (she says that's Hamid's role), they steal and sell her clothes. Driven to distraction, Saida turns to a female friend for advice. Despite all her beliefs, she agrees to use witchcraft, consulting a local *fqih*, but this act of desperation is, of course, of no help at all. As Saida begins to have nightmares of killing Hamid, she tries for one last time to resolve matters with him. The film ends as he issues his terms for agreeing a divorce: her inheritance, plus all the contents of their shared flat.

This is no real resolution (who thinks Hamid will honor his side of the bargain?), and Noury's focus on male attitudes is unflinching. Men openly proclaim that educated women are an "abomination," that it is "unthinkable" for a woman to be in a position to give orders to a man at work, and that men only strive to get rich so that they can divorce and take a new (younger) wife. There is no support for an abused wife from any of the women around Saida: they all accept the situation of unquestioned male authority, which they see as a key element in maintaining "traditional values." Though there are a few awkwardly placed flashbacks in *A Woman's Fate*, the overall narrative line is clear and powerfully affecting. The compositions are excellent (by Kamal Derkaoui, for *A Simple News Item* as well as *A Woman's Fate*) and the music (by Moncef Adyel, for all three films) is used to telling effect. Noury's three realist dramas discussed here are all well argued pleas for social change and constitute a valuable addition to the development of Moroccan cinema. At the end of the 1990s, Noury's career took an unexpected turn. As he has explained: "I set out from the principle that when you are a filmmaker, you make any kind of film. So I wanted to prove to myself that I could do something other than purely social or committed cinema. One of my dreams is, one day, to make a western."[109]

The result was not a western but a comedy that achieved enormous box office success, *She Is Diabetic and Hypertensive and She Refuses to Die / Elle est diabétique et hypertendue et elle refuse de crever* (2000). Despite the fact that two of the most popular films with audiences in Maghrebian film history—Ferid Boughedir's *Halfaouine* (1990) and Mohamed Abderrahman Tazi's *Looking for My Wife's Husband* (1993)—are comedies, few North African directors have tackled the genre.

In a perceptive study, Kevin Dwyer uses a comparison with Tazi to bring out the specific characteristics of Noury's work. In order to give his film a universal appeal, Noury has chosen as his subject the situation of a young man, Najib, totally dominated by his mother-in-law. Hadja is in complete control of him at his workplace (she is the incontrovertible boss of the company set up by her late husband) and at home (where she insists that he and her daughter, Souad, have separate bedrooms). Najib is such a weak character that it is difficult to sympathize with him, and Noury has admitted, "You can't identify with any of the characters." They are stereotypes—the domineering mother-in-law, the weak son-in-law, the infantilized wife—rather than fully rounded individuals. The tone is one of farce, and we are encouraged to laugh at the characters rather than with them. Noury plays various tricks with his audience, "to underline that this is a film meant to amuse, that the filmmaker is enjoying himself as much as the actors, and the spectators should be entertained even more when they realise this."[110]

The film's commercial success led to its similarly named sequel, *She Is Diabetic and Hypersensitive and Still She Refuses to Die / Elle est diabétique et hypertendue et ell refuse toujours de crever* (2005), and even a third variation on the subject directed in Spain by his sons, Imad and Sohael, from a script that he provided. Noury established an unchallenged reputation as one of Morocco's true film pioneers and was the most prolific of Moroccan feature filmmakers in the 1990s decade. He also directed one of Moroccan cinema's most commercially successful film comedies. But after just one more feature, *The End of the World / Le bout du monde*, in 2012, he became totally disillusioned with Moroccan television production structures and government film support schemes. He moved to Spain, where he has continued his career as an actor, appearing, for example, in three films directed there by his sons.

Mohamed Abderrahman Tazi, who was born in 1942 in Fez, followed his studies of film at IDHEC in Paris with mass media communication studies at Syracuse University in New York. On his return to Morocco, he made a number of shorts, worked on foreign productions shot in Morocco (including films by John Huston, Francis Ford Coppola, and Martin Scorsese), and also served as director of photography on a number of shorts and features, most notably Hamid Benani's debut film, *Wechma*. Unlike most of his contemporaries, Tazi is not a natural writer-director, and all his work has been made from scripts furnished by others. In the case of his debut feature, *The Big Trip / Le grand voyage / Ibn assabil* (literally, "the traveler" in Arabic) (1982), the script was by Noureddine Saïl, who also produced the film and went on to become head of the Moroccan film service (CCM). The film is essentially a roads movie, following the trajectory of a single truck driver. Tazi has said he was attracted to the genre for practical reasons, because it offered the possibility of "a series of encounters, all tied together by one main character, a film with movement; a film that travelled that would free me from the restrictions of unity of place, that would allow me to express the countryside, with travelling shots, the truck, and so on."[111]

Omar, a naïve and basically taciturn man in his thirties—played by a non-professional actor—is hired to drive a truckload of dates from southern Tunisia to Tangier, a route that will take him through several major Moroccan cities. His encounters along the way vary from the humorous to the desperate. From the start, he shows his consideration for others, helping a woman repair her car, which has a puncture; picking up a couple of Western tourists; and agreeing to transport a religious teacher (*fqih*). But then his encounters get more serious: he mislays his jacket (containing all his money), he is involved in a barroom brawl, and, while sleeping at the roadside, his cargo is stolen. Undeterred, he befriends a girl who is thrown out of a passing car. They spend some time together in Tangier, and the question of going abroad comes up in conversation. She helps him sell his truck and puts him in touch with someone who can transport him. He is to be towed to Europe in a small rowing boat, and all seems well. Tired out by his efforts, he falls asleep, and we see his dreams retracing his journey. When he awakes, he finds he has been betrayed again. The rowing boat has been cut adrift, and he is alone at sea. The terror on Omar's face as he confronts his predicament is as real as it seems. The actor could not swim and had never rowed a boat. This bleak ending, which was not in Saïl's original script, was devised by Tazi himself, anticipating a tactic he adopted in subsequent films.

After this low-budget and unpretentious debut, Tazi had to wait eight years for another opportunity to direct. During this time, he lived for a while in Spain (he has a Spanish wife), and the new film, *Badis* (1988), emerged as a Moroccan-Spanish coproduction, with French funding support. While Tazi chose the setting and theme of the film, the first draft was once again written by Noureddinne Saïl, with the writer-director Farida Benlyazid brought in to revise the whole script and so allow the film to express "a feminine sensibility"—ironic in view of the response the film received from Moroccan feminists.[112]

Badis is a Moroccan village on the Mediterranean coast, situated alongside a centuries-old citadel that is still controlled by Spain and used to detain political prisoners. The visually striking location is well explored in the opening shots of the film, which also establish the identities of key characters. One of the young villagers, Moira, who has a Moroccan fisherman father and a Spanish mother (who has left to go back to Spain), is attracted to one of the Spanish soldiers, who returns her feelings. The social dynamic of the village is further disturbed by the arrival of two townsfolk from Casablanca, an authoritarian Koranic teacher and his oppressed wife, Touria. Their lives, like that of Moira, are closely scrutinized by the villagers, particularly the postman and the café owner, who both like to interfere in other people's lives.

Touria becomes Moira's teacher, and the two grow close—they dance together, rather than bothering with formal lessons, though Moira does learn Arabic well enough to read the Koran. Despite this, Touria's husband becomes more and more tyrannical, and when Moira finally receives the letters from the young soldier inviting her to join him in Spain (previously held back by the post-man), the pair decide to run off together to assert their independence. But when they are caught, encircled and confronted by the villagers, Moira asserts her lib-erty by dancing in defiance. It is a woman who throws the first stone, and the pair are stoned to death by the angry crowd.

This is another, beautifully shot, tale of defeat: to be an outsider in this closed community is not acceptable and is even punishable by death. The film was well received by festival audiences abroad but failed totally in Morocco. According to Kevin Dwyer, "It closed after one week, drawing a total of barely three hundred spectators."[113] As can be imagined, it was the ending, devised by Tazi against the wishes of his scriptwriters, that caused controversy among feminists, among them the distinguished sociologist Fatima Mernissa. She asserted that *Badis* "shouldn't have ended in that defeatist, pessimistic manner, because the film was made at a time when Moroccan women were starting to take their lives into their own hands."[114] Tazi's interpretation of the scene is very different: "The woman who throws the stone is doing it, in a way, to protect the girl, to protect the family, to protect women as a sex. She's not throwing it to punish but to stop this girl's indecency, to stop men being bewitched by the spectacle."[115] Ignoring the fact that the rest of the work is filmed in a realist style (even the real name of the vil-lage is used in the film), he asserts that the scene should be read as symbolic and that he was "sounding an alarm."[116]

Tazi responded to the failure of his film to reach Moroccan audiences and the criticism of the film for its negative ending by turning, in his next film, to that rarest of forms in Maghrebian cinema—comedy. In the process, he made the film that became the biggest box-office success to date in Moroccan film history.

Looking for My Wife's Husband / À la recherche du mari de ma femme / Al-bahth an zaoui imaraati (1993) is thus a fresh departure for Tazi. The protagonist, Hadj Ben Moussa, played with real comic flair by Bachir Skirej, initially lives an idyllic life in the medina of Fez, where he has his jeweler's shop. There is no jealousy or antagonism between his three wives, each of whom has a specific role: Lalla Hobby is the mother figure, Lalla Robbea the child rearer, and Houda the young (still childless) mistress figure. Nor is there any criticism from outside the immediate family, not even from Lalla Hobby's daughter, Miriam, who is a doc-tor living outside the medina. Houda, who has known no other situation than her parents' traditional home and the hadj's polygamous establishment, abides by the rules, though she is attracted to the idea of romantic love. The intricacies of this web of relationships are beautifully captured in the script, written by Tazi in collaboration with fellow director Farida Benlyazid, which shows the varied strengths of the women, as well as the overall crushing male dominance.

The film's crisis comes not from any infidelity but from Houda, alone in the house, answering the door unveiled ("naked" in traditional Moroccan terms).[117] Hadj Ben Moussa is totally outraged and repudiates her on the spot, a fatal error, as he soon discovers from his lawyer. Under Islamic law, a third renunciation is conclusive. The couple cannot be reconciled and continue to live together (except as socially reviled fornicators). The only solution is for Houda to remarry, consummate this marriage, and then divorce. She agrees to this proposition, as her inexperience has made her find life alone outside the confines of the medina and traditional society very difficult to handle. Obviously the remarriage provides problems for Ben Moussa, but a willing husband is found, a young Moroccan who usually lives and works in Belgium. The wedding night focus of the film is not on the newlyweds but on Ben Moussa, alone and in agony (neither of his other wives has the slightest sympathy for his predicament). Worse is to come. The next morning, the husband vanishes back to Belgium, and Ben Moussa is unable to arrange the planned divorce.

Throughout the film there is an easily tolerated discrepancy between the scenes in the media (enacted in 1950s style décor and reflecting Tazi's own childhood) and the bustling views of the rest of 1990s Fez. But in a concluding scene not contained in Benlyazid's original script and not disclosed to the cast before shooting, we are brutally translated, in virtually improvised documentary footage, to the realities of 1993 and the difficulties of illegal immigration, as Ben Moussa boards one of the frail boats attempting the crossing to Europe, in search, as he says, of his wife's husband.

Introducing his new feature, *Lalla Hobby*, Tazi has said:

> When finishing the first part, *A la recherché du mari de ma femme*, I realised that this wasn't the end of the story, that I had to continue. *Lalla Hobby* is, from this point of view, the logical extension of a process which was started in the first part of the story. The first film reveals certain social aspects as well as people's attitudes in their home country compared to those they adopt once they find themselves in a foreign land. *Lalla Hobby* is also an attempt at sketching a comic and cheerful portrait, of taking a look at illegal immigration, a burning social issue affecting a number of European countries today.[118]

Making a comedy dedicated to those who risk their lives every day in the Straits of Gibraltar, is no easy undertaking.

Hadj Ben Moussa, now played by Amidou (Hamidou Ben Messaoud), an actor who has attained star status in Europe, is not a good traveler and is standing gesticulating when the boat runs into trouble. He topples over and is rendered unconscious. He is rescued and wakes up in a Tangiers prison cell. When his family in Fez learn what has happened Lalla Hobby, his first wife, sets out for Tangiers, only to find he has been released and made a successful clandestine voyage to Spain, en route for Belgium. The film alternates his actions with scenes depicting the responses of his wives. The sought-after Houda (now played by a newcomer, Samia Akkariou), for example, has been abandoned by her new husband and is suing for divorce, while Lalla Hobby has taken over the shop in Fez, making it more profitable than the hadj ever did. In Belgium, after the criticism leveled at *Badis*, he now shows women well able to run their own lives. Hadj has various encounters—in Antwerp with a Jewish jeweler friend from Fez and later with an attractive Belgian girl, for example—but all end in disaster. He is successively cheated, mocked, beaten, and eventually arrested and deported. He is, however, able to make a suitably spectacular arrival in Fez, where the whole family await him at the airport. He emerges from the plane with an attractive Belgian blonde—but this is merely the custody officer, to whom he is handcuffed.

Tazi spent several years as a production director at the Moroccan television channel 2M, before returning to feature filmmaking with the historical drama, *Abou Moussa's Neighbors / Les voisines d'Abou Moussa* (2003). He has since made *The Old Maid / La vielle jeune fille / Al-bayra* (2012).

Throughout his career Tazi has retained his belief in narrative simplicity: "As far as narration is concerned, I don't think it's appropriate for Moroccan films to narrate in the style of Bergman or Antonioni. I think simplicity is primary—we don't need to create a complicated scheme in order to construct a narrative. We need a linearity in narration, in telling a story."[119]

He has chosen stories that are inspired by contemporary issues, such as rural backwardness, polygamy, and immigration, that pose problems for his protagonists, but he does not make films that are polemical. At the same time, as Kevin Dwyer points out, he has developed a style that respects the privacy of these protagonists: he shuns intimate scenes (there are no depictions of sexual intimacy), and his camera keeps a distance from his characters, who are customarily depicted in medium shots rather than close-ups.

In the 1990s, a new and more challenging tone was adopted by Abdelkader Lagtaâ, who was born in Casablanca in 1948 and trained at the Lodz film school in Poland. He has described himself as more influenced "by Polish cinema or, more generally, by the cinemas of Eastern Europe, than by Western cinema or, for that matter, by Egyptian cinema."[120] One Moroccan critic, keen to define the particular stance of his work, has dubbed his approach "sociopolitical," as opposed to merely socially concerned, because of the filmmaker's willingness to "unveil the unspoken and to confront taboos."[121] These are concerns to which Lagtaâ constantly returns in his interviews and presentations of his films.

A Love Affair in Casablanca / Un amour à Casablanca / Hubb fi al-dar al-bayda (1991), Lagtaâ's debut film, was made with limited, purely Moroccan funding, which created difficulties during the shooting. Made "in dramatic circumstances and with derisory resources," the film has defects that the director recognizes, but these did not prevent the film from being a great success with Moroccan audiences.[122] The film has a complicated plot that depicts an eighteen-year-old schoolgirl, Saloua, who is oppressed at home and runs off with a fifty-year-old man who has seduced her. When she leaves him for her true love, a boy of her own age, she finds that he is the elder man's son. There is a real sense of the messiness of adult and parental problems flowing out over the young, seen here with fresh eyes as a new generation involved with drink, sex, and drugs. The imagery, particularly with regard to the sexual involvements, is very restrained by Western standards: this is a film about the bodies it cannot show. Yet the frustrations in the life of a young woman caught in a society where men make the rules to suit themselves, are spelled out very clearly, as are the difficulties of a girl living away from her family and the humiliations of a lost virginity. The film ends with the boy's suicide and recriminations among those left behind.

Lagtaâ's second feature, *The Closed Door / La porte close* was shot in 1993 but not released until 2000 because of censorship problems. As Lagtaâ explains, this was because "it shows a homosexual schoolteacher, which the censors considered to be degrading for that profession, as if homosexuality was completely foreign to our reality. So they asked me to mutilate my film in order for it to be distributed. I refused because I think a film should be presented in its entirety: that's the right of the spectator as well as that of the director."[123]

The Casablancans / Les Casablancais (1998), which received coproduction funding from the Moroccan Fonds d'Aide, as well as from France and Canada, offers a bleak image of the Moroccan city. The tone is set by the first of the three loosely interlinked stories that the film contains. The life of the bookseller Mostafa Ziani is turned upside down when he receives a summons from the police. He does help his clients by obtaining for them books not distributed in Morocco and imagines this is the reason for the summons. His anxiety is increased when he witnesses an unmarried couple arrested on grounds of gross indecency merely for talking to each other on the street. Mostafa feels he is being spied on wherever he goes and fears every knock at the door. He is on the point of trying to go into hiding, when his son actually reads the whole summons and discovers that it is in fact addressed to his neighbor, M. Zaïm.

This first episode vividly illustrates the widespread pattern of fear induced by the Moroccan authorities in citizens who remember the 1970s, when oppression was at its extreme. The second episode shifts its focus to the situation of women in a culture that offers them little freedom or respect. Just because she is beautiful and dresses in Western style, the young teacher Saloua is leered at in the street and spied on at home. Her underwear is even stolen by one of her salacious neighbors, who assumes that because she is unmarried and lives alone, she must be debauched. It is a telling comment on Moroccan society that the official charged with investigating her morals when she applies for a passport sees his job not as uncovering the truth but as confirming every rumor. His way to promotion, as he sees it, is to establish her guilt, thereby confirming his superiors' suspicions. If she were innocent, he thinks, there would be no inquiry. This official is one of the few comic characters in the film, and the episode ends in farce with him deciding to approve her application and to get a passport for himself, "so he can go to the top of the Eiffel Tower with her."

More sinister is the third episode. Kamal, whose little girlfriend, Houda, is in Saloua's French class, is at the start a boy like any other. But he and his friend Adil have their thinking corrupted by their teacher, Lhaj Kabouss, who is an Islamic extremist and gives them free extra lessons. Kamal comes to think his parents will go to hell as sinners and tries to get his mother to cover her head and his father to give up drinking beer. A chilling moment comes when his mother tells him he can expect a little brother or sister. Left alone, he murmurs to himself that this is "a child conceived in sin." He even takes a knife toward his parents' bed but is disturbed at the last moment. Coming to realize what he is doing, he runs off to drown himself but is saved by Houda, supported by Kamal's parents and friends.

Lagtaâ's first three features troubled the censor but shocked and delighted a mass audience with their very striking image of modern life in an Arab society, where alcohol, drugs, prostitution, and casual sex abound. The authorities are scorned and derided, while corruption is exposed as commonplace.

Given his committed stance, it was inevitable that Lagtaâ would be one of the first Moroccan filmmakers to tackle the hitherto taboo subject of the years of brutal repression under Hassan II, the so-called Years of Lead. The opportunity came when Hassan's son and successor, Mohamed VI, loosened censorship restrictions. *Face to Face / Face à face* (2003) is set at the beginning and the end of the 1990s, a period very important to Lagtaâ, since it was then that he began his feature filmmaking career. The film is not a direct representation of the Hassan II years but rather an exploration of that period's residue, its continuing influence on people's awareness and behavior in the decades that followed.

The film begins in 1993. Kamal and Amal are a happily married couple with a three-year-old daughter. There are tensions when Amal wants to finish the final year of her degree (abandoned because of the birth of their daughter) and when Kamal revives the idea of immigrating to Canada, but there is no hint of a split in the relationship. There is, however, a foreshadowing of what is to come when a play that Amal is planning to see is abandoned and those who have gathered for the performance are brutally dispersed by the police. Kamal, an engineer by profession, continues to think that repression is a thing of the past and miscalculates the effect of a report he has prepared on corruption at the huge construction site where he is working. His report is seemingly welcomed, but he is immediately ordered to transfer to another project in the South.

Knowing nothing of this, Amal goes to the station to meet Kamal's brother, Redouane, on his release from prison but is brutally assaulted by a drunk in the parking lot. At this point, we are not told what then happens to her, but it seems she is arrested by the police, who use the opportunity to search the empty flat. When Amal eventually reemerges, she is visibly shaken and unwilling to talk to anyone about what has happened to her. She tries to contact Kamal, but his company now refuses to recognize him. Obsessed with his own situation, Kamal accepts all too easily the idea that Amal has gone off with a lover. Arbitrary incidents and missed timings have resulted in a tragic misunderstanding, each thinking that he/she has been abandoned by the other.

Seven years later, for reasons we are not told, Amal, accompanied by her brother-in-law, Redouane, sets out to find her husband. It is a painful journey into the Upper Atlas Mountains, territory that she knows less well than the Alps. Confessions, surprises, and quarrels abound. Redouane talks about his fiancée, Nour, who cracked up and committed suicide while he was in prison. Amal reveals, for the first time, that she was arrested and sentenced for "incitement to debauchery" and that she was raped in prison. Souad, who was Kamal's nurse after his car accident and now lives with him, finds herself confronted by a wife she did not know existed. Kamal, who is now an amnesiac, comes face to face with a brother he does not recognize and told about a wife and child of whom he has no memory. Amal obtains the agreement to divorce, which Redouane thought was the purpose of the trip, but rejects it. Nothing is resolved. The last words in the film, as the screen turns to black, are those of the daughter, Leyla, on her mother's mobile phone, "Daddy, can you hear me? I'm Leyla, your daughter." We do not hear Kamal's response, if, indeed, there is one.

Face to Face is a slow-moving film, making great use of long takes, straightforward in narrative terms on one level and totally enigmatic on another. Why has Amal determined on this trip at this time? Was Kamal, whom his brother recalls as uninterested in politics, really involved in the Berber uprising? The uprising preceded his car accident, which occurred while he was being pursued by the police. What will any of the characters do next? Will Leyla get a response from her father?

No one is at home with the situations they find themselves in. Amal seems uncertain of her relationship with her new lover, Mounir. Redouane can find no place for himself in the changed circumstances of contemporary Morocco—his old political certainties have been crushed. Kamal can make no links with his own past. Souad is left feeling betrayed and lied to by everyone. A society that cannot come to terms with its past, the film tells us, cannot provide a secure base on which people can build secure lives. For Lagtaâ, "It's the main characters' existential quest which constitutes, the principal content of the film." These personal predicaments are a reflection of Morocco as a whole, a society that cannot progress toward modernity and that is weighed down by the conservative attitudes prevalent in the South. In the same interview, he admits, "Personally, I'm like my characters: I don't know the countryside and it doesn't seem to me to carry values I want to defend."[124]

Lagtaâ continued his self-appointed role of "questioning society, questioning social practices, questioning how people behave and the kinds of relationships they have with each other"[125] in *Yasmine and Men / Yasmine et les hommes* (2007).

Lagtaâ subsequently made a medium-length, French-language documentary study of Moroccan cinema: *Between Desire and Incertitude / Entre désir et incertitude* (2010). He opens the film with a homosexual love scene from his own second feature, *The Closed Door*, banned by the censors in 1993 and cut by distributors when the film was finally released to a Moroccan audience seven years later. The difficulties faced by filmmakers—caught between tight censorship regulations and traditional social attitudes on the one hand and a public accustomed to an alien imported cinema on the other—form one of the key themes of the film. *Between Desire and Incertitude* builds on comments from a number of leading Moroccan film critics and statements by filmmakers ranging from veteran Latif Lahlou to relative newcomers, such as Ahmed el-Maanouni, Najiss Nejjar, Nabil Ayouch, and Faouzi Bensaidi. There are fourteen well-chosen clips from films made by the filmmakers discussed, many of them showing scenes where the filmmakers' concern is to subvert the censors or to challenge audience preconceptions. The latter part of the film widens out to take in the role of the Moroccan Film Center (the CCM) and the impact of foreign—particularly Hollywood—movies shot on location in Morocco. But at the very end, it returns to the immediate problems facing Moroccan filmmakers, with el Maanouni talking about the declining international audience for Moroccan films and Nejjar emphasising the growing need to confront Muslim fundamentalism.

Half the Sky / La moitié du ciel (2014) is a feature-length, French-language docu-drama based on the autobiographical novel *La liqueur d'Aloès* by Jocelyne Laâbi, the French wife of the Moroccan poet Abdellatif Laâbi, who collaborated on the screenplay. The film, Lagtaâ's first opportunity to confront directly the oppression of the 1970s, received support from French funding organizations and also, remarkably, from the Moroccan film support body, the Fonds d'Aide. Instead of making a mere political denunciation of the regime or offering an explanation of how its "security" operation worked, the director concentrated on the lives of those directly involved: the detainees and their families. The narrative is strictly chronological (except for one brief moment when Jocelyne remembers her own father's involvement with the French anti-Semitic Vichy regime). The film does not use any of the conventional structures of narrative suspense but instead keeps strictly to the characters' own level of knowledge, with a voice-over by the actress playing Jocelyne. We, the audience, know as little as they do. A seemingly stable life (Jocelyne and Abdellatif have two children and are expecting a third) is torn apart by the unpredictable actions of the state authorities, who are, of course, accountable to no one but themselves.

The couple's situation is clear to us from the precredit sequence, at the beginning of which Abdellatif is arrested. Jocelyn, though she keeps her French nationality, was brought up in Morocco and sees it as her home. Abdellatif is the director of the literary review *Souffles* ("Whispers"), which has gradually become more politicized, and he and his colleague Abraham (who is also arrested) have together founded a nonviolent underground movement, *Ilal-Amam* ("Forward"). Arrested in February, they are released, only for their arrest to be sought again in March, when Abraham escapes and goes into hiding. Unable to find him, the police arrest his sister, Évelyne, who is tortured so badly that she dies two years later. When Abraham is finally arrested, Jocelyne is implicated, as she has been in communication with him. In custody, she is badly treated, if not actually tortured, and released only after she has surrendered her passport. When she desperately needs it to take her youngest child to France for medical treatment, she turns to the French embassy for help but finds none.

Jocelyne has already begun to work actively in the protest movement, which brings together the families of the detainees, and this—combined with a hunger strike by the prisoners—brings improvements in prison access. Small successes can be celebrated, but the overall picture remains bleak. Despite a spirited defense, Abdellatif is arbitrarily condemned to ten years in prison, and a little later, Abraham is sentenced to life imprisonment. The struggle continues, as Abdellatif serves the first eight years of his sentence with the date of his release never mentioned. Then out of the blue and without warning, he is set free. The film ends with Jocelyne and the children celebrating as they drive to meet him.

Lagtaâ vividly brings to life the personal suffering and doubts of the detainees and their families, who no longer have any control over their daily lives. The authorities act arbitrarily and are impervious to reasoned arguments. The result, in Jocelyne's case, is almost a decade of total uncertainty. Even after his release, Abdellatif has no idea when, or if, the police will intervene again. Hassan II's police state (which, of course, asserts that "torture does not happen here") is revealed in all its inhuman barbarity. *Half the Sky* is a fitting high point in Lagtaâ's lifelong effort to show the pressures and contradictions that confronted Moroccan citizens in all walks of life during and after the years of overt oppression.

Alongside his latest film, Lagtaâ has also begun a new career as a French-language novelist, publishing three novels in quick succession: *Québec je me souviens* (2014), *Éloge d'errance* (2014), and *Perte d'équilibre* (2015).

*

The beginnings of a renewal of Moroccan cinema, bringing it in line with developments elsewhere in the Arab world (again backed by both the CCM and the Fonds Sud), came with the appearance of a major figure from a slightly younger generation, Daoud Aoulad-Syad. Aoulad-Syad was born in 1953 in Marrakesh and was originally a teacher of physical sciences at Rabat University. Inspired by an exhibition by Henri Cartier-Bresson while still a student, Aoulad-Syad turned his attention to photography. He has published three books, *Marocains* (1989), *Boujaâd, Espace et mémoire* (1989), and *Territoires de l'instant* (with Ahmed Bouanani, 2000), and continues to exhibit regularly. Mouna Mekouar has compiled an excellent selection of the photographs that figured in the exhibition organized by the Maison Européenne de la Photographie in Paris in 2015–16.[126] Aoulad-Syad's involvement with cinema began at FEMIS in Paris in 1989, and he subsequently made a number of short films, many in collaboration with the veteran Moroccan director Ahmed Bouanani, who also scripted his first two features.

Bye-Bye Souirty / Adieu forain (1998) is set in the drought-stricken south of Morocco and brings together three disparate characters. Kacem is an aging traveling showman whom, we sense from the beginning (and from the French title), is about to undertake his last mission. Larbi, his son, is a disgruntled ex-boxer who has spent time in prison for violence. As the film progresses, he becomes more and more frustrated by the fact that women are more attracted to gay men than to macho males like him. The third character, Rabii, is a homosexual transvestite dancer, at a low point in his life since his lover of five years has just decamped, taking all Rabii's savings with him. No bonds develop between the three, and they remain isolated individuals as they travel from place to place with their lottery booth and a performance routine that generates little popular interest. The characters they encounter do little to raise their spirits. For example, the female teacher they meet is totally frustrated in her career because the villagers want a "real" teacher—that is to say, a man. Very little happens as the film progresses, and there are no moments of high dramatic tension. Even Kacem's death in the hospital in Marrakesh occurs offscreen. The two younger men are left alone, Larbi driving off alone and Rabii vanishing into the night.

The Wind Horse / Le cheval de vent / Aoud rih (2001) remains Aoulad-Syad's best-known film. It is a sort of (very understated) road movie that brings together two very disparate characters, the aging ex-blacksmith Tahar and the thirty-or-so-year-old Driss, whose past includes a spell in prison for theft (but only from the rich, as he is keen to make clear). Brought together by the breakdown of a bus, they build a tentative relationship that is, itself, always threatening to break down. They set out from very different positions. Tahar is leaving a totally unhappy domestic situation (he lives with his son and nagging daughter-in-law), while Driss has been kicked out of a hospital (though we never know what his illness is or was). Each has an immediate goal, Tahar to visit the grave of his second wife in Azemmour and Driss to visit his mother, who moved out when he was a small child and who is now in a hospital in Essaouira. But beyond that, everything is in doubt. In Casablanca, where he has an uneasy relationship with his brother, Driss picks up his motorbike and, with Tahar in the sidecar, they head south, each driven by a personal "wind horse."

They move through a landscape where poverty is rife and where there is a sense that a traditional world is passing away. As Tahar puts it, from his blacksmith's point of view, "There aren't enough horses left in the world." The people they encounter have an awkward present, a past that haunts them, and usually an impossible dream. Most also have a little story to tell. The pair comes by chance upon a traveling fair, where Driss *almost* has a romantic encounter with the Wall of Death rider Malika (but she has a fiancé in prison). They also encounter Rabii (from *Adieu forain*), who is still traveling. As they continue their journey, they become ever closer. Driss is mistaken at one point for Tahar's son, and Tahar arranges for the pair to be photographed together side by side (he has no such image with his actual son, Mestafa). Each of the two achieves his immediate goal; however, Tahar finds little solace at his wife's grave, and Driss's mother has had a stroke and cannot even acknowledge his presence. They have, nevertheless, discovered each other, and when a despairing Driss tries to drown himself in the sea, it is Tahar who saves him. But as the film fades to black, the future is totally uncertain for both of them. *The Wind Horse* is a very underplayed film, with no obvious dramatic excitements. But we do become invested in these two very divergent personalities, and throughout, there is the pleasure of the formalized shooting of a film that was created with a photographer's sense of composition and feeling for the precise moment to frame and cut.

Tarfaya (2004) is the least known of Alouad-Syad's films. Though written by Youssef Fadel rather than by Mohamed Bouanani, it is in the same vein: a film that holds the viewer's attention, but where very little happens. Miriem, a young woman of twenty-eight, arrives in a little village in the North hoping to be able to emigrate. But there is a long wait, which allows the director the opportunity to describe the everyday life of a village where inhabitants make their living thanks to the delays suffered by would-be emigrants. As an anonymous reviewer notes, Alouad-Syad's camera "follows Meriem, a young girl tempted by the idea of exile. We do not know much about her history. The film shows her here and now, in the present, without a past or future. And each of the sequences in which she appears, lost in an ocean of dunes and waves, is a true photograph."[127]

Alouad-Syad established his own distinctive voice in these first features. The films are muted narratives that go nowhere, deal with indecisive characters and are full of encounters that lead to nothing. The past—from which the characters are mostly fleeing—weighs down on them, but there is no sense of a future opening up. The films are slowly paced and meditative, with everything underplayed by a director who never pushes his material to make big dramatic scenes or confrontations. Instead, Aoulad-Syad's films are full of silences, words are seldom tools of communication and dreams are largely unfulfilled. The visual compositions reflect the director's status as a professional photographer whose work continues to receive regular major exhibitions in Morocco and France.

The director's most recent films form a closely linked pair, with the open ending of the second allowing the prospect of a trilogy. *Waiting for Pasolini / En attendant Pasolini / Fi ntidhar Pasolini* (2007) is the story of a film extra who was befriended by Pasolini while the latter was shooting *Oedipus Rex* on location near Ourzazate in 1966. Ourzazate is the usual studio base for foreign filmmakers shooting on location in Morocco, and many celebrated Western films—from *Laurence of Arabia* to *Gladiator*—have been made there. Such productions account for some 90 percent of all finance invested in Moroccan-based filmmaking, dwarfing the local output. And, of course, the neighboring villages profit enormously from money expended by producers, crew, and cast.

Thami now works as a television repairman, but when he was younger, he worked as an extra on a number of foreign-made films. The fact that he became Pasolini's friend and was able to buy a house with his earnings has given him some status in the village. When he and the villagers hear that another Italian feature is to be shot in Ourzazate, Thami is overjoyed, as he assumes that Pasolini will be returning. When he learns that it is to be a cheap biblical epic and that Pasolini has been dead for some thirty years, he keeps this news from his fellow villagers. The villagers are willing to queue for hours for a part in the film, which will involve dressing up and spouting a few words of Italian, a language they do not understand (the words will, of course, be subsequently dubbed). Disaster comes for Thami, when the villagers discover that this is not a Pasolini film and that he has no direct access to the producers. Even more devastating for all is the news that production of the film is to be suspended. Thami makes his own attempt to remedy matters by dressing up to resemble the priest played by Pasolini in his own film (Thami has kept the headpiece worn by Pasolini as a souvenir). Followed by a crowd of villagers, he harangues the Italians in an awkward variant of the words expressed by the priest to Oedipus.

In her comparison of *Oedipus Rex* and *Waiting for Pasolini*, Gian Maria Annovi stresses the film's link to the form of cinema practiced by Aoulad-Syad's slightly older contemporaries. *Waiting for Pasolini* "stands as an excellent case of the 'social-realist style' that . . . characterizes contemporary Moroccan cinematography. Moroccan filmmakers working within the context of the contemporary social-realist genre openly criticize the limitations of traditionalism and Western modernity. . . . In *Waiting for Pasolini*, Aoulad-Syad does exactly this by addressing the neo-colonialist aspect of today's Moroccan film industry."[128]

But this is only one aspect of a complex and beautifully realized film. *Waiting for Pasolini* also uses humor to make its points, and this implies rethinking aspects of plot structure and positing a different relationship between the spectators and the characters. The film is also a reflection on cinema itself, opening the way for the more radical approach adopted in his next feature. All Maghrebian filmmakers need their own production companies in order to maintain their freedom. But, of course, making independent films for what is essentially an art house market is not lucrative, hence the need for filmmakers to work from time to time in television. Aoulad-Syad's account of what this involves allows us to understand the roots of his sympathy for the exploited villagers: "I've made téléfilms for television, because that's the way you earn money, I understand that, but when it's not my own production, I'm just a paid technician and that's all."[129]

Waiting for Pasolini gives a vivid picture of the dreams and aspirations aroused by the production of a film among poverty-ridden villagers, particularly the prospect of what is, in their eyes, untold wealth. In contrast, *The Mosque / La mosquée / A jamaâ* (2010) makes clear the unforeseen physical consequences of film production on rural communities and on unsuspecting villagers who get involved. The film deals with the outcome for Moha, one of the participants in this film, when villagers refuse to demolish the film set of a mosque that he allowed to be built on his land. Instead, they begin to use it for religious purposes, since they have no other mosque in the village, and choose one of the actors from the film to serve as their new imam, sidetracking the objections of the previous holy man. Without his land, Moha has no option but to work as a laborer for others if he wishes to support his family. As he constantly complains, it's not a mosque—it's a film set. But for the villagers, it *is* a real mosque, and all the relevant religious and secular authorities support this view. Moha's attempts to bypass them and knock down the film set, with the aid of the ousted imam, are thwarted, and he can make no progress. Instead, he is told he will receive the reward for his good deed in paradise. The arrival of a documentary television crew reveals how the village has been tidied up and embellished for the film. It also allows Moha to make an impassioned plea to the camera. But the only result of this is that he is arrested, which leaves the film itself unresolved and allows the possibility of another film to continue and conclude the narrative.

The Mosque is remarkable in many ways. The film did not derive from a carefully structured script but from the actual events that arose from the shooting of *Waiting for Pasolini*. For filming purposes, Aoulad-Syad had built just the façade of a mosque, with no concern that the minaret did not face Mecca: it was designed in such a way as to reflect light in the best possible manner. The crew then went off to film studio sequences in Ouarzazate, and when they returned, they found that at the time of prayers, four villagers came to pray. The crew all found that very funny, but next day, there were ten worshippers. When the workmen stripping the set refused to demolish the mosque façade, Aoulad-Syad did not know what he was able to do, since destroying a real mosque would clearly be a serious offense. Was his film décor now real?

The Mosque is therefore not simply a fiction but, in a very real sense, a documentary reconstruction, using actual scenes, confrontations, and dialogue expecienced or overheard by the director. All the performers, apart from Moha, are nonprofessionals who were found as the filming got under way. Aoulad-Syad also further develops the self-reflexivity we have seen in his earlier films. He admits that he had always told himself that one day he would make a film about cinema: "All the great directors I admire have done that." The character Rabii from *Bye Bye Souirty* makes a reappearance in *The Wind Horse*, which gives a new dimension to the film. *Waiting for Pasolini* can be read in part as a critique of the film *Oedipus Rex*. And, finally, *The Mosque* opens with an appearance by the director himself, presenting a screening of his previous film to an audience that includes some of its participants. For Aoulad-Syad, "the best film school, is seeing films," and he has admitted influences as diverse as Iranian cinema and John Ford.

The role of humor is also very important in Aoulad-Syad's films. He approaches it not as a thought-out element of the script but as an outcome that arises from the film's subject. Apart from engaging his audience, this form allows him a way to deal with religion. As he explains: "It's delicate to talk about religion in Morocco. At heart, I'm a believer and I live in a family of believers. I don't want to stir things up. With humour you can communicate a huge amount of things without saying them."[130]

Perhaps Oliver Barlet has given the best summary of the work of this complex director: "Daoud directs in a way that recalls Chaplin: a structure choreographed with great precision, a great attention to framing and to objects, a light humour, which is subtle because it is understated and plays with the unexpected, a generalised social critique which does not deny the psychology of the characters, and finally a whole human metaphysic in the reduced space of a village."[131]

Tunisia

In Tunisia, the state organization Société Anonyme Tunisienne de Production et d'Expansion Cinématographiques (SATPEC) has been active from the late 1950s and offers opportunities to many, especially the new filmmakers who returned from film schools abroad in the 1970s and 1980s. But the first significant director of post-independence Tunisia is Omar Khlifi, whose films are currently not available. He was a member of an older generation, born in the mid-1930s. Self-taught and already the director of a number of short films, he did not study abroad but emerged from the flourishing Tunisian amateur filmmaking sector in the 1960s. Khlifi was passionate about cinema and in 1970 published a book about the films shot—mainly by the French—in Tunisia, concluding with an array of critical accounts of his own first feature, the first Tunisian feature film.[132]

Between 1966 and 1970 Khlifi made a loose trilogy set at various stages of the Tunisian liberation struggle. *The Dawn / L'aube / Al-fajr* (1966) is set in 1954 and focuses on three young people from diverse backgrounds who fight against the French and, as a result, lose their lives. The film ends with an epilogue showing the return to Tunis of the nationalist leader (and first president) Habib Bourguiba on June 1, 1955. Touti Moumen sums up the importance of the film: "*The Dawn* was a film that had to be made, firstly because we needed a film that was 100% Tunisian, and secondly—considering Algerian cinema and what it has produced in terms of films on the war—it needed to be a film illustrating the struggle for independence against French colonisation, and Omar Klifi has responded to this challenge."[133]

There were obvious technical problems, as Khlifi was operating with a crew of whose members none had previously worked on a feature film and with a cast of actors who had never before appeared in a fictional film for cinema release. Tunisian critics, at the time of its release, had mixed reactions. They all saluted the effort, while being aware of the deficiencies. Several of them wished it had been the film they themselves could conceive—but Khlifi had made his own film. Perhaps the best account is that of Victor Bachy:

> It was the first Tunisian feature: it was long awaited. People expected too much, hoped too much of it. In anticipation, everyone had imagined it in their own way. *The Dawn* is not filled with the spirit of revolution, it does not exalt a national epic. *The Dawn* is not full of vibrant anti-French hatred, nor is it a catalogue of the misdeeds of colonialism. *The Dawn* is not a lyrical firework glorifying the martyrs. . . . It is an episode in the very simple life of three militants, who are not depicted as out-right heroes, but who participated with discretion and self-sacrifice in the general movement of clandestine insurrection. They did not know where the orders came from or who gave them. But they carried them out confidently, blindly. They were simple Tunisians.[134]

The Rebel / Le rebelle / Al-moutamarred (1968) is a film that looks back at the internal struggle against tyranny in southern Tunisia in the 1980s and was received with even more reservations by Tunisian critics. One called it "a pseudo-historical Tunisian western: acceptable in terms of its genre."[135] Again Victor Bachy gives a more balanced account: "The narrative is driven by a single man, Salah, turned into a rebel, initially by family matters, then by national issues. Next to him are two women who remain a little in the shadows but determine his conduct: His mother, who reminds him of the offense to the family honour which he must avenge, and a young Bedouin woman ready to love him. The character of Salah forms the film's structural axis. Except for the opening sequence . . . the editing of the film is straightforward and chronological."[136]

Khlifi was quite open about his intentions with his third feature, *The Fellagas* / *Les fellagas* / *Al-fallaga* (1970), which traces stages in the liberation struggle and post-independence conflict with the French from 1951 to 1961: "Firstly, I have to say that I'm not inclined to shoot protest films, because I don't they [*sic*] would get released. . . . What's the point of making films no-one will see? *The Fellagas* does not claim to paint a picture of the Tunisian revolution: it simply tells a real-life story. . . . For the moment, I repeat, I want to make films that get seen. That's my objective. Afterwards, we'll see."[137]

Khlifi wants to discuss issues of national identity, but only in the form of conventionally constructed films designed primarily to offer entertainment. In this case, *The Fellagas* is a further variant on the tale of a young man Mosbah, for whom domestic problems lead to a sense of rebellion that is channeled into fighting for the national cause. Along with his rival, Ali, who married the woman Mosbah loved in spite of her protests, he is killed in the last battles of the war.

Screams / *Hurlements* / *Çurakhh* (1972) is a fresh departure for Klifi. Leaving behind the world of male commitment to the cause of independence, he focuses instead on a story about two daughters, as told by their mother. Shot on a miniscule budget, it is a film intended to shock its audience: "It's a question of awakening people's consciousness. Of course, certain ancestral practices cannot vanish from one day to the next, but filmmakers can certainly contribute to progress being made."[138] The action is set at a time deliberately not defined: this could be a cautionary tale from the past or it might be contemporary rural Tunisia. Saadia fought off the man who raped her and subsequently killed him. She is condemned to death by the village elders. Selma loves Hédi but is threatened by a forced marriage by her father. She goes mad when she finds Hédi, who has returned to rescue her, drowned and dead at her feet.

For once the critics were virtually unanimous, as the selection of 1973 and 1974 reviews compiled by Touti Moumen makes clear. Halim Chargui has reservations, but "*Screams* seems to me the best of the author's four films." For F. B. (in *El Moujahid*), "It's an absolutely detestable and completely marvellous film. In fact, you detest it at one moment because it hurts, troubles, disturbs. And you immediately love it, because what it says is true and it therefore reassures you." M. S., a reviewer in Tehran, writes: "*Screams* is a clear and striking work on the condition of Tunisian village women and on a society whose backward-looking ideas and beliefs Omar Khlifi attacks." Abd-Essatar Latrech is equally full of praise: "We can never thank our friend Omar enough for having shot *Screams*, a work which honours our young cinema." For Abdelhamid Gmati, "The contributions and qualities of the film are numerous, situated on three levels: the script, the photography and the direction." For Monique Hennebelle, finally: "*Screams*, Omar Khlifi's fourth film is without doubt his best, on both the visual and the political level. . . . The violence with which Omar Khlifi denounces the oppression of women because of out-dated ancestral customs is unexpected."[139]

There was a fourteen-year break before Khlifi's final return to filmmaking and his old subject matter with the resistance tale, *The Challenge / Le défi / Al-tahaddi* (1986), coproduced, as one of its last films, by SATPEC. In presenting his film, Khlifi wrote: "This is an authentic film, whose protagonists are still alive and which values authentic acts of bravery. It's my own choice to deal with men, militants on the ground. An action film in Tunisia hardly corresponds to our reality and we cannot compete with the latest American or Italian series. . . . I believe that it is our duty not to forget and to show to the young and not-so-young certain aspects of our struggle for national independence."[140]

As Klifi's own words make clear, this is a return to the world chronicled in his trilogy. The style is much the same, though this time there is a budget enabling helicopter shots to open and close the film. This is a film that is always shaped as an action film, with little concern for period detail (it is set in 1952). If the shooting is sometimes a little clumsy, the approach at times somewhat naïve, and the music often overemphatic, there is no doubting where the director stands on the issues with which he deals. *The Challenge* shows the director's continued respect for the characters whose activities he follows and again reveals his sincere commitment to the cause of Tunisian independence.

Since this date, Khlifi has pursued a new career as the sometimes controversial chronicler of contemporary Tunisian political issues.

*

At the end of the 1970s and beginning of the 1980s, SATPEC produced or coproduced some remarkable feature debuts, such as, in 1982, those of two European film school graduates, Taïeb Louhichi and Mahmoud Ben Mahmoud. Their shift away from everyday reality and toward formal abstraction, points to one of the new directions Tunisian cinema would take in the later 1980s and early 1990s. Though their first features could hardly be more different, both are major works that obtained international success, a trajectory their directors never quite matched in their subsequent highly accomplished work. Both directors have interspersed their feature film production with significant documentary work.

Taïeb Louhichi, who was born in 1948 in Mareth in Tunisia, studied at the IFC and the École de Vaugirard in Paris. His debut work, *Shadow of the Earth / L'ombre de la terre* (1982) is a seemingly simple but, in fact, highly sophisticated work for which he assembled a team including two key collaborators who would themselves direct major feature films before the end of the decade: Nacer Khemir (who designed the film) and Moufida Tlatli (who edited it). The film tells of an isolated rural family community—patriarchal father, with his sons and nephews and their families—whose life is slowly but inexorably torn apart both by natural forces and by the impact of the modern world. The decline of the community is reflected in the gradual departure of the men (who, one by one, emigrate with their families or are conscripted into the army), until the patriarch rules over a community lacking in able-bodied men and therefore no hope of economic survival.

During the opening sequences the general air is that of a sympathetic documentary or ethnographic study (Louhichi has a doctorate in sociology). Even here at the beginning of the film, there is no attempt to individualize the characters. The fate of the community—rather than the destinies of the individual family members—is at the center of the film, yet the community's precise status is left undefined. We are never told specifically that we are in Tunisia, and the city harbor at the end of the film is unnamed. The sense of abstraction is enhanced by the fact that, though the rural camp is situated on the border of another country, this, too, is never specified. The border is, we are told, a locus of war, but the activities we see—from a distance—are ambiguous incidents apparently involving border police and smugglers. The film as a whole is a beautiful, slow-moving elegy for the passing of a traditional way of life. Ill equipped to cope with modernity, the characters are as little likely to prosper in the city or abroad as in the arid wasteland where they were born. There is, quite simply, no way out. Fittingly, the film ends with the frozen image of a coffin, in which the body of the elder son, who had chosen emigration, is being returned to his family.

Despite the realism of its detail, *Shadow of the Earth* is an abstract fable with universal application. Louhichi's later work explores a variety of styles and subjects. *Leila My Reason / Layla ma raison / Majnoun Layla* (1989) is a reworking of the classic Arabic love story of the poet Qays and the beautiful Leila. The setting is again a timeless desert community, but this time the emphasis is not economic survival but the traditional notion of family honor. When Qays returns home from his travels at the beginning of the film, he is hailed as a poet and welcomed into his extended but closely knit family. The marriage between Qays and his beautiful cousin Leila, who are known to love each other, is agreed to by the two fathers. But Qays cannot remain silent; poetry proclaiming his love—not only praising Leila's beauty, but also celebrating her body—pours out of him. This is anathema in a traditionally minded society, resulting in his future father-in-law feeling himself and his family dishonored and breaking off the engagement.

Leila My Reason is full of lushly photographed desert landscapes through which, from the opening images of Qays's return, individuals and groups are endlessly making their way. The photography is sharply focused and excellently framed, but there is no actual dramatic development and very little for the two leading players to do, apart from look increasingly anguished. The outcome is totally predictable. The two families are driven apart and not even an emissary from the ruling prince can bring them together again. Qays's madness steadily increases, until he is a virtual hermit in the desert. Leila pines and is unable to re-create the happiness of her former life when she is married off. Eventually (but very elegantly), Leila dies and Qays follows her, his poetry looking forward to their reunion in another world. Surprisingly little use is made in the film of Qays's poetry, though it is the key feature in the plot, and nowhere is there any repost to the poet's equation of passion and madness.

Moon Wedding / *Noces de lune* / *Urs al-qamar* (1998), by contrast, is a contemporary tale of friendship and betrayal set in present-day Tunis. A group of five rich and idle young people enjoy a sense of freedom, closeness, and friendship in agreeable surroundings. Almost as a joke, they they bring together Pierrot and Madonna, a pair of seemingly ill-suited lower-class contemporaries (he has mental problems, she is illiterate) and arrange their marriage. This proves to be the film's turning point. While the couple comes ever closer together by helping each other, the group itself falls apart. Tensions emerge, quarrels develop and one of their number is killed. But there is no real resolution, and the death goes unprobed and unpunished. For Louhichi, "The young people are not to be condemned. I blame them for nothing. They are victims. They must be forgiven, they needed to be understood before they commit the murder." Though Louhichi wanted to play with some of the codes of the thriller in this film, his own relation to violence is distinctive: "Our youth isn't violent, and if there is violence it is silent, deaf, interior. It is expressed in ways other than bloodshed."[141]

Wind Dance / *La danse du vent* (2004) is a more introspective piece, dealing with the thoughts and imaginings of a film director (played by Mohamed Chouikh) lost in the desert while exploring locations for his new production. In 2006, Louhichi was seriously injured in a car accident, which left him wheelchair-bound. But in 2014, he was able to make a fifth feature film, *Child of the Sun* / *L'enfant du soleil*. This begins with a group of three young people (two boys and a girl), who have been drinking in a nightclub, breaking into a house and making themselves at home there. They are confronted by the owner, a writer who is now confined to a wheelchair. One of the group, Yannis, thought he recognized his own family in the writer's last novel, and so what began as a seemingly random break-in becomes a search for identity.

Mahmoud Ben Mahmoud was born in 1947 in Tunis and attended INSAS in Brussels. Feeling this training was too concentrated on technical matters, he took further courses in art history at the Free University of Brussels.[142] His first feature, *Crossing Over / Traversées* (1983), is a most sophisticated and universally relevant parable about emigration, exile, borders, laws, and bureaucracy. Like Louhichi, Ben Mahmoud created a production team involving several of his fellow filmmakers (and some of those about to become filmmakers): Selma Baccar as executive producer, Moufida Tlatli as editor, and Fadhel Jaïbi as lead actor. Unlike that of *Shadow of the Earth*, the setting of *Crossing Over* is precisely located—a cross-channel ferry sailing between Ostend and Dover—and the passing of time is noted minute by minute on the screen. Crucially, the film begins on December 31, 1980, when two travelers attempt to land at Dover but are refused admission into the United Kingdom. By the time they reach Ostend on the return voyage, it is January 1, the start of a new bureaucratic year. Their visas have now expired, and they are unable to disembark. The film (based in part on Ben Mahmoud's personal experience) plots the very different but parallel stories of the two refugees, a Polish working-class dissident and an Arab middle-class intellectual.

Temperamentally, they are very different, with the extrovert Bogdan always trying to involve himself with others, while Youssef remains silent and haughtily aloof. A possibility of escape seems briefly to offer itself in Ostend, but after an adventurous night ashore, both are back on the ferry the next morning. Separated by language, class, and culture, they are unable to find common ground, and each goes his own separate way. The Pole—in despair—indulges in the suicidal shooting of a British policeman, while the Arab retreats into an inner world, strengthened by a casual, but intense, sexual encounter. A settled life in Western Europe is never a possibility in this Kafkaesque tale, which moves with total narrative logic from the almost documentary style of realism at its beginning to Youssef's inner world of myth and imagination at its conclusion.[143]

Ben Mahmoud went on to make three more features. *Chichkhan / Poussière de diamants* (1992, codirected with Fadhel Jaïbi) is a deliberately dark and enigmatic work, much closer in style to Jaïbi's earlier collaborations with Fadhel Jaziri than to *Crossing Over*. Jaïbi's theatrical background is very clear in the concentration of the action in a limited number of largely interior spaces, often at nighttime, and the heavy reliance on dialogue. Many of the shifts and changes, which might normally be expressed through facial expressions and gestures in cinema, are here verbalized in the wealth of dialogue the film contains. Paradoxically, in a film that is so claustrophobic, the characters are always haunted by other worlds and other times, particularly by Italy—origin for some, destination for others. One key to the narrative is the fact that the old aristocrat Si Abbes's closest friend and neighbor, who has just died, was Pippo, an Italian who had settled in Tunis with his wife and sister.

The two directors, who cowrote the film, consistently and deliberately hold back information. It is only much later in the film that we learn the identity of the young thug who attacks Si Abbes in the precredit sequence and seems to know him intimately. It is, in fact, his illegitimate son—the product of an encounter with his fiancée's maid—a child, we are told, he has never acknowledged. But we never hear his side to the story and have no knowledge of the son's life before the point when he turns up to assault his father at the beginning of the film.

The film's cutting often adds to the mystery. Does Si Abbes's old love, Pippo's sister Renata, actually throw herself from the upstairs window after saying she wishes to look at the sea again, just after she and Si Abbes have been reminiscing about their affair decades before? The cut away from the scene is too quick for us to know this for certain, though Si Abbes's son talks enigmatically of her death toward the end of the film. Throughout the film, it is not merely factual information but also the characters' reactions to fresh and unexpected developments that is kept from us in this way. Here, for example, we are not shown the reactions of the other people in the room at the time, including Si Abbes himself.

Similarly, what is the meaning of the *chichkhan*, the jewel that gives the film its title? Was it in fact stolen by Si Abbes from his Italian neighbor? How is it to be defined? Touti Moumen's attempted answer only poses new questions: "Chichkhan, this coveted jewel, where does it come from? What is its origin? Is its origin Arab, Spanish, Berber, Greek, or . . . ? It is all things at once. This jewel, is it not the memory of Tunisia, a multi-cultural, multi-facetted Tunisia?"[144] The passing of the jewel from hand to hand—given by Si Abbes to Kinza, returned by her, then given again only to be discarded, found by Kinza's daughter, and returned by her to Si Abbes—seems to parallel the emotional shape of the film. But finally (and we are never told how) it ends up in the son's hands, and he simply discards it (though he is, he tells his father, desperately in need of money.

In the climate of uncertainty the film creates, we can never be sure of the characters' own inner feelings or their unstated relationships with others. The son aggresses Si Abbes and threatens to burn his flat down, but he weeps inconsolably at what he thinks is his father's deathbed. Does Si Abbes really mean what he says when he aims a shotgun at his son and threatens to kill him if he ever returns? And what of Kinza? It is she who rescues Si Abbes when he collapses after his son's attack. She drives him home and is given the *chichkhan* by an evidently besotted old man as his way of thanking her. When she mocks his infatuation, telling him he needs a girl of fifteen, she can hardly be thinking of her own teenage daughter, Rym. Yet it is Rym who forms the closest relationship with Si Abbes. When she returns the bracelet, she announces she wants to stay the night with him and sleep in his arms. This is a troubling moment, as we have just seen Si Abbes sexually abuse a young woman hardly older than she is. Kinza'a attitude toward Rym's growing affection for the sixty-eight-year-old is as hard to fathom as her own actual feelings for Si Abbes. *Chichkhan* is a demanding and disconcerting film, not least in its view of the impenetrability of human emotions.

The Pomegranate Siesta / Les siestes grenadines / Kouaïl erroummen (1999) was written in Brussels and intentionally presents—through its principal protagonist—an outsider's view of contemporary Tunisia. Ben Mahmoud is keen to make clear that he visited Tunisia four months before the shooting "and tested the script against reality. There is a moment when the script has to come out of the computer and be tested against the real."[145]

The film's title refers to the season of the year when that fruit ripens, traditionally a mellow season. As the film twice shows, pomegranates are also used to predict a person's fortune: open one without spilling a seed and you will be rewarded with good luck. After living in Senegal for ten years, during which time she has been kept from contacting her French mother, the teenage Soufiane is brought back to Tunisia by her father, Wahid, who wants to make her "a real Tunisian." But, as the film's opening sequence of Soufiane dancing on the plane with a black music group hints, Wahid has miscalculated. In keeping her from her "white" European mother, he has introduced his daughter to real African culture—she is referred to on one occasion as that most paradoxical of entities, "a white negress." She has great difficulty in fitting into Tunisian society, which she sees as inherently racist.

Wahid, too, finds reintegration more difficult than he had thought. After ten years, the old values no longer hold in Tunisia, and Liman, the friend he relies on, cannot be trusted. For him the season is far from mellow, as his life gradually disintegrates. He had seen himself as sacrificing his life for his daughter, but now he has to admit that there have been too many silences (about his mistress), too many lies (about his ex-wife, Muriel, who has been seeking all along to contact Soufiane), and too much blind faith (in Liman). For Soufiane, this is a period of self-discovery, including a brief affair with Liman's son, Charfik, who has deserted from his military service, and the prospect of meeting her mother again after so many years. Wahid's choice of upbringing for the daughter he loves has made her into a forceful, outspoken, assertive young woman who is no longer willing to follow her father's lead. The film ends as it began, with Soufiane expressing her individuality through dance.

The Pomegranate Siesta touches on a wide range of themes—immigration, emigration, the rural exodus, old cultural values, and new dynamic fusions. But Ben Mahmoud's principal concern is with examining Tunisia's place in the African world, at a time when the nation's black roots are being denied. As he himself has said: "If *Chichkhan* represents a bridge extended towards Europe with which we willingly share at least the Mediterranean heritage, *The Pomegranate Season* is a had [*sic*] extended towards black Africa and an invitation to less arrogance towards this continent."[146]

The Professor / Le professeur / Al-oustadh (2014) was shot during the Arab Spring, which led to the ousting of President Ben Ali, but deals with an earlier period, when Ben Ali first rose to power as director general of national security.

According to the official, synopsis: "Ahmed Hafiane plays Khalil Kalsaoui, a university law professor appointed by the government to head Tunisia's League of Human Rights, a largely toothless talking shop whose chief purpose seems to be whitewashing state oppression and undermining the 'red gangrene' of Communist opposition. An urbane and respectable married man in public, Kalsaoui is also having [an affair] with one of his radical, young students."

Stephen Dalton, who provides this synopsis, notes that "Ben Mahmoud shoots this thoughtful suspense drama in straight, sombre traditional style. . . . Hafiane is especially impressive in his pleasingly layered, prize-winning portrait of a suave apologist for tyranny slowly facing up to his own guilt, hypocrisy and moral vacancy."[147]

Interspersed with Ben Mahmoud's later feature output are a number of video documentaries, many of them striking pieces of historical research. *Albert Samama Chikli* (1996) examines the extraordinary life of the Tunisian film pioneer who explored every aspect of photography, including aerial and underwater photography, before discovering the cinema, becoming the Lumière Brothers representative in Tunis, and organizing the first film screenings there. With the aid of his daughter, Haydée, the film explores Chikli's ventures into filmmaking, first in documentary and then with fictional films. While still a teenager, Haydée not only wrote the scripts of Chikli's short fiction, *Zohra* (1922), and the feature-length *The Girl from Carthage / La fille de Carthage / Aïn el-ghazel* (1924) but also appeared in the leading roles. She subsequently had a role in Rex Ingram's *The Arab*, but she had to refuse Ingram's invitation to Hollywood, as her father insisted that she stay in Tunis to finish her *baccalauréat*.

The Beys of Tunis / Les beys de Tunis (2006), which chronicles the complicated history of Tunisian regal rulers, was similarly made in collaboration with the descendants of the family, in particular Prince Fayçal Bey. Having succeeded in freeing the country from direct Ottoman rule, the beys established Tunisia as a nation, only for it to be taken over as a French protectorate in 1881. They achieved a great deal, from the abolition of slavery in 1846 to the banning of polygamy (the last act of the last beys). But in the mid-twentieth century, they had to cope not only with the French but also with a German invasion, which was quickly overthrown after the Allied landings. More complicated still was the beys' relationship with growing Tunisian nationalism, spearheaded by the Destour Party. While Moncef Bey achieved great popularity for his support of the national cause, others, such as his successor Lamine Bey, were accused of collaborating with the French. In 1956, Tunisia became independent as a constitutional monarchy, but within a year, the great advocate of independence, Habib Bourguiba, proclaimed a republic (giving himself untrammeled power).

Ben Mahmoud's full feature-length study of Arabic music, *A Thousand and One Voices / Les mille et une voix* (2001), begins on a personal note. It was inspired by the director unexpectedly hearing his father's voice when visiting his grave (it later transpired that a record he had made was being used in a tutorial group). It is Ben Barka's own voice that guides us on a journey of exploration that investigates the various branches of Sufi musical tradition, each founded as a specific discipline by a particular founding father (often a religious poet, of whom the best known is Jalal al-Din al-Rumi). The journey does not begin in Tunisia, since the Sufi tradition is now moribund there. Instead, the film opens at the Al-Azhar mosque in Cairo and then moves on to very different traditions in Radjastan and Istanbul, where the ancient art of the whirling dervishes is still preserved. As in *The Pomegranate Siesta*, Ben Mahmoud is fascinated by Africa south of the Sahara, and his voyage takes him to the annual Baye Fall musical celebrations in the Senegalese city of Touba, where a fresh Sufi-inspired tradition was founded by Sheikh Hamadou Bamba. The festival currently draws two million pilgrims a year. After a brief return to Cairo, the film ends by citing the Prophet himself: "Allah never sent us a prophet who did not have a good voice."

From his very first feature, *Crossing Over*, Ben Mahmoud has been concerned with borders and, more particularly, with what is contained within borders. The first exploration of this theme—a Slav and an Arab trapped together on an English cross-channel ferry—is a personal recollection, a matter of individual circumstance, rather than an issue of wider significance. Ben Mahmoud grew up in a multicultural Tunisia, where Arabs, Jews, and Christians belonged to the same community and had lived side by side for centuries. Independence, together with wider Middle Eastern developments, has created a very different Tunisia, and the director is concerned to probe some of those aspects of Tunisia's rich history that are wiped from the official records. These include the now vanished Italian community (dealt with in the 1992 Italian-commissioned documentary, *Italiani dell'altra riva*); the final ties with a Russian émigré community, which once numbered six thousand (*Anastasia de Bizerte* [1996]); the links with black Africa (*The Pomegranate Siesta*); the influence of the beys, who ruled for centuries (*The Beys of Tunis*); and even Tunisia's role in the birth of cinema (*Albert Samama Chikli*). His own rediscovery of his Sufi background (though he now lives a secular life in Belgium with a French wife) came with the commission to make *A Thousand and One Nights* and is a personal response to growth of Islamic extremism. As Ben Mahmoud has rightly observed, when questioned about his residence in Brussels, "My roots are in Tunisia and I continue to draw my inspiration from that country. . . . My situation as an emigrant allows me to have a distance and yet to preserve the links to popular spaces which were mine when I lived here. . . . Geographical distance can give a filmmaker in exile a pertinence which may be lacking in those who do not live abroad."[148]

*

Long before Fadhel Jaziri played the lead in *Crossing Over* and Fadhel Jaïbi cowrote and codirected *Chichkhan*, both had been actively collaborating on theater and film projects. Jaïbi, who was born in Ariana in Tunisia in 1945, studied at the Sorbonne, the Institut des Études Théâtrales de Paris, and the École Charles Dullin. He founded his first theatrical company in France. Jaziri, who was born in Tunis in 1948, followed his first performances in Tunis with further study in London. In 1972, the pair founded the Théâtre du Sud in Gafsa and then moved to Tunis, where, in 1976, they were key members, alongside Jalila Baccar, Mohamed Driss, and Habib Masrouki, in the collective that founded the Nouveau Théâtre de Tunis. Three of the group's productions were videoed and two filmed for cinema release. In turning to film, the group's explicit aim was to renew Tunisian cinema, which members described as hovering between a "Zorro" level and a "zero" level and "to narrate through fables the relations between people, class relations, sexual relations."[149]

The Wedding / La noce / Al-urs (1978) was a free adaptation of a 1919 one-act play by Bertolt Brecht, *Die Kleinbürgerhochzeit* (known in English as *A Respectable Wedding*). The film proved a critical success abroad but flopped in Tunisia, where, as they wryly confessed, they had thought "that they going to beat imperialist productions in their own field."[150] *The Wedding*, which opens with the Kurt Weill song *Mack the Knife* sung in German, has a visual style that borrows from German expressionism and the work of Fritz Lang. This was the contribution of Habib Masrouki, who shot the film and who studied cinematography at IDHEC in Paris. Shot on 16mm and in black and white, but with a very elaborate sound track, the film makes few concessions to the audience. It was shot in a single location (an old and crumbling flat) and concentrates claustrophobically on a couple alone for the first time on their wedding night. The camera focuses implacably on their words and smallest gestures as they spend the night discussing sexuality and jealousy, potency and failure, life and fantasy—more like an old married couple than newlyweds. It is a film unlike any other in Tunisian cinema, except *Arab*, which followed ten years later.

Jaïbi and Jaziri are credited as coauthors of *Arab / 'Arab* (1988), another adaptation of a play first produced by the Nouveau Théâtre de Tunis. This time, they shot in 35mm color and with international financial backing. Yet the film has the same claustrophobic atmosphere as *The Wedding*, having been shot largely in a deconsecrated basilica on a hill at Carthage just outside Tunis, built by the French and representing for the authors "the Occidental umbrella which protects and decimates at one and the same time."[151] Jalila Baccar again plays the lead, this time as an air hostess, Houria, who arrives in Tunis to seek news of her lover, who has disappeared, from the last person known to have met him, Khélil, a photographer wounded in the fighting in Lebanon. The film is not a realistic account of current political events but a fable in which Houria is transported back into the

Arab past, a time of chivalry but also of fatal rivalries, abductions, jealousies, and honor killings. In the course of a very complicated action, the characters kill one another, with only Houria left alive. At the end of the film, she flies back to Lebanon, pregnant with Klélil's child. Despite the many deaths, the directors claim that *Arab* is "none the less a film of hope. You have to have reached the extreme of tragedy and violence for change to be possible."[152] As its title indicates, *Arab* sets out to question Arab identity—not to show the fate of individuals, but to point to the collective failure of Arab culture, as expressed both in its historical past and in its present wars and conflicts.

Since the end of their collaboration, Fadhel Jaïbi has made one other screen adaptation of one of his plays, *Junun / Démences* (2005), while Fadhel Jaziri has made a film record of one of his theatrical spectacles, *Hadhra* (2001), featuring Sufi music and dance, and a first solo fictional film, *Thirty / Trente / Thalathoun* (2007).

*

The international reputation established by Tunisian filmmakers from the late 1980s onward is partially due to two supportive factors: the funding from the French Fonds Sud Cinéma, which began in 1984, and the emergence of innovative and creative independent producers in Tunisia after the collapse of the government organization SATPEC. The later feature work of Louhichi and Ben Mahmoud consistently received Fonds Sud funding, as did that of all the other innovative Tunisian directors who emerged in the late 1980s and 1990s—in all, about thirty feature films made by around twenty filmmakers received such support. Among the new producers, the key figure was Ahmed Attia.[153] He produced the first films of four major new directors who have very different histories and showed distinctive personal approaches when they turned to feature filmmaking: Nouri Bouzid, Ferid Boughedir, Moncef Dhioub, and Moufida Tlatli. Though all four of these Tunisian directors made strikingly successful debut features, only Bouzid has been able to establish himself with over half a dozen features in thirty or so years. In addition to his own features, his screenwriting skills enabled him to help launch the careers of his three contemporaries.

Nouri Bouzid, born in Sfax in 1945, has a complex past—training at INSAS in Belgium and extensive work as an assistant on foreign features shot in Tunisia, as well as five years imprisonment for left-wing political activities. He is the director who most clearly combines the decade's key themes of intimacy and sharp political critique. With seven feature films directed since 1986 and contributions to the scripts of six others (including the first features of Ferid Boughedir, Moncef Dhioub, and Moufia Tlatli), he has emerged as a major figure in Maghrebian cinema. He denies that any of his films are autobiographical: "I don't make films to tell my life story. Believe me, that direction does not interest me at all."[154]

But given what we know of his background—enduring torture in prison for example—it is difficult not to see his films as having autobiographical elements, though this form is rare in Arab cinema. They are also examples of what he promoted as a "new Arab realism," colored by the 1967 Arab defeat in the war against Israel. The aim of the new filmmakers was, in Bouzid's view, "to subvert norms, refuse prohibitions and unveil sensitive areas such as religion, sex, the authorities, the 'father figure.'"[155] Bouzid's own first three films (all produced by Ahmed Attia)—*Man of Ashes/ L'homme de cendres* (1986), *Golden Horseshoes / Les sabots en or* (1989), and *Bezness* (1992)—feature damaged male protagonists who are defeated by experiences rarely mentioned in Arab or African cinema: childhood sexual abuse, torture, and male prostitution.

Man of Ashes brings a quite new tone to Maghrebian filmmaking in its focus on two troubled young men, Hechmi and Farfat, growing up in Bouzid's native city of Sfax. We gradually discover that they share a common past: as ten-year-old carpentry apprentices, both were raped by their foreman, Ameur. This is an experience that has shaped their entire lives, and neither is now at home in a society dominated by the aggressive attitudes of their fathers. Crisis looms for both of them on the eve of Hechmi's arranged marriage. Farfat, thrown out by his father, becomes more and more erratic, even throwing himself into the river at one point, while Hechmi finds the thought of his wedding night hard to cope with. One of Bouzid's audacities is the choice of an old Jew, Monsieur Levy, the carpenter for whom Ameur worked and who knew nothing of the assaults, as the one adult to whom Hechmi can talk openly. The scene between the two of them is central to the film, in terms of both meaning and structure, a lament for a lost age of innocence when Tunisia had a mixed culture of Arabs, Jews, and Europeans.

From this point on, the film becomes much darker in tone and with many scenes now played out at night. Levy, who has treated Hechmi as a son and is the only nonaggressive older man in the film, dies. The supposedly respectable Arab fathers are all violently abusive in some way: Ameur raping his charges, Farfat's father disowning him, and Hechmi's beating him physically, an aggression to which the young man makes no response. A visit by Farfat, Hechmi, and some of their drunken friends to a brothel run by the old woman Sejra, a former beauty and relic from the same era as Levy, is not a success. The evening ends with Farfat relieving some of his self-hatred by stabbing his abuser, Ameur, to death. The more introspective Hechmi, however, is left as troubled as ever. There is no hint in the film that he will ever be able to shape his own fate: the wound to his body and mind can never be healed. He remains a fixed, submissive character, forever mutely recalling an act that can never be undone.[156]

Golden Horseshoes was described by Bouzid in 1994 as his favorite film— "it's the film closest to my heart, my existence and my life"—but insists that it is not autobiographical: "There's a little of me in all the characters, but it's not my life. . . . Maybe it's even a film against myself."[157] But though he uses several distancing devices—a protagonist very different from himself, a voice-over in which the protagonist talks of himself in the third person—the sense of direct, lived pain is one of the film's strongest qualities. The former political activist Youssef Soltane returns to Tunis in winter, when everything is wet and cold, after two years in hiding, six years in prison, and another two years since his release. The chosen time is the festival of Ashura, which has a double face: "It celebrates the salvation of the prophets. . . . Soltane, who saw himself as a prophet, will not be saved, [but] Ashura is also the night on which Hussein, the Prophet's grandson, was murdered. That's why there's lots of blood in the film."[158]

There is, in *Golden Horseshoes*, a total unity of protagonist, plot, and style. Structurally the film reflects Youssef's efforts. As he tries successively, but in no perceptible order, to pick up the broken pieces of his life, so too the film sets off, seems about to make a significant breakthrough, and then falls away, only to start again on another track. The actions do not fit together to form a coherent whole: over and over again the film gets itself under way, only to shudder to a sickening halt. There is no creation of suspense and no possibility for a successful resolution of the action. The film is shaped as a succession of encounters, almost all of which are broken up by memories or imaginings of past events and circumstances: with his mother; his youngest daughter; his wife, Zeinab; his son, Adel; his elder daughter; and, finally, his brother, Abdallah, an Islamic fundamentalist, with whom he has his bitterest exchange.

Everything we see and hear in the film relates directly to him, but significantly there are no images that relate to even an imagined future; Youssef is caught between a past that no longer makes sense to him (he has no answer to those who treat his ideas as outdated and mock his former ambition to shape, as an intellectual, the rule of his country) and a present with which he cannot connect. His only real personal contact is with his old friend and mentor, Sghaier, whose basement is the sole location left untouched from the past. But when the pair venture out to buy more wine, they encounter a dark and labyrinthine world largely in ruins.

Memories of past torture now fill Yossef's mind, and even a passionate chance sexual encounter cannot remove the pain. Bouzid's audacious handling of this nude love scene, like his treatment of the torture sequence and the shots of animal slaughter, shows to what extent his approach to the body is key to the intense physicality of his cinema: "The body is the key to one's identity. I'm all for a cinema of the body."[159] One of the strongest unifying features of the film, lifting it out of a purely realistic mode, is the recurrent paralleling of Youssef's tormented life with that of the crippled white stallion that serves as a symbol of endangered freedom and gives the film its title. The figure of the horse recurs regularly in the narrative, sometimes as a dream image, sometimes as a nightmare reality. At a rare moment of peace in the film, when the dissidents are together before their capture, we hear the song (from a prison poem written by Bouzid himself): "Run, run over the waves, you lovely horse." The song returns during the sequence with Sghair and, most important, at the very end of the film, when the symbolic role of the horse is unambiguous. We see shots of the horse galloping free and hear once more the Arabic song with its simple musical accompaniment: "Would you be surprised to know / That your shoes were made of gold? / Run, run, over the waves, you lovely horse."

Bezness traces the interaction in the tourist resort of Sousse of three characters, each of whom is given his or her short spell of voice-over to reveal dreams and doubts, aspirations and frustrations, that are illustrated in the ensuing scenes of dramatic interplay.[160] The first we meet is the French photographer Fred, who gets lost in the old city but is rescued by a small boy who becomes his companion. He is here on a photo assignment to document the *bezness*, the young Tunisian men who prostitute themselves to the (mostly older) foreign tourists, men and women indifferently. When Fred emerges onto the beach, he can capture the image that most perfectly epitomizes the clash of cultures that underlies the film's action: two attractive young women emerge side by side from the sea—one a topless tourist, the other a Tunisian woman covered from head to foot in traditional dress. Fred tells himself he is here to understand this alien culture, to pierce the invisible veil, but in fact, he finds himself drawn to a beautiful young woman, Khomsa, whom he meets by chance. Her plight is very clear: she is in love with Roufa (Fred's young companion's much older brother), who expects her—like his sister—to follow the traditional rules in her own life while accepting that he works as a *bezness*. Roufa's situation is the most problematic. Whatever excitement his job once gave him has long gone. He is growing too old for this kind of work, the tourists are too knowing, and even his dreams of settling in Europe are now fading.

The film shows all Bouzid's skills at weaving together narratives, and there are scenes of real intensity. Roufa, the archetypal Bouzid hero, is tormented by a wasted sixteen years but has nowhere to go. All his anger is ultimately directed at himself, and though he circles Fred menacingly on his motorbike, he makes no move against him. *Bezness* shows all Bouzid's immense skills as a writer-director, but it lacks the emotional intensity of the two previous works, and Bouzid has made the reason very clear himself. While he was deeply involved with the fate of Hechmi and Youssef Soltane, Roufa leaves him cold: "I had no sympathy for these *bezness*, for their universe, for their way of behaving and speaking."[161]

By breaking taboos in this way, Bouzid gave realist cinema in Tunisia an unprecedented edge and bite, and the emotional involvement with the tormented male figures is often intense. Perhaps because he was tired of being asked about how autobiographical his first three films were (even *Bezness!*), Bouzid's subsequent feature focuses on female protagonists. An even stronger influence was Bouzid's work coscripting Moufida Tlatli's *Silences of the Palace*.[162]

Bent familia / Tunisiennes (1997) is a study of three women who come together in their shared efforts to find space for themselves in a male-dominated world. The film opens in an archetypal female space—the residence of a clairvoyant who listens to the women's stories, gives them charms and amulets, and basically tells them to submit and accept God's will. The film's central figure, Amina, is the familiar Arab victim, pale and troubled, neglected and deceived by her husband. Her sister, Meriem, by contrast, is fat and bubbly, quite happy to be a subservient woman in a male world, complacent with marriage and all it brings. She longs only for a son. Amina's old friend Aïda has carved out a very different life for herself. She is an academic, divorced for seven years now, with a Palestinian lover but no plans for remarriage. Always positive and optimistic, she strives for an independent life, but, as a single woman, she has to face the continual rebuke of most of the men she encounters, even that of her young son. The fourth woman, Fatiha, is even more forthright but has very different and deeper problems as a refugee from the civil war in Algeria. As a trio of women seeking space in a male world forms, she replaces Meriem as the third.

Bouzid's approach is clearly illustrated by the events in the film: "What I observe, what I see, in the street, in everyday life, is that the aggressions, the demands, the provocations of all sorts are, above all, directed at women."[163] The film does not have a particularly strong dramatic plot—nothing is actually resolved for the three women—and its structure has been aptly described by Amira Ben Youssef as "a sort of motionless road-movie."[164] But it does contain a succession of beautifully constructed and powerfully acted scenes. There is the family dinner party, the tone of which is captured in Amina's father's idea of a joke: "Women are like cars: test the upholstery and the motor, never buy second-hand, and keep everyone else away from driving it." At home, Amina is brutally raped by her husband, who then goes out for dinner with a whore. The three women's joint outing ("like bachelors") to a beach visually dominated by an abandoned shipwreck offers a welcome interlude, as they wander through the ship, exchanging confidences and intimacies, even telling each other painful truths. Most moving of all is Fahita's account of a girl's (Fatima) murder that she witnessed in Algeria and has left her scared of men. The monologue is so powerful that it some ways it unbalances a film otherwise mostly concerned with more everyday aggression toward women, particularly as it is followed by a scene of Amina at the mirror examining her face for signs of aging. There is no resolution as such to the film: the prejudice against women's freedom is as strong among boys (like Aïda's son) as it is in Amina's uncomprehending husband (who sees himself as a liberal). Many women, including Amina's mother and sister, are complicit. Yet Fahita gets her visa, and Aïda will no doubt hold her life together;

however, there is every indication that Amina, after being abused and punished in her own home, will go back to living—in even greater daily fear—with her husband.

Clay Dolls / Poupées d'argile (2002) focuses on young girls from outlying villages sold into domestic service in Tunis, an operation organized by Omrane, a typical Bouzid protagonist. He wants to do good but has failed and is an alcoholic. His role toward his charges is totally ambiguous: he wants to be their protector, but he is the one who puts them in danger. He sets out to find and help Rebeh, the most rebellious of his protegées, who has left her employer, but he is accompanied on his journey by the eight-year-old Fedhah, the latest of his victims. Fundamental to the film is Bouzid's view of the gulf in Tunisian society between Tunis and the rural areas, where there are only two sources of income: making clay pots and selling their daughters into service in the capital: "The trade in domestic servants seems to me to reveal all that and more. It is, at one and the same time, informal, unrecognised, scattered and widespread. Though masked, it is at the heart of Tunisian society."[165]

At the center of the film is Rebeh (played by Hend Sabri, who made her debut in Moufida Tlatli's *Silences of the Palace*). She is Bouzid's most striking female character. As he has explained: "I have always been attracted by individuals who escape, or find themselves driven out of family structures which are patriarchal, extremely strong and dominating. Inevitably they find themselves marginalised, problematic, conflictual, carrying their own conflicts within themselves and, paradoxically, strongly rooted."[166]

The violent male world of drinking and fighting, where male "honor" is paramount, is vividly depicted in all its squalor. By contrast, in Rebeh, Bouzid offers a striking portrait of a sexually active young woman: rebellious, provocative, and genuinely sexy (as in her dance scene). She cannot be contained or imprisoned, but at the same time, she has been abused and is four months pregnant. In the bleak world of Bouzid, the despair is so deep that there is hardly the possibility of narrative progression, let alone the possibility of a positive outcome. *Clay Dolls* is a film full of energy, tightly focused on its main characters and a powerful addition to the director's œuvre.

Making Of (2006) is Bouzid's most unexpected film in terms of both structure and subject matter. The title employed for the film has a double meaning. "Making of" is the term customarily used in France for short documentaries about the shooting of a film, often found accompanying DVDs. It also, of course, has the normal English connotations of shaping, forming, creating. But we only find the real significance of both meanings later on in the film.

The opening gives a vivid portrait of disaffected young people in Rades in 2003, at the time of Iraqi war, which is experienced as a humiliation by all Tunisians and especially the protagonist, Chokri (who calls himself Bahta). The young people move around in rival gangs and are noisy, vulgar, and competitive, spraying grafitti on walls and indulging in petty crime. Their passion is break dancing, at which Bahta excels, but their public displays of this bring them into conflict with the police. Bahta has the customary family life of a Tunisian adolescent: a doting mother and a stern father, who beats him brutally when he catches him stealing from his grandfather's wallet. Bahta has no job; a sort of relationship with his well-brought-up girlfriend, Souad (who passes her *baccalauréat*, while he fails his); and an all-consuming dream of immigrating to Europe. His cousin is exactly the opposite: quiet, polite, and considerate. He serves in the police force and is at home in Tunisian society. After Bahta has been arrested for causing a public scandal and is humiliated yet again, he dresses in his cousin's uniform and enacts a splendid harangue, in the role of a policeman, at the clients of the local café, who, oddly enough, do not recognize him.

Up to this point, Bahta has been a typical Bouzid protagonist, unable to fit into society and constantly facing defeats and humiliations, screaming his frustrations at the sea on a dark night. But compared with the physical abuse suffered by Hechmi and the torture endured by Soltane, the frustration of Bahta's dream of Europe seems comparatively trivial. Yet after the café scene, the plot takes a dramatic and unexpected turning. Bahta's peformance has attracted the attention of two bearded Islamists previously unseen in the film. Presumably recognizing his vulnerability beneath the swagger, they introduce him to a middle-age stonemason who gives him a bed and a job. Father figures are customary in Bouzid's films, but this one is different: he sets about what will be the long task of converting Bahta to fundamentalist Islam. The indoctrination is largely verbal, and Bahta seems an unlikely choice for the role for which he is being prepared. The concepts are totally alien to him (he does not even know who Nasser was or what the word "adultery" means). But the encouragement, the questioning, and the lessons get under way, beginning with the doctrine that dancing is a sin.

At this point, and to the spectator's initial bewilderment, the film breaks down. The actor Lotfi refuses to say his lines and to participate further in what he describes as "a dangerous game." Lotfi is confusing his own situation with that of the character he is playing. The director, Nouri, has to be called, and the shooting is interrupted. Bouzid is troubled by the mess and says this will be his last film. But almost immediately (before we have got over our shock), the film resumes with Lotfi in the role of Bahta, trying vainly to organize his departure for Europe, suffering a fresh humiliating beating, and then resuming his work as an apprentice and struggling to come to terms with questions of world politics and religion.

At this point, again unexpectedly, the narrative breaks down as Lotfi demands a discussion with the director. This allows Bouzid to give his own understanding of the Koran and its place in modern life, to explain that his film is not anti-Islam but antiterror, and to express his own (secular) views on the necessity of separating religion from politics. It would seem that Lotfi has not been given a full script, so the situations that are new to Bahta are new and unexpected to him, too. When Bouzid finishes, the action resumes again, this time with work on the monuments in a graveyard and a discussion of martyrdom that Bahta initiates. It is clear that the teaching is having a great effect on him, and he begins to want to take on the role martyr.

The narrative now breaks down for the third and final time as Bouzid has to explain to Lotfi the difference between a film and reality. If Lotfi is identifying with Bahta and feeling his fears, then this is all the better for the film. But Lotfi is not convinced: he believes more and more that the film is a monster. When the action resumes, Bahta prepares himself for martyrdom, but he is judged not to be ready and is not given a mission. When the Islamists, who now see him as a danger to themselves, lock him in an unused winery, Bahta cracks up. The final scenes of the film, after he finds a cache of explosives and escapes, are a plunge into madness, involving ever more vicious confrontations with those nearest to him and a climax in which, fleeing from the police, he blows himself up. The final credits are accompanied by a somewhat enigmatic song: "Be who you want, but be a country for us."

Though the film won the *tanit d'or*, the top prize, at the JCC in 2006, *Making Of* is, at the very least, an awkward film. It is directed with the characteristic Bouzid energy and gives the familiar close view of the characters' emotions. It treats a major theme in contemporary Arab culture and is structured to surprise us at every turn. Bouzid has consistently said that his task as director and scriptwriter is not deal with problems and bring solutions but to provoke the spectator to think and to interrogate the situations he depicts. But *Making Of*'s premise, that a breakdancer blocked from getting to Europe can be turned by verbal arguments into a potential suicide bomber, seems dubious. The three interventions by Bouzid in the film also seem to convey personal uncertainty about the undertaking rather than constituting a Brechtian distancing effect. What the film most certainly constitutes is the most spectacular plunge into despair and madness undergone by any Bouzid protagonist.

Hidden Beauties / Millefeuille / Ma nmoutech (2012) is a return to the female world that Bouzid explored with such success in *Bent familia*. The idea of the project, cowritten with Joumène Limam, predates the Arab Spring, and it originally dealt with two young women's differing views on virginity. Noting the revival in the wearing of the hijab—even in Tunis, where it had been previously almost unknown—Bouziz resurrected the project, now to be focused on differing responses to the wearing of the veil.[167] The film opens and closes with images of male violence, beginning with the killings associated with Ben Ali's initial attempts to stamp out the protests and ending with interfactional disagreements among the Islamist extremists as the fall of the government is announced. But the film is essentially the story of two young women, cousins and close friends, living in Tunis and working in a local *pâtisserie*.

Aicha, who works downstairs in the kitchens to support her two younger sisters, is happy to wear the hijab. For Zeinab, on the other hand, who works as a waitress in the café, going bareheaded is essential to her sense of her own free identity. Everything changes when Hamza (Zeinab's brother and Aicha's fiancé) gains his release from prison. For him, the fact that Zeinab refuses to wear a veil and works in a café makes her little better than a whore. He receives support from his mother and aunt (though significantly not from his father) and also, less expectedly, from Zeinab's fiancé, Brahim, a French-based businessman. It would seem that Hamza had dealings with the Ben Ali administration, but after his release, he sees the Islamists as his best commercial bet. Aicha finds herself in the opposite situation. Hamza, to whom she remains deeply attracted, tells her she should give up work, though he is unable to offer any financial support. Meanwhile, her boss is pressuring her to renounce her veil and work in the café upstairs as a waitress.

Nothing is resolved in *Hidden Beauties*. The Arab Spring brings fresh hope but also leads, paradoxically, to new and unwelcome pressures on young women. As so often in Arab society, when patriarchal values are reasserted, it is older women who provide the physical support, attempting to put young women— even their own daughters—"back in their place." For Bouzid, the early 2010s were a time of intense complication. In 2011, he was awarded France's highest honor, being made a chevalier de la Légion d'Honneur at the Cannes Film Festival. The same year, he was placed on a death list by the Tunisian fundamentalist Islamist party, Ennahda, and was attacked by a young activist who stabbed him in the head. The director's inner turmoils are very apparent in *Hidden Beauties*, made at this time and released in 2012. Bouzid himself takes on the role of the blind accordion player Ammou, who is one of the anonymous victims of violence associated with the Arab Spring. Throughout the film we see disconcerting shots of a male body being washed and prepared for burial. Only toward the end of the film do we realize that this is Ammou and, at the same time, Bouzid enacting his own death. Explaining the circumstances after the release of the film, Bouzid said: "It's my way of replying to the death threats I received after the revolution."[168]

Bouzid's cinema has always been a physical cinema, in which the body is the focal point. One example among many would be the meticulousness with which Bahta prepares himself for martyrdom in *Making Of*. Bouzid has admitted that, as a child, he loved the Italian spectaculars featuring imported Hollywood stars with Tarzan-style physiques, such as Gordon Scott and Steve Reeves, playing the legendary heroes like Hercules and Maciste.[169] But his own cinema is not about such triumphant heroes. His is a cinema of male defeat: "All my films talk about people's humiliation, how they are broken. They are all wounded characters. I did

not want to be demonstrative. I wanted it to remain at the level of emotion: entering the characters' depth and solitude, without explanation. I'd like the spectator
to be trapped into identifying with these characters."

Hechmi, Youssef Soltane, Roufa, Omrane, Bahta—even Majid (Amina's husband in *Bent familia*, who is humiliated, despite his outward success, when his
wife challenges him)—all correspond to this type, as Bouzid sets out to under-
mine the myth of the strong Arab male. None is a match for the women whom
they are so often able to dominate or exploit, thanks to the patriarchal traditions
of Arab society. *Hidden Beauties* explores the new parodoxes of male dominance
as Tunisian society moves away from the dictatorship of President Ben Ali. The
other major characteristic of Bouzid's cinema is that the filmmaker becomes a
witness: "I lift the veil on society. I unveil what is hidden."[170] He has also said
that his role "is to raise even more problems, to interrogate, to shake people's tor-
por, to instil doubt."[171] Bouzid is very happy to confront taboo subjects head-on,
and his adherence to these principles with seven features in some thirty years is
exemplary.

Ferid Boughedir, who was born in 1944, received no formal film training
but codirected a feature, *Murky Death / La mort trouble*, with the Frenchman
Claude d'Anna in 1970. Boughedir is the complete cineast: feature filmmaker,
documentarist, academic, film historian, and critic. Boughedir's *Halfaouine /
Halfaouine, l'enfant des terrasses* (1990) was an equally striking debut as Bouzid's
Man of Ashes—though in a totally different register. This striking comedy is one
of the most popular films ever made in the Maghreb and certainly the greatest
box office hit in Tunisian film history. It is fresh, funny, and inventive. The hero,
Noura, is depicted at just that point where his small stature allows his unsuspecting mother to continue to take him to the women's baths (or hammam), while
he is in fact, like his taller friends, developing a growing obsession with women's
bodies. Inevitably, his true motivation is eventually discovered, and he is expelled
from the hammam. He spends the latter half of the film attempting to rediscover
the world he has lost and eventually succeeding. *Halfaouine* is not a film concerned with the manipulation of time and the creation of suspense. It follows a
totally predictable pattern, moving gently from the initial arousal of sexual interest to the gratification of desire with the body of a beautiful, submissive young
girl. Boughedir is open about the autobiographical aspects of the film. It was
"very largely inspired by events I personally experienced in Halfaouine, the old
popular district of Tunis'"[172] This first autobiographical feature is neither a precise historical reconstruction nor the depiction of contemporary issues. Rather,
the film's aim is to create a timeless, dreamlike world of childhood and the subsequent acquisition of experience.

But there is another autobiographical thread, as the film's coscriptwriter,
Nouri Bouzid, points out. Boughedir "celebrates the act of becoming a man in

discovering the female body. It's interesting, you could almost say that about cinema. Cinema is the art of discovering and seeing: this can be an aim in itself, and it's Ferid's cinema."[173] Indeed, in the four successive scenes that have the hammam (or its reconstruction) as their setting, we have a metaphor for the birth of a filmmaker: moving from a childish, indifferent gaze to a more focused look, on to spying (looking—or trying to look—without being seen), and then finally to a restaging (with suitable props) of the paradisiacal space that has been lost.

As in several of Bouzid's films, the protagonist of *Halfaouine* has an amiable father figure, in Noura's case, the shoemaker-cum-poet Salih, a drinker and womanizer. It is by watching Salih seduce his aunt Latifa that Noura learns the lessons that he proceeds to apply to the family's beautiful young servant girl, Leila. She is a willing participant in his game of re-creating the hammam at home (she is desperate to know all about this essential woman's space) and ends up naked in his bed. The next morning, Noura is totally reinvigorated, defies his father, and leaps across the rooftops of the old quarter. This gives the film a seemingly appropriate ending, at a first viewing. But, on reflection, it is less satisfying, since, as the sociologist Fatima Mernissi has observed, seduction "is a way of seeming to give yourself and of procuring great pleasure without actually giving anything."[174] Noura shows absolutely no concern for the young girl, who is returned in disgrace to her family because of his actions.

Boughedir's second feature, *One Summer at La Goulette / Un été à La Goulette* (1995), is a study of three families—Muslim, Catholic, and Jewish—living by the sea at La Goulette in Tunis in the 1960s. The film's tone is set by the opening song celebrating La Goulette (reprised at the end of the film) and by a gang of boys spying on the local Muslim religious leader, Hadj Béji. They are happy to accept the story that he is unmarried because he has murdered seven "inappropriate" fiancées and buried them in his garden. The bulk of the film comprises the boisterous interactions at home, on the streets, in the local cafés, and at a wedding of three families that have been linked since childhood. But domestic strife is provoked by the three adolescent daughters—Meriem, Gigi, and Tina—each of whom chooses to fall in love with a boy from a different religious community. But it is the shadowy figure of the hadj who dominates the community, claiming religious authority. Known as the "double hadj" because he has been to the Middle East twice (without, it would seem, ever actually reaching Mecca), he is also a ruthless property developer. He takes an inappropriate sexual interest in his "niece" Meriem, persuading her family that she should be veiled. At the film's climax, she takes her revenge by stripping naked in front him, causing him to fall dead at her feet.

One Summer at La Goulette is a noisy and disjointed work that includes a return to the community of Claudia Cardinale, Tunisia's most celebrated actress, in a locally celebrated but narratively irrelevant and anachronistic sequence. A final title, locating the film's action as ending on July 4, 1967, underlines that this is a world that will be swept away by global events. The film is uneven but remains a deeply felt plea for tolerance that contains the warmth, humanity, and humor so characteristic of all Boughedir's work.

Another strikingly original film, with a mood quite the opposite to those of Boughedir, is *The Sultan of the Medina / Soltane el medina* (1992). The director, Moncef Dhioub, was born in Sfax in 1952 and is a product of the Tunisian amateur film movement (Fédération Tunisiennes des Cinéastes Amateurs, [FTCA]). He worked in street theater and puppetry before making a series of three remarkable short films that gave him an international reputation.[175] In *The Sultan of the Medina*, the timeless world of the Tunis medina is depicted as bleak and hostile, static and cut off from modernity, and full of mysteries and enigmas. The film is essentially a fable involving two innocents in a violent, enclosed, male-dominated world, racked by gang rivalries and power struggles. The medina is a world of cruelty to the weak (a cripple, for example) and violence toward women (a bride locked up so her virginity cannot be lost). Moments of humor—such as those involving an old man employed to paint out the nipples on film posters—are rare. Fraj is the holy fool of Arab legend, able to move through the male world of the medina as well as through the women's world (but only naked, like a small child, to be used by women seeking curses or spells). His counterpart, Ramla, is an innocent virgin, with dreams of leaving her medina prison for a prince's palace. This is not destined to be. Hesitating on the threshold of escape, she is raped and destroyed by her future husband's own men through his connivance. *The Sultan of the Medina* does not have the easy accessibility of *Halfaouine*—it is bleak and uncompromising, a black tale of defeat. But it is crisply made, with good performances from its actors and with the sense of control one would expect after Dhouib's short films.

The director has, however, directed only one subsequent feature, a light-hearted comedy, *The TV Is Coming / La télé arrive* (2006), made fourteen years later. The film's premise, Robert Lang informs us, "is self-reflexive, much like that of a Hollywood backstage musical. When the municipal cultural committee of El Malga in southern Tunisia hears that a German television company is planning to make a documentary in their dusty, rural village, they busy themselves with the preparation of events, including a pageant representing three thousand years of Tunisian history." In addition to its primary aim of creating an amusing comedy, the film can also be read as an allegory. To cite Robert Lang again, "The allegorical form, which plays here in registers of ambiguity, ambivalence, and contradiction, allows *The TV Is Coming* both to uphold the myth of Tunisia as a historically progressive state and to undercut this narrative at the same time."[176]

The fourth major filmmaker to emerge in the late 1980s and early 1990s is Moufida Tlatli, who was born in 1947 and is a graduate of IDHEC and a one-time trainee in French television (ORTF). What makes her unique is that she worked for eighteen years as a film editor with many of the leading Arab filmmakers—Abdellatif Ben Ammar, Taïeb Louhichi, Mahmoud Ben Mahmoud, Ferid Boughedir, Nacer Khemir, Merzak Allouache, Farouk Beloufa, and Michel Khleifi—as well as three very significant female directors making their debuts: Selma Baccar, Néija Ben Mabrouk, and Farida Benlyazid. Tlatli's debut feature, *Silences of the Palace / Les silences du palais* (1994), is a study of relationships within a family—reflecting the director's thoughts about her own mother and her concerns for her teenage daughter. Like *Man of Ashes* and *Halfaouine*, *Silences of the Palace* is a deeply felt look at the past while not being directly autobiographical.

Maghrebian female directors tend to be more influenced by Egyptian cinema than their male colleagues—several record having regularly watched Egyptian movies on television as children, at home with their mothers—and Tlatli's debut film is consciously structured as a melodrama. It involves a typical interplay of past and present, tracing the instinctive revolt of a young singer, Alia, who returns to the palace where she grew up and where her mother, Khedija, was a servant. Other standard features of the melodrama also play a key role—the importance of the musical score, the uncertainty about the protagonist's parentage, the use of surprise (as when Khedija suddenly emerges as an oriental dancer) and coincidence (Khedija enjoys the delicate love of Sid Ali and is raped by his brother on the same day).

Equally important is the way in which space is used in the film. The divisions of space in Arab culture express, in Fatima Mernissi's phrase, "the recognition of power in one part at the expense of the other,"[177] and this distinction is a key feature of the film's structure. The division between the upstairs of the palace and the servants' quarters is absolute, and the masters visit the latter space only to demand services or to give orders. There is the constant and very explicit threat from upstairs to the young Alia's virginity. Khedija's death from a failed abortion forms the film's downstairs climax. The Tunisian princes, the beys, compromised by their collaboration with the French protectorate, display a veneer of culture, but this cannot disguise their sense of absolute power. The servants mount the kitchen stairs only to offer the services demanded of them, including sexual ones. The disregard of any individual female identity is most shocking when the bey Si Bechir rapes Khedija (his brother's mistress) before her daughter's eyes while openly contemplating taking the daughter too at some point. But nothing is said; no complaint is raised. As the old housekeeper Khalti Hadda tells Alia at the end of the film, "We were taught one rule in the palace: silence."

The early part of the narrative of *Silences of the Palace*—up to the midpoint, constituted by the rape of Khedija—is devoted largely to the lives of the servant women and the personal relationship of mother and daughter. The beginning of serious political discussion comes only after the rape, when the comments of the servants listening to the radio in the kitchen ("if the bey leaves, the country is lost") are paralleled by comments upstairs on the bey's precarious situation and the condemnation of the nationalist song, "Green Tunisia." Political information increases, spread by the radio: "Upheavals and riots are spreading throughout Tunisia. The French government has refused to receive the nationalist delegation. There have been demonstrations for independence in several cities. A nationwide strike has been declared."

The powerful climax of *Silences of the Palace* brings together the passing of the beys, the death of Khedija, the freeing of Alia, and the independence of Tunisia. At the end of the film, Alia explicitly compares her life to Khedija's: "Like you I've suffered, I've sweated. Like you I've lived in sin. My life has been a series of abortions. I could never express myself. My songs were stillborn." *Silences of the Palace* demands to be read as another instance of the "national disenchantment" of which Hélé Béji wrote so eloquently in 1982.[178] But Tlatli does not end without hope. Rediscovery of the past together with the recovery of her mother's story make Alia determined to keep the child Lotfi wishes her to abort: "This child, I feel it has taken root in me. I feel it bringing me back to life, bringing me back to you. I hope it will be a girl; I'll call it Khedija." A new future, however painful, begins. We can see Alia as a symbol of Tunisia. As Zahia Smail Salhi notes, looking back on the film ten years after it was made, *Silences of the Palace* is an invitation for women of her generation "to take the achievements of yesterday's revolution towards new horizons through a new social revolution."[179]

The Men's Season / La saison des hommes (2000), Tlatli's second feature, has an even more complex twenty-year time scale but was less successful, perhaps because the lead actors were required to play themselves both as newlyweds and as adult parents one and two decades later. The focus is characteristic of Tlatli: a group of women of varying ages on the island of Djerba joined in unity, their mutual friendships compensating at least in part for the absense of their menfolk, who spend much of the year living and working in Tunis. Their return constitutes the "men's season" of the title. A key figure in the film is the autistic son of one of the women; his situation is totally ambiguous, in that he both liberates his mother (through his gender) and imprisons her (through his disability). The film is full of beautifully realized scenes reflecting both the difficulties caused by lives lived largely apart and the surprises for the women, who find an unexpected independence and self-realization in this lifestyle. The film is audaciously edited and ends with a typical Tlatli multiple climax (here bringing together childbirth, seduction, and marital reconciliation). The film is a tribute to women's survival of years of lack and longing and confirms Tlatli as a major director.

*

There are two additional Tunisian directors, both born in the 1950s, who made their appearance in the mid- to late 1990s: Mohamed Bensmaïl and Mohamed Zran. Both studied in Paris and have spent much of their lives there, but their trajectories have been very different. Ben Smaïl came to direct his sole feature film after establishing his career as an actor. Zran, by contrast, was trained in filmmaking and, during the 1990s and 2000s, has completed major work in both documentary and fiction.

Mohamed Bensmaïl was born in 1953 in La Goulette. He studied drama at the Université de Paris VIII and in Los Angeles and subsequently worked as an actor—playing the lead, for example, in Mehdi Charef's *Miss Mona* (1987). He also starred as a director in his own debut feature, *Tomorrow I Die / Demain je brûle* (1998). The film follows the trajectory of Lotfi, who has lived in France for a dozen years or more and has a French wife and two daughters in Paris. Lotfi, visibly ill from the outset, has returned to Tunis in order—as we eventually discover—to die in his native country. He meets up with his parents and family, but there is no way of rekindling old relationships; he terminates all his encounters abruptly. When he seeks out his childhood haunts, he has a number of chance meetings, but again nothing of significance occurs. He is not, it seems, in a position to make true human contact and becomes increasingly an observer of, rather than a participant in, Tunisian life. As Sonia Chamkhi concludes, "His final quest is to bear witness to the absurdity of two worlds, that of his origin and that of his exile, which condemns men and women to despair and disenchantment."[180]

Mohamed Zran, who was born in 1959 in Zarzis and studied filmmaking at ESEC in Paris, has a more substantial output. He followed his graduation piece, *Comma / Virgule* (1987), with two more noted 35mm short films, *Le casseur de pierres* (1989) and *Ya nabil* (1993), both dealing with aspects of immigration. He made the feature-length documentary, *The Song of the Millennium / Le chant du millenaire* (2002) between his two features, *Essaïda* (1996) and *The Prince* (2004). More recently he has completed a second feature-length documentary, *Being Here / Vivre ici / Zirziss* (2010).

Both Zran's documentaries begin in his hometown of Zarzis. *The Song of the Millennium* uses Zarzis as the starting point for an exploration of the length and breadth of Tunisia at the beginning of the millennium. Aware that the country is experiencing rapid change, he tells us in an opening voice-over that he felt an urgent need to bear witness, to wander through the country without plans or preparations: "Tunisia is all mine. And I need to film today something true to myself, something which can reconcile me to my country."

In all, he visits over a dozen locations that, frustratingly, are not named or identified by region, even in the end credits, though the names of the principal interviewees are given there. Zran is keen to allow his interviewees the chance to give their views directly to the camera. He does not appear in the shot during the interviews, and his questions are heard only when he is dealing with children. Though the film ends in Tunis, its principal focus is on rural Tunisia, where life largely follows the traditional pattern, though oddly discordant or incongruous aspects of modernity intrude. The film ends somewhat inconclusively in the capital city, largely around Avenue Bourguiba. Though we meet a poet, Ouled Ahmed, who published a slim volume of verse in 1992, there are no substantial interviews to bring out the current situation in the capital or to contrast urban and rural life in Tunisia.

The Song of the Millennium deals with ordinary people leading ordinary lives. The range of interviewees is pleasingly wide, the landscapes often beautiful. Though most have (often severe) financial difficulties, they remain remarkable cheerful and optimistic. Many of them are reconciled to a life of toil and take a pride in their work. Both men and women are committed to their families, and none are attracted by city life. But virtually all, adults and children alike, have a project to undertake or a dream to cling to. Mohamed Zran offers here a vivid and positive kaleidoscope of Tunisian life.

Being Here is presented by Mohamed Zran as a "documentary-fiction," but it is not apparent how much fiction the film contains. The characters play themselves, but how far the film was prescripted is not immediately clear. Unlike *The Song of the Millennium*, which offers a broad-based portrayal of rural Tunisia for which Zarzis is the starting point, the new film presents itself as an intimate portrait of Zarzis itself. There is no unified narrative as such and certainly no dramatic highpoints. Instead, Zran offers a patchwork of events in the lives of seven characters, to whom nothing much happens in the weeks in which the film was shot. Some talk directly to the camera—though Zran himself is neither seen nor heard—but most are filmed in their everyday interactions and conversations. Apart from those in the chemist shop of the main character, there are very few domestic scenes. Instead, we see lives lived in the community and shared by people who see each other every day. The mood is captured by the cheerful, lyrical musical score provided by Amin Bouhafa.

The central figure is Simon, a Jew who, with the help of his daughter, runs the chemist's shop that serves the local inhabitants. He has done this for some fifty years, supplying a wide range of goods and providing traditional medicines for humans and animals. He is confident enough in his cures that he proposes to ask for payment only after the patient has recovered. Most of the characters are his clients; they come by to make their regular purchases, meet, gossip, do deals, or indulge in (rather incoherent) philosophizing. As Zran says, "He embodies the unerring attachment to the local collective memory."[181]

The themes of Zran's two documentaries, showing Tunisians caught between poverty and aspiration, are remarkably similar. And in *Being Here* he succeeds very well—though perhaps in a slightly oblique way—in his stated ambition "of using a small town like Zarzis to grasp the deep changes and upheavals which societies of the South are experiencing because of internal and external factors . . . changes which are experienced as a confrontation between tradition and modernity."[182] The filmmaker's sympathies are always with those who continue to respect their local traditions, and here he offers a vivid range of well-differentiated portraits.

Zran's first fictional feature film, *Essaïda*, is one of the few features to concentrate on class differences within Tunisian society. Essaïda is the popular quarter, situated on the outskirts of Tunis, which is largely inhabited by people drawn to the capital because of rural poverty. Zran, who had lived for fifteen years in France before making this film, tells us that it all stems from a chance view from a window in a flat overlooking Essaïda, a district totally unknown to him at the time. In a similar way, the film's protagonist, Amine, a fashionable but dissatisfied painter, is struck by the appearance of an adolescent, Nidal, and follows him back to his home in Essaïda. In many ways, Amine is a projection of the filmmaker himself: Westernized, cosmopolitan, and artistically gifted but needing inspiration from an environment quite alien to his own and hence needing to draw, too, on the lives of the local inhabitants of Essaïda to nurture his art. Perhaps some of the film's occasional awkwardnesses stems from this closeness of filmmaker and main character.

Though Zran maintains his opposition toward social differences and his support for artistic integrity, the film, as it unfolds, loses some of its clarity, with the plot plunging toward melodrama: Nidal's involvement in crime grows, which leads eventually to his death, and a symbolic figure, a blind old man full of poetic wisdom, is introduced. *Essaïda* remains a remarkable first feature, providing insights into aspects of Tunisian life mostly ignored in Tunisian cinema and offering a reflection on the role of the artist (painter or filmmaker) in providing truth within a fundamentally divided society.

There is also a social gulf between the two leading characters in Zran's second feature, *The Prince*: Adel, an apprentice flower-seller on Avenue Bourguiba, and Donia, the maturely beautiful, divorced manager of a bank situated near his place of work. In this film, the two are linked not by artistic aspiration, as in *Essaïda*, but by the power to dream the impossible (and to hold on to that dream). Zran does not see dreaming as an escape from reality. Instead, for Adel, whom the director describes as "having the characteristics of an artist, a creator," dreaming is "a way of rejecting abdication to social and emotional wretchedness."[183] The links between Zran's two films are close, to the extent that *The Prince* also has a symbolic blind man, this time one selling mirrors and calling to passersby to stop and see themselves as they really are. For Zran, Avenue Bourguiba plays a crucial role in the film, allowing him to focus on the key aspect of his project: "Asking myself about the identity of Tunisians today, faced with the profound changes to our society in the era of globalisation."[184]

Zran has cast his film as a comedy, full of little moments of misunderstanding and humorous confusion. It concentrates on a handful of individuals, but it has the clear aim of raising wider issues in Tunisian society. This is in line with Zran's earlier films, and a concern with wealth and poverty, with tradition and the demands of modernity, is common to all his films. Zran shows clearly that he has both a deep concern with, and an original approach to, the depiction of Tunisia's problems.

*

Female pioneer directors began to emerge very slowly in Tunisia during the 1980s and 1990s, and only Moufida Tlatli, who served as editor on both *Fatma 75* and *The Trace*, achieved a truly international reputation. Three other female filmmakers—Selma Baccar, Néjia Ben Mabrouk, and Kaltoum Bornaz, all born in the 1940s—were able to make first feature films, but all three experienced hindrances in their careers. Both Baccar and Ben Mabrouk had to wait several years for their debut features to be shown to the public, their release being blocked by the censors and / or the state film production organization, SATPEC. Kaltoum Bornaz did not experience delays with the actual release of her first feature, but she had to wait until 1997—when she was fifty-two—to be able to set it up.

Selma Baccar (sometimes known as Salma Baccar), who was born in Tunis in 1945, had her first experiences of cinema in the context of the Tunisian amateur filmmaking movement, which flourished alongside (and independent of) the state filmmaking organizations. Her first short film, *The Awakening / L'éveil* (1964), characteristically about women's issues in Tunisia, was made within this context. Subsequently, she studied psychology at Lausanne in Switzerland, no doubt fulfilling her parents' wishes, and then filmmaking at the IFC in Paris, undoubtedly her own choice. After completing her studies, she worked for a while for Tunisian television and in various production roles on shorts and feature films, including Mahmoud Ben Mahmoud's *Crossing Over* and Néjia Ben Mabrouk's *The Trace*.

One of President Habib Bourguiba's most widely recognized achievements after independence was to give Tunisian women a new legal status (unique in the Arab world) and to offer young women the same educational opportunities as their brothers. It would have been expected therefore that Baccar's sixty-minute docu-drama, *Fatma 75*, begun in 1976 and dealing with the history and role of women in Tunisia since the times of Carthage, would have met with official approval, and indeed, it did receive some government funding. After its opening, the film concentrates on three stages of development: the 1930s, the pre-independence period, and the situation since independence in 1956. Our guide through these stages (who gives the film its title) is a young fictional student at the University of Tunis in 1975, Fatma Ben Ali, who is preparing her thesis on the topic. The film's mixture of fiction and documentary reflects Baccar's view that there are no barriers between the two genres, and one of her major concerns was "to maintain a homogeneity despite the different genres employed."[185]

The credits of *Fatma 75* acknowledge and thank Habib Bourguiba for his role in promoting women's equality. But as Florence Martin observes, "It also showed that the condition of women in 1975 constituted 'the logical end point of a long history' . . . and that in progressive Tunisia there was still ample room for improvement (for example, women did not have equal pay, and when applying for a passport, they needed their husband's authorization)."[186] President Bourguiba was apparently not pleased with these observations, and the film was banned from screening in Tunisia until 2006, though a copy was smuggled out for limited foreign screenings.

Baccar has since gone on to make a number of television series and two fully fictional features a decade apart. *Dance of Fire / La danse du feu / H'biba M'sika* (1995) begins with a group of Arabs drawn to a Jewish circumcision ritual by the power of the singer's voice. This is our introduction to Habiba Msika, a historical figure to whom Baccar was attracted on two counts: firstly, "as an excuse for the representation of the condition of women from various aspects, Tunisian and Jewish, woman and artist at a moment when this is not yet habitual in people's ways of thinking," and secondly, because the life of Habiba Msika (who was all of these things) allowed her to portray "a search for the absolute, in relation to this woman's freedom and her creativity as an artist—an artist who exceeds her own limits and the limits of society."[187]

In 1928 Tunis, Msika is a star who crosses the barriers into the world of men—she is a thoroughly Westernized figure who openly smokes and drinks alcohol. Though in so many ways an outsider, Msika has her own group of admirers—nationalists, artists, journalists, and poseurs. This is a very different Arab world than that which emerged after the foundation of Israel. Jews and Arabs mingle freely, and Mzika is invited to perform before the bey of Tunis. She is the mistress of a rich man, Mimoumi, who gives her jewels but who becomes a hostile force in the background when she rejects him for the shy nationalist poet Chedley, who, for a while, becomes her next lover.

Her fame growing, Msika travels to Berlin and Paris, in both of which she finds a traditional world in turmoil (with the first signs of the rise of the Nazis in Germany, for example). In Paris, she finds a new lover (the ambiguous playboy Pierre) but is most attracted to her better-known (in the West at least) contemporaries: Sarah Bernhardt, Isadora Duncan, and Loie Fuller, models she strives to emulate. Ironically, it is in Paris, too, that she makes her first real discovery of Arab poetry and song. On her return to Tunis, she is welcomed and resumes performing. Bad reviews merely incite her to be more provocative still, and the result is the dance of fire, which comes as a real shock for her audiences. But while still at the height of her fame, her personal life begins to fall apart, and Mimoumi reemerges to set fire to her as she lies sick in bed. This is, in a sense, the inevitable ending for anyone who leads a flamboyant lifestyle—it can only end badly. As Baccar herself says, "The dance of fire is a dance of death. The dance prefigures her death. She is like a moth who knows it will burn if it goes too near to the light, but cannot help itself from doing so."[188] *The Dance of Fire* is a remarkable work, both for its celebration of a star little known in the West and its re-creation of her performances. It also draws a fascinating and detailed picture of the Arab world of the 1920s, so different from that of today.

Flower of Oblivion / Fleur de l'oubli / Khochkhach (2005) is also a narrative about a woman addressed specifically to women—and Tunisian women in particular. It deals with the possible effect of giving opium (*khochkhach*) to mothers to ease the pain of childbirth, a practice once common in Tunis. As Baccar records, "My mother drank *khochkhach* when she gave birth to us. So did my aunts. So did my grandmother." Addiction was rare (none of her family suffered from it), but Baccar decided to explore this possibility.[189] *Flower of Oblivion* is "the story of Zakia, who is forcibly sent to a psychiatric asylum to cure her addiction to the opium tea she started to drink when she gave birth to her daughter, Meriem, some twenty years before. Her stay in the hospital constitutes a framing narrative which spans eight to nine months, in which the story of her life is embedded, narrated via flashbacks in a nonchronological order."[190] This narrative is located—mostly through radio broadcasts—as occurring during the short reign (1942–43) of one of the most popular of Tunisia's beys, Moncef Bey. For a full, if highly theorized, account of the film, see Florence Martin's *Screens and Veils*.[191]

In 2011, Selma Baccar began a new stage in her career when she was elected to the National Constituent Assembly as a representative of one of the newly emerged democratic parties, Al Massar, of which she subsequently became president.

Néjia Ben Mabrouk, who was born in El Ouediane in 1949 and studied French language and literature at the University of Tunis, went on to study filmmaking at INSAS in Belgium. She grew up in southern Tunisia, "in a village in which most residents were French or Italian. Since there were only a few Arabs, we were allowed to go to the local movie theater. So I became familiar with European cinema very early. . . . Every Friday at school [at the local cinéclub] I got to watch the great films in the history of cinema: Eisenstein, Griffith and of course the French classics."[192] At the age of fifteen, she read an article in *Les Temps modernes* about the Czech director Vera Chitilova and, realizing for the first time that a woman could become a film director, decided that this was to be the path her own career would follow.

There was no hindrance from her family, who were supportive of education for their daughter as well as for their sons. Her father gave his permission (despite his low opinion of filmmaking, which his viewing of Egyptian cinema had reinforced). Her mother had always wanted to be an actress and was able to fulfill this ambition by appearing in her daughter's film.[193] After graduating in Tunis, Ben Mabrouk moved to Belgium, where she financed her own film studies in Brussels at INSAS, where she was the only woman (Arab or otherwise) in the classes she attended. She graduated in 1975, with her short film, *To Serve You / Pour vous servir*, and worked for a while in Belgian television. She has lived in Brussels since the 1970s and has Belgian nationality.

Ben Mabrouk's first and so far only feature, *The Trace / La trace / Sama*, was difficult to set up in Belgium, though she received support from the German television company ZDF, from her fellow student Michel Khleifi (through his personal company Marissa Films), and, eventually, from SATPEC in Tunisia. It was a legal dispute with SATPEC that caused the delay of the film, which was shot in 1982 but released only in 1988, with fresh participation from Ben Mabrouk's own aptly named production company: No Money Company.

The Trace is a tale of a young woman's struggle for the education that she feels from an early age will be what will give her life real meaning. Ben Mabrouk was seven when independence was achieved in 1956, yet suprisingly there is no reflection in *The Trace* of any of the changes in society or women's lives brought on by President Bourguiba's policies; it is far from being a celebration of the new opportunities she herself experienced. Instead, life for the film's heroine, Sabra, is a chronicle of the successive obstacles for women in a traditional society. *The Trace* seems in so many ways an autobiographical work, with the protagonist following Ben Mabrouk's trajectory from a mining village in the South to study in Tunis and then abroad. But Sabra does not get to enjoy the discovery of cinema that shaped Ben Mabrouk's own life: she is denied the opportunity to see a Tarzan film because the cinema is an exclusively masculine world.

The film cuts, sometimes confusingly, between two periods of Sabra's life: when she is a child of ten in Gafsa (in the neglected South of the country) and as a twenty-year-old setting out as a student in Tunis. As a child, she grows up in a world ruled by her father. Though he is seldom seen, he makes the decisions and brooks no opposition. The young Sabra longs to be outside, riding a bicycle around the streets, but instead she is enclosed in the dark interior world of women's confinement and domestic work.

The film's first image is of a stone, carefully wrapped and put into a box, that Sabra's morther, who shares many of her society's superstitions, imagines will help protect Sabra's virginity. Initially, she is full of foreboding, threatening not just to kill Sabra if she sins but also to drink her blood and go willingly to prison, which, she says, won't be worse than her present life. Yet the mother is a fascinating character, illiterate, of course, but proud to have given birth to a daughter as well as two sons. As Sabra grows up, her mother comes to support her daughter's ambitions more and more strongly. Touchingly, when asked by her young daughter for a story, she tells her, "I only have one story, my own"—that of a mother who acccpts her domestic role and loves her daughter.

Though she eventually gets to continue her studies in Tunis, life does not improve for Sabra. The troubles begin when she is turned down for a room at the college hostel. Her difficulties come to be symbolized by that familiar female lack—a room of her own. None of the public spaces are available to a single girl wishing to study—they are all male dominated. Nor can a single girl rent a room on her own. Sabra is forced into cramped shared bedrooms, where she has to study by candlelight. We see little of college life, but her one scene with her tutor shows her to be a stubborn student, keen to present her own views directly (with no reference to others' opinions and no use of quotations, for example), though she is told bluntly that if she continues this way, she will fail. This is indeed what happens, but though Sabra burns her books and notes, she cannot be put off her chosen course of action and announces that she will go abroad to study alongside her brothers, who are already in Europe. Our last view of her is on her way to the airport.

The Trace is a very downbeat film, without even a touch of humor. Apart from her mother and, at the very end, her father (who offers a few coins for the journey), Sabra is on her own. Her friends in Tunis keep to the old female superstitions and rutuals, which are of no interest to Sabra (particularly as the aim now is to attract men rather than to seek protection from them). She does not seem to make friends with her fellow students or have good relations with the staff. But her dedication to achieving the ambitions she sets for herself as a child demands to be admired.

Since the delayed release of *The Trace*, Ben Mabrouk has been able to contribute only one fifteen-minute episode, "In Search of Shaima / A la recherche de Chaïma," to the collective film *After the Gulf* (1991), produced by Ahmed Attia. The budget was small, but Ben Mabrouk managed to get to Baghdad by joining the crew of a team making a documentary there for Belgian television. Her idea for her own film was simple: find and interview the young woman whose anxious, suffering face appeared on world television while she watched or participated in a funeral procession in the El Amyria district of Baghdad. The attempt to find the girl is fruitless, but it confronts Ben Mabrouk with the grim reality of the aftermath of the US air strike there, which resulted in a direct hit on a shelter in which dozens of families had taken refuge. Ben Mabrouk emphasizes the universality of wartime grief and suffering by including media images from struggles elsewhere in the world (Lebanon, Chile, Cyprus, and others) and by setting all this material against the message of hope contained in Martin Luther King's celebrated "I Have a Dream" speech.

Kaltoum Bornaz, who was born in Tunis in 1945, initially studied Engish language and literature in Tunis. She followed this with studies of filmmaking at IDHEC in Paris and the University of Paris III. She subsequently worked as an assistant on foreign productions and as an editor on Tunisian films, including some features. She also made a number of short films but had to wait almost thirty years after graduation to make her first feature.

The title of *Keswa—The Broken Thread / Keswa—le fil perdu / Kiswâ, al-hayat al-dhâi'* (1997) refers to a very heavy traditional gown, woven with silver thread, that is worn by Tunisian women on special occasions, such as weddings. In the film, which is based on an actual incident in the director's own life, Nozha, who has just returned home from France, where her marriage has ended in divorce, is persuaded to wear such a garment for her brother's wedding. But she has the misfortune to be left behind when the wedding party departs and realizes, too late, that she does not know where either the wedding or the reception is to be held. With the help of a willing taxicab driver, she spends the rest of the day and much of the night traveling across Tunis in search of her family. This allows a vivid and, at times, surprising image of the city to emerge, as Bornaz intended: "Through my heroine Nozha and her family, deep in my heart, I wanted to portray life in Tunis today with its maze of contradictory and coherent elements, liberties and barriers." This is the first aim set out in the film's publicity material, and it is certainly achieved. But if the film at times loses its focus—as she does in Tunis by night—this is perhaps because the director had so much more in mind. She goes on in her statement of intent to list half a dozen other intentions, ranging from reappropriating sterotypes and lifting the veil off matriarchy to lightening the weight of tradition and celebrating "exuberance, humor and sensuality."[194]

The heart of the film remains Nozha's own experience. As she wanders, the threads of the gown start to unravel and the weight of the garment lessens. Nozha is perhaps becoming reconciled with the traditions she rejected in marrying against her parents' wishes. Certainly this was Bornaz's intention. Nozha certainly does not conform to the stereotypical view of the the submissive Arab woman: "There are many films showing Arab women like chronic victims trying to fly away from tradition and authority—and Nozha is doing the opposite of that."[195] Instead, she "tries to solve the puzzle of her identity—to be a free, modern, Arab Muslim woman."[196]

Bornaz has since gone on to direct a second feature, *The Other Half of the Sky / L'autre moitié du ciel* (2006), which deals with one of the continuing injustices prevailing in Tunisia, despite the transformation of many aspects of women's lives undertaken by Habib Bourguiba: "Selima learns that Muslim girls only inherit half as much as their brothers, leaving her with far less than her twin brother, Selim, when their father dies. Selim then goes to live abroad, leaving Selima to cope on her own."[197] The Tunisian film historian Sonia Chamkhi's initial response to the film was totally positive: "*L'autre moitié du ciel* is a good film, supported by the look of a [real] filmmaker and served by a sense of framing, plasticity, length and rhythm. . . . It is above all a film of atmosphere, which one watches with evident aestheic pleasure."[198]

*

Quite apart from the rest of Tunisian cinema is the totally distinctive creative world conjured up by the multitalented Nacer Khemir, who was born in 1948 in Korba. Khemir is a sculptor, a graphic artist, a designer, a book illustrator, an actor, a performing storyteller, and the author of numerous children's books, as well as video- and filmmaker. All of these other activities have fed into his filmmaking. He says of himself: "I consider myself a *hakawati*, a storyteller, not only of stories and narratives but also that of a culture, one who tries to add to *The Thousand and One Nights* other stories that cover the past and express the present—and I hope—embrace the future."[199]

Unsurprisingly, he brings very special qualities and concerns to his filmmaking. In the four feature films he has made in the course of the past thirty years, he has developed a style that is unique in both form and content. Central to his concerns are the worlds of children's imaginations and the power of myth and memory—particularly that of the lost domain of the legendary Andalusia, the Arab empire that stretched from Damascus to Grenada. In dealing with these themes, his films explore, in a totally personal and original way, the potential of narrative film forms derived from oral storytelling.

In many other ways, too, Khemir is a distinctive figure. He is self-taught and never formed part of the flourishing Tunisian amateur film movement in which some of his contemporaries took their first steps in directing. Similarly, though he has been based largely in Paris for many years, he did not receive any higher education or formal film training there, as has been virtually the norm for Maghrebian filmmakers. The roots of Khemir's storytelling lie in his family background. Several of his works, books as well as films, are dedicated to his grandmother, "the Andalusian, who opened for me the gates of the invisible." Khemir's own children's books are written in memory of this world where the invisible had its place, following the Arab tradition that only "a thread separates the human world from that of the supernatural."[200]

During the 1970s, Khemir began with a number of short films, followed by two longer fictions, both made for television—*L'histoire du pays du Bon Dieu* (1976) and *L'ogresse* (1977)—as well as a fifty-two-minute documentary, *Somaa*

(1978). His first feature film, *Searchers of the Desert / Les baliseurs du désert* (1984), begins with a young teacher (played by the director himself) arriving at the remote, ancient village to which he has been posted by the government. From the beginning this is a place of mystery: the bus driver denies that it even exists. Already, from the bus, the teacher has seen a group of young men, hunched and chanting, marching by in the desert. These turn out to be the young men of the village, cursed to wander endlessly, "marking out" the desert. The village is a place cut off from time and modernity, with no schooling or family life. The children are dressed like figures out of a storybook, and the village represents perfectly a child's imaginary world, where a djinn at the bottom of the well is as real as a boy's aged grandmother.

The only girl is a mysterious fifteen-year-old, kept secluded by the teacher's host. The new teacher has a number of encounters with her, some seemingly real, others clearly imaginary. When the villagers set out on a three-day pilgrimage, the young teacher is entrusted with a book to hand over to the cursed young men, who, it is believed, will return during the villagers' absence; the book's secrets will free them from the curse. But instead, the teacher himself is led off into the desert by an aged, blackclad woman who emerges from a picture in the ancient volume. The narrative could logically end here,[201] but *Searchers of the Desert* is not about logic. New story lines develop, involving a pompous white-uniformed police officer and a boat that appears out of nowhere in the middle of the desert and then vanishes. The boat's supposed captain, Sindbad, sends the villagers a tangible present, a Chinese mechanical bird, and a little boy, Housin (seen in the earliest scenes in the village), who also sets off into the desert. As this new story is about to begin, the "searchers of the desert" are heard passing on their endless march, and the credits roll.

There is a profound ambiguity about the "searchers" or "wanderers" of the title. For Khemir, they represent "all those young people, all those lost generations of the Arab-Muslim world, whether they are young emigrants or not."[202] Denise Brahimi links *Searchers in the Desert* to various realistic films in her discussion of the "void" in Tunisian society but notes that the young men could be "bent to the soil like convicts" or "mystics in prayer marching towards their God."[203] The depiction of the village is equally stylized and troubling, hovering between the real and the imaginary. Ferid Boughedir, who raises the issue of an orientalist gaze, notes that "the costumes and characters, inspired by miniature engravings, make no reference to any real Arab country" but concludes that Khemir's sincerity "convinces or seduces" the spectator.[204]

Khemir's second film, *The Dove's Lost Necklace / Le collier perdu de la colombe* (1990) is an homage to the golden age of Andalusian culture. As before, there are a number of narrative threads that run alongside each other, sometimes interweaving, sometimes going in their own directions. The principal thread involves

Hassan, an apprentice calligrapher who is seeking the meaning of love by collecting as many of the sixty Arab terms for love as he can. He is fascinated by his master's daughter and employs Zin, a little boy longing for his missing father, to act as an intermediary. These opening sequences depict an idyllic tranquility, an ordered world of learning and calligraphy where everyone is safe. The master calligrapher is playing a game of chess, by pigeon post, with a Christian friend. The city is full of tiny shops selling books and luxury goods and alcoves of scholars instructing their followers. The men (and there are only men) on the streets are sumptuously dressed, and the perfume seller proclaims that three things were precious to the Prophet: perfume, women, and prayer. This is a stunningly beautiful world—a dream Andalusia, inspired by Arab-Islamic miniature paintings—filled with the elements of fairy tales: a monkey said to be a prince who has been bewitched, a poet driven mad by love, a nobleman setting out on a quest (to find the princess of Samarkand), a master calligrapher who is completing the prince's version of the Koran for delivery to Mecca, and an old man who is finishing the embroidery of the prince's shroud.

But the idyll cannot hold, and gradually discordant images and incidents break in to disturb it. The linear normality of the opening narrative is disrupted, as the boundaries separating dream and myth from the everyday are dissolved. We can no longer be certain of whether what we are seeing is real or imagined. Hassan's passion is triggered by an image of the princess of Samarkand, found on the sole remaining torn page of a book. Later he sees her on horseback below the old cliff-top cemetery, or perhaps he imagines her. Zin has a vison of the great mosque at Cordova and meets (or imagines he meets) his long-lost father, who takes him down into another world and out of the narrative.

Hassan has ever more mysterious, dreamlike encounters: with a strange horseman, Aziz, who is, perhaps, the princess disguised as a man; with the princess herself in a vision corresponding exactly to the book illustration; and with a servant who hands him the ancient book, now miraculously intact. But since the prince's death, the ordered world has collapsed, and barbarians invade and burn the outskirts of the city. The barbarians' threat of violence leads Hassan and Aziz to jump from a cliff. Aziz vanishes, the book is lost in the waters, and Hassan returns alone to the now devastated city. On the way, he meets by the roadside an old man, who gives him the pen of his old master, a calligrapher who spent twenty years of his life striving to perfect the letter *waw*. The film ends with an image of the letter *waw*, which, the old man tells him, is the only letter of the alphabet to have its own meaning: it is unique and manifold, like God. It is the letter of the traveler.

Khemir is keen to define Arab-Islamic storytelling, not only as an oral tradition, but also as a written form, within a culture in which all books are significant and where one, the Koran, is indeed sacred. It is a culture where the act of writing, calligraphy, has a religious significance.[205] *The Dove's Lost Necklace* takes its title (with the addition of the word *lost*) from the classic book *The Ring of the Dove*, written in 1027 by Ibn Hazm (993–1064), which opens with the words "Love, my friends, begins jestingly, but its end is serious."[206]

This final recourse to the timeless beauty of calligraphy helps Khemir give the film the meaning he intended: "The opposite of death and destruction; it is an anthem of love and life."[207] There are many visual and narrative continuities with *Searchers of the Desert*: the same setting of an exotic mud-built desert town, the constant interplay of the real and the imaginary, a narrative that steadly loses its initial apparent linear coherence. Again, we have a sensitive young man and a boy as the central figures. The enigmatic image of the adolescent girl (the sheikh's daughter) in the earlier film has blossomed into the highly ambiguous figure of the princess of Samarkand, who occasionally ventures forth on her henna-adorned gray horse as a man, Aziz, who befriends Hassan. In Khemir's world, the characters are not individuals but types (the teacher, the boy, the scribe, the object of passion). Passion is the affair of the lover alone, and the pursuit of its path leads to death, not domesticity. The clearest definition of love in Khemir's world is the story of the three butterflies in his third feature, *Bab Aziz*. The first approaches a burning candle and says, "I know love." The second flies closer and brushes the flame: "I know the burning of love." The third plunges straight into the flame and is consumed: he alone knows real love.

Khemir's prime visual inspiration—the source of the strikingly beautiful composition and rich palette of colors—lies in the miniatures so often found in ancient Islamic manuscripts and on decorative pottery, and it was from one of these that he found the initial inspiration for his third feature, *Bab' Aziz / Bab' Aziz, le prince qui contemplait son âme* (2005). The idea of the prince came, Khemir tells us, "from a beautiful plate that was painted in the twelfth century. It shows a prince leaning over a beautiful pool of water, and it carries the inscription, 'The prince who contemplated his own soul.' This image stuck me as something I had to build upon, which is why it seemed obvious that the movie should be shot in Iran."[208] There are again continuities with the earlier works. Our last view of Hassan in *The Dove's Lost Necklace* showed him similarly sitting by a well. Ishtar, the little girl who accompanies Bab Aziz on the travels, was, Khemir points out, "born from from the sand, like the Arabic language" and "is reminiscent of the letter 'waw' which means in Arabic 'and.' The Sufis call it the letter of Love, because without it, nothing can come together."[209]

Bab' Aziz completes a loose trilogy of films devoted to the positive aspects of the Muslim heritage. Whereas the first two films looked back to the glories of Andalusia and the role of the word—especially in its written form as calligraphy—within the Arabo-Islamic tradition, in *Bab' Aziz* Khemir looks beyond Tunisia and toward Iran and is concerned with mystical Islam: the dances, songs, and sayings of Sufism. There are no national boundaries in Khemir's world, and the various locations are fused inextricably through the film's editing. Khemir was particularly taken with a scene in which "you can see a character walking in a palace in Tunis, looking out of a window at a landscape . . . in Iran." This provides a perfect example of Khemir's syncretic vision: "This moving world (moving like the desert, never really different and never quite the same) stretches between the window of the Tunisian palace and the Iranian landscape."[210]

The pattern established in the first two films is echoed in both the pattern of the narrative and the dialogue and the voice-over narrations in *Bab'Aziz*. These draw extensively on the thirteenth-century mystical Iranian poets, Attar (author of the celebrated *Conference of the Birds*) and Rumi (founder of the Sufi "whirling dervishes" sect), as well as the contemporaneous Arab-Andalusian Sufi poets, Ibn al-Arabi and Ibn al-Farid. *Bab'Aziz* opens with the desert and the emergence from concealment of Bab' Aziz and his granddaughter, Ishtar, who have been sheltering overnight from a sandstorm. Bab' Aziz is on his way through the desert to a meeting of dervishes that happens once every thirty years. There is no one direction to follow: each will follow his own path, yet they will all eventually meet up at the appointed place. In fact, at the end of the film, we learn that the dervishes he is to meet are already dead. They rise from their graves to greet him before setting off (like the "searchers" of Khemir's first film) into the desert, leaving him to prepare himself for his own death.

Along the way and to please Ishtar, who says stories help keep her warm, Bab' Aziz tells the story of the Prince Who Contemplated His Soul, and the narative reverts to this at intervals throughout the film, with the final episode coming just before Bab' Aziz's final separation from Ishtar and his own death. While traveling through the desert, the pair make numerous acquaintances, each of whom has his own story. Among these, there is Hassan, who is seeking the red dervish, who, he claims, killed his brother; Zaïd, a wandering singer with no particular goal; and Osman, who once fell into a well and saw a vision of a heavenly palace that he has been trying to find again ever since. The trajectories of the characters interweave and separate as each follows his own destiny, and the film's epigraph, that "there are as many paths which lead to God as there are men on earth." The stories of Hassan and Osman could well have come from the *Arabian Nights*, but they are incorporated into the film's narrative present tense. Only Zaïd, with his baseball cap, introduces a presumably deliberate discordant contemporary note. Similarly, Zaïd's story of his passion for Nour involves unexpected modern elements, such as an airliner and a hotel bed after a night of lovemaking. Otherwise, it is the largely lost traditions of the Sufis on which the film concentrates. In a hidden Sufi mosque buried in the sand and at the city of Bam, they enjoy a feast of Sufi songs and dances. At the end, in Bam, Zaïd finds Nour again, enabling *Bab' Aziz*, like its two predecessors, to end with a new story about to begin.

Khemir's vision is unique in African and Arab cinema. His imagined fairy-tale world has a total coherence, with certain constantly recurring themes and characters—a mixture of dream and reality; a beautiful and mysterious virgin; little boys and girls; the lost grandeur of Andalusia and the Islamic past; tales of journeys, treasure, magic, and, always, the mysterious power of love; and the key significance of the word, written, spoken, and sung. This world is created through precise framing and camera work, sumptuous color imagery, and a multitude of expressive faces and exquisite costumes. Khemir's narrative style, too, is unique. The characters are not individuals who develop and change but types who are multiplied to create a richer narrative world. Echoes and resemblances are constant, and very different characters in divergent stories suffer the same fate or adopt the same actions. Just as the desert shifts in the wind, constantly uncovering and obliterating, so Khemir's stories start up but peter out, rarely reaching a climax. His characters hold stage for a while and then vanish in some unexplained or magical way from the narrative. The endings of the embedded stories are abrupt and truncated: there is never a true resolution, just the potential beginning of a new story.

Khemir's fourth feature-length film, *Sheherazade /Schéhérazade* (2011), is a fascinating epilogue to this trilogy of filmed stories. Here we have the art of storytelling in its purest form, an oral recitation of the kind Khemir has performed to audiences throughout his career. Here it is the word that is dominant, principally through the voice of Khemir, filmed before an audience (that we never see) on a small darkened stage, sitting alone on a chair surrounded by dozens of small candles. His voice is supplemented by that of Sheherazade, who tells the story of *The Thousand and One Nights*, and by a set of visuals that complement or contest the spoken narration but are never developed to constitute narratives of their own.

To embark into the desert, Sherherazade tells us, is to embark into poetry, the metric rhythm of which is derived from the beat of camels' hooves. Khemir begins with a story he likes to tell because it has no real ending—it is up to the audience to determine. Throughout, the same human themes recur: love, freedom, and the confrontation with death, against which words—a new story—are the best defense. The stories abound in duplications, coincidences, and variations to constitute a narrative labyinth from which there is no escape, except into a new story. *Sherherazade* brings to the fore the oral tradition on which all Khemir's fictions are based. As he has said elsewhere, "Storytellers open the doors of the imagination and unroll their tales like carpets of sand or stones. Their stories intermingle like little streams that jin to become one vast river. Listening to storytellers means being unsure whether one is going backward or forward in time."[211] Here, in *Sheherazade*, as so often in Khemir's work, there is a contemporary counterpoint to the timeless narrative world: the film ends with Khemir sitting and drinking coffee in a Paris café and then setting off toward the Sorbonne in pursuit of a young student named (of course) Sherherazade. As Khemir says of his own practice, "The storyteller does not perform in a theatre, he installs a theatre in his listeners' hearts."[212]

Virtually all contemporary Arab filmmaking has a national focus, but there is little that is specifically Tunisian about any of Khemir's films, even when they are shot in Tunisia (as *The Dove's Lost Necklace* was—in Sousse, Kairouan, Tozeur, and Nefta). Khemir's vision is syncretic. The clothes of the children in *Searchers of the Desert* are not traditional Tunisian costumes but modern designs, created, like those in all his films, by Maud Perl. In *The Dove's Lost Necklace*, he casts an Indian as Hassan, a Palestinian boy as Zin, and a Syrian actress as the princess. Questioned about this, Khemir replied: "In the same way that I tried to re-create an image of a city in the eleventh century, giving it the Arab-Islamic touch of those centuries, I also tried to re-create a human group that could have and—at least presumably—would have inhabited that splendour and framework. The process of pasting [*collage*], and combining things, happened over several stages, and this pertains to architectural as well as human constructions."[213]

Khemir's overall concern, throughout his work, is to show "an open, tolerant and friendly Islamic culture, full of love and wisdom . . . an Islam that is different from the one depicted by the media." For him, fundamentalism "is a distorting mirror of Islam," and *Bab' Aziz*, like its predecessors, is "a modest attempt to give to Islam its real face."[214]

Egypt

We have already noted Youssef Chahine's inspirational role in offering the example of a new kind of Arab filmmaking from which younger filmmakers across the region could draw inspiration. His work in the1980s also offered a specific new model of production finance, drawing on foreign funding sources, such as the French Fonds Sud Cinéma. This allowed Chahine to create an internationally recognized Egyptian cinema, acclaimed at festivals worldwide, that was not wholly dependent on local Egyptian box office receipts. His own production company, Misr International Films, gained valuable experience that could be passed on through coproduction agreements. This was the particular mode of independent production followed by two of his most talented former assistant directors, Yousry Nasrallah and Asma El Bakry (the name is variously spelled in different transliterations) from the late 1980s and early 1990s onward. Both worked consistently outside the structures of the Egyptian commercial industry.

Yousry Nasrallah was born in Cairo in 1952 and, like Chahine, was born into a Christian family. After studies of economics and sociology at Cairo University, he followed the conventional pattern of those wishing eventually to become film directors in Egypt. He studied at the Cairo Higher Cinema Institute, had a spell as a film critic in Beirut, and then worked as assistant to a number of directors, including Volker Schlöndorf, Omar Amiralay, and Youssef Chahine. He worked as assistant to Chahine on a number of films, from *Farewell Bonaparte* onward, and coscripted *Alexandria—Now and Forever*. In return, Chahine produced Nasrallah's first features and used the contacts made through his production company to help him receive support from French coproducers and from the Fonds Sud Cinéma.

Nasrallah's debut film, *Summer Thefts / Vols d'été / Sariqât sayfiyyah* (1988)—which is, according to Benjamin Geer, "largely autobiographical"[215]— offers a vivid look at Egypt in the summer of 1961, as Nasser's land reforms began to take shape. The previous social organization had clear boundaries between the wealthy landowners and the peasants who worked in their fields and owned nothing. Nasser, heard several times on the radio, promises a radical social reform that throws everything into confusion.

The previous situation established clear social distinctions between the two classes, though there were inevitably relationships that crossed the boundaries, examples of which are portrayed in the film. There is a tentative relationship between the feminist-minded Dahlia and Abdallah, a young peasant boy offered an education by the family, and there are also complex emotions for the women who spend their lives as servants in the big house and develop particularly close relationships with the children growing up there, who spend more time with them than with their parents. It is in this context that a friendship develops between Yasser and a peasant boy, Leil.

The film concentrates on the people in the big house who are deeply affected by Nasser's proposals. Since the land has been inherited by three sisters, there are inevitably tensions between them and their husbands about how to deal with the situation and whether to sell. There are also marital complications. Yasser's parents are divorcing, and Yasser, who is close to his mother, will have to go to live with his father. Things come to a head on Yasser's birthday, when a celebration planned to bring patricians and peasants together fails totally. Yasser is confined to bed with a disease picked up swimming in the local stream with Leil. The male peasants have left for Alexandia for a Nasser rally (that they are paid to attend) and domestic relations worsen among members of the family at the big house. Yasser has always been attracted by the legend of Robin Hood, and he involves Leil in a plan to rob the rich to enable his mother to afford to keep and support him. Their plot is uncovered, but it is only Leil who is arrested, revealing that the reforms have not changed everything.

The film has an epilogue twenty years later. Yasser returns, having spent the last four years in Beirut, to reconcile himself with Leil, who, like many of the young men in the village, is off to Iraq, where the Iran-Iraq war is brewing. This is a striking debut film with a minimal story line that nevertheless offers complex insight into a key moment of Egypt's political history.

Mercedes / Mercedès / Marsîdès (1993), Nasrallah's second film, begins as a satirical melodrama narrated by Warda, with a prologue in the 1950s entitled "Family Stories." Warda is a beautiful upper-class young woman who is about to be married off by her mother to a rich suitor. Meanwhile, she falls in love instead with a black diplomat. They do not manage to elope, but the result is what the doctor calls "not a slight cold, but a slight pregnancy." Warda is left potentially disgraced, but her mother arranges marriage to an extremely rich old man, Mansour, who conveniently dies before the child is born. Though he is not black, Warda names her son Noubi, literally "the Nubian." Warda is now potentially very rich, but her money has been stolen by her brother-in-law, Youssef, who has absconded to Paris. She follows him, seduces him, reclaims her money, and leaves him with a son, Gamal. Back in Egypt, she devotes herself to her "real" son Noubi, who unfortunately falls under Nasser's spell. After Nasser's death, he vows to devote all his wealth to the socialist cause. Deeply concerned, Warda has him committed to a mental hospital.

From this point on, the film becomes a progressively more confusing melodrama, toying with many of the genre's conventional themes and relating the action not so much to political events as to the sadly inadequate progress of the Egyptian national football team in a world cup event. Noubi is released, white-haired and looking, as someone later remarks, like his mother's elder brother. Oddly, he bears no resentment toward his mother for his years in custody; indeed, he goes on to fall in love with a girl, Afifa, who resembles her, raising all the melodramatic concerns about incest. His first social engagement is his uncle Youssef's wedding, which does not go without incident and culminates in Youssef's sudden death on his wedding day. His dying words give Noubi a quest: to seek out his half brother, Gamal, whom he never knew existed.

There are further plot complications involving child trafficking and drug smuggling, overt homosexuality and violence. But, according to the conventions of the genre, Noubi, Gamal, and Afifa are united in a soft-focus happy ending. The film remains totally enigmatic, including the meaning of its title. Youssef's dying word is "Mercedes." This is the name of his first wife, a character we never see. She raised Gamal but plays no part in the action. It also refers to the automobile to which there are frequent references in the film. As Nasrallah has said, "At the time, there were a lot of Mercedes cars. . . . Their owners would drive them in the most outrageous way, as if they owned the country."[216] Noubi is told at one point that not wanting to own a Mercedes is un-Egyptian (to which he responds that he longs for a Rolls-Royce), yet it is in a Mercedes that the trio drive into their happy ending, in a seemingly inevitable if totally ambiguous final image.

On Boys, Girls and the Veil / *À propos des garçons, des filles et du voile* / *Subyan wa-banat* (1995) is a feature-length documentary that received positive reviews abroad but was never commercially released in Egypt. An exploration of the confused relationships between young working-class people in contemporary Egypt, the film has, as its central focus, the twenty-four-year-old Bassam Samra, who played Gamal's gay friend in *Mercedes*. We see Bassam going about his everyday life, teaching at a technical college (where the pay barely covers his travel costs) but also going to an audition for a shampoo advertisement, because he has ambitions to establish himself as an actor. He is under pressure from his father, and even from his barber, to settle down and get married. For Bassam's father, this entails following the same path he himself did—spending three years working in Saudi Arabia to acquire the money that would allow him to set up a minibus business.

Most of the film comprises discussions set up by Bassam with members of his family, his friends and work colleagues, and some female acquaintances. The young men talk about how they like going out with girls—to the cinema, perhaps sharing a kiss—but all make it clear that this is not a liberty they would under any circumstances allow their sisters to enjoy. The girls have almost all been pressured into wearing a head veil and accept that it will be an inevitability after marriage. At the same time, there is a disconnect in the boys' own lives: a girl you like and go out with is not a girl you would conceivably marry. Marriage is a family business, whether or not it is parentally arranged, and has nothing to do with mutual attraction. The few words of explanatory voice-over in the film are provided by Bassam, from his own very personal perspective. Nasrallah does not intervene himself or open out the film to offer other, wider opinions and experiences that might contextualize the issues. In a fascinating comment captured by Geer, Nasrallah said of Bassam, "It's not really him. It's the image of himself that he wants to give you. . . . In a sense he plays the role of the director."[217]

Despite its title, Nasrallah's next feature, *The Medina* / *La ville* / *Al-madina* (2000), is in fact about two cities: Cairo and Paris. For financial reasons, it was shot on video and blown up to 35mm. The tone is set by the opening quote from *The City* by the Greek poet C. P. Cavafy, who spent most of his life in Alexandria: "No new lands, no new seas—the city will follow you. You will grow old in the same neighbourhood, your hair will grow grey. . . . No ship will carry you away. You wasted your life the world over, just as you ruined it in this little corner."

The film begins as a kind of fictional replay of *On Boys, Girls and the Veil*. The central role, that of Ali, is again played by Bassam Samra. Here he is a young man working with his father in the market district of Cairo, Rod al-Farag, but dreaming of becoming an actor. There is even an audition scene, with the director casting for a documentary about "a loser like you who wants to be an actor." The film offers a vivid picture of the market and the intimately entwined lives of those who work in and around it, including Ali's closest friends. His decision to leave to try for a new life with his actor friends in Paris is triggered by the government decision to move the market to a new site in the name of urban regeneration. It is a painful and emotional farewell for Ali, who has a final row with his father, who belittles his ambition and disowns him.

Two years later, Ali is in Paris, not working as an actor. Instead, he is taking part in rigged boxing matches, staged by a man who is also engaged in smuggling illegal immigrants into France. As he gets more and more dissatisfied with his role, Ali begins to protest and act badly in the ring. As a result, he is first beaten up and then run over by a car driven by his previous assailants. When he recovers from his coma in the hospital, his life has changed totally. He is an amnesiac who does not even know his own name. In the hospital and subsequently on the streets, he encounters real friendship, but he is totally lost and eventually hands himself over to the police.

Presumably deported as an illegal immigrant, he finds himself back in his old surroundings in Cairo, but he is now unable to remember his mother's name or to recognize his father, his old friends, or even his fiancée. In Nasrallah's view, "Losing his memory is the best thing that ever happened to him, because he can now separate people he can't stand from people he likes. . . . He be comes a free human being."[218] Throughout, Ali has been sure of one thing: he is an actor. And the film ends on a positive note with a scene of him acting in a film called *The Village*. Like much of the film, this positive ending is highly ambiguous. Introduced by Ali in voice-over as something that happens to him, it could be a memory, a dream, or a current event. The blurring of the distinction between Samra as a person and the character he plays points to a key characteristic of these early films. One is aware of a certain unease between the director himself—from a wealthy background but a one-time Communist Party member—and his chosen working-class subject matter and also a reluctance to impose himself too firmly on his film material. Characters seem to choose their own trajectory and events are left to tell themselves.

Gate of the Sun / La porte du soleil / Bab al-chams (2005) is a reworking of Elias Khoury's highly respected five-hundred-page novel about the Palestinian struggle, coscripted by Nasralleh, the author Khoury, and the Lebanese writer-director Mohamed Souheid. For Khoury, this involved a reshaping and restructuring of the narrative, but this was something he willingly accepted: "It was certainly a little frustrating for me to make this kind of choice, but it was also fascinating to see how I could rewrite this novel which can be infinitely rewritten."[219] Though the work was arduous, it proceeded in an agreeable way. The three would meet up every evening to work on the dialogue and, as Khoury relates, it was an agreeable experience: "As Yousry is a very good cook, each evening was a festival of good words, excellent food and marvellous wine."[220] As director,

Nasrallah confronted head-on the issue of creating a story out of the events relating to the Palestinian conflict: "The thing is, we are expected to be ambassadors, politicians, judges. Anything but storytellers. I see this as a form of repression . . . of fear of living. . . . We can only be commentators. . . . There is nothing more disconcerting and upsetting than fiction. And that's a good thing. This is what Elias, Mohamed and I tried to do when we wrote the screenplay. This is the line I tried to take when I made the film."[221]

Gate of the Sun is a massive four-hour, thirty-eight-minute epic, divided into two parts: *The Departure / Le départ* and *The Return / Le retour*, each running for well over two hours. It has a cast drawn from across the Arab world and, since Palestine was obviously not accessible to the filmmakers as a location, it was shot in Syria and Lebanon. It had international financial backing but no Egyptian support apart from that of Misr International. It was intended for both cinema and television screenings. Like Nasrallah's earlier works, it received excellent reviews from Egyptian and foreign critics but was granted very few screenings in Cairo.

The film weaves together the stories of two Palestinian resistance fighters of different generations, Younès, also known as Abou Salem, and his younger compatriot, Khalil. It focuses in particular on the loves that have shaped their lives. *The Departure* opens in the Shatila refugee camp in Lebanon in 1994, where the aging Younès is lying in a coma, tended by Khalil. In the hope of bringing him back to consciousness, Khalil talks constantly to Younès, retelling the story of his, Younès's, life. He begins in 1943, when traditional family customs still ruled the life of villagers, for whom the olive harvest was the highpoint of their year. The sixteen-year-old Younès is cajoled into a marriage with the twelve-year-old Nahila, arranged by his blind father, Ibrahim, and opposed by his mother. There is no voice-over in the film, but we regularly revert to Khalil at the bedside, praising or sometimes attacking Younès's career and questioning his love for his wife. We also get occasional interventions by Om Hassan, the old woman who is sheltering them, who has a very different perspective on Younès: "A peasant knows nothing about love."

The film's main narrative is basically a chronological account of Younès's life. At the beginning, he and Nahila are just children and cannot consummate their marriage. Younès's departure the next morning to fight the British occupiers sets the pattern for his life: he is a man constantly on the move, always trying to protect his people. Obviously, there is no Palestinian victory in his lifetime, but he never deviates from his path; his constant refrain is "We must start again from zero." When he returns to the village of Deir al-Assad a few years later, he and Nahila have both matured, and they fall in love at first sight. They make love, and Nahila becomes pregnant with their first child. This sets the pattern for her life: their relationship is mostly one of separation, but when they are reunited, Nahila again becomes pregnant and is left to bring up yet another child on her own.

When Younès becomes a fugitive from the Israelis, they arrange their meetings in the grotto, which provides the film's title, the Gate of the Sun.

As the film progresses, Nahila grows into a stronger character, seeking education for herself, taking charge of the children, and becoming a leader of the women in their revolt against those who oppose them. The couple are well matched, but their lives are set against the savage reality of the *Nakba*, the expulsion of the Palestinians from their lands in Galilee by the overwhelming might of the Israeli army. Much of the central part of the film is a record of this Palestinian humiliation at the hands of the Israelis, who drove them into Lebanon. The Israeli refrain—"This zone is forbidden to Arabs. We will kill the men and rape the women"—is a threat they do not hesitate to carry out. As always in Nasrallah's work, we, the audience, are left to make up our own minds about the protagonists. Younès's constant struggle is in vain: he is away seeking arms in Syria when Deir al-Assad is burned to the ground. We see little of his actual resistance activities, except the moment when he blows up the children's dormitory in the kibbutz, in revenge for the killing of his own son. Nahila's growing authority is apparent in the two final scenes of the film. In the first, she defiantly proclaims herself a whore and claims she does not know the name of the father of the child she is carrying to avoid betraying Younès's whereabouts to her Israeli interrogators. In the second, she summons the whole village to proclaim that her fourth child is that of the hero they all know and revere.

The story of *The Departure* is a straightforward narrative, setting the protagonist's constant struggle and relationship with Nahila against the implacable and overwhelming force of the Israeli armed forces—the *Nakba*. *The Return*, looking at events a generation later, has a much more complex dramatic structure, full of unexplained incidents, that reflects the subsequent disjointed Palestinian experience—marked by separation, loss, and dislocation. The precredit sequence brings to the fore Om Hassan's 1980s experience of disappropriation as she visits her old home in Galilee, now occupied by an Israeli-Arab settler. This sets the tone for the film.

Khalil's life in Chatila in 1994 is marked by his love for Chams, but he is thrown off course when she kills a neighbor (for reasons never made clear) and is subsequently executed by Palestinian forces. When Khalil is arrested, humiliated, and accused of being an accomplice, he is confronted with events from his earlier life. These are elaborated and explained in the film'a main narrative but do not form any sort of simple chronological pattern. Khalil's voice forms a linking thread, but his life does not have the straightforward drive that animated Younès. This is a Palestinian cause characterized by division, mistrust, inner strife, differences, and rivalry.

After we have seen Khalil humiliated in 1994, we go back to his presence at the expulsion of the Palestine Liberation Organization (PLO) from Beirut in

1992, when he first met Chams. We are then shown images of his childhood, which are followed by his adolescent enthusiasm for the revolution. In 1976, he experiences the Lebanese war from within the camp at Tal El-Zaatar, is wounded and sent to China for training. He fails his physical examination and is given a three-month medical training: he becomes a hospital nurse, not the doctor he claims to be in Chatila. We return to the treatment of Younès, but the interaction of patient and carer is interrupted by Khalil's two encounters with an extroverted shampoo seller and his contact with a film crew exploring the camp as research for their production of a Jean Genet play. There is a tentative interaction with the French lead actress, Catherine, and a partially successful telephone call with his estranged mother, made from a side of Beirut he has never been able to visit.

The film, now increasingly marked by death and loss, achieves its unity when it reverts to its original pattern, focusing again on the love experienced by the two men. There is a long portrayal of what is presumably the last encounter of Younès and Nahila, who now have seven children. Here, for the first time, she gives her side of their story (it has always been Younès who has done the talking). She is worn out by stories and dreams. We are also shown Khalil and Chams together before the shooting incident, and their night of lovemaking means that Khalil is absent when Younès dies (just as Younès was absent from the burning of his village, Deir al-Assad). Again, as in *The Departure*, the last word is given to Nahila, as we hear her dying letter to Younès and see final images of the grotto that played such a large part in their lives.

Gate of the Sun is a highly impressive film, covering a huge sweep of the Palestinian experience over fifty years. The key aspect of the film is that it does not simply praise Palestinian valor. The Palestinian society depicted at the opening of part 1 is not an ideal world—it is shown to be patriarchal, constraining, and backward looking. The catastrophe that overwhelms it—the *Nakba*— overthrows all existing assumptions, but it is at least a communal disaster. The story of Younès and Nahila shows vividly that, for individual Palestinians at this time, relationships could endure. Younès's absences are compensated for by his stories and ambitions, typified by the creation of the Gate of the Sun. At the same time, the Palestinian nation is shown to survive, not least because each of this couple's reunions gives birth to a new generation.

Part 2 shows unflinchingly the impact of the *Nakba* on the subsequent generation. The sense of a Palestinian identity persists, and new social values are embraced (exemplified by the contrast between the open sexuality of the relationship between Khalil and Chams and the first encounter of Younès and Nahila on their wedding night). But this is a world where every individual is essentially on his or her own, bearing a particular burden of spatial dislocation and of separation from family. Chams has no involvement with the life of her daughter, Dalal, and Khalil has huge problems making contact again with his estranged mother. Elias Khoury has said of his work, "This is a novel about women, a novel where women incarnate both the continuity of life and the idea of revolt. Women understand things much better than men."[222] This is fully reflected in the film, where the spirit of Nahila infuses the whole narrative.

The Aquarium / L'aquarium / Genenet al-asmak (2008), Nasrallah's most stylistically innovative film to date, focuses on the power of words to shape an individual's personality. The two principal characters are well matched. Both are well-to-do, attractive people, who dress well. Neither has married or had children, but each has one surviving parent, with whom the relationship is not easy. Above all, they are both night people, addicted to words. Laila is a radio presenter who runs a late-night talk show, *Night Secrets*, which invites listeners to phone in with their fears and problems. Youssef is an anaesthetist who is fascinated by the words and confessions uttered by patients as they drift into unconsciousness. He supplements his earnings from daytime employment at a hospital with nighttime earnings working in an illicit abortion clinic.

We, the audience, obviously wait for them to meet up, come together, and fill the essential loneliness of their lives, but Nasrallah frustrates us. Youssef, who prefers to spend his nights sleeping in his car, rather than spending time in his apartment overlooking the Nile, does phone in to Laila's show. He talks about his anxiety concerning the huge Cairo aquarium, which he sees as a maze from which he fears he may never escape. But Laila does not select this conversation for inclusion in her show. Youssef does in fact go to the aquarium, but their anticipated meeting does not occur. Another night, they are both in the same nightclub, where Laila's frenetic dancing reveals her frustrated sensuality. Nasrallah's camera tries to link them, panning from her to him, but Youssef has his back turned to her, absorbed in his own concerns. When they do eventually meet up, she recognizes his voice in an abortion clinic where she is accompanying a friend. But their conversation comprises just a couple of sentences. Did he go to the aquarium? "Yes." Did he get out of it? "I don't know yet."

Nasrallah is always keen to step back to let us draw our own conclusions about his characters. Here, both of the two principals are addicted to words, but neither of them makes a personal presentation, either by a direct-to-camera statement or by means of a voice-over comment. Instead, it is the actors playing the secondary roles—their colleagues, friends, acquaintances—who step out of character to tell us, direct to camera, how they conceive the parts they play and how they, as actors, view the two protagonists.

None of the stylistic novelties of *The Aquarium* form part of Nasrallah's subsequent film, *Scheherzade, Tell Me a Story / Femmes du Caire / Ehky ya Shahraza* (2009). This is is a fresh departure for Nasrallah, an attempt to bring together his own personal approach and the structures of Egyptian commercial cinema, using a popular star, Mona Zakki, in the leading role. Based on a script proposed to him by Waheed Hamed, the writer of the internationally successful feature *The Yacoubian Building*, this is the first of his films where Nasrallah was not present at the very first stages of the writing. Nasrallah was tempted by the challenge of making a popular melodrama because "melodrama allows the telling of paradoxical, yet real, relationships between men and women" and because he wanted "to renew a great tradition of Egyptian cinema: superb melodramas and magnificent women."[223] The film is also an inversion of this tradition, in that here the desired objects are the men who betray the virtuous women who fall in love with them.

Hebba and Adnam seem to be a perfectly matched couple, successful, well off, and in love. She is a popular television talk show host, while he is a successful journalist, possibly in line for promotion as editor of one of the state's principal newspapers. But their professional choices drive them increasingly apart. She strives fearlessly to expose uncomfortable social and political problems, while he wants a quieter life, happy to follow government wishes and guidelines, if this will help him in his ambition to be promoted. Yielding to Adnam's concerns, Hebba agrees to follow his requests to steer clear of political issues. The new focus in her television program, *Dusk Till Dawn*, will be the personal issues of women, a subject she will research personally, going back to her journalistic roots.

The first three episodes of her new series, in which women feature as witnesses to the abuse the have received, form the core of the film. Their initial statements to the presenter give way to direct reenactments of the events to which they refer, without any voice-over intrusion or clarification. The first is that of a self-confessed "old maid" who was happy to marry her mother's choice of husband, until she learned the terms he would impose. He would control every aspect of their life together. She would wear a veil, give up driving, hand over her wealth and earnings, and be accountable to him for every penny she spent. (Why would she need hair shampoo, when she was going to be veiled?) The second episode concerns a woman released after fifteen years in prison for murder. She was one of three young sisters left to care for the family business after their parents died. Initially robbed by their opium-addicted uncle, they turned to their father's trusted young assistant. But he seduced all three of them in turn with promises of marriage. When the truth comes out, the eldest of the three, Saffa, kills him, an act for which she has no regrets. The third story concerns a professional woman who falls in love with a very successful man, goes through a formal (future) marriage contract with him, and then falls pregnant. When he claims not to be the father, she has an abortion.

This latter episode proves politically lethal, as the man concerned (who is not named in the program) is appointed to be one of Hosni Mubarak's ministers just as the story is transmitted. Adnam (wrongly) sees this as the reason why he is refused promotion, confronts Hebba, and beats her savagely. But this is not a woman who can be put down that easily. In a splendidly melodramatic conclusion to the film, the fourth episode of her television series features Hebba, openly revealing her bruises, as both presenter and witness to the abuse she her-self has suffered.

Nasrallah returned to his favorite subject matter—the gulf between rich and poor in contemporary Egypt—and was reunited with his preferred actor, Bassam Samra, in *After the Battle / Après la bataille / Bad al-mawqia* (2012). The film is precisely situated, beginning on February 2, 2011, with the disruption of the first Tiananman Square demonstration and ending with the march against the state television center eight months later, when the government troops open fire, kill-ing many of the participants. Rim is a well-educated, upper-class woman, who is passionate about social change and a member of a group of social reformers. She is also in the process of divorcing her husband. By chance, she is taken by her friend Dina to the village of Nazlet, from which the horsemen and camel drivers who disrupted the February demonstration were recruited. These are men who made their living by taking tourists around the pyramids and who are now—after the uprising—without work and penniless. As an activist, Rim cannot ignore their plight, but she is also attracted by one of the horsemen, Mahmoud, and he to her.

They assume that their contact, which amounts to no more than a kiss, is a private matter, but it shapes their subsequent behavior as the connection is clear to all. Rim's new enthusiasm for Nazlet is derided at a meeting of her commit-tee, and she is warned not to confuse life and work. Things are even worse for Mahmoud. He is derided by the villagers, since he was caught on television being thrown off his horse and abused by demonstrators. Worse follows. His children are taunted and told their father is not a real man, and when Rim returns to mobilize the village, he is derided as Rim's "toy-boy." Rim's efforts do lead to some awakening awareness—on the part of Mahmoud's wife, Fatma, for exam-ple. But there is no happy outcome. Mahmoud, following Rim, does get to chant "Bread, freedom, dignity, humanity" at the October demonstration, but he is one of those shot by the government forces. *After the Battle* has an overcomplicated narrative, and its commitment to change is constant. But, ultimately, it offers no hope of renewal for Egypt after the Arab Spring.

Asma El Bakry, who was born in 1947 in Cairo, studied French literature at Alexandria University and history in Paris. She received no formal film train-ing but served as assistant to Youssef Chahine and Salah Abou Seif on major films and also worked on a number of foreign productions shot in Egypt, including *Death on the Nile*. She made five documentaries before beginning her feature film career and has also worked as a freelance writer. Her links to Chahine were noted in a review of her first feature by Philippe Royer, who wrote that this work "renews an acquaintance with an older Egyptian cinematic tradi-tion, lyrical and delicate of which Youssef Chahine was thought to have been the last representative."[224]

The best known of El Bakry's three features remains the first, *Beggars and Noblemen / Mendiants et orgueilleux / Chahhâtin wa noubalâ* (1991), adapted from a novel by Albert Cossery. The film is precisely—if initially somewhat enigmatically—set in time, in terms quite alien to Egypt. It opens with a newspaper headline referring to the Allied entry into Berlin and ends with radio reports of the nuclear attacks on Hiroshima and Nagasaki. This is a time when, in Egypt too, old values are vanishing. There are comic references to this in the opening account of local voting results—referred to by Gohar as "the most intelligent election in history": Baghouti, a water-carrier's donkey, is unanimously chosen by voters in Mit Abou Dahoud, one of Cairo's electoral districts. On a deeper level, doubt, change, and uncertainty pervade the whole film. The physical setting of the action is a lively, realistic portrayal of street life in the poorer quarters of the city, but the central characters operate on a quite different level, constantly discussing the ways in which the Hiroshima bomb alters everything. History and geography are mere systems of lies that should no longer be taught: there are no certainties, even here.

When we meet the film's protagonist, he is pursuing what he regards as a free life. Though he is still respectfully addressed as Professor Gohar, he has opted out, given up his job, and is sleeping on the stone floor of his flat, dependent on a daily dose of hashish from his friend Yakan. He is well known to the beggars on the street and is a regular frequenter of the local brothel. It is there that, quite unexpectedly, he strangles one of the girls who has been left in charge in the absence of the madam and the other whores. At this point, the audience's expectation is of a conventional detective drama that will reveal Gohar as the killer and uncover his motivation. Our expectations are heightened by the entry of an immaculately uniformed and totally self-confident police officer, Nour el-Din, who is initially in total command.

But the film, which El Bakry describes as "a fable,"[225] develops in a quite different direction. Even Gohar, who feels no guilt or remorse, cannot explain his own act; it is part of the new unknowable world in which they are now living. Gohar, Yakan, and their friend Kordi all accept this new conception of society, and this makes them impervious to the logical methods of enquiry pursued by Nour El-Din. They openly mock him and obstruct his investigations, Kordi making false confessions, Yakan refusing to talk even when he is savagely beaten by the police, and Gohar smiling as he openly admits his guilt. Instead of being cowed by the police investigation, they confront the very basis of Nour El-Din's methods, telling him he is a tormented soul whose reality must be a nightmare. As the action proceeds, the initially confident police officer increasingly grows to fit their description of him. Because the killing was gratuitous, he cannot find the logic and proofs he needs and is plunged into despair. In the end, he accepts their vision of the world, and our last sight of him is dressed in civilian clothes, visiting the brothel as a friend and, presumably, as a client.

For her second feature, *Concerto in the Street of Happiness / Concerto dans la ruelle du bonheur / Kunchirtu fi darb sa'ada* (1998), El Bakry turned to comedy. Again the film is structured around an interplay between domestic and street life in the Cairo district of Darb Saada on the one hand and an outside force, Western classical music, on the other. There may be acceptable noise and chaos when the children play on the street, but to ordinary Egyptians, even those working backstage at the opera house, Western music is nothing but banging, screaming, and whining, while musical notation is seen as incomprehensible scribbling. These cultural tensions tear apart the life of the film's protagonist, Azouz. At the beginning of the film, he is happily married to Mabrouka and fully integrated into his community. But then he is charged with looking after a celebrated violinist, Sonia El-Minshawy, who is returning to her native Egypt after fifteen years of studying and performing in Europe.

As Azouz takes her around Cairo and on a tourist trip to the pyramids, an interesting counterpoint—which is continued throughout the film—arises between the Egyptian landscape and a totally alien accompanying musical score, drawing on the orchestral work of eight European composers and three operas (*La Bohème*, *Tosca*, and *Aïda*). Azouz becomes totally captivated by Sonia's French appearance and attitudes, and, though he is in debt, he buys himself a Western suit for their excursions together. He has no understanding of classical music, but he becomes totally caught up in it, spending all his time listening to the orchestra and singers from the back of the hall, coming back home late, and sleeping on the sofa. But all this passes unnoticed by Sonia, who is similarly emotionally caught up when she runs into Sherif, the man who was her first love, for the first time in fifteen years.

There is plenty of humor abstracted from Azouz's comic mishaps and the misunderstandings of Mabrouka's friends and neighbors (who are these women Bellhova and Aida whom Azouz in now obsessed with?). The disintegration of Azouz's marriage and the interventions of his neighbors are also handled lightly. When Mabrouka becomes particularly distraught, one of her friends proposes a love charm comprising the eye of a migrating cow and the genitals of an orphaned mouse, ground in oil. But, in comedy at least, all obsessions have to come to an end. Sonia realizes there is no future in her relationship with Sherif and leaves abruptly for Europe. As Azouz's cousin observes while trying to get him away from his foreign obsessions, you can never recover your roots once you've tasted the fruit of foreign lands. Sonia's abrupt departure, without a word to Azouz, also brings him to his senses. His reintegration into his community comes when he chooses to take care of Ayoub, the child flautist now left alone after the death of the aged beggar whose companion he was.

El Bakry's third feature, *Violence and Derision / La violence et la dérision / Al-unf wa al-sukhriya* (2005), is an adaptation of another Albert Cossery novel but lacks the stylistic innovation of her first. In accordance with the title, the film opens with a violent explosion in the flatlands that leaves one of the unknown perpetrators dead and the other wounded. The film then follows the activities and arguments of two distinct but overlapping groups of would-be revotionaries, and the narrative structure reflects their hesitations and confusions—there is no sense of the action moving smoothly and clearly toward a climax. The setting is an all-too-plausible future vision of Cairo where all forms of street activity are progressively banned: begging, street vending, throwing down litter, picking up cigatette ends, assembling in groups, and even driving a horse-drawn vehicle through the city. Any transgressions are forcefully confronted by an aggressive police presence.

One group of the activists—whose loudest voice is that of Tahar, newly emerged from prison—advocates violence against the governor. But they spend most of their time in mutual recrimination or suspicion, constantly afraid that their activities may be betrayed by one of their colleagues currently being beaten and tortured in prison. Only at the end of the film, with Tahar's individual decision, is the initial, failed explosion followed up with real lethal action. The second group, involving the schoolteacher Orfi and the film's central figure, Karim, is led by the secretive Heikal. This group has a more imaginative strategy: mockery. Early on they respond to the ban on begging by setting up a fake beggar, who spurts out what looks like blood when its hair is tugged by a policeman. They publish a stream of texts praising the governor to a ludicrous intent—even comparing him to Alexander the Great—and their major project is filling the city with caricature images of the governor, proclaiming, "Together we'll make all our dream and hopes come true." All the citizens who assemble to laugh at the image and at the pretensions of the slogan are savagely beaten by the police. Their final act of mockery is to produce a scheme for the erection of a statue to the governor.

Apart from Karim, who makes kites for the enjoyment of children and plans to marry his live-in girlfriend, none of the revolutionaries is presented in a positive light: Tahar beats his sister, Aïcha, and Heikal merely uses Souad, who is in love with him and is the daughter of one of the governor's ministers. As Heikal later says, "Women are nothing but trouble." The film offers a very disillusioned image of political action. In the end, the two groups' collective revolutionary actions come to nothing. Wanting to protect the purity of the revolution, Tahar kills the governor by blowing up his car. But the television reports do not talk of revolution; they proclaim that the governor is a martyr, state that the bomb was foreign-made, and claim that Tahar was mentally unstable. Heikal brushes aside the fact that the principal outcome of his campaign of mockery has been the beating up of hundreds of innocent citizens. He has, it emerges, no belief that getting rid of one tyrant will not result in the emergence of another. For him, revolution is a game, a fantasy that allows you to never stop enjoying life. At the end of the film, he has, of course, a new and even better plan of derision.

Asma El Bakry is a distinctive voice in Egyptian cinema and, though her work varies in tone, there are a number of constant features. Of course, there is no positive Western-style protagonist who can—in the end—achieve his goal. Female characters—the whores, Azouz's wife, Souad—are, as usual in Arab cinema, depicted as being ill-treated by men, but this is not the central focus of El Bakry's work. There is always a background of ordinary people living ordinary Cairo lives, but El Bakry's male characters are not at home in this world. At the same time, they lack the power to change it. All have to acquiesce: Nour El-Din gives up trying to impose order and authority, Azouz abandons his Western dream, and the revolutionaries see their efforts come to nothing. El Bakry's world is full of challenges and inequalities, but transforming it is beyond the characters' abilities.

The independent stance of these two filmmakers, despite the fact that they have won numerous awards at international film festivals, has generally not been well received in Egypt. El Bakry's third feature, *Violence and Derision*, seems not to have been released in Egypt, and *Gate of the Sun* is not included in official Egyptian film listings, since it is regarded as a foreign production. But the work of the pair inspired the efforts in the 2000s of several younger Egyptian filmmakers, including Khaled El Hagar and Atef Hetata, whose work has been considered elsewhere.[226]

Lebanon

Heiny Srour, Borhan Alawiya and Jacqueline Saab are three distinctive filmmakers who fit perfectly Hady Zaccak's classification of a group he calls "filmmakers of the Lebanese intelligentsia." All were born in Lebanon in the 1940s but were shaped by study abroad in France or Belgium. Along with a handful of their contemporaries, they were crucial in the transition of Lebanese cinema from the 1970s to the 1980s, creating "a cinematic practice that corresponded to a structure of feeling deeply rooted in Arab culture."[227] All three mixed documentary and fiction during their very different careers and did significant work abroad and with foreign funding.

Ibrahin al-Ariss sets out three ways in which their projects were "radically different from what Lebanese cinema had known in the past": "First, they saw the relationship between Lebanon and the rest of the Arab world as an organic one, which gave Lebanese filmmakers the prerogative to make films in any part of the Arab world and about any of its issues. Second, in their films about Lebanon they sought to understand the social and political reality of Lebanon, and to express it without fear or reticence. Finally their film practices were new."[228]

Heiny Srour, who was born to Jewish parents in 1945 in Beirut, studied sociology at the American University in Beirut and social anthropology at the Sorbonne in Paris. It was there, through the influence of Jean Rouch, that she became interested in cinema. But, as she has noted, Rouch's course "was so underfunded, that we mostly watched ethnographic films and hardly trained in actual filmmaking. The students were overwhelmingly male, Rouch always in Africa, so I was still having doubts about my path."[229] In Paris, she was impressed by films as diverse as Fellin's *8½* and Fernando Solanas's *The Hour of the Furnaces*, but neither proved a model for the films she wanted to develop. Srour, with her twin passions for feminism and Third World national liberation, is an iconoclastic figure in the context of Lebanese cinema.

Though both her feature-length works—made ten years apart—have attracted considerable critical attention, she was never able to establish a real career, and she has largely lived abroad, in London or Paris. She did, however, manage to make a handful of video works in the 1990s, the first of which was *The Singing Sheikh* (1991), a ten-minute contribution to the Channel Four South series. Shot securely within the conventions of mainstream television, it is an affectionate portrait of Sheikh Imam Mohamed Ahmad Eisa, a blind Cairo musician. Far from lamenting his fate, he is happy with it. Blindness has made him "blessed with more vision"; learning the Koran by heart has been a further "great blessing," while his gift for music is "a talent given only to angels." His heroes are Che Guevara and Ho Chi Minh, and an ongoing concern is Palestine. The song that resonates through the piece is "The Oppressed Are Rejoicing." Living in the old quarter of Cairo, he is a much-loved and revered member of the community and is respected for his free thinking, which led to half a dozen spells in prison in the 1970s.

Srour began her career with the feature-length documentary *The Hour of Liberation / L'heure de la libération a sonné / Sa'at ad-tahrir daqqat* (1974). She has recorded that she had great difficulty getting her family, especially her father, to accept her career and her lifestyle. As she admits, she accused male Arab filmmakers of having problems with their mothers only to find that she was "a woman filmmaker who had just as many problems with her father."[230] In fact, as she records, "I experienced the first day of the Lebanese Civil War in a very symbolic way, by being cast out by my father from the paternal home, after he had humiliated me to the core in the presence of a colleague [the Algerian filmmaker, Abdelaziz Tolbi] who had regarded me as a heroine for having made the film *The Hour of Liberation* among the resistance fighters in Dhofar."[231] There were also considerable difficulties in both finding funding for the film as well as actually shooting it.

The Hour of Liberation is a film totally committed to the Popular Front for the Liberation of the Occupied Arabian Gulf (PFLOAG)—there are no ambiguities and no space for questioning any of the organization's claims and activities. The origin of the film is intriguing, since it results from an interview commissioned by the editor of the journal *Africasia*. At first, Srour found the topic unpalatable. For her, as a Lebanese, "anything related to the Gulf carried a stinking trail of moral and political corruption."[232] She was not initially impressed by the PFLOAG representative, until he mentioned that one of the aims of the struggle was to "liberate women from their oppression," since women "suffered a double oppression in an underdeveloped country."[233] Immediately, she was determined to make a film, dropped her research at the Sorbonne, and began to sort out financing. This proved extremely difficult, as she had no prior experience or formal technical training. Eventually she obtained an initial £500 from a German television producer, and the project could get under way. She spent a month researching on the border with Yemen before her French (all-male) crew arrived, and they were allowed two months shooting in the province of Dhofar, "an underdeveloped, roadless mountainous, desertic area."

The tone of *The Hour of Liberation* is set from the outset: a sequence of carefully posed still images of the revolutionaries, alternating with titles bearing political slogans, and accompanied by a patriotic song and a male voice-over denouncing imperialism and pointing to the British government's real interest in the area: its oil deposits. The complicity of local rulers in this colonial system is constantly stressed. There is a limited use of archive footage, but most of the material comprises direct, straightforward imagery shot by Srour's two-man team working with basic 16mm equipment. A key to the film is its stress on the role of women in the struggle, training and bearing arms alongside the men, whom they equal in number. There are no direct-to-camera interviews. Srour shows but does not interrogate the freedom fighters. Emphasis is placed on the positive activities of the revolutionaries: their efforts to construct the road network denied them by the British, to replace ancient sorcery with modern medicine (though supplies are limited), and to develop schools, always with a stress on collaborative effort. Even more impressive are the debate sessions involving both children and adults in discussion with their leaders about issues felt important by them. The film ends with demonstrations of support in the United Kingdom and by representatives from as far afield as Algeria and Vietnam.

The Hour of Liberation is a forerunner of much of what was to come in Lebanese documentary, with filmmakers struggling under adverse conditions, with minimal budgets and at the risk of their lives in war situations. This sixty-minute study of the then little-known liberation struggle in Oman was the first film by a woman and the first from the Middle East region to be selected for screening at the Cannes Film Festival.[234] In the Soviet bloc, it was treated with some reserve, withdrawn from both the Moscow and Leipzig festivals to which Srour had been invited.

The strengths of *The Hour of Liberation* are its simplicity and straightforward commitment. A key to Srour's second full-length work and first fictional feature, *Leila and the Wolves* (1984), is a statement in one of her interviews: "Those of us from the Third World have to reject the idea of film narration based on the nineteenth-century bourgeois novel with its commitment to harmony. Our societies have been too lacerated and fractured by colonial power to fit into those neat scenarios."[235] The film is an ambitious experimental fiction that brings together enacted scenes (with the cast taking on multiple roles) and newsreel footage, some of it dating back to the British Mandate and some recording Israeli massacres (such as that at Deir Yassin). Many of the scenes re-create events in a realistic manner, with Rafiq, for instance, cast at different times as both hero and villain. Others are purely symbolic, often reinforced by an imaginative use of music (as in the dance of death toward the end of the film, when Leila dances with a group of men in skeleton masks). Overall, the film adopts the kind of loose narrative pattern used, for example, by Merzak Allouache in his Algerian fantasy, *The Adventures of a Hero*.

The heroine, Leila, like the director herself, works in London as an exhibition curator. When she notices that the exhibition set up by her partner, Rafiq, has no images of women's roles in the struggles across the Arab world, she resolves to put this right and travels through time and space to reveal aspects of women's repression and resistance in the Arab world. The wolves of the titles are the males who continually thwart women's freedom. The film's iconic image is that of Leila, clad in the flowing white gown she wears through much of the film, addressing a silent and repressed semicircle of black burka–clad women (while the men splash freely about in the sea nearby in their bathing trunks). The same actresses (all nonprofessionals) are also seen at one point in a guerrilla training camp, their eyes blindfolded as they learn to load and handle weapons. But the liberation of the women on the beach is a timid one: at the end of the film they do remove their veils but remain black-clad as they paddle timidly in the shallows.

Borhan Alawiya (known in French as Borhan Alaouié) was born in 1941 and studied filmmaking at INSAS in Brussels. He has had an unusual shape to his career. To begin with, he was commissioned by the Syrian General Organisation for Cinema and the Établissement Arabe du Cinéma in Beirut to make a feature film, *Kafr Kassem*, immediately after his graduation in 1973, at the age of just thirty-two.

Kafr Kassem (1974) is a complex work, quite remarkable as the debut feature of a young man just emerging from film school. A documentary drama reconstructing one of the worst Israeli massacre—the killing of forty-seven helpless Palestinians—it creates an enormously powerful impact while eschewing all the key devices, such as suspense and surprise, customarily used to create dramatic effect. As Claude Michel Cluny has noted, "Free from the dramatic tension which a traditionally conceived film would undoubtedly have sustained up to a spectacular ending, the script can bring to the fore the wheels of the killing machine, while revealing the contradictions which surround it on both sides: Jewish racism and Arab resignation."[236]

The film is tightly shaped, with captions giving the time and date to locate the action. Each victim is named at the end. There is a double focus: on the massacre itself and on the Israeli legal reaction to it. The chilling precredit sequence of the Israeli trial after the massacre sets the tone. The accused border guard Shalom Aoufar proclaims that he has been taught to hate all Arabs and had no doubts about participating in the massacre. When the hypothetical question is posed—what would you do if you encountered a harmless woman ten meters from her home twenty minutes after the imposition of a curfew that she had no way of knowing was in force—he replies, "I would shoot her immediately."

We know from this moment on how the film will end. But while we know that many of them will die, the inhabitants of Kafr Kassem continue their lives in blissful ignorance. On July 23, 1956, for example, they gather at home or in the village café to hear Nasser proclaim, on the radio, his solidarity with the Palestinians and announce the nationalization of the Suez Canal. Most acclaim the news; only the communists have their doubts. But elsewhere things have changed. The Israelis have enacted laws to permit the confiscation of land "vital to national security" and declared uncultivated land to be public property (while at the same time prohibiting Palestinians from entering their own farmland to cultivate it). After the Nasser speech, the dispossessed villagers, now forced to work as laborers for the new Israeli owner on what was once their own land, protest against their low wages. But their protests have no positive result. The arrival of the Israeli radio truck, allowing those with permits to send messages to relatives abroad, underlines the anguish caused by the expulsion of so many Palestinians and the resulting breakup of families after the 1948 establishment of Israel. As September 29, 1956, proceeds toward evening, the daily routines of domestic life—herding sheep, harvesting the crops—continue as usual, with no incident of any kind to provoke what is to follow.

The handling of the massacre is masterly, setting out the sequence of events with total precision, preparing us for the full horror of what is to follow. For the first time in the film, we go back in time, to 2:00 p.m. on September 29, and the perspective shifts to that of the Israeli forces. The immediate planned Israeli response to the nationalization of the Suez Canal is the invasion of Sinai. To ensure that this occurs without problems, a clampdown on the Palestinian Territories has been decreed. The local commander Colonel Shadni interprets his required actions in the harshest possible terms. The curfew in Kafr Kassem is to operate from 5:00 p.m. on that day until 6:00 a.m. the next morning. There are to be no arrests; anyone breaking the curfew is to be shot—men, women, and children alike.

At this point, the film again moves forward in time, to the trial with which the film opened. All those involved in the massacre of dozens of Palestinians are found guilty by the Israeli court, but they are given minimal sentences and allowed to keep their military rank. As dusk falls, the shepherds and farmworkers begin to return to Kafr Kassem. They are all—including a truckload of female workers—lined up and shot. Only two or three escape death. At this point, orders arrive to abort the curfew, and the people of the village spill out to search for their dead husbands, wives, and children. The film concludes with a title detailing the verdict passed by the Israeli court on Colonel Shadni (found guilty, fined one Israeli cent, and allowed to retain his rank). The anger of Alawiya, who scripted the film as well as directed it, is clear throughout. But the presentation of the massacre is sober and measured, giving the film its immense power. One can only agree with Claude Michel Cluny's judgment in 1978 that *Kafr Kassem* "is one of the most important work [*sic*] in Arab cinema, thanks to its themes and search for an obective language."[237]

Alawiya subsequently received funding from UNESCO to make a first feature-length documentary, *It Is Not Enough for God to Be with the Poor / Il ne suffit pas que Dieu soit avec les pauvres / La yakfi an yakoun allah maal foukara* (1976), cowritten and codirected with a fellow INSAS graduate, the Tunisian Lotfi Thabet. It deals with Arab architecture and features the Egyptian architect Hassan Fathi, for whom, as the opening title indicates, there is a contradiction between Western modernism and a modernity dominated by natural values, founded on a scientific spirit, and based on a real confidence in people's potentialities. Fathi places his faith in Arab modernity and appears in person to argue against the import of Western architecture into the Arab world, contrasting the layout and values of a traditional Arab city with the neighboring modern architecture that towers over it. Fathi advocates for the type of Arab house in which he himself lives, finding that its spaces correspond to human needs and desires.

The film concludes with Fathi's concern for the peasants of Upper Egypt, still living in traditional ways on the fringes of the modern monetary system. Here the focus is on the village of Gharb Assouan, brick-built in traditional style by the peasants themselves, and the ancient village of Gourna, where Fathi himself was involved involved in building a new residential quarter in the traditional style. *It Is Not Enough for God to Be with the Poor*, which stands apart from most of the rest of Alawiya's work, is a perfect illustration of the "critical documentary approach" that Néjia Ben Mabrouk defines as fundamental to INSAS teaching.

In 1982, Alawiya settled in Paris, where he has lived ever since. There he has made half a dozen or so short films, mostly documentaries, since the mid-1980s, many of them concerned with exile. Alawiya is a filmmaker who does not make a distinction between documentary and fiction: "For me, this separation does not exist; I can understand that it is a useful terminology to sort things out. But either cinema exists, or it doesn't."[238] Two fifty-two-minute films that capture the particular flavor of Alawiya's work and the delight he has in playing with fiction and reality are *Letter in a Time of Exile* / *Lettre d'un temps de l'exil* / *Risala min zaman al-manfa* (1984) and *To You, Wherever You May Be* / *À toi, où que tu sois* / *Ilayk aynama takoun* (2001).

Letter in a Time of Exile moves among Paris, Brussels, and Strasbourg to tell four tales of exile that look to be documentary studies but all turn out (from the final credits) to be acted performances. A recurring theme is transport, with the first two stories, both narrated by Alawiya, set largely in the *métro*. For Abdallah, the *métro* is a lonely place where he spends three hours because he has loaned out his room to a friend to allow him to spend time with a girl. For Karim, it is a place of magic, a great illusion, a darkroom in which colors emerge from the negative. In Brussels, Rizkallah, the only one of the four characters to talk directly to the camera, speaks at length of the pleasure of living in Brussels and of his frustration that his brother will not join him from Beirut. In Strasbourg, Alawiya tells the story of Nassim, a doctor mourning the death of his father. The four contrasting stories offer no single coherent vision of exile and little that is specific to the Lebanese experience. Instead, they are meditations on the very diverse ways in which exile is experienced. The choice of the first-person letter format is significant. As Hamid Naficy has noted, "Exile and epistolarity necessitate one another, for distance and absence drive them both."[239]

To You Wherever You May Be, the answering piece, is a letter from Alawiya addressed from Beirut in 2001 to the (fictional) Karim from *Letter in a Time of Exile*, with whom Alawiya claims to have lost contact. Again, Karim is treated as a real person. The film begins with footage from the earlier film to introduce Karim and contains interviews with people who are referred to as his "favorite poet" or his "best friend." The core of the film is one of the constant themes of exilic literature and film: the home from which you have been separated for years, during which time you have kept its image alive in your memory and imagination, no longer exists if you actually revisit it. In the circumstances, with Karim known to be a fictional character, the veracity of the ten interviewees, whom Alawiya summons to support his verdict on Beirut, must be in some doubt. Some, such the poet Ounsi al-Hajj and "Karim's best friend," Ahmed Beydoun, have an air of authenticity. Some of the minor figures, marked by the civil war years, are the kind of witnesses customary in Lebanese documentary. But several of those who talk of Beirut by night and are referred to only by a first name could be either dramatic constructions by Alawiya or self-dramatizing individuals. Alawiya's filmic approach allows no clear distinction to be made. The final message to Karim is that "nothing remains of those nights that we had in Beirut, the realm of our dreams and memories—except the music."

Alawiya, who also contributed one episode to the Tunisian-produced collective film *After the Gulf? / La guerre du Golfe . . . et après / Harbu al-khalîj wa ba'du?* (1992), is the ideal chronicler of the complex experience of exile, where the now and the then are inextricably entwined. For him, "The essential work of a filmmaker is to construct a film by putting one time on top of another, as an architect places brick upon brick." What he appreciates in cinema is "what is between the shots, the ellipses," because "cinema is a construction in time, a mosaic of time."[240]

Beirut: The Encounter / Beyrouth, "la rencontre" / Beirut al-liqa' (1981), Alawiya's second fictional feature, was a Lebanese-Belgian-Tunisian coproduction, produced by one of the most talented of the new generation of Tunisian producers, Hassan Daldoul. The film was shot in 1980–81 but set "one day in 1977," and the key figure is arguably the divided city of Beirut itself. The protagonist, Haïdar, awakens to the sound of rubbish being cleared from streets outside the flat where he is staying with his brother and his family. The actual fighting in Beirut remains in the background, but the film stresses the different impact of the conflict on the two sides of the city. The main contrast in the film's pared-down visuals is that between Muslim West Beirut, where Haïdar is staying, and the affluent Christian suburb of Achrafieh, where Zeina, the woman he is trying to contact, lives with her family. The streets of West Beirut are full of destroyed buildings, and there is evidence of gunfire and shelling everywhere, whereas Achrafieh has peaceful tree-lined avenues.

Though the film distinguishes so graphically the differing effects of the war on the two halves of the city, there is no attribution of blame in the film. The uncontrolled power of armed militants is apparent in both communities. Politics are barely touched on, except in an early scene where Haïdar, reading a headline that East and West will soon to be reunited, comments, "What about the South, will that be abandoned?" The war has a paradoxical effect on Muslims and Christians alike: while Haïdar, a refugee from the South, feels ruined West Beirut is a place where he can be active, Zeina's family has decided to leave the apparent security of the Christian neighborhood to live as exiles, despite the uncertain future that awaits them in the United States.

This is the context in which Haïdar tries to arrange a first encounter with Zeina, whom he knew at university. The tightly focused narrative, which unfolds over a twenty-four-hour period, concentrates exclusively on the couple's thoughts, words, and experiences. Two years before, when they last met, Haïdar and Zeina had been attracted to each other, though this attraction had been expressed by nothing more than intense conversations. Now they twice attempt, unsuccessfully, to meet up. The meeting is to be at two o'clock in the café in the Christian quarter where they used to meet. But the encounter does not take place. Zeina arrives early but is driven out by the aggressive behavior of three militants, playing at one of the newly installed pinball machines. Haïdar, caught up in the traffic, arrives late, and he, too, is made apprehensive by the militants' behavior.

As an alternative, Zeina suggests that they each make an audiotape that can be exchanged as she passes through the airport into exile the next morning. Each of them, in their bedrooms, separately records a message revealing their intimate thoughts and recounting their experiences of the last two years. Though Alawiya cuts regularly from one protagonist to the other, these recordings remain monologues. The next day, it is Haïdar who arrives early, and, after a few inconclusive encounters, he grows impatient and (for reasons not explained in the film) leaves before the flight departs. Zeina, who is the one delayed by traffic on this occasion, arrives late. She weeps when she does not find him, while Haïdar, in his taxi back from the airport, destroys his tape. For Lina Khatib, though the two attempts fail, "they remain an example of the Lebanese people's resistance to the logic of segregation imposed by the war."[241] Another interpretation of *Beirut: The Encounter* would be that the director demonstrates with implacable logic the impossibility of communication across the boundaries created by the war.

Khalass (2007), which followed sixteen years later, was funded from French, Belgian, and Lebanese sources. It is by far Alawiya's most conventionally structured film, a chronologically narrated, extremely violent revenge drama, complete with a few dance sequences and an unexpected happy ending. Ahmad, a freelance journalist, and Rouby, a documentary filmmaker, are longtime friends and flatmates. On the same day, both their lives collapse. Ahmad loses his job and his girlfriend and is beaten up in a taxi. Rouby finds Wissam, a young boy he has been filming, lying in the street, knocked down by a hit-and-run driver. In the hospital, Wissam is left to die because Rouby cannot immediately come up with the money for treatment. Dejected, the pair vow revenge and take out their guns: somebody has to pay.

After stealing a car, they hunt for the man who beat Ahmad. Failing to find him, they beat and humiliate his cocaine-dealing friend. The next victim is the hospital manager, whom they gun down in his flat, along with a friend. The walls of the pair's flat are covered with photographs of victims of the civil war, along with a portrait of the man responsible, William al Ayouk. He is their next victim. Dressed as Saudis, they track him down in a luxury hotel and, wearing masks, make him drink sufficient cocaine to kill him. For Ahmad, the next victims are to be his ex-girlfriend, Abir, and her new husband, Raymond. But at the last moment, Ahmad finds himself unable to kill the woman he still loves. At this point, the film's tone changes completely, as both men are redeemed by love. Rouby takes his little daughter Leyla to rejoin her mother, Habiba, in Tunisia, while Abir returns to Ahmad and together the couple flies off to Australia, where his sister lives.

Khalass is a perplexing film from the author of *Kafr Kassem*. Ahmad and Rouby are a physically unattractive pair, and their actions are totally reprehensible. Abir is shown willing to sell herself in order to break into the movies. There is no law and order in Beirut, and no sense of morality in the film: the murderers' actions are never questioned, and they make their escape unchallenged. The tone is uneven: the killing of William, for example, is played out as a kind of farce, not as a serious act of long-contemplated revenge.

Jacqueline Saab was born in Beirut in 1948 and studied economics at the Sorbonne in Paris. She describes herself as having grown up in a sheltered world, within "a very bourgeois, cultured family" and given a French-language education. Of her initial time in Paris, she has said: "I became interested in the Arab world. I wanted to know who I was."[242] As a result, she worked for a time as a journalist, and though she had no formal film training, she turned to documentary filmmaking in 1973. Because she was a woman "who could think and was an intellectual, and was different from the image they had of women," certain possibilities opened to her, and she was able to begin her career with a fifty-two-minute *Portrait of Gaddafi / Portrait de Khadafi* (1973). Over the next two decades, she made over two dozen, mostly short, 16mm documentaries, covering a whole swath of issues in the Middle East.[243] She also made three feature-length documentaries that show the range of her interests: *Lebanon in Torment / Le Liban dans la tourmente / Lubnân fi al-dawâma* (1975), *The Sahara is Not for Sale / Le Sahara n'est pas à vendre* (1977), and *The Lady from Saigon / La dame de Saïgon / Saida Saighon* (1997).

Saab's documentary work contains social and political analysis across a range of Middle Eastern countries: Libya, Syria, Iraq, the Palestinian Territories, Mauritania, and, especially, Egypt and Lebanon. By contrast, her three varied feature films, made over a period of twenty years—*A Suspended Life / Une vie suspendue / Gazal al-banat 2* (1984), *Once Upon a Time, Beirut / Il était une fois, Beyrouth / Kan ya ma kan, Beirut* (1994), and *Dunia* (2005)—explore the more intimate world of women's existence in the Arab world.

Like most of Saab's feature work, *A Suspended Life* is known by a number of titles. The US-distributed video gives an (unused) alternative title, *The Razor's Edge*, while its Arab title, *Ghazal al-banat 2*, is a direct allusion to Anwar Wagdi's 1949 popular mainstream Egyptian feature about love across class, the title of which translates as both *Candy Floss* and *The Flirtation of Girls*.[244] The film was shot in West Beirut, ten years into the civil war, and no doubt reflects Saab's personal situation at the time, when she was, by her own account, pregnant, homeless after a kidnapping attempt, and living "in a mental or inner exile in Lebanon."[245] Certainly, the impact of the continuing conflict is always there in the film's background, except for the small children, who have known no other way of life and whose mock funeral ("for South Lebanon") has a touching innocence, as does their indifference to Karim's death at the very end of the film. Virtually all the adults in the film are haunted by memories (for example, Samir's father's recollection of his lost life as a fisherman in South Lebanon) or trapped in repetitive behavior (a gunman continually shooting at birds in the trees, a drunken sniper playing his deadly game with an unseen opponent). Donatien spends his time collecting old newspapers, "because they are all the same," and Samir's father obsessively collects tiles to repair all the roofs of Beirut (he claims to have 32,875). Everyone, it seems, is torn between the need to leave Beirut and the desire to stay. Beirut is both an unreal, nightmare landscape and a place where real killing occurs, in one instance depicted in documentary war footage.

A Suspended Life is a complex and, at times, perplexing film, since the boundaries between the real and the imagined are seldom clearly marked, and the dialogue constantly shifts between ordinary conversation and poetic declamation. The fourteen-year-old Samir is a product of the war years, allowed to roam free in the torn city, but the film is not a realistic depiction of her situation; rather, it is a tale of her unfolding consciousness, mixing naturalistic recording of her everyday life with dream and fantasy sequences. For example, she recalls or imagines a wedding morning (her own?), with the mother waving a blood-stained cloth. Samir is like a figure from a fairy tale, drifting into a pink house—the "palace" she dreams about, but in reality the studio of a middle-aged artist and widower, Karim. She steals an old watch, leaving a black footprint on one of the canvases spread out on the floor. She returns, bringing strawberries as a gift, and is forced to admit that the footprint is hers. For her, the war is good, because it allows her encounters that would otherwise be impossible. She is free, while the adult world is stifled, seemingly untouched even when she sleeps with a boy for money and has to have her vagina repaired.

Yet the film is always enigmatic—her relationship with Karim is both intimate and impersonal, full of concealments as well as moments of openness. She accuses him of always painting the same picture, but at the same time, she proclaims her love for him. For Karim, she is just a child, but she identifies herself with Beirut and its five-thousand-year history. Toward the end of the film, the pair enter an abandoned theater, where Hakim performs a soliloquy of despair. But then the stage mysteriously fills with characters from earlier in the film, now performing in front of an audience of mummified figures covered in cobwebs. Samir announces her father's death and is reconciled with her brother. All that remains is for Samir to say goodbye to Karim before he is shot dead by an unseen sniper in the empty street outside his house.

Once Upon a Time, Beirut, Saab's second feature, is often given the subtitle *The Story of a Star / Histoire d'une star / Qissah najmah*. The film was made after the end of the civil war and has a much more optimistic tone, though it opens with a very serious quote from Marguerite Duras's script for Alain Resnais's

Hiroshima mon amour: "Why deny the evident necessity of memory?" This was a time during which, Saab has said, she "felt totally free" but that also "brought up memories of my country, and I decided to make a feature film about Lebanon."[246] As so often in Lebanese films, Beirut is at the cinema of the film's focus, as Saab has made clear: "For a long time, Beirut was the West's Oriental 'favourite.' It had no rival in the Near East. It was a city for people from all cultures, a place of business, pleasure and drama, but also a place of myths. . . . But, although the myths associated with Beirut did so much over the years to enhance its wealth and fame, they were also largely responsible for its downfall. The idea here is to review these great myths."[247]

In *Once Upon a Time, Beirut*, two young girls, Leila and Yasmine, just emerging from their teenage years and clad respectively in jeans and miniskirt, set out on a project to discover the real identity of Beirut. Enlisting the support of the reclusive Monsieur Farouk, who began by projecting films at the Rio cinema at the age of thirteen and went on to own ten cinemas in Beirut, they make their exploration by using his personal archive to uncover the cinematic depiction of Beirut and the state of Lebanon.

The result is a (literally) fantastic voyage through cinematic depictions of Beirut and Lebanon, using episodes from around forty Lebanese, Egyptian, European, and Hollywood movies, including Volker Schlöndorff's *The Forger* (on which Saab worked as assistant) and her own preceding feature, *A Suspended Life*. Leila and Yasmine are able to comment on these films and occasionally participate in them, through carefully edited reconstructions staged by Saab. There is no logical chronology or order in which the film extracts are shown. As Saab has said, she sought to work by "going back to Arab narrative traditions: not like those in the Occident with the beginning, the middle, the end."[248] Hence the film juxtaposes clips from silent French black-and-white films from the Protectorate era, full of pious sentiments of the essential unity of Maronite Christians and Muslims, with Egyptian movies where Beirut is a city devoted to pleasure (with the requisite oriental dancing and broad comedy), as well as Hollywood blockbusters featuring international spy rings and (potential) mass destruction. The images of Lebanon in the past that emerge are often moving, both for the two girls and for anyone who knows Beirut's subsequent history. This is never more so than in a silent film depicting the love of Princess Daoulah (meaning "state") and Prince Salam (meaning "peace"), facilitated by a dwarf, Itak, who, thanks to a virginal kiss by Daoulah, is restored to his proper identity as the prince of Beirut.

Even Leila and Yasmine come to see that old movies, whatever their origin, recycle clichés, myths, and fantasies about Beirut. They therefore adopt a donkey as their new professor of history. This leads well into the projection of the second reel of film, which they have offered to Dr. Farouk as the justification for their visit, namely passages from Jacques Baratier's 1958 Tunisian-shot feature, *Goha*. Here Goha, the traditional Arab figure of a holy fool, accompanied always by his faithful donkey, proclaims, "Truth is a monkey, it pulls all sorts of faces."[249]

Dunia (2005), also known as *Kiss Me Not on the Eyes* (after the popular song by Abdel Wahab), is of particular interest, since it is virtually the sole fictional feature (alongside Moumen Smihi's *The Lady from Cairo*) to be made in Egypt by a noted Arab filmmaker from outside the country. It is, however, far from being a mainstream commercial product, though it does contain an abundance of song-and-dance routines, to the point that, in the words of Anny Gaul, "the entire film sings and dances, from the splish-splash of a woman pounding laundry with her feet to the murmur of city traffic."[250] The film also features an Egyptian singing star, Mohamed Mounir, in the leading role, and his songs provide much of the film's sound track.

Saab had great difficulty in finding funding for the film. There were problems too with the Egyptian censorship board: "They said my film was anti-Islamic, pornographic, and anti-Egyptian."[251] The reason for this hostility is clear. The film deals openly with female sexuality, attacks restrictive censorship practices, and deals, head-on, with the practice of female circumcision (excision, or *kittan* in Arabic). There were also problems with casting the film, since many of the actors approached were fearful of the effect the film would have on their future careers. Saab's eventual choices were excellent, however. Mohamed Mounir is totally convincing as the prominent academic and activist, Professor Bashir, who is currently campaigning against proposals to enhance censorship, while Hanan Turk is beautifully vibrant in the role of Dunia.

Though Saab's background is in documentary and she is passionately concerned about the issues raised in the film, this is by no means a social tract. It does, however, draw on recent real happenings in Egypt—the debate about the banning of *A Thousand and One Nights* and the assault, on the street, of one of Egypt's greatest novelists, Naguib Mahfouz. Essentially this is the story of a spirited young woman of twenty-three with a double ambition: to write a thesis on love in Arabic poetry and to emulate her late mother, who was a noted belly dancer (and in Dunia's eyes) a true artist. In these efforts, she is supported by two spirited older women, her tutor and her aunt, the latter of whom works as a taxicab driver.

The film's opening scene—a dance audition—makes clear where Dunia's difficulties lie. Responding to criticism about why she, as an aspiring dancer, makes so little expressive use of her body when reading a love poem, she responds by crouching down in a position where as little of her body as possible is visible and admitting that she has seen a naked woman's body only once, two years before in French film. The implication throughout the film is that Dunia herself was excised as a child, but this is never made explicit.

Against the odds perhaps, Dunia is successful in her audition and sets out to undertake further dance training in a bare studio decorated only by a large portrait of her mother and with a teacher who makes rigorous demands of her, in particular that she *feel* her body as she dances. Her enthusiasm also persuades Dr. Bashir to become her supervisor, and they begin a series of one-on-one tutorials, in which words like desire and ecstasy are discussed in the context of poetry readings. But just as she cannot dance with the required freedom, so she is unable to recite Sufi poetry with the required passion. Progress is also threatened when Dr. Bashir is attacked and blinded in a street attack motivated by the views that he has expressed on television about the need for more liberal censorship. But blindness does not make him hesitate or stifle his views. He fights back, and his therapy sessions—learning to trust himself walking now that he can no longer see—parallel Dunia's dance lessons, where she, too, must learn to trust her body.

Dunia has a boyfriend, Mamdouh, but their relationship is troubled. Even when she is leaning over the balcony, watching a love scene from an old Egyptian movie on the neighbor's television, she cannot bear to be touched. All the same, she agrees to marry Mamdouh, hoping that in this way she will find freedom. Her wedding day, when she wears a stiff white paper dress, is the only time in the film that she is not dressed in red. But despite Mamdouh's apparent gentleness, she cannot open up to him, and when she dances sensuously in front of him, he sees it as her way of taunting him and hits her. The experiment has not been a success, and she leaves him, writing her farewell note on her white paper wedding dress. This is the lowest point for Dunia, since she also has to cope with Yasmine, the little girl downstairs, who is deeply troubled now that her grandmother has organized her excision—shown in graphic detail in the film.

But all is not lost. Dr. Bashir slowly recovers his sight and the first image he sees—albeit mistily—is Dunia. Now that her marriage has ended, Dunia is emboldened. Borrowing the dress and bracelets belonging to his mistress, she gives herself to Bashir, who recites, "You are Dunia. You are the world. You are life" as, for the first time, he touches her face. After their lovemaking, Dunia is finally free, and the film ends with an image that is the very opposite to that of the film's opening scene. Casting aside her mother's scarf, which she has worn throughout, the red-clad Dunia can finally dance with true passion and sensuousness. The film should perhaps end here, but Saab, always the documentarist, presses home her point with an end title that announces that, according to Amnesty International and the United Nations, 97 percent of all Egyptian woment have been genitally mutilated.

Saab's fictional output, varying in style and tone from film to film, is always engaging and original. We are given a succession of portraits of young women struggling to discover themselves in difficult circumstances, Saab's own personal views are never hidden, but she allows the individual lives she has chosen to chronicle to proceed at their own pace, without didactic or sociological intrusions.

*

Two major figures in Lebanese documentary who began their joint careers in the 1980s are the Jordanian-born Palestinian documentary filmmaker Maï Masri and her husband, the Lebanese filmmaker Jean Chamoun. Masri was born in 1959 and educated at San Francisco University in the United States, while the slightly older Chamoun, who was born in 1944, studied at the Université de Paris VIII and began a solo career in the late 1970s. Since the early 1980s, the couple has worked together consistently, dealing mainly with Lebanese topics. The documentary work of both filmmakers, though totally reliant on foreign funding, is passionately committed to the Arab cause in Lebanon and Palestine.

The couple's collaboration has always been extremely close; whenever one has a solo directing credit, the other almost always acts as producer. Together, they have made around twenty 16mm documentaries about Lebanon and Palestine, mostly with the standard television length of fifty minutes or so. Many of these documentaries have support from NGOs and charitable organizations, and, according to their publicity material, they have been broadcast by more than one hundred television stations around the world.[252] Crucial in their output is a series of films that allows us a direct and immediate insight into successive developments in Lebanon over a period of twenty-five years.

The pair's work together began with *Under the Rubble / Sous les décombres / Tahatal ankad* (1983), which dealt with the Israeli invasion of 1982 and, especially, with the resistance of the inhabitants of Beirut under seige and faced with constant Israeli bombing. The film, which has a powerful text by Roger Assaf, is a moving and troubling depiction of a war waged largely against defenseless civilians. But even it can find no words for the event with which the film ends, the massacre at the Sabra and Shatila Palestinian refugee camps, in which an estimated two thousand men, women, and children were slaughtered.

Wild Flowers: Women of South Lebanon / Fleurs d'ajonc, femmes du Sud du Liban / Zahrat al-qandal (1986) is a feature-length study of the role of women in the struggle against the Israeli invaders. The direct accounts of women's acts of individual bravery, actual participation in the struggle, and subsequent imprisonment and torture are interspersed with domestic scenes, landscape shots, and songs celebrating the South and its women so that the final emphasis is on the women's growing self-awareness and confidence.

War Generation—Beirut / Beyrouth, génération de la guerre / Jil al-harb (1988) looks at Beirut's young people thirteen years after the outbreak of the civil war, again using direct-to-camera interviews. All four of the main participants—a child of twelve, an adolescent who has just become a militant, a Palestinian caught up after the 1982 massacre, and a young man who became involved in what seemed an idealistic cause in 1975—have shattered lives: "We're the war generation. We don't know anything."

Suspended Dreams / Rêves suspendus / Ahlam mu'allaqa (1992), made after the end of the civil war, looks at the legacy of the fighting through the eyes of four people closely involved. Nabil and Rambo, who spent ten years shooting at each other across the green line, find that, after peace is declared, they have enough in common to work together and even become friends. They feel totally deceived by their leaders. Wadad, whose husband disappeared, is most aware of the loss and the challenges of bringing up her two children. Rafiq, a satirist and performer, talks of the postwar assault on memory and culture, embodied in the grandiose plans for a new and shiny steel-and-glass Beirut. Though the war is officially over, there are still ominous signs: car bombings, uncontrolled pollution, and the Israeli shelling of the Litani River.

Hostage of Time / L'ôtage du temps / Rahinat el-intizar (1994) is set after the 1993 Israeli offensive, which caused 300,000 to flee, and tells of a young female doctor who returns after ten years study abroad. South Lebanon is now under Israeli occupation and also subject to indiscriminate shelling and bombing. The savagery of the Israeli onslaughts on defenseless civilians—for which the only explanation is an intention to drive them from their land—is laid bare. The physical and mental problems of the Lebanese population and Palestinian refugees living under this enormous pressure are vividly illustrated, and the doctor's discussions with her own family show the conflicting views of Lebanese citizens about how they should try to shape their future. But the film, like most of Masri and Chamoun's work, ends on a note of hope.

Two very different studies of third-generation Palestinian refugees, whose grandparents alone have actual memories of Palestine, show some real change in living conditions. *Children of Shatila / Les enfants de Chatila / Atfl Shatila* (1998) looks at those growing up in the Lebanese camp, now the home of all the dispossessed, who face hopeless lives. They dwell in the past, recounting tales of the 1982 massacre they are too young to remember and growing up with no prospect of integration into Lebanese society. The only link with the outside world is the one-day visit of a troupe of French clowns, and their sole touch of modernity is the video camera loaned them by the filmmakers. But in *Frontiers of Dreams and Fears / Rêves d'exil / Ahlam al-manfa* (2000), just two years later, the Chatila children have access to computers and can communicate with other refugees children in the camp at Dheisha near Bethlehem. The two groups of children are even able to meet up face to face, if only through barbed-wire fencing, at the Lebanese-Palestine border. But the adolescent excitement this triggers soon evaporates, as both groups of fourteen-year-olds become involved in the *intifada*.

In 1995, Maï Masri made her first solo fifty-minute documentary, *Hanan Ashwari: A Woman of Her Time / Hanan Ashwari, femme de son époque*, a personal portrait of the Palestinian spokesperson. From the very beginning, the film sets her personal, domestic situation against vividly shot images of the (largely Israeli provoked) violence on the streets of Palestine. Her situation is beautifully symbolized by the fact that the house where she lives with her husband and two daughters is situated just across the road from the huge prison, used successively by British, Israeli, and now Palestinian authorities.

Ashwari first came to prominence as an articulate, forceful female spokesperson for Yasser Arafat's PLO at the time of the Madrid talks in 1991, breaking all the stereotypes of the submissive, victimized Arab woman. She carried out this role for two years but did not participate in the subsequent Gaza Political Authority, preferring to concentrate on human rights issues. These, as she soon came to understand, meant a confrontation with the Palestinian authorities misusing their power, as well as opposition to Israeli oppression. This latter is made vividly apparent by her own difficulties in traveling the few miles through the Israeli checkpoint separating her home in Ramallah from Jerusalem, "a place where the whole Palestinian reality comes together."

We learn of Ashwari's background, which has undoubtedly given her the confidence to assert herself in a male-dominated world. Her father was a Christian doctor who was one of the founders of the PLO, and she herself was educated, first in a Quaker school, then at the American University in Beirut, and subsequently at the University of Virginia, where she completed her doctorate (a trajectory that parallels that of several Palestinian filmmakers). The bulk of the film shows Ashwari's human rights activities, as much concerned with Palestinian abuse of the law as with Israeli violence. We see her addressing a joint Palestinian-Israeli women's rally, where she shows that her commitment to peace and understanding is absolute. But the film cannot find an optimistic resolution, as we witness scenes of Israeli demolition of Palestinian homes and the destruction of ancient vineyards to create the network of Israeli-only roads linking the settlements to Israel (a program still in operation a decade after this film was made).

In the 2000s, Masri directed two feature-length documentaries both dealing with Lebanon. *Beirut Diaries: Truth, Lies and Videos / Chroniques de Beyrouth: vérités, mensonges et vidéos* (2006) deals with the Beirut Martyrs' Square camp set up in opposition to the Syrian occupation, which grew up, seemingly spontaneously, immediately after the assassination of the Lebanese prime minister and billionaire entrepreneur, Rafic Hariri, on February 14, 2005. The diaries are those of a participant, a young woman, Nadine Zaidan, who was in her flat, three minutes' walk from the St. George Hotel, when the killing took place. The beginning is full of euphoria, with a real sense that their demands for "truth, freedom and national unity" must be met. The huge rally by Hezbollah in Riad Solh Square on March 8 is more than matched by the opposition's Martyrs' Square rally on March 14, involving one million Lebanese (a quarter of the entire population). Dialogue between the young people is constant, but the differences in their approaches become increasingly obvious. The Syrian withdrawal offers hope, but a (curiously joyous) rally to celebrate the thirtieth anniversary of the outbreak of the civil war only underlines the lack of comprehension among the young of the older people. The latter's lives continue to be locked within the civil war, and they are still seeking news of the seventeen thousand people from both sides who disappeared without trace. After seventy-two days, when the camp is dissolved, the old guard are back in politics, and a new sectarianism has been born, with a fresh wave of assassinations and car bombs. Like so many Lebanese before her, Nadine is left with the sense of having been manipulated by outside forces and deceived by her own Lebanese leaders.

The narrative of *33 Days / 33 jours / 33 yaoum* (2007) is intercut with newsreel footage of the Israeli invasion that began on July 12, 2006, but deals with the conflict indirectly, focusing on journalists involved in reporting the conflict and on those working through drama to maintain the spirits of the displaced children whose lives have been torn apart. There is a sense of victory for Hezbollah, but not for the refugees, even as they are finally able to return to their devastated villages in the South. The great strength of Masri and Chamoun's work lies in the personal statements of the ordinary people whom they encounter and interview, creating an immediacy to the horrors that their documentaries confront.

In 2008, Chamoun directed *Lanterns of Memory* for Al Jazeera Documentary, dealing with the unresolved issue of the estimated seventeen thousand Lebanese kidnapped and missing from all sides of the conflict. For the now aging mothers of those lost, the need is for the truth, for the known mass graves to be opened up, and for the victims to be given proper funerals. Chamoun opens the film with the return of Samir Qantar, Lebanon's longest-serving prisoner (he spent twenty-seven years in Israeli prisons), who is enrolled in the mothers' cause. But the focus is mainly on the efforts of Wadad, first seen in *Suspended Dreams*, who is still seeking news of her husband after over a quarter of a century. Chamoun also finds again the two frontline militants, Rambo and Nabil, still friends but now with families of their own. Though the pain is deep, there seems little real hope for the victims' families—the powerful in Lebanon have no wish to reveal the truth and, perhaps, their own personal guilt and responsibility.

*

Two distinctive filmmakers pursuing a very different kind of documentary form—the personal filmic statement, which it emerged in the 1990s—are Olga Nakkas and Mohamed Souheid.

Olga Nakkas has an international background, having been born in 1953 in Turkey and subsequently educated in the United States and France. She has directed two feature-length works, made fifteen years apart: *Lebanon: Bits and Pieces / Le Liban, fait de pièces et de morceaux / Lubnan min taraf ila taraf akhar* (1994) and *Mother, Lebanon and Me / Maman, le Liban et moi* (2009), which exemplifies the more personalized, digitally made documentary style of the 2000s. She has said of her documentary work and her relationship to Lebanon (which she originally left when she was fourteen): "*Lebanon, Bits and Pieces* is the first film into which I really put a lot of myself. It deals with my relationship with my past and with a country I love and hate at the same time. . . . It is the story of my anger and reconciliation with Lebanon, a story of my love affair with this country. It's a love-hate relationship, a country that I always leave and come back to, a country I cannot live with but at the same time cannot be too far from."[253]

Ibrahim al-Ariss notes that "with minimalist style Olga Nakkas presented a perplexing and bewildering Lebanon emerging from the silence of the canons, through a series of meetings between her, the returnee, and some of the friends she seeks out, in whose demeanor and behavior she observes the new Lebanon."[254]

Mohamed Souheid was born in Beirut in 1959 and has had a varied career. He first studied at the Lebanese University but made an initial career as a writer. He has worked as a film critic in the daily press and has also written a number of books on cinema in Arabic. He published his first novel, *Cabaret Souad*, in 2004 and served for a time as professor of film at the Université Saint-Joseph in Beirut. He has also worked in television and collaborated on the scripts of several feature films, including Yousry Nasrallah's Egyptian adaptation of Elias Khoury's novel *Gate of the Sun*. In 1990, he made the first of a number of short personal video documentaries. He began his feature career in the late 1990s with a trilogy of autobiographical works: *Tango of Yearning / Tango du désir / Tango el-amal* (1998), *Nightfall / Jusqu'au déclin du jour / Indama ya'ti el-massa* (2000), and *Civil War / Guerre civile* (2002).

Tango of Yearning has a title seemingly derived from a ballad, *Tango of Hope*, by the singer Nur al-Huda. It marks Souheid as a filmmaker unlike any other in Lebanese cinema. The film is a subjective outpouring of love, loss, grief, and self-justification—the ultimate in autobiographical (not to say narcissistic) film-making. There is an opening quotation from Andrei Tarkovsky and frequent references to films and filmmakers (from Mohamed Abelwahab to Marlon Brando). But there is no attempt at a coherent narrative, and the recurring sequence of titles imposed on the film offers little sense of a sequence of events or references. There is frequent mention of a failed television series, *Fond of Camilia*, but this does not appear in any of Souheid's published filmographies (perhaps it is a disguised reference to the TV miniseries *Women in Love*, which he did direct). The film never follows the basic rules of conventional documentary, so there is doubt about how much of it is literally true and how much of it is simply the director's subjective "truth."

Tango of Yearning frequently separates sound and image to make creative juxtapositions and to avoid a logical sequencing of material. One is inclined to believe the old man who tells of his attempt to keep cinemas open in Beirut during the civil war (even instituting women-only matinees), but whether the testimonies of Souheid's friends, given to him, direct to camera, are spontaneous or prescripted is uncertain. As Souheid says, "I was hopefully looking for the moment that revealed how much people were eager to reconstruct their own stories with their own language(s), as well as mine."[255] Against the background of a devastated Beirut, where no systematic attempt has ever been made to establish the truth of the civil war years, *Tango of Yearning* offers its own tentative, highly personal account of love and loss.

In *Nightfall*, the emphasis is on another aspect Souheid's past, his participation during the early 1970s in the so-called Student Brigade, a group aligned to the Palestinian liberation movement, Fatah. This was a coming together of a number of committed young Lebanese whose aspirations were defined at one point as "a mixture of innocence and hypocrisy, political revolution and personal expression." Souheid is his own cameraman, and much of the action is filmed during an increasingly drunken evening, where the surviving (and now much older) members of the group try to remember why they chose Fatah rather than one of the Lebanese movements of the time (such as the Communist Party). We see a group of men (and a few women) struggling incoherently (partly because of the quantity of alcohol they have consumed) with their own experiences and motivations from twenty-five years before, remembering dead colleagues, beginning stories that they cannot finish, reciting snatches of poetry, and singing half-remembered patriotic songs. In all, there are a dozen or so old colleagues who share their memories with Souheid, the most celebrated of these being the novelist Elias Khoury. Again, there is no attempt to present a coherent narrative or to give any information beyond that of the firsthand accounts by Souheid's informants. Laura U. Marks, for whom Souheid is "a central proponent of the experimental video documentary movement, which is perhaps Lebanon's greatest contribution to contemporary Arab and world cinema," aptly writes of his "passion, compassion, love of lost or unlikely causes and taste for slapstick."[256]

Civil War, Souheid's tribute to Mohamed Douaybess, a film technician who disappeared in 2000, begins with characteristic Souheid wry humor, "Mohamed, Mohamed, there are too many Mohameds in this country." Later he shouts, "Mohamed!" in the street, and four or five men and boys turn round to look at him. The film also contains the customary mix of direct-to-camera interviews, songs, voice-over comments by the filmmaker, and digressions (for examples, on the relationship between tooth decay and stress, a theory that the civil war was caused by sexual frustration, a treatise on what kind of beating for a child is allowed in Islam, the death of the actress Souad Hosni), as well as unexpected enacted scenes (a woman wanting her one-thousand-page observational novel filmed, an implausibly overweight karate fighter in training). There are juxta-positions of image and sound (Beirut street scenes overlaid with jungle sounds) and unexpected visual effects (some of the testimony by the dead man's friends superimposed on the windows of ruined buildings).

The sense of continuity in this loose trilogy of works is strong. Mohamed, a film technician who trained in Greece, is described as embracing his camera as if it were his girlfriend, just as Abou Hassan in *Nightfall* compared holding a wom-an's breast to holding an arak glass (the latter is better, he proclaimed). Mohamed, who never allows himself to be filmed, is torn between his hopes and his reality, just as the friends in *Tango of Yearning* reflect on their ideals and the actual-ity of the war. The film seems always to find a way not to reach its conclusion, which, when it does eventually arrive, contains unnecessarily graphic descrip-tions of the decomposition of a body. At the end, the director is again shouting, to inform Mohamed of Souad Hosny's death and Youssef Chahine's new movie, and demanding to know who is Mohamed's favorite director: Mohamed Souheid (first of course) or Akram Zaatari, Ghassan Salhab, Roger Assaf, or Jean Cham-oun? The film ends with still photographs of (presumably) the real Mohamed Doaybess, though, since even his name has been called into account earlier in the film, one can never be sure.

Souheid has recently completed another feature-length documentary, *My Heart Beats Only for Her / Mon cœur ne bat que pour elle / Ma hataftu li ghayriha* (2008). The title is derived from one of Fatah's anthems, and the "Her" of the title refers to Beirut. The film again deals with the now largely forgotten revolutionary era of Beirut in the 1970s (Souheid's own youth), when the dream of many young militants was to make it an "Arab Hanoi." The central thread concerns a militant, Hatem Hatem, who took the name Abu Hassan Hanoi and dreamed of making the revolution, visiting Vietnam, and working in Hollywood. A search by his son reveals that, in fact, Hatem soon left Fatah and ended his life as a provincial wedding photographer. Subsequently, the film, rather confusingly, explores the son's own life through a comparison of three contemporary cities: Beirut, Hanoi, and Dubai.

Interestingly, one reviewer has described *My Heart Beats Only for Her* as being about Souheid's discovery of his own father's earlier activities. In a sense, Souheid's documentaries are all self-portraits as much as they are studies of their ostensible subject matter, particularly as so much of the meaning is carried in his own voice-over narrations and interjections (though even these are often fiction-alized and read by another voice). The characters address Souheid directly, and he gets drawn into the discussion, with the result that *Civil War*, for example, is addressed as a kind of shared letter to his dead friend. Souheid likes to draw out aspects of his subjects that correspond to his own preoccupations. There is the constant series of references to films and film viewing and also an ambivalent relation to women, combining both attraction and, simultaneously, a lack of commitment.

Often the links in Souheid's films are idiosyncratic and become clear only as the film unfolds: in *Civil War* we only fully understand the early references to dentistry when we learn that Mohamed Douaybess could be identified only through his dental records when his body was eventually found. The meaning of many incidents in any given Souheid film can only be guessed at. What are we to make of the revelation that the car apparently being driven off in the final shot of *Nightfall* is actually a wreck being rocked side to side? For Laura U. Marks, "Life is like that in Mohamed Soueid's world: a ride that goes not forward but moves at the whim of (not necessarily hostile) outside forces."[257] This is an ingenious explanation but not a thought that would occur to any first-time viewer of the film. The sequence, like so much of Souheid's work, is fundamentally (and intentionally) ambivalent and ambiguous.

*

The civil war that began in 1975 inevitably brought the collapse of existing Lebanese commercial filmmaking structures, as studios and cinemas were destroyed and filmmakers scattered. As Ariss notes: "A whole generation of filmmakers combined their political activism with their creative artistic expression—a generation with no relationship to the Lebanese cinema heritage. These were the young Lebanese who combined political and cinematic vision, similar to other such movements emerging at that time in Egypt, Czechoslovakia and Latin America."[258]

Unable to fund their films from local sources, most of these Lebanese filmmakers have had to look for foreign coproduction finance. But this creates problems, in that European producers, looking for films successful at international festivals, have very different tastes from ordinary filmgoers in Beirut, whose viewing habits have been shaped by decades of Egyptian comedies and melodramas. The responses by individual filmmakers to dependence on French funding recorded by Lina Khatib are varied. For Danielle Arbid, France is "an oasis for getting funding,"[259] whereas Ghassan Salhab's experience is that French funders "feel that they can dictate what we do,"[260] though this has not prevented him from creating a totally personal style.

Despite the pressure of events, a successful new generation of feature filmmakers emerged, additional members for the group Hady Zaccak's aptly terms "the filmmakers of the Lebanese intelligentsia." Among these is the real pioneer of contemporary Lebanese feature filmmaking, Maroun Bagdadi (also spelt Bagh-dadi) (1951–1993). He abandoned his studies of political science, begun at the Université Saint Joseph in Beirut, in order to study filmmaking at IDHEC in Paris. He also worked for a while as a journalist and regularly made documentaries, mostly for television, while he lived in Lebanon. He made his first feature as early as 1975, though he had to wait until 1982 to complete a second. In all, Bagdadi made five features for cinema release in Lebanon or France and achieved a reputation as one of Lebanon's leading filmmakers. He planned another Lebanese feature, *Zawaya*, in 1993, but he died in a mysterious accident while researching it in Beirut.

Maroun Bagdadi's *Beirut Oh Beirut / Beyrouth ô Beyrouth / Beirut ya Beirut* (1975) was made with a largely amateur cast and on a very small budget. It draws a picture of Beirut after the 1967 defeat by tracing the lives of four young people, Christians and Muslims, that all end in defeat. The film now seems to be lost—certainly Lina Khatib could not locate a copy while researching her book *Lebanese Cinema*. She does, however, give us a brief account of the film: "Set between 1968 and 1970, *Beirut ya Beirut*, revolves around four characters: a bourgeois woman; two men (another bourgeois and 'an ideologically-committed man'), who fail in their relationships with her; and a third man, a refugee from the South who rejects Beirut and goes back to the South to participate in the resistance movement."[261]

Hady Zaccak notes that, despite its technical faults, the film "already exposes the elements which will lead to the conflict."[262]

Bagdadi's subsequent feature traces the downward spiral of the increasingly violent civil war. *Little Wars / Petites guerres / Houroub saghira* (1982), shot with an American crew provided by Francis Ford Coppola, for whom Bagdadi had worked in the United States, looks at the situation in 1975.[263] As Bagdadi stated in his presentation of the film at Cannes, *Little Wars* looks specifically at the reversion to tribalism in Lebanon and at the lost generation of Lebanese youth who were in their twenties when the war broke out: "A lost generation. A disfigured generation."[264] Khatib records that it

> revolves around the story of four young Lebanese men and women who are caught up in the war and who try to cope with it in different ways. One of them, Nabil, realizes that the only way of survival in the city is through death. . . . One of the most haunting scenes in *Little Wars* is one where Nabil decides to create martyr posters of himself and to declare himself dead. . . . It is in this way that Nabil's body is shown as merging with that of Beirut to form one entity, scarred by the war, but unable to escape from it.[265]

In 1984, Bagdadi left Beirut for Paris, where he lived until has death, working in both film and television, making three features and two téléfilms. It was in Paris that he made the French-language feature *The Veiled Man / L'homme voilé /*

al-Rajul al-muhajjah (1987), which was financed and marketed as a French film but which is totally shaped by events in the Lebanese civil war and their repercussions in Paris. The opening sections of the film, many of which take place at night, are deliberately enigmatic and largely without dialogue. The opening location (to which the film constantly returns) is, appropriately enough, that of the slaughterhouse where meat is cut for the meal of Kassar, a wealthy member of the Christian Lebanese community. He immediately recognizes Pierre as he checks in at a run-down hotel in the Lebanese district and has him followed as he explores Paris in search of his sixteen-year-old daughter, Claire. We know little about Pierre at this stage, except that he is clearly a man with scores to settle, as his first act in Paris is to kill an Arab he has followed. We never learn the reason for this killing, but it is clearly an action he has carried out before, since he behaves in the ruthless manner of a professional killer, complete with a silencer attached to his gun. Our initial view of Pierre is contradicted by that of Claire, when they eventually meet up. She sees him as a hero: a doctor and member of the *Médecins sans frontières* who has spent three selfless years in humanitarian work, saving lives in Beirut. The enigma remains, as he refuses to talk about his recent past, even when she takes him to a restaurant, coincidentally owned by Kassar. Back at her flat, Claire imitates for her father the oriental dance they have just witnessed, but still he remains silent.

The film depicts the Lebanese community in Paris as a dark world, where clan rivalries and loyalties persist, violence is just below the surface, and old Beirut battles are refought. Bagdadi's fluent camera work captures perfectly the complex interactions between the more peripheral characters, as well as the intimate, half-spoken links between the characters in the foreground. Bagdadi is masterly in his treatment of the growing tenderness between Pierre and his daughter, Claire, as they rediscover each other. Equally well scripted and directed are the more tense and edgy relationships, such as that between Pierre and Kassar, who reminds him of the need to fulfill his side of the bargain that allowed his release in Beirut. The distances and the passionate love linking Claire and Kamal, who was sent out by his mother onto the streets of Beirut to kill at the age of just sixteen, after the assassination of his father and brother, are well conveyed as well. He is a survivor, defined by one of the characters as the person who shoots first. When Claire contrasts Kamal with her father, he gives her a tape to prove that Pierre was indeed a combatant and a killer. There is huge pathos when Pierre finally breaks down and reveals the truth about his past, for the first time, in an intimate scene with Claire's close friend Julie. The slaughter of twenty-two orphans he thought he had saved from the Beirut violence by hiding them in a mountain village turned him from caring doctor to avenging killer. In the film's final scene, father and daughter are united in their grief, as she witnesses Kamal's betrayed wife throw herself at him in a passionate embrace (celebrated in music and by a camera circling the couple) and then promptly stabs him to death. *The Veiled Man* is indeed a tale of broken lives: Pierre and Claire face an uncertain future, though they have each other for support.

Outside Life / Hors la vie / Kharij al-hayat (1991) is a French-Italian-Belgian coproduction, with most of the dialogue in French. It was made while the war was still going on, and Bagdadi's intention was to show both sides of what was occurring: "From my background culture I can evoke the situation from within. At the same time, I do not live there any more, so I can show the other side of the subject."[266] It treats a subject that Bagdadi had already dealt with in one of his French téléfilms, the ironically titled *Lebanon: Land of Honey and Incense / Liban, le pays du miel et de l'encens* (1988). *Outside Life*, based on the actual experiences of the journalist René Auque, deals with the kidnap and torture of a French journalist and photographer, Patrick, who never learns why he was seized, why he is being tortured, or why, eventually, he is released. The film begins with the grim statistics of the civil war: 148,000 dead, 427,500 wounded, 25,000 missing, and 5,000 of these known to be taken by militia groups from both sides. In the vividly depicted sequence that follows, Patrick, who always acts with professional detachment, is constantly seen in the midst of the action. He films abductions, killings, and bombings, as well as the victims and victors, celebrating by firing their guns into the air. Only when he is forced to film two militants grinning and celebrating beside a victim who has been hanged does he show disgust by tearing the film from his camera. Then, suddenly and for no apparent reason, he is snatched and bundled into a car.

Apart from a brief coda at the very end, the rest of the film is devoted to Patrick's imprisonment, shown as he personally experiences it (there are no sequences devoted to activities on the outside, at the French embassy, for instance, or in the French press). He is confused about why he has been abducted. Though he does not know it at the time, the fact that he has to wear a blindfold whenever one of his captors enters the room is actually a positive sign, indicating that they intend to ransom or exchange him, not kill him. Similarly they show concern when he gets sick—a dead hostage is worth nothing. He is told at one point that he is to be exchanged for the brother of Walid (the leader of this little group), who is in prison on drugs charges in France. But he has no way of knowing if this is true or whether it is a change of leadership at the French embassy that makes the deal fall through, since at other times he is regularly lied to. Equally we, the spectators, are never told whether his eventual release is part of a deal agreed with the French government. Imprisoned and isolated, he loses all sense of identity. Only once does he briefly meet a fellow hostage, and this encounter offers little encouragement. Farid, a French-speaking Lebanese played by actor-director Roger Assaf, whom he heard screaming during a savage beating, is not required to be blindfolded, indicating clearly, he tells Patrick, that his captors intend to shoot him.

Patrick is constantly moved from place to place, always tied up in some way and on one occasion taped up from head to toe, like a mummy. No one calls him "Patrick"; indeed, the most sympathetic of the captors always refers to him using the name of his own small son. As they explain, all the militants themselves use pseudonyms, the most striking being that of the English-speaking captor, who demands to be addressed as De Niro, claiming he spent five years in Hollywood working as a film extra and bodyguard to Robert De Niro.

Patrick's experience of being a hostage is one with which we are familiar from other real-life accounts—pointless petty humiliations and savage beatings when he tries to escape on the one hand but also small kindnesses: the offer of a game of draughts or having the photograph of his girlfriend, Isabelle, restored to him. Nothing is predictable. On one occasion, he is allowed into the open air, after being warned not to try to escape. In what seems to be a demonstration designed just for him, a white horse is set free to gallop down the apparently empty street in front of him, only to be shot dead after a few yards. Patrick's eventual release, after he has been bizarrely made to dress in a burka, comes as a complete surprise to us and to him. Up to the last moment we fear that he could be taken to be executed. After his release, he stumbles into the French embassy and is blinded by photographers' flashlights. There is then a brief scene of his celebrating with Isabelle and friends in a Parisian *bistrot*. He tries to call Philippe in Beirut, but there is no reply—the flat is empty, seemingly ransacked. The film concludes with repeated shots, taken from a speeding car, of desolate Beirut streets.

Perhaps the most fascinating aspect of *Outside Life* is the treatment of Patrick's captors. They are leading double lives. The one who calls himself Philippe and is passionate about France is both a militant (and presumably a killer) while being a family man. He takes his little boy hand in hand to school and lives a normal domestic life with his wife and child (as we see when his flat becomes Patrick's last place of imprisonment). His captors all envy Patrick's life in Paris—free and, in their terms, rich, with a beautiful girlfriend. They enjoy no such freedom. They can choose to be fighters rather than jailers, as Omar, one of the least sympathetic of their number, does. But the almost inevitable result is martyrdom. To quote Zaccak once more, "The kidnappers sometimes appear as executioners, sometimes as victims, sometimes as sick people. Their existence is often contradictory: they cling to life, but they like torturing and killing. In the end, they do not know what they want, or what they are doing, and live in a nightmare."[267]

Outside Life is brilliantly shot and edited, capturing perfectly the shifts in mood and circumstance of Patrick's life, both as a photographer on the streets and as a captive. Though of necessity shot in part in Palermo (with only some exteriors shot in Beirut), the picture presented by the film of the devastated city of Beirut is always totally convincing. Nidal El Achkar, who plays a mother whose son has been kidnapped in scenes shot in Palermo, has recorded that the reconstruction of Beirut there was so convincing that she felt she was actually in her native city as she improvised her role.[268] The film's portrayal of its characters—victims and militia men—caught up in the conflict is equally persuasive. As Bagdadi has explained, "In the routine of horror, there are only victims and hostages." In one sense, Patrick's situation can be understood as a metaphor of the captive city of Beirut. But, to quote Bagdadi once more, "The film's metaphor shows that in fact all Lebanese are hostages in their own country, since they have not chosen this situation."[269] This is a major work, one of the finest portrayals of the Lebanese civil war.

Bagdadi's last completed film, *The Girl in the Air / La fille de l'air* (1992), is a conventionally financed, purely French action film based on the real-life exploits of Nadine Vaujour—escapades that often made the headlines in the French press. Renamed Brigitte in the film, the character develops from domesticated housewife, unaware of her husband's (Daniel) gangster lifestyle, to the courageous and ingenious woman who rescues him from jail in a spectacular helicopter raid. The film, which was well received, is a smoothly directed work, always engaging, if somewhat slow paced.

All three feature films made by Maroun Bagdadi between 1987 and 1992 are based on published accounts of real-life experiences. *The Girl in the Air* differs from the rest in having a female protagonist with a simple motivation (love for her husband) who uncomplicatedly achieves her single (if criminal) ambition. The lives of Bagdadi's male protagonists are more complicated: they are weighed down by violence experienced in the past (Pierre) or currently endured in the present (Patrick). As Lina Khatib notes, "There are no silent, solitary heroes in Bagdadi's films. There is no exaggerated masculinity to be admired. There is no good and evil. Instead, what we see in the films is a frustrated masculinity that is both a result of the war and a catalyst for it'"[270]

*

During the 1990s, a number of Lebanese filmmakers also made their fictional feature debuts with funding assistance from the Fonds Sud Cinéma, among them Jean-Claude Codsi, Randa Chahal-Sabbag, and Leila Assaf.

Jean-Claude Codsi was born in 1948 in Beirut and trained at INSAS in Belgium. He subsequently worked as assistant to his fellow INSAS graduate Borhan Alawiya on *Kafr Kassem* and several of his most distinctive documentaries. Since 1997, he has taught at the Institut d'Etudes Scéniques et Audiovisuelles (IESAV)— part of the Université Saint-Joseph in Beirut. He made his first feature in 1994 but had to wait seven years to screen his second.

Time Has Come / Il est temps / An al-awan (1994) was produced my his own company, Aflam, in Beirut, with backing from Moscow and Paris. The film begins with the abandonment of preparations for a Christian wedding in 1975, at the very start of the war, when the groom, René, a Christian militia chief, is ambushed. We learn the full circumstances surrounding this event only toward the end of the film. The action proper begins with Kamil, an unsuccessful hippy musician and failed gambler, being commissioned by an old family friend, "Uncle" Georges, to make a music video for the World Union of Lebanese Refugees. On the boat from Cyprus, he meets up with Raya, a beautiful young woman who is clearly attracted to him but who initially keeps key aspects of her real identity secret. She does not tell him the true situation of her son, Antoine, who, she claims, has been kidnapped, or the meaning of the word *hambalambasset* written on the plaster protecting her damaged ankle. Their arrival allows us to see two very different aspect of Beirut life, that of the Christian upper bourgeoisie, to which Raya is chauffeured away, and the situation of ordinary citizens, including those living on the demarcation line, which Kamil explores as he works on his video and tries to find people who can help him solve the enigma of Raya. This is a city still under fire, where snipers operate and Kamil's nephew is injured in a car bomb incident.

In a film full of scenes of friends and families reunited, there is a powerful sense of the changes wrought during the dozen or so years that both Kamil and Raya have spent in exile. The strongest sentiment, however, is nostalgia for a more distant, innocent past, symbolized by the summer camp that Raya and her friends Ohanness (now a war photographer) and Atef (a restaurant owner in Paris) enjoyed as children. This was the adventure they dubbed *hamalambasset* (using the nonsense word that Ohanness's father, a portrait photographer, used to make his clients smile). Issues from the past are resolved. Raya tells her son, Antoine, the truth about his birth, and we learn that René did not die from his wounds but shot himself in horror at the summary execution of Muslims, carried out by his own followers in the aftermath of the ambush. But the issues in the present are left open. Raya, after making love to Kamil, returns to Paris, and the last words in the film are those of his letter to her as he looks out over the sea separating Beirut from Cyprus.

A Man of Honor / Un homme d'honneur (2011) begins with a chance meeting in Beirut that causes Brahim, now a wealthy, if solitary, car dealer, to attempt to sort out things that happened in his life some twenty years before in his native country, Jordan. The woman he has met is Leila—now accompanied by her nineteen-year-old daughter, Sarah—whom he and his brother-in-law, Riad, were supposed to have shot in an honor killing. In a still tribal society, Leila had "disgraced" her family by falling in love with a foreigner, Rick (to whom she is still married). In fact, when the moment came, Brahim had saved Leila by shooting his own brother-in-law, who totally accepted the concept of an honor killing. Subsequently, Brahim had put out a false story about Riad's death, covered up the escape of Leila, and then faked his own death in a car crash, emerging with a new identity and nationality in Lebanon. As a result of Brahim's deceit, Riad is thought to have brought shame to his family, whereas Brahim is remembered as "a man of honor."

Brahim's attempts to resolve matters in Jordan meet with total failure: his mother rejects him (preferring the myth to the reality); his wife, Asma, who is dying of cancer, turns her back on him; and his son, Farid, who, of course, does not recognize him, cheats him as a gullible foreigner. When Farid spends the money he was given to pay for Asma's treatment (buying a bright-red mustang instead) and Brahim confronts him, Farid beats him savagely (still not knowing that Brahim is his father). The extended family is brought together at Asma's funeral, but the result is further violence, a beating for Brahim and the stabbing of his uncle. But all is resolved, on the surface at least, in the traditional tribal manner by the payment of blood money. Now Leila can introduce her daughter, Sarah, to her own mother. The film ends with two extremely well-written scenes. The first is a meeting between Brahim and Leila pointing to the unspoken affection between them. Her desire to break away from the constraints of tribal society may perhaps explain Brahim's decision to save her by shooting Riad. The second scene is a meeting between Farid and Sarah. He proclaims that as cousins they should marry annd tries to amuse her with a succession of Arab "jokes" about violence in family relationships. Sarah, who has been brought up in England, responds with total incomprehension and splendidly expressed contempt.

A Man of Honor is a very revealing example of the creative potentials and tensions faced by Arab filmmakers of this European-trained generation. Like the first film, it was produced by Codsi's own Lebanese-based production company, Aflam Films, with initial Fonds Sud Cinéma backing and subsequent French coproduction financing. Codsi worked on the script with a number of local collaborators, including the director Ghassan Salhab, but also developed it at the Francophone Production Forum at the Namur film festival and at a Euro-Mediterranean program held in Marrakesh. He wanted "this movie, which addresses foremost the Arab and Oriental audience, and whose subject concerns primarily this audience, to be easily accessible." For this reason—to meet the assumptions of an audience familiar with Western as well as Egyptian popular styles—he opted for "a classical and linear narrative structure." After discussions with members of his crew, he finally adopted "the scope format and landscape dominance of the American Western," using Toufic Farroukh's musical score to emphasize this choice"[271]

Randa Chahal-Sabbag (1953–2008) was born in Tripoli, to an Iraqi Christian mother and a Lebanese Muslim father. In 1973, she moved to Paris, where she studied filmmaking at the Université de Paris VIII and the École de Vaugirard. She has since moved constantly between Paris and Beirut, returning to Lebanon to shoot all her feature films. She began her career with a number of short films and longer video documentaries, including two fifty-two-minute works—*Our Imprudent Wars / Nos guerres imprudents / Hurubina al-taisha* (1995) and *Souha, Surviving in Hell / Suha, survivre à l'enfer* (2000), the study of a Lebanese communist activist, Souha Béchara. After a failed assassination attempt on a collaborationist general, Béchara spent ten years of torture and solitary confinement in a Khiam prison. After her release, she arrived at Chahal-Sabbag's Paris home, bursting with things to say. The director recorded and edited these and also accompanied Béchara on her trips to the places of her past: her home village, the site of the failed assassination took place, and the Khiam prison.

Our Imprudent Wars is an initial attempt to make sense of the civil war, a war that defies comprehension. As the director notes, the all-too-real hostilities are halted and a ceasefire arranged, just so German filmmaker Volker Schlöndorff can shoot his *fictional* version of the war, *Circle of Deceit*, "playing war games," as she puts it; two hundred thousand people have died—but for what purpose? How can it be safer to be with the enemy (whether Syrians or Israelis) than with your friends, simply because the Lebanese themselves are constantly changing sides and alliances?

In the film, Chahal-Sabbag mixes 16mm documentary footage that she shot both at the beginning and the end of the war with probing interviews, shot direct to camera, with her own family: her mother, who is both a lawyer and a feminist; her sister, who is a left-wing militant; and her brother, who fought in the war. As Hady Zaccak notes, the absence of her Marxist father, who died before the end of the war, "marks the disappearance of a Lebanon which was still idealistic."[272] Nothing makes sense to her family or to the filmmaker herself, who confesses that Beirut is a place "which I no longer love, but cannot stop filming." Nothing adds up, and the family are left with a sense of futility, combined with what is almost a feeling of guilt for just having survived. The film ends with tourists having themselves photographed in the ruins of Beirut, against a backdrop of demolition (intended as a prelude to rebuilding). Though completed in 1995, *Our Imprudent Wars* was not shown in Beirut until 1999 and then only in a film society context. As Lynn Maalouf notes: "The film's harsh criticism, unhindered by any self-censure, of all parties involved in the war is certainly a reason for this long delay. At a different level, this also denotes the physical resistance of the Lebanese to face any remembrance of things past, of the war, and its implications. No matter how strong this resistance, however, Chahal's film is certainly a catalyst, if not an incentive, to open the way to vital questions."[273]

Chahal-Sabbag subsequently completed four fictional features before her early death from cancer at the age of just fifty-four. Three of them—*Screens of Sand / Écrans de sable / Shasha min al-raml* (1991), *The Infidels / Les infidèles* (1997), and *A Civilized People / Civilisées / Moutahaddirat* (1998)—were outspoken in their attacks on aspects of Lebanese society. A new serenity was reached with her last film, *The Kite / Le cerf-volant / Tayyara min waraq* (2003), which won the Silver Lion at the Venice Film Festival in 2003.

Screens of Sand was shot in Tunisia and in French, but, as the director notes, "just as in the written Arabic language, the camera movements are always from left to right. We are the heirs of a very aesthetically minded civilisation." The film, which deals with the oppression of women in the Arab world, was not well received. Deborah Young in *Variety* writes that the film "is shot with a handful of actors and lots of sand, giving it a pleasing elemental simplicity. What's too pared down is the practically non-existent story, and [the] film winds down after an intriguing start full of atmosphere."[274]

The Infidels, made in France, received an even worse reception, presumably because it tackled the issue of homosexuality head-on, chronicling the affair between a Muslim fundamentalist and a French diplomat living in Cairo. As Rebecca Hillauer reports: "On the one hand, Lebanese government officials returned her screenplay with the comment 'threat to state security,' but—mystery of the Orient—Randa Chahal-Sabbag received permission to make the film. On the other hand, she received a letter from the French Embassy accusing her of damaging the image of France. France then withdrew all financial assistance for the project (apart from Arte TV, which continued its support)."[275]

Chahal-Sabbag's third fictional feature, *A Civilized People*, aka *The Civilized*, was equally abrasive. Set in 1980, the middle of the civil war, it shows the disruptions caused by the conflict, focusing in particular on the foreign servants left behind to guard their possessions by the rich bourgeoisie who have fled Beirut. As Marina Da Silva notes, the film oscillates between documentary and fiction: "The director shows the snipers who controlled flats, streets and whole districts, and who ruled without concern for the law. She demonstrates that children were used in the fighting and sent to the front." The lesson of the film is "that the war was made from the inside, by the Lebanese themselves, who have killed, tortured, abducted, who were all responsible, regardless of which political party or faith they belonged to."[276]

This was never going to be a popular message for the authorities, and Chahal-Sabbag made things worse (in the eyes of the censors) by "using dialogue which disturbs and shakes up the viewer, Randa Chahal has opted for a bitter language, where sex is continually mocked and religion blasphemed, and where the machismo and power which weapons confer are attacked."[277] There was inevitably a fresh conflict with the Lebanese censors: "In 1999 the government went as far as cutting 47 minutes of Randa Chahal's *The Civilised*—just over half the film—blaming its decision on the film's 'vulgar language and slurs against both Christians and Muslims.' This censorship was coupled with the denunciation of the film's director in some Beirut mosques. In addition, Randa Chahal and her crew also received death threats. The film has only been seen in Lebanon once (at the Beirut Film Festival in 1999)."[278] In France, only four cuts were required, but the release of the film was delayed by four months.

The Kite is set in South Lebanon in a village cut in two by the Israeli occupation. The two halves are separated by barbed wire and a minefield and dominated by a watchtower manned by a couple of armed Israeli soldiers. The exclusion is complete; only the occasional coffin and, as we later discover, a solitary bride without her bridal party can cross the arbitrary border—provided the relevant pass has been obtained. The women of the divided village try to keep in contact, but they have to use megaphones to speak to each other, broadcasting loudly and publicly things better kept secret, whether they are intimate family details, the qualities that make their offspring special, or quite pointed mutual abuse. On the Lebanese side, villagers try to keep to the old ways, and the elders decree that Lamia must marry her cousin Samy, to whom she was promised before the occupation, even though this means that she will rarely, if ever, be able to return to her family.

Though the family feel she must be married off, as she is approaching her sixteenth birthday, Lamia is still a child, happily flying her kite alongside her younger brother and his friends. She shows her spirit, however, by clambering over the barbed wire when her kite gets caught up on the wrong side. The Israeli soldiers, anxious that she may stray into the minefield, can only watch her through their binoculars and fire warning shots in her direction. There is meant to be no real communication between Israelis and Lebanese—the relationship is always to remain occupier and occupied. One of the soldiers—on his first days of military service—is Youssef, a conscripted Arab Israeli who is warned by the lieutenant that though the people of the village are his cousins, he must treat them as enemies. This, as we shall see, Youssef finds himself unable to do.

The attitudes in the village are totally bound by tradition. Arranged marriage is unquestioned, and a woman accosts Lamia and her friend as they set off for school, asking why they are studying, as they are young women now. The girls' conversation, however, shows that they have been brought up in total ignorance, with no knowledge about what sex involves or how a woman gets pregnant. The level of conversation is not much higher in the watchtower, where the seventeen-year-old Youssef is constantly harangued about sex and marriage by his older colleague, whose own drunken sex life is appalling. Yet the wedding must go ahead and the families exchange videos, which allow Lamia and Samy to express their aversion to marriage and their animosity toward each other. The "wedding" is unlike any other in Arab cinema. The bride sits enthroned in the splendid white wedding dress and high heels, surrounded by weeping women, but no groom appears. Instead, Lamia has to make her way alone across the village divide, splendidly dressed in her flowing gown but without a wedding party, to meet her new husband for the first time. The couple take an instant dislike to each other and behave more like a pair of sulky children (which they are) than a married couple. The worried families agree that the only solution is for Lamia to go home to her family, which scandalizes some of the Lebanese villages.

Amid all this, love is born between Lamia and Youssef, though they have virtually no possibility of coming together, except when Lamia crosses back to her family. They are largely confined to looking at each other from afar with binoculars. But in their thoughts and dreams they can be together. The film ends with a long sequence in which this happens. The barbed wire parts to allow Lamia to pass and a mine exploding cannot harm her. Lamia and Youssef are alone on the watchtower—touching, talking tenderly, with Youssef divested of his Israeli army jacket and star of David—when the film cuts abruptly to black and the credits roll.

The Kite is a charming romantic comedy, understated but capturing perfectly the discovery of young love, even though this can only be in a dream. The simplicity of the narrative exposes the social reality in which the film is set: a rigid patriarchal Arab society, the beginnings of a shift in attitudes and expectations among those living under occupation and the pointlessness of the Israeli occupation (guarding whom against whom?). The new restrained tone meant that *The Kite* was the first of Chahal-Sabbag's films to obtain a full release in Lebanon. This brought her a new recognition in Beirut and the award, in 2004, of Lebanon's highest presidential honor, as she was made chevalier of the Order of the Cedar.

Leila Assaf, who was born into a Christian family in Beirut in 1947, returned from Sweden, where she had trained and worked extensively in television, to make her sole Lebanese feature, *The Freedom Gang / Le gang de la liberté / Al-sheika* (1994). This is a sympathetic study of street children in the Beirut slums, set during the last days of the civil war. The ten-year-old al-Sheikha and her nine-year-old brother try to escape from the dominance of their drunken father and form a gang of thieves on the streets of Beirut. But their attempts to break free are met with only further abuse and exploitation by adults. A spell in a Catholic nunnery offers al-Sheikha some respite, but only for a while. Assaf can offer no way forward to resolve the social problems she exposes, and her chosen ending underlines Lebanon's social divisions, offering no hope of a better future for the poor. As a group of well-dressed middle-class children sail off on holiday, singing French songs, al-Sheikha and her brother are left, ignored in their ragged clothing, trying to sell chewing gum on the quayside. As Lina Khatib notes, "The film's representation of the war is complex. The war is not shown as directly contributing to the children's misery. For most of the film, the devastation of the war is almost irrelevant to the children's everyday lives. The film even shows the children taking advantage of the panic accompanying the start of shelling. . . . The general side lining of the war in the film highlights its tackling of a problem 'created by the war that persisted after the war ended.'"[279]

*

A figure apart in Lebanese cinema (in a place akin to that occupied by Nacer Khemir in Tunisian cinema) is Ghassan Salhab, who was born in Dakar in 1958 and grew up in Senegal. He saw Lebanon firsthand at the age of thirteen and subsequently pursued his studies, first in Beirut and then in Paris. He has collaborated in various ways on the films of several of his younger compatriots, and, though he received no formal film training, he has taught in Beirut, at the Académie Libanaise des Beaux Arts and Université Saint-Joseph. He began his career in 1986 with the first of a series of a dozen or so experimental video shorts, mostly about fifteen minutes in length. He also made a forty-minute video, *A Brief Meeting with Jean-Luc Godard; or, Cinema as Metaphor / Brève rencontre avec Jean-Luc Godard, ou le cinéma comme métaphore*, in 2005.

The title of Salhab's first feature, *Beirut Phantoms / Beyrouth fantôme / Ashbah Beirut* (1998), refers to Beirut as a phantom city, but the real ghost is the protagonist, Khalil, who returns to Beirut after ten years of exile. We do not see him arrive at the airport, and our first awareness of his presence is a long-held forward-tracking shot through the front window of a taxi. He is briefly glimpsed by one of his old colleagues, but his taxi disappears in the traffic. The reason for his old colleague's astonishment is eventually made clear. Khalil is officially dead, killed alongside his close friend Khaled in fighting during the civil war. Photos of them both, hailed as martyrs, had subsequently been displayed on dozens of walls around the city. Initially, Khalil hides away in his hotel room. When he does emerge, he inevitably frustrates all his old friends and, in particular, to his former girlfriend, Hanna.

The story line follows a simple path—Khalil arrives, explores Beirut largely in a hired car, meets up with former friends, and vanishes again—but there are many gaps in the narrative. He will not explain to his friends why he has come back and offers no explanation about his departure ten years earlier. He has no answers when they question him about the money stolen from his militant group a week before he disappeared, money that would have allowed it to mount a serious offensive. Khalil remains an enigma. We never learn whether he is a Christian or a Muslim—sectarian issues are of no interest to Salhab, whose sympathy extends to both sides of the conflict. We eventually learn why Khalil has returned: to buy a new set of papers from the petty crook Ghassan (played by Salhab himself) who sold him the previous ones, which allowed his escape. There is a nice irony here. He wants papers that will allow him to live abroad under his real name, Khalil Chams. But these papers have to be faked because he is officially listed as dead by the Lebanese authorities. He will therefore base his new life on a similar falsehood to that of ten years before. Whether he will be able to take up this new life remains unknown at the end of the film, when his empty car is found riddled with bullets. According to Salhab in interviews, he will be fine. He has been kidnapped by a gang who have mistaken him for someone else—a fitting dramatic end for a man who has lived ten years of his life denying his own identity. But that is an outcome that does not figure in the film.

Beirut is always present in the film, pressing in on the characters physically in the present and shaping their lives through memories of the past. Initially Beirut seems to be a city finally at peace with itself. But soon there are signs of the underlying tensions: blocked-off roads, armed men patrolling the streets, checkpoints. The violence is still there. There is an explosion outside Hanna's flat while Khalil is staying there. When Hanna takes her television crew to film on the demarcation line, they come under heavy shelling and have to take shelter overnight with the locals in a cellar. Salhab captures beautifully the sense of an all-pervading underlying violence in the city that brings back memories and shapes people's perceptions. At one point, the film shows Khalil looking out of the flat, watching the people idling on the promenade. The film cuts to couples and families posing one after another to be photographed against the backdrop of the sea. But each time a photograph is taken, what we hear is not the click of of the camera but a gunshot—a telling reminder of the countless numbers of people who were lined up and shot during the civil war.

Beirut Phantoms is a very formally structured film. Salhab's most striking innovation is the series of direct-to-camera comments by the characters interspersed throughout the film. We are shown that these statements are shot in a studio, filmed in close-up by an immobile camera. All the main themes of the film are made explicit here: identity, the influence of the past, the impact of living in present-day Beirut. The range of views is extraordinarily wide. For some, the war years were a vivid period of openness and immediacy, and for some these were times heightened by the sense of danger; for others, they were the times that blighted their lives. The exact status of these statements to camera is left deliberately imprecise. From a viewing of the film, there is no way of knowing whether these were prescripted by the director or improvised by the actors from material provided by him. A third possibility, that these could be accounts of the actors' personal experiences, is raised by the fact that with each first statement Salhab includes a title naming the actor or actors involved, who include Darina al-Joundi and Rabih Mroué.

Beirut Phantoms is a remarkably accomplished first feature. It captures our attention both through the depth of its analysis of what it means to live in Beirut and to have experienced the civil war and through the originality of the formal methods by which these experiences are conveyed.

Terra incognita / Al-ard al-majhoula (2002) focuses on a similar group of "thirty-somethings" in Beirut, the unknown land of the film's title, but the emphasis here is not on the weight of the past but on the elusiveness of the present, which does not allow the characters to root their lives in Beirut.

Salhab brings a double focus to the city. He stresses, even more than in *Beirut Phantoms*, the sea, the sky, and the beauty of the surrounding landscape. But Beirut itself is strangely intangible, largely filmed either at night or from the interior of moving cars or taxis, with the image obscured by windscreen dirt and the lack of a stable focus. The effect is to create an instability that, in turn, is reflected in the characters. The very foundations of the city have been uncovered by the massive destruction. Evidence of seven successive conquests and ensuing destructions of Beirut have come to light, uncovering buildings and monuments that have yet to be dated and identified. The authorities' response—to tear down and rebuild in a new modern style—is creating a new Beirut, to the extent that even those who have lived there all their lives will not be able to recover the past or find their own roots.

The film concentrates on three members of a Beirut-based group—Soraya, who is a tourist guide; Nadim, an architect; and Leyla, who has no apparent occupation. As with the characters in the previous film, their lives are disturbed by the return from abroad of one of their number, Tarek, but he plays a less crucial role than does Khalil. Early on, another member of the group expresses their joint belief, namely, "Expatriates should remain abroad and invite us to stay with them." The group are constantly in contact on their mobile phones, trying to set up meetings that, for one reason or another, do not happen. Nadim has virtually given up human contact, in order to spend all of his time at his computer, devising more and more abstract designs for the new city he hopes to help build. But the others all have phrases that, in some way, sum up their lives. Questioned about the destination they are setting out to reach, Soraya tells her tourists, "Is it far? I don't know, I've never reached the end." Tarek asks his own reflection in the mirror the same question that all his friends put to him, "Why did I come back?" Asked why she refuses to give directions to a passerby, the introspective Leyla, a lesbian with an unrequited passion for Soraya, offers her personal motto: "You have to know how to get lost." Even the maid in the Soraya household, who is preparing to go back to her native country, has her own philosophy: "It's not just about living in poverty, but in a way that escapes us." In the circumstances, even Salhab seems to feel he has to demonstrate that he does not have an identity problem. His director's credit at the beginning of the film is an image of his passport, giving his parents' full names, his religion (Shiite Muslim), and marital status (bachelor).

The opening images introduce us to two of the key figures of the film: Haîdar and Soraya. Haïda is not part of the group but a radio commentator whose

comments on political developments (particularly the threat from Israel) dominate the sound track throughout the film, backed up by the constant arrival of
Israeli warplanes breaking the sound barrier over Beirut. Soraya is the film's principal character, whose role as a tourist guide allows us to see numerous aspects of
the city and its surroundings. But her life does not offer the film a conventional
dramatic shape. Though Tarek maintains that he came back because of her, she
does not take him seriously, and they do not resume their relationship. She also
seems incapable of any other sort of emotional commitment. She collects visas
in her passport but takes no actual steps to leave Beirut. She currently has no
permanent relationship in her life and instead picks up men in bars and clubs for
instant sexual gratification. She wants nothing further from any of the men she
sleeps with and even refuses to acknowledge one of them when they meet again
by chance on the promenade. This offends his male pride, and, in one of the film's
final sequences, he follows her and her tourists for miles in his car, in order to
punish her. The film's final image is a close-up of her face with a black eye. This
is a surprising but not satisfying climax. It seems that, for once, Salhab has suc-
cumbed to the clichéd "rules" of conventional film narrative—namely, that an
erring woman must be punished.

Though they are all caught up in differing ways with the city, none of the
characters has any real roots in Beirut. Salhab talks of there being two bodies in
the film, Beirut's and Soraya's: "They are similar but they don't come into contact.
How could they? In Beirut, at most, one crosses paths."[280] Soraya does not know
why she stays, just as Tarek does not know why he has come back. Both Soyaya
and Nadim, though in their thirties, still live with their parents. Ironically, only
Tarek, who does not know whether he will stay or leave, has a flat. Nadim is passionate about the rebuilding of Beirut, but for him, this involves devising ever
more elaborate patterns on a computer screen, not an engagement with bricks
and mortar. Unlike the characters in *Beirut Phantoms*, these citizens of Beirut are
not weighed down by the past; instead, they live—hover—in an eternal present
that leads nowhere. Their only real future concern is a vague, but persuasive, fear
of another war, of another Israeli invasion. As Salhab has observed, "Characters
are suspended in the present, without daring too much to look back, and even
less to look into the future. . . . What lives, what stories are left to invent after a
catastrophe?"[281]

The fragmentation of Soraya's life—a different man every night—is reflected
in the film's stylistic patterning. Here only Leyla is lifted out of her context to
address the camera (not another character) in an extreme close-up. But scenes
involving the other characters are not allowed to have shape or to develop. Salhab constantly cuts abruptly and jaggedly, from image to blank screen, from
character to character, from interior to exterior, from day to night. The film is
full of music, Arab popular songs as well as secular and religious chanting (both

Muslim and Christian). But this is never used to smooth the cuts from one situation to another through a conventional sound overlap. Instead, the sound is cut in exactly the same abrupt way as the images, creating startling transitions for the spectator. When an overlap does occur, as, at one point, between Christian and Muslim chants, the result is a clash that creates a total cacophony.

The result of Salhab's stylistic choice is to create an unsettling image, both of Beirut and of the characters. In this respect, it fulfills perfectly his aims, as set out in an interview with Lina Khatib: "*Terra incognita* reflects a frozen time, a country stuck in the present, but not in a positive way. . . . I wanted to make the viewer uncomfortable when watching people being lost, to enter the viewer into a physical experience of being lost through the film's structure. I wanted to remove the viewer from the comfort zone of linear structures."[282]

The Last Man / Le dernier homme / Atlal (2009) is Salhab's idiosyncratic take on that old Hollywood staple, the vampire film. The setting in Beirut no longer has a real significance—this could be any city draped in darkness. There is also a move away from the group and its social interactions to the inner experience of a single individual. But though the focus is new, the film contains much of Salhab's favorite imagery: it opens with shots of the waves breaking on the shore, there are lots of tracking shots from inside cars, and there is plenty of underwater imagery. As in the previous film, the sound track contains popular Arab film songs but is dominated by radio commentaries on political issues and the threat from Israel. A novelty in the opening part of the film is a display of flamenco dancing, with a single woman performing direct to camera against a black background: stamping, turning, gesticulating, posing. The familiar stylistic patterns also recur, and the roots of Salhab's work in the techniques of experimental video are clearly visible. As before, the spectator is deliberately made to work hard for his or her enjoyment.

All is darkness, shadow, mystery, the unknown, but, as one might predict, the story line is minimal. A succession of bodies is discovered in the city, with their throats cut and their blood sucked dry. The person charged with dealing with the bodies is Dr. Khalil Chams (the same name as that of the returnee in *Beirut Phantoms*), who works at the local hospital. Dr. Khalil is a troubled character, and there are many signs that he may himself be the vampire. The first victim is a neighbor whose windows his flat overlooks. He has trouble with his eyes and is advised to wear sunglasses. He is happy in the rain but shrinks away from direct sunlight. A snorkeler who spends much of his time exploring the seabed, he survives an explosion that might be expected to kill him. There are ambiguous scenes in the darkness with his mistress, Zeina, but she is not assaulted or killed. It is very suspicious that he spends most of his nights prowling the streets and is out there when victims are killed. When he discovers a dead man, he tries to help him, but when he gets blood on his hands, he licks it off. Khalil also has some knowledge of vampires, realizing instantly that when the police arrest a suspect and parade him on television, this cannot be the guilty man, since vampires cannot be photographed.

Dr. Khalil does indeed prowl the streets at night, not because he is in search of fresh victims, but because he is a man in quest of his own identity. He senses an affinity with the vampire, fearing that the vampire may in fact be his double. Several times he can sense the vampire's presence, but his shouts and challenges go unanswered. Eventually he does surprise the vampire while he is sucking blood from his latest victim, but Khalil does not attempt to apprehend him. Instead, he takes up the vampire's position and in turn sucks blood from the victim's throat. The ending is enigmatic. The two men meet and come face to face. The vampire, his double, does not resemble him in any way. Dr. Khalil kisses his neck, then the men separate and vanish into the darkness. Nothing is resolved. In a typical Salhab joke, the vampire, who looks nothing like Dr. Khalil, is played by the actor Aouni Kawas, who played Khalil, the returnee hero of *Beirut Phantoms*, and hence is, to a certain degree, Salhab's own alter ego.

Salhab does not make a strong distinction between documentary and fiction, and the lessons of his first two ventures into fictional feature filmmaking are borne out in his later documentary video work. The twenty-eight-minute short *(Posthumous) / (Postume)* (2007) is an excellent demonstration of Salhab's creative and highly individual use of video. It utilizes to the full the medium's possibilities for the startling combination and juxtaposition of images and sounds, the potential for abrupt cutting and very slow dissolves, forward and reverse tracking shots, and sudden cuts to a black screen. The whole is held together by a continuous, if varied, sound track. Though there is some use of archive material and television footage, the bulk of the imagery is very personal, much of it derived from Salhab's feature films. We are shown images of Beirut, often desolate or in the process of being demolished (by the Lebanese themselves, because of the bomb damage), interspersed with close-ups of faces or the backs of people's heads. The shots of Beirut largely comprise images of destruction (the constantly repeated impact of a bulldozer and a crane on an already devastated building or incessantly recurring identical tracking shots through the ruined city). The close-up images of people are motionless and silent (though there is no direct address to the camera) and record the faces of actors and actresses from Salhab's first feature films. Four of these share the voice-over narration, though there is no way of identifying them individually, and no attempt is made to allow them to record their own views of the shared experience.

This is perhaps because the core of the film's narration comprises Salhab's own poetic thoughts and reflections on his personal situation of being in Beirut at a time of intense Israeli bombing. At one level, the concern is with the citizens and the city and, on another, with the intense relationship of Salhab to Beirut.

The first reflections concern the situation "where time loses its function" so that we have a continuous sense of drowning, our senses almost numb, anaesthetised.

Salhab reflects on the fact that, though the Israelis have the capacity to destroy Lebanon's electricity plants (and have previously done so systematically), this time the electricity remains accessible, and hence the Lebanese can still watch television: "I suppose it was the Israelis' desire to allow us to constantly follow news bulletins, so that we could witness our own deaths live, on air." Lying wounded in a hospital bed in a luxury akin to a five-star hotel increases the temporal dislocation: "It's as if we were crying without tears, without pain, without contractions of the face or body, without bitterness. We were crying as only the dead could cry." This is also a time of confusion: "There is a narrowed difference between what happens inside us and what happens in the outside world." Back home in his own world, Salhab goes "into a third time dimension," waiting to get back to his own time and space. Ultimately, the narration comes to an end, as he confesses: "I tell myself a lot of things, but I have nothing more to say." (*Posthumous*) is a moving, engaging, totally personal response to being confronted with overwhelming foreign aggression.

The sixty-nine-minute video documentary *1958* (2009) is entitled a "self-portrait of yesterday" but is far from being the straightforward autobiographical work that this might imply. As the film constantly reminds us, 1958 is not only the date of Salhab's birth but also the year when, in Lebanon, the first revolts and uprisings occurred. These would, within a few years, lead to full-scale civil war. The key thread of the film is a long statement by Salhab's mother, who is lifted out of her domestic context and filmed in extreme close-up, just like the fictional characters of *Beirut Phantoms*. She talks directly, without interruption, to an immobile camera that never shifts from its single fixed point of viewing. Her statement is constantly intercut with black-and-white newsreel images from the unrest in Lebanon as well as threads of images less directly related to 1958, such as contemporary color images that depict an overgrown graveyard of abandoned tanks together with undersea footage of marine wrecks. The newsreel images, which are undated and unlocated (mostly showing Lebanon, it would seem, but some shot in Senegal and others in Egypt), are never used to form a coherent, documentary-style account of the period. The nearest we get to this is a firsthand account of the events in Beirut by an unnamed garage owner who was directly caught up in the demonstrations and eventual armed conflict.

Salhab himself is markedly lacking from his own self-portrait. We see, fleetingly, just a couple of photographs, a professional photographer's image of mother and son and his own (canceled) first passport. Equally, we see repeated shots of someone who is presumably Salhab walking through the streets or at sea in a boat. But we cannot be sure if it is him or an actor lookalike, as we see only the back of the man's head and there is no synchronised voice track to accompany the images. There are also enigmatic shots of a man stripped to the waist and toying with a rifle. Perhaps this unnamed individual is, in some way Salhab's alter ego, since the actor involved is Aouni Kawas, who played the returnee in *Beirut Phantoms* (as well as the vampire in *The Last Man*). We do hear Salhab's voice, but his poetic mediations (in French) form only one thread of the complexly constructed and interwoven sound track, full of abrupt shifts and occasional conflicts (the mother's narrative is occasionally drowned out by other voices).

Just as we see no images of Salhab's boyhood haunts in Dakar and meet none of the friends he must have had then, so too is his mother equally reticent about him. Salhab's sole intervention in her lengthy monologue is to begin by asking his mother whether she remembers his birth. But instead of giving us childhood reminiscences of her eldest son, she talks essentially about her own life: the abrupt shift from being a schoolgirl to suddenly becoming a bride and the dislocation of moving from a secure home life in Beirut to bringing up children in a foreign country, where Arabic was hardly spoken and not taught in school. She talks of the change that a first child makes in a woman's life but does not refer specifically to Salhab by name. She is perhaps most animated when talking about the street demonstrations she participated in as a schoolgirl and about her enduring passion for Nasser and pan-Arabism. When she has finished speaking, we see her, still immobile, listening to a romantic song by Asmahan (which she apparently chose herself). *1958* is a typical Salhab work. He treats the documentary form with the originality and fluidity with which he handles fictional narratives to produce what is, essentially and paradoxically, the portrait of an invisible man.

Salhab has subsequently made two more fictional features, the first of which is *The Mountain / La montagne* (2011). This is Salhab's most pared-down and enigmatic feature, filmed in black and white and largely comprising very formally composed static, long-held images. In his statement of intent, Salhab says of the film that it "attempts to track the journey of a man at a crucial time of his life—at a breaking point. However the film does not get ahead of the main character, nor knows as much. Instead it moves along at the same speed as him, if not following closely behind."[283]

The Mountain is focused on a single unnamed figure (played by Fadi Abi Samra). Though partially financed by the Doha Film Institute, this is a totally personal work. The sequence of events in the film is simple. We see the protagonist in his room. He is then driven to the airport by a friend. He does not take a flight but instead hires a car and checks into an anonymous hotel in or near an unknown city, asking not to be disturbed. The brief snatches of conversation with the (unnamed) friend, the car hire assistant, and the hotel receptionist constitute the only dialogue in the film. A solitary fragment of a radio broadcast locates the action in time: ten years after the Israeli withdrawal from Lebanon. The protagonist does, on occasion, murmur to himself in English, but this is clearly not his native language. He seems to be a writer (though he claims, speaking with the receptionist, to be a singer), but what we see of his writing makes no sense. It largely consists of strings of disconnected nouns, but the only meaningful fragment of a sentence, "On the way to Dakar," does link him directly to Salhab.

About an hour of the film's eighty-three-minute running time is devoted to the protagonist alone in his hotel room. Though he is largely filmed in close-up, his face betrays no emotion: we are offered no clue about what is going on in his head. He closes the curtains, disconnects the phone and the television, and seems troubled by the slightest sound coming in from outside, though there is nothing to be disturbed about. The only development within the room is that he starts off fully clothed, later has a shower and wanders around with a towel wrapped around his waist, and then has another shower, after which he is shown totally naked (though always discretely filmed, especially when he is apparently masturbating).

There are two moments depicting the aftermath of violent action in the film, but on both occasions, the protagonist is merely an onlooker. Early in the film, when driving, he comes across a crashed car with two dead occupants, He stands by impassively as it catches fire. The very end of the film contains a similar incident, but the way this is presented is totally ambiguous. The protagonist, now fully dressed again, either leaves his room or imagines leaving his room—there is no way of telling which. Outside, in the woods, he discovers the body of a man who has killed himself with his shotgun. Again, there is no visible response.

There are many unexplained aspects of the film, such as the repeated cut-away shots to close-ups of footprints in the snow, though the film is not, it would seem, set in the winter. More puzzling still is the film's final shot: a two- or three-minute fixed shot of the same snow, now without footprints. *The Mountain* is a rare example of a film, professionally produced and precisely realized, for which there seems only one intended spectator: the filmmaker himself. Or, to quote Salhab in his pressbook, "According to the teachings of Tao, the goal matters less than the path one takes."[284]

Salhab has subsequently made another feature, *The Valley / La vallée / Al-wadi* (2016), set in the Bekaa Valley, well known as a war zone and as a site for opium cultivation. *The Valley* is a much more accessible film than its predecessor. It makes full use of color, atmospheric music, and its striking mountain setting, and it even has an embryonic plot. The dialogue is extremely sparse and largely inconsequential, such that the final credit to Mohamed Souweid for "help with the dialogue" is presumably a customary Salhab joke. The director's familiar style of static, long-held images and abrupt cutting from setting to setting (instead of creating a traditional narrative flow) is, however, retained. Most importantly, the unnamed protagonist is a typical Salhab figure: an anonymous man who emerges from a car crash (that we hear but do not see). He is badly wounded, but he is able to help start the car of a group of stranded people whom he meets as he staggers down the road in the midst of the empty Lebanese mountains. When he faints, they decide to help him. Their first idea is to take him to a nearby hospital, but when they find the police waiting there, they change their minds and take him back to their farmhouse, near an unnamed village.

It transpires that the group members are, in fact, drug smugglers, keen to pass unnoticed and protected by armed guards. The atmosphere is understandably tense, and the presence of the protagonist makes it worse. Is he spying on them, perhaps feigning amnesia? The members of the group become increasingly hostile and threatening, especially after he attempts to escape through a window. They desperately want to know the truth, and one of the women even tries to seduce him, in vain. All he can apparently remember is an old Lebanese love song, sung, it seems, by Aziza Jalal: "I am waiting for you, my love . . ." The protagonist makes no visible attempt to recover his past. We are intrigued by this mystery, as are his hosts, but when the truth does eventually emerge, it is banal and inconsequential: he has been away from the area for ten years and has returned to see and photograph the old family house, now occupied by the Syrian military. There is no development of the characters—they merely wait—and there is no drive toward a climax on any personal level.

The climax to the action in fact comes from outside, as the previously silent, empty landscape now becomes filled with the sights and sounds of war. There are helicopters overhead and the gunfire is getting nearer. Smoke from the explosions can be seen on the horizon. They arm themselves with machine guns, but why they think these will protect them against a heavily armed invading force is unclear. The radio works only sporadically, but the reporters' fragmentary phrases that do come through increase the tension: "Beirut has been erased," "Why have you abandoned us?," "I have lost my way." But in typical Salhab fashion, nothing happens on screen. The unidentified army destroys the neighboring village but passes by the farm. There are no explanatory farewells as the group disperses. The final panning shot takes in the now quiet landscape and ends with the image of the protagonist's back. When he turns to look, inscrutably, at the camera, the film cuts to black and the credits roll.

The Valley is again a totally personal work, made by a director in total command of his medium. It is clearly a reflection of the recurrent pressures and terrors that Lebanon has suffered for decades. But the detail is impenetrable. Why does the film open with the image of a red rose? Who are these people whom we have watched for a hundred minutes or more? What will happen to them all, including the protagonist, in future? Is there hope for Lebanon?

Ghassan Salhab has made a unique contribution to Lebanese cinema. His work is totally personal, making no concessions to dominant cinema practices. It is marked by his insider / outsider status. He spent his childhood years in Dakar and then, for seventeen years, divided his time between Paris and Beirut before finally deciding to settle in the Lebanese capital. Though Beirut features very prominently in his work, he has no interest in the sectarian divide. His concern is with individuals. Stylistically, his work is marked by his lack of concern for realism, the construction of gripping linear narratives, and the separation of fiction and documentary. He refuses the conventional "rules" of continuity editing and the use of sound to smooth the transitions from one setup to another. On the other hand, his work is full of little ironies, paradoxes, puzzles, and even contradictions. He posits an active spectator, and his innovations have had a clear influence on the new styles of filmmaking that emerged in Lebanon in the 2000s.

Recently, Salhab has turned to writing, publishing *Fragments du livre du naufrage* in 2011. As Jacques Mandelbaum says in his preface to the book, "This is a sombre collection, joining together an absurd humour, a polite despair, and an indecipherable hope. . . . What emerges from these *Fragments du livre du naufrage*, and from Ghassan Salhab's work as a whole, is that melancholy equates to hope."[285]

Palestine

Though her own work with her husband, Jean Chamoun, has dealt almost exclusively with Lebanon, the Palestinian documentary filmmaker Maï Masri has offered one of the best definitions of the role of Palestinian cinema:

> Cinema can create an imaginary Palestine, but it can never replace a real Palestine that consists of land, rights, and freedom for millions of dispossessed Palestinians. In the meantime, our cinematic Palestine can play a powerful role in preserving and developing Palestinian identity and in nurturing the personal and collective dream of a real Palestine. Much Palestinian cinema is concerned not simply to show things as they happen in the present, but to write history from the perspective of those who lost in the unequal struggle, to [emphasize] the link with the disputed land of Palestine and to define Palestinian identity.[286]

It is customary, for example in discussions of Palestinian literature, to make clear distinctions between three groups: those Palestinians who live in the Palestinian Territories, those who are Israeli citizens, and those who live in exile and have foreign citizenship. Given the small number of filmmakers involved, and the fact that the bulk of the film funding almost always comes from abroad, I have chosen here to treat all those who define themselves as Palestinians as comprising a single entity, united in supporting a single cause, while offering some definition of their personal status in individual discussions of their work. This does not imply that they have equal freedoms or equal opportunities, when, for example, they attempt to film in the Palestinian Territories.

Another crucial question of identity that has to be addressed is the relationship of Palestinian filmmaking to Israeli cinema. A fascinating insight into the impact of the new Palestinian cinema that emerged in the 1980s and 1990s is offered by the two editions of Ella Shohat's book *Israeli Cinema*. The first, which appeared in 1989, is a virtually unaltered version of the doctorate dissertation she completed in 1986, while the new edition was published in 2010. In the first edition, Israeli cinema is defined as "a film culture that, for the most part, saw itself firmly grounded within the Zionist ethos,"[287] but the emergence, since the 1980s, of a considerable number of internationally acclaimed films by Palestinians who are also Israeli citizens (including key figures such as Michel Khleifi, Elia Suleiman, Hanna Elias, Nizar Hassan, Hany Abu-Assad, Ali Nassar, Mohamed Bakri, Tawfik Abu Wael, and Ula Tabari) has changed this. From her Israeli perspective, Shohat argues that Israeli and Palestinian cinemas cannot be discussed separately: "It is virtually impossible to speak of Israeli cinema without 'Palestine,' just as it is virtually impossible to speak of Palestinian cinema without 'Israel.'"[288]

While it is clearly the case that the work of all Israeli citizens (Arabs as well as Jews) must be included if one is to define an Israeli national cinema, the argument here is that the self-defined notion of a "Palestinian cinema" does have a valid, independent identity. In a study of this kind, looking at cinema in the global era, when so many filmmakers are exiles working with foreign funding, using their personally stated national adherence can be a useful way of grouping related filmmakers. This in no way implies that the concept of a "national cinema" in the traditional sense has any ongoing relevance or continued critical validity. The time of such clear-cut definitions has long passed. Palestinian filmmakers have collaborated on projects with Israelis. Michel Khleifi, for example, worked with Eyal Sivan on the epic four-and-a-half-hour *Road 181: Fragments of a Journey* (2004). But this does not mean that knowledge of the history and ideology of Israeli cinema is needed for an understanding of these films or other Palestinian productions: the Palestinian film vision has its own autonomy.

Palestinian documentary has played a vital part in informing the world (or at least that part of it that wishes to listen) about the past sufferings and present plight of the Palestinian people. The films are often passionate and compelling, setting out the Palestinian narrative of the *Nakba*, so often drowned out by the triumphalist tale of the founding of the state of Israel. They make the strongest possible case for the restoration of Palestinian territory, the ending of the Israeli occupation and the restoration of basic Palestinian rights and freedoms. But it must always be borne in mind that many of these documentaries are polemical works, and the filmmakers are often drawn toward fictionalizing events. This occurs from the very beginnings of Palestinian documentary, with Michel

Khleifi stating openly and without apology that, in *Fertile Memory*, he "tried to push the real scenes from daily life towards fictionality."[289]

The same process can be found, too, in the work of younger Palestinian film-makers. Nurith Gertz and George Khleifi note that Hany Abu-Assad revealed in an interview that his documentary *Ford Transit* "includes more than a few staged scenes" and that the protagonist, the transit driver, "is actually an Arab news station cameraman, who had acted in one of Abu-Assad's films."[290] Similarly, in Mohamed Bakri's *Jenin Jenin* there is a scene showing a tank driving toward a group of captured Palestinians that suddenly blacks out, suggesting they were run over. Questioned about this scene, Bakri "admitted to constructing the footage himself, as an 'artistic choice.'"[291] Abu-Assad speaks for a considerable number of Palestinian documentary filmmakers in his defense of his own actions: "I'm not the first to have blended the documentary genre with fiction, but for some reason people believe that when a director uses documentary style he needs to adhere to the [literal] truth. I didn't make up events that never happened; the scenes in the movie happen every day."[292]

*

The founding work of Palestinian cinema is Michel Khleifi's documentary *Fertile Memory / La mémoire fertile / Al-dhâkira al-khisba* (1980). Khleifi, who was born in 1950 in Nazareth, was trained at INSAS in Belgium and began his professional career making reports and documentaries for Belgian television (RTBF) and radio. Through Marisa Films, the production company that he founded in Belgium, Khleifi coproduced not only his own early films but also the debut features of two of his fellow INSAS graduates, the Tunisians Mahmoud Ben Mahmoud (*Crossing Over*, 1982) and Néija Ben Mabrouk (*The Trace*, 1983–88).

In *Fertile Memory*, Michel Khleifi brings together the personal stories of two Palestinian women who do not know each other at all and whose lives are very different. As Khleifi has explained, the film "doesn't claim to explain all the problems of Palestinian women. Its purpose is to make audiences (Arab and others) sensitive to the reality of woman as a fundamental protagonist in history, and to show how woman's liberation would deeply influence the course of events towards a better future for Arab society."[293] As in his own later films, and many of those of his contemporaries, space plays a key role. As Gertz and Khleifi note, on the one hand, place "is an imagined place that revives the past, drawing on the pre-traumatic era, and thus functioning as a national, unity-constructing symbol that presents an idyllic home and homeland created out of an exilic state.' But, simultaneously, this abstract space is portrayed 'as a concrete, familiar, and revered place, where daily life occurs in the here and now.'"[294]

The first of the women is Roumia, a widowed grandmother in Jaffa who works in an Israeli clothing factory. She has lived in poverty since her family's land was expropriated by the Israelis (who have founded a kibbutz on it). After thirty years, she still clings to the land as well as to the old ways of living, disapproving of young people's lives in general and her own daughter's remarriage in particular. The other, younger, woman featured in the film is Sahar, who lives a very different life as a divorced single mother in Ramallah, teaching at Bir Zeit University and working as a novelist. Both women are victims of the assumptions of Arab patriarchal society (one accepts, at a very real cost to herself; the other rebels, but thereby causes herself fresh problems). They are also victims of the Israeli occupation, which denies Roumia her land rights and involves Sahar, even if she is not herself a militant, in the student struggle.

Fertile Memory not only comprises two very different stories but also involves two distinct documentary procedures, with Sahar questioned by an unseen interrogator, while Roumia gives her own account, largely in voice-over, and participates in what seem to be staged scenes of domestic life. One focus of the film is on the everyday gestures of the two women, but Khleifi has said that he intended the film to be "not just about women, but also for women."[295] The structural pattern of the film was consciously intended by Kheifi, who has said, "In *Fertile Memory*, Palestine—its history, its reality, its future, and its contractions—appear through the portraits of two women. . . . I tried to push the real scenes from daily life towards fictionality, by exploring the two women's external and internal worlds. I had to suppress the boundaries between reality and fiction, document and narration."[296]

The director has also expressed his satisfaction that the film "turned the PLO's militant cinema upside-down. It demonstrated that it is more important to show the thinking that leads to the political slogan rather than the expression of this slogan that is political discourse."[297]

In *Fertile Memory*, Kheifi's fluent camerawork and evocative use of music offer a lament for Palestine's lost lands and autonomy. Throughout this beautifully edited film, there is a concern with the dignity of simple interior spaces and the beauty of the empty landscape. The inclusion toward the end of black-and-white newsreel footage of the Israeli response to the first *intifada* adds a fresh poignancy to Khleifi's restrained, contemplative stance.

Following *Fertile Memory*, Khleifi alternated documentary and fictional works. The thirty-minute documentary *Maaloul Celebrates its Destruction / Maloul fête sa destruction / Ma'aloul tah'tafel bidamariha* (1984) was apparently made in part from footage shot for *Fertile Memory* that did not find a place in that film. The film opens with a brief, seemingly conventional montage of the Israeli capture of Palestinian land in 1948: images of damaged buildings, of dead and wounded civilians, and of Arabs trying vainly to fight off Israeli tanks while armed only with rifles. According to Bashir Abu-Manneh, this montage includes images of the 1982 Israeli invasion of Lebanon because, for Khleifi, "Lebanon leads back to Palestine: to understand Lebanon one has to understand 1948."[298]

Maaloul is just one of the 250 or so villages whose inhabitants were displaced by Israeli fighters in 1948 and have since been denied the right to return. What is distinctive about Maaloul is that once a year, on Israeli Independence Day, the former inhabitants are allowed to return with their families—to explore and explain, to picnic and play. Three threads run through the film: discussions about the past by the older people group around a mural depicting the village as it once was, shots of the jean-clad legs of someone striding through the ruins of the village today, and a lesson taught to Arab schoolchildren about the founding of Israel. The film mixes black-and-white archive footage from the past and shots of the villagers in the present, some talking directly to camera, with dreamlike, reenacted color scenes, shot in soft-focus and slow motion, purporting to show the village before 1948. The most moving scenes are those depicting an old man, Abu Zeid, trying to pick out the outlines of his own house and garden from the ruins. Gertz and Khleifi capture perfectly the effect of Kheifi's editing together of the different levels of time and reality: "It transforms the static narrative of the past resurrected in the present into a story of remembrance of the past, its recognition and processing, as a working through, as a stage toward a return to life in the present and its continued progression to the future."[299]

Khleifi does not make a clear distinction between fiction and documentary, so his first purely fictional work, *Wedding in Galilee / Noce en Galilée / Urs fi al-Jalil* (1987), is a natural follow-up to *Fertile Memory*, made six years earlier. The lead producer in the credits is Khleifi's own company (Marissa Films, based in Brussels), and the film is essentially a European-funded project, with most support coming from Belgium and France. It was shot with full permission from the Israeli authorities, though (as Khleifi admits) on the basis of a slightly edited script. The film was shot in Palestine, not at a single location, but through the fusion of settings from five separate villages—three in Galilee, near Nazareth, and two in the West Bank. The opening scene with the military governor was shot in Jerusalem. The casting is very mixed, partly because there is no theatrical tradition in Palestine. The roles of the governor and the cousin Bassam are played by professional Palestinian actors working in Israeli theater. The first Israeli officer is played by the Palestinian Arab Juliano Mer Khamis, who in 2004 was to make one of the most striking of all Palestinian documentaries, *Arna's Children*, about his activist mother. The *mukhtar* (the traditional head of the village community) is a nonprofessional, illiterate, semi-bedouin farm laborer (chosen for his physical appearance), while the grandfather is Khleifi's eighty-four-year-old uncle. The women's roles are all played by outsiders, the mother by an Arab-born theatrical actress living in Detroit and the groom's sister by a *beur* living in Paris, while the bride, because the role stipulated nude scenes, had to be played by a French actress. It is remarkable, at this period of Arab filmmaking, how so many of the most forceful and memorable female leading characters are played by non-Arabs.

Wedding in Galilee is very much a prescripted film, conceived as a five-act structure, and Khleifi kept strictly to this during the shooting. The concentration of the bulk of the action on a single day and night, together with the use of a single location (the village) calls to mind the structure of classical European drama. Khleifi, like so many of his film school–educated generation, has a keen awareness of film history and theory, and, talking about this film, he uses Deleuze's terminology in admitting to the influence of Hollywood: "I wanted to take the image-action mechanism of American cinema and make use of it for the image-action of my own cinema."[300] Khleifi is self-evidently an outsider to the story he tells. But the film expresses the intense feeling of identification with the homeland, which so many exiles experience: "The experience of this Palestinian society which is my own, Palestinian society inside Israel since 1948, is such that our problem is how to express ourselves within this power structure, how to find forms and subjects which, in addition, can become universal."[301]

The first act of *Wedding in Galilee*, the shortest and the only part of the film located outside the village, gets the action under way. It features a confrontation between the *mukhtar* and the Israeli military governor. The *mukhtar* wants the curfew lifted for the grand celebration of his son's wedding. The governor initially refuses outright. This is an extremist village, and its inhabitants have to learn to respect the Israeli will. The governor's lieutenant suggests a form of compromise: the curfew can be lifted, but only if the governor is invited as guest of honor. This is agreed, with the stipulation that the governor will stay until the end of the celebration.

On the bus traveling back to the village, the *mukhtar* has time to reflect on the decision he has made. The way in which Khleifi intercuts shots of him on the bus with scenes of the villagers summoned to receive the news shows his constant concern to drive the physical action forward, to set the scene swiftly. In contrast, the slower pacing of the central scenes surrounding the wedding is such as to allow space for the inner feelings of the individuals most closely involved. Inevitably, in the village the response to the *mukhtar*'s compromise is hostile. His brother (the father of the bride) vows not to attend: "There is no celebration without dignity and no dignity under the army's heel." Three of the young villagers are already thinking of assassinating the governor, and scenes of their not-very-well-planned plotting recur throughout the film. The Israelis make things worse on the day of the *mukhtar*'s return, showing their authority by bringing the curfew forward by one hour.

At dawn on the wedding day, there is no sense of drama, even though the Israelis are expected. The rituals of the traditional ceremony are well known, and everyone has their role and place in what is intended as a celebration for all. People come together, interacting without tension. There is a mosaic of little scenes, featuring all and favoring only the bride and groom. Hassan enjoys his grandfather's stories, and the grandmother upsets the adults with tales of her adventures (real or imaginary) with men. The older women busy themselves preparing the food, while the plotters try to get the Israelis drunk and hesitate about what to do next. As Khleifi has stated, his cultural action "aims at liberating spaces where everyone can be moved, can rediscover the real nature of things, marvel at the world, think about it and immerse oneself in the world of childhood."[302]

As the narrative proceeds, the younger women bathe Samia, the bride, while the men prepare Adel for his wedding, getting him drunk. Samia is the sensual focus of what is a very sensually shot film. We first see her naked at the preparations for the ceremony, and she will be similarly naked at the film's climax in the bedchamber. We are told nothing about her view of the arranged marriage and know nothing of any previous relationship with Adel. But it is she who tries to make the wedding night succeed, while Adel is filled with self-pity. She speaks little but her final words offer a challenge to all the men of the village and beyond: "If a woman's honor is her virginity, where do you find the honour of a man."

Samia is, it seems, naturally reticent, and her act of cutting herself comes as a shock. Her sister-in-law Soraya offers a very different image of the younger generation of women. She is naturally outgoing and far from submissive to her boyfriend, Ziad. It comes naturally to her to taunt an Israeli guard: "If you take off your uniform we'll dance with you." At one moment she acts as no woman of her mother's generation would ever have done, standing in front of a mirror and wearing male headgear, she pulls up her blouse to examine and touch her breasts. Fully dressed again, she asks the boy Hassan who is the most beautiful girl in the village, to which Hassan replies tactfully, "Today the bride. All the rest of the time you."

As the day proceeds, everything looks toward the final celebration of the wedding and everyone uses the confusions of the gathering to follow their own trajectory. To this point there has been no real tension or suspense. This comes when the *mukhtar*'s prime Thoroughbred is accidentally let loose and races through the fields ending up in the middle of a minefield (the devices planted to stop the villagers using their land). The Israeli soldiers' response is to fire in the air in the hope of driving the horse in the right direction. The *mukhtar*'s response is more successful, luring it to safety through familiar calls and endearments.

When it is time for the marriage to be consummated, traditional rituals are followed, but when the couple find themselves together, it is soon clear that this is an arranged marriage between cousins, not a love match. Adel blames his father, not himself, for his impotence. While tension among the parents grows outside, Samia takes matters into her own hands. Asking Adel, "If a women's honor is her virginity, where do you find the honor of a man?" she cuts herself to provide the requisite bloodied sheet.

When this is displayed to widespread rejoicing, the tensions that have been growing are eased. The governor can leave safely—albeit to a peaceful protest from the villagers—and the day finally comes to an end.

Wedding in Galilee is a complex and ambivalent work, as is clear from the director's published statement of intent: "Only everyday life is real. Politics, religion are myths; Palestine, is a mythic country par excellence."[303] The early attacks on the film for its lack of opposition to the Israeli occupation, made by Arab critics generally not known for their personal opposition to their own corrupt dictatorships, are clearly misguided and based on a very superficial reading of the film. Khleifi does not deal with political polemics, as he himself makes clear: "Politics excludes the imaginary, unless it can be used for ideological or partisan ends. But my films' cultural world is made up of both reality and imagination, both of which are vital to the creation of my films."[304]

But his handling of the issue of Palestine land, for example, is subtle but significant. Mostly we see landscapes only through windows (from the bus, when the *mukhtar* returns from Jerusalem, and a couple of lingering shots from the house during the wedding ceremony). The only time the camera is free to explore the land around the village is when the Thoroughbred makes its spirited escape—and the horse ends up in a field mined by the Israelis to prevent the villagers from cultivating it.

The Israelis are not caricatured—we see an army carrying out what it sees as its task of occupation. But the threat always implicit from the armed soldiers in their jeeps contrasts totally with the solicitous attitude of the older village women, when one of the occupiers, a female soldier, is overcome by the heat. The trio of young men are shown to fail in their dream of assassinating the governor, but the village is united in its peaceful opposition at the end of the film. The *mukhtar*'s strategy of accommodation with the governor is not a successful ploy. Though the wedding goes ahead without incident, this act of submission provokes real hostility from the men of the village and, in his own mind at least, the groom's impotence on his wedding night.

Set against the Israelis' overwhelming might is not an Arab revolt in the present but an evocation of their past traditions, the wedding ceremony that no occupation can devalue. Khleifi re-creates with loving care the smallest detail of the festivities, down to the bunch of grapes that the bride must step on as she enters the bridal chamber. Young and old all know the traditional songs, steps, and gestures; the ceremony unites the villagers in the present. While the film alludies to a past freedom and autonomy, the passage between past and present is a complex one, as Gertz and Khleifi make clear: "Reviving a lost past while integrating the daily sequence of life in the present and creating a flow and connection between tradition and modernity, between the past revived in the present and the actual present occurring separately from it."[305]

Canticle of the Stones / *Cantique de pierre* / *Nashid al-hajjar* (1989) is the least known and, in some ways, the most enigmatic of Khleifi's feature-length Arab works. Certainly it does not fit any neat division between documentary and fiction. Though it is generally considered to be a documentary—by Bashir Abu-Manneh, among others—the ratio of fiction to documentary is far higher than in the partially fictionalized *Fertile Memory*, and it could easily be described as a fictional feature set against a real-life background. Few critics have dealt with it, and Khleifi himself devotes just a couple of paragraphs to *Canticle of the Stones* in his chapter in Hamid Dabashi's book.

As in *Maaloul Celebrates its Destruction*, a number of strands run through the film. The scenes of the *intifada* have a ring of truth, but the parallel love story between two unnamed characters is clearly fictional and in many ways dominates the film. Indeed the woman, a filmmaker returning from exile, articulates all Khleifi's own concerns about how to deal with the *intifada* in an appropriate filmic manner. The stylistic differences between the two continuous threads of the film could not be more marked. The formal composition of the images of the two lovers in their hotel contrasts sharply with the jagged, reportage-style shooting of the disturbances on the streets, and Bashir Abu-Manneh points out that "the intellectualized love encounter is spoken in classical Arabic, while the *intifada* footage is in colloquial."[306] The love scenes are given a romantic musical accompaniment, often by the trio of instrumentalists seen at intervals throughout the early part of the film, while, on the streets, the harsh dominant sound is that caused by the Israeli military crackdown.

Khleifi's own two paragraphs offer fascinating insight into the development of the film. Significantly, he does not talk of making a documentary: "The initial project was to make a poetic impressionistic investigation based on the portraits of some of the children killed by Israeli repression." But as he worked on this concept, he turned the problem around and "started filming the theme of sacrifice as a subject of the *intifada*. This was a universal approach, since sacrifice is part of all human experience." When the time for scriptwriting arrived, he "wrote a poetical dialogue with two voices: she and he" and, while writing it, realized "that there was some similarity with *Hiroshima mon amour*, by Marguerite Duras, adapted in Alain Resnais' outstanding film." He asked himself what was to prevent him from having "the literary and cinematographic references of *Hiroshima mon amour?*"[307] As a result, the opening exchange of offscreen voices can be read as an homage to (or even a parody of) the Duras text:

MAN: All you'll see is moments in time. You'll see nothing.

WOMAN: I'll see mutilated bodies. I'll see destroyed souls. I'll see poverty. I'll witness resistance and denial.

MAN: You'll see nothing of all that, because unless you live here, it is all invisible.

Canticle of the Stones is perhaps the most enigmatic of Khleifi's films. The two halves of the double story line do not illuminate each other. Instead, the transition from one to the other constantly jars. The lovers' intense introspection never acquires an emotional power—it has no momentum—and the reality of what we see and hear happening between them is unclear. Indeed, the very real suffering happening on the streets seems trivialized by the proclamations of a couple who give no attention to the *intifada*, the ostensible reason for the woman's return. As has been noted elsewhere, Khleifi's "refusal to condone the 'children of the *intifada*,' whom he saw as victims and not heroes, and his resistance to revolutionary clichés" led to his work finding little support in Palestinian and Arab circles, with the result that "increasingly, he began to feel marginalized and misunderstood."[308]

In contrast to *Canticle of the Stones*, Khleifi's next documentary, *Mixed Marriages in the Holy Land / Mariages mixtes en terre sainte / Al-zawaj al-mukjtalit fi al-aradi al-muqaddisa* (1995), is one of his most directly accessible works. It was inevitable that the subject of inter-racial marriage would attract Khleifi, given his interest in peaceful personal struggle and his rejection of national and racial boundaries. The film, which runs for sixty-six minutes and was shot on Beta SP, is a conventionally structured documentary focused primarily on the experiences of eight couples in mixed marriages. Their comments to the camera, as they are interviewed by Khleifi (who does not himself appear in the shot or offer any personal commentary), are interspersed with statements by representatives of the three Middle Eastern monotheistic religions, giving their (at times very divergent) orthodox views. All support tradition and oppose mixed marriage. Only in Islam is it permissible for men to marry outside their religion, and then only if the woman converts. For women, marriage outside Islam is forbidden, indeed punishable by death under sharia law.

Much of the film deals with the initial family reaction to their mixed relationship, and here the experience is consistent. Whether they were Jewish men marrying Arab women or Arab men taking Jewish wives, they virtually all lost contact with members of their family and most of their friends. Some were openly branded as traitors. Most would now like contact with their loved ones but realize that this is impossible, the price they have to pay for the life they have chosen. The greatest problem they now foresee concerns the fate of their children, who do not fit into the community in which they live and go to school. Even here one mother finds humor. When their small son was taunted for having a Jewish mother and an Arab father and asked what he was, he replied: "A communist." *Mixed Marriages in the Holy Land* is not a major work, but Khleifi's sympathetic approach to both filming and questioning shows both his desire to give these couples a voice and also his own immense respect for those who, out of love, have chosen a very difficult path in life.

Speaking of his third, and least known of all his fictional features, *The Order of the Day / L'ordre du jour* (1993), Khleifi has said, "I was excited about the idea of making a film that would give a fictional, anthropological reflection on the life of this bureaucratic class, the largest class in today's developed countries." But the reality was very different: "After the Gulf War, I directed my first Belgian film. The subject, location and characters all came from the novel of my friend Jean-Luc Outers. As I explained, it was an almost anthropological look at the bureaucrats at the end of this century. . . . I won't dwell on that film, which to this day remains a painful memory for me: through the irrational rejection of this film in Europe, I discovered that European society refuses, in an intolerant manner, any external viewpoint on its own reality."[309]

Khleifi's approach to his next fictional feature, *The Tale of the Three Jewels / Conte des trois diamants / Hikayat al-jawaheral-thalatha* (1996), a characteristic mixture of the real and the imaginary, is very clear from his statement of intent in the film's pressbook: "Youssef, a young, 12-year-old Palestinian boy, is a child of the Intifada: With his father in prison and his brother sought by the Israeli army, he lives with his mother and sister. Although his life is punctuated in the refugee camp and escaping into the countryside of Gaza."

As in *Canticle of the Stones*, Khleifi chooses a double pattern of narration, but this time it is the adults who are fighting on the street; the people in love are just children. The two strands are kept apart: Youssef does not even want to visit his father in an Israeli jail, and the children are stopped only once when out on the streets after curfew. His elder brother is an active resistance fighter and Youssef's mother and sister tend and shelter one of his wounded companions. But none of this involves Youssef. The only time the two narrative strands come together is in the film's disconcerting ending. Youssef is shot, pointlessly, by an Israeli patrol seeking resistance fighters. He is dead (we assume) before his family can reach him. As they approach, the Israeli soldiers inexplicably turn and run away. When his mother reaches him, Youssef is miraculously alive and well—presumably thanks to the logic of the indestructible fairy tale hero.

Stylistically, the two strands are treated very differently. The film was shot entirely in Gaza, just at the time of the Hebron mosque massacre. The ten weeks of preparation and shooting had to follow the rhythms of the Israeli curfews, the same rhythm as that governing the lives of the Gaza inhabitants. Khleifi chose to shoot the various confrontations and killings in television newsreel style, sharp and immediate.

Aside from the two dream sequences, which shape the beginning and end of the film, the rest of Youssef's adventures are filmed in a more laid-back style, with plenty of time for the telling details of which Khleifi is so fond. Though a child of the refugee camp, much of his time is spent outside it, on the beach, around a palm-lined oasis and, later, in an orange grove. It is at the oasis that Youssef meets a gipsy girl, Aïda, with whom he falls in love and vows to marry when he grows up. She is full of tales of the supernatural and even gives Youssef some djinn soap that will give him "the strength of Goliath, the courage of David and the wisdom of Solomon." To win Aïda's hand, Youssef has to accomplish a task she gives him—namely, to recover the three jewels missing from her grandmother's necklace that, unfortunately, were lost in South America. Much of the middle part of the film is concerned with Youssef's attempt to cope with this: Where is South America? What is a visa and why do you need one? *How* much money do you need to fly there? Eventually, he decides to stow away in a crate of oranges that his friend Salah's father is exporting to Europe. Immediate dispatch is prevented by a new Israeli curfew, and Youssef awakes next morning to the sunshine and the song of his pet goldfinch, which has been released to find him. It is the song of the goldfinch that leads the family home. *The Tale of the Three Diamonds*, like its predecessor, *Canticle of the Stones*, reflects Khleifi's long-held belief in a peaceful solution to Middle Eastern conflict and an eventual reconciliation between Palestinian and Israeli societies.[310]

Road 181: Fragments of a Journey in Palestine-Israel / Route 181, fragments d'un voyage en Palestine-Israël (2004) is a documentary shot on Beta SP over a period of two months in the summer of 2002 and codirected with Israeli director Eyal Sivan. The film takes its title from the 1947 United Nations General Assembly Resolution 181, which, as the sparse precredit sequence tells us, envisaged a partition of Palestinian land in which 56 percent would go to the Jewish minority, 43 percent would go to the Arab majority, and the rest would be designated "an international zone." *Road 181* is a massive, overloaded but understated four-and-a-half-hour road movie (divided into three feature-length sequences) in which the two filmmakers follow this 1947 partition line that was proposed as a solution to the problem of how to establish the independent state of Israel. The partition line never existed as a border, but it nevertheless "caused the first Arab-Israeli war, which has yet to end."

In their interview (recorded in January 2004) included in the boxed set of DVDs, the filmmakers make clear their shared personal stance, which is never explicitly stated within the film. The Zionist project, for them, can be understood only in terms of the nineteenth-century European concerns with developing a national state and with fostering colonialism. Equally, the three stages of the journey represent, for the filmmakers, three distinct areas: the South, which has been ethnically cleansed; the Center, around Jerusalem and in the shadow of Gaza, where the conflict has its heart; and the North, where the colonial project began and where Sephardic Jews from the Arab Middle East are now settled, in a sort of buffer zone. For Khleifi, "there is a lot of hope in the film," because when you begin to "understand a process, its mechanisms, you can reflect, create, propose a new path, a new vision of the world." None of these attitudes is made explicit in the film. Instead, the spectator is left free to create his own connections and to draw his own conclusions.

The film largely comprises a series of interviews with individuals, mostly Jews but some Arabs, encountered on the journey and presented in strictly chronological order. The interviews are separated by brief shots of the car journey itself. The emblematic linking shot is of the view through the front window of the car, with the maps strewn on the dashboard. There is a paradox at the heart of the film, in that the filmmakers are constantly searching for traces of earlier Arab occupation of this land, though they well know that all such traces—even the place names—have been obliterated, as this is, of course, territory now occupied, and partly settled, by Israelis. The shaping of the film reflects the sequence of the filmmakers' random encounters. There is no voice-over commentary to offer explanations or give historical background beyond that provided by the interviewees. Nor is there any factual documentation to back up assertions made by the participants (who are mostly unnamed), nor is there any graphic material within the film itself to enable an audience to track the progress of the journey along the imaginary border.

Route 181 is less a conventional documentary than a massive audio-visual archive, capturing the tensions (largely within the Israeli population) at a particular moment in time and raising a whole series of issues related to this divided land. It is less a statement of verifiable factual information—beyond the known obliteration of former Arab villages—than the revelation of the extent of the contempt and ill will that the Israelis the filmmakers encounter direct toward their Israeli Arab cocitizens and their Palestinian neighbors. The openness with which this hostility is expressed—even by otherwise mild-mannered people—is breathtaking, rendering the notion of any peaceful, two-state solution unthinkable.

Khleifi has said that he regards the film "as a political work of art," adding, "this is our history in Palestine. We have the right to film this history and we won't let that be taken away from us."[311] In fact, the initial screening of *Route 181* in Paris led to huge media debate and extreme hostility from the Jewish intellectual community. The result was a partial ban on further showings, including during the Festival du Cinéma du Réel held at the Paris Pompidou Centre. The outcome was particularly serious for Eyal Sivan, who was attacked as a "self-hating Jew." He became involved in libel proceedings, which had an ambiguous legal outcome but led to the loss of his teaching position at the French Ministry of Education and the television channel Arte's the decision to cease commissioning his films.[312]

Zindeeq (2010), which was made fourteen years after Khleifi's previous fictional feature, is a complex, introspective, low-budget film (shot on Super 16mm and blown up to 35mm). The protagonist, unnamed in the film but referred to as M (for Michel, possibly) in the press release, is a figure very close to Khleifi himself, if not directly autobiographical. He is a European-based, Palestinian-born filmmaker who has a French passport and can pass himself off as a Frenchman unable to speak either English or Hebrew at an Israeli checkpoint. The role is played moreover by Mohamed Bakri, an actor (and director) of Khleifi's generation who in real life made the very film Khleifi's protagonist is working on, a documentary entitled *1948*.

The film is basically a road movie. Newly arrived in Palestine but already at odds with Rasha, his attractive young Palestinian assistant, M arrives in Nazareth ostensibly for the funeral of his uncle; he is in fact there to seek out his parents' graves (a further autobiographical allusion, since Nazareth is Khleifi's own birthplace). Back in Ramallah, he learns that, because of a blood feud involving his nephew, it would be unwise to return to Nazareth. Inevitably, M sets off for Nazareth, and the film develops as one man's solitary nighttime journey to and through Nazareth, where he is constantly refused a room at all the hotels he visits. The vision that emerges from the nighttime shots of Nazareth is bleak in the extreme: marauding gangs beat up passersby at random, and feral children are camped in and roaming through the streets. M seems totally lost and has nothing positive to propose, even after a nighttime meeting with a prophetic drunk at the well of the Virgin Mary. The question that haunts M is a purely personal one—why did his parents stay in Nazareth in 1948? He receives no answer that will satisfy him and restore his identity as both a Palestinian and an exile.

The film begins in a firmly realistic mode, but as it progresses, there is a growing confusion about the status of the images, which mix M's actual encounters and what he has recorded, what he remembers and what he imagines or longs for. He is constantly filming with his camera (as he tells a young boy, "We Palestinians don't make war; we make films") and rewinding the camera to view the material he has shot. But some of the images we see him watching are clearly imagined ones, and the shots of the countryside include scenes from *Fertile Memory*. Whether he has a series of sexual encounters with girls half his age in the early part of the film is uncertain. What is clear is that the film does not separate itself from M's views—those of stereotypical Arab cinema in which any woman is either mother, virgin, or whore.

The film's title, *Zindeeq*, means atheist or nonbeliever, and for M the old unquestioned truths—such as simply blaming Israel for everything—seem no longer to make sense. This was presumably the purpose of M's project on the *Nakba*, but, for him, it is no longer valid. *Zindeeq* is perhaps the only recent Palestinian film that sees no hope in the future, even for the women of Palestine. The film is full of doubts, questions, and controversial assertions. Eman Morsi describes it as "the latest instalment in an emerging sub-genre of Palestinian experimental films that see nothing in the Palestine-Israel conflict but a surrealist, incoherent and absurdist muddle."[313] This view is borne out in the final lyrical image of the film, where the down-to-earth Rasha is transformed into a white-clad virgin walking on the Sea of Galilee. Khleifi did little to explain the ending when he was questioned about it at a festival presentation of the film: "A man from Nazareth was the first to walk on water, so it's appropriate that the first man to make a woman walk on water is also from Nazareth."

*

Two other documentary Palestinian filmmakers of this generation have very different and contrasting backgrounds. Mohamed Bakri is an Israeli Arab and thus formally an Israeli citizen, while Samir Abdallah is a representative of the Palestinian diaspora. The pair give complementary views of Palestinian society and its problems—one from the inside, the other very much from the outside.

Mohamed Bakri, a self-taught filmmaker, was born in 1953 in the village of al-Bi'na in Galilee and has made an international reputation as an actor in over twenty Palestinian, Israeli, and foreign films. Bakri has also made four major documentaries, beginning with *1948*. Gertz and Khleifi describe the film thus: "Mohamed Bakri's *1948* (1998) depicts a diversified and polyphonic past. The different points of view include the perspective of the people who experienced the events, that of the historians attempting to understand them, and that of the artists describing them (Muhamad Taha, Emile Habibi). It is also both the perspective of past days, when the events actually occurred (supported by archive photographs), and that of the present time, when the tale is being narrated."[314]

Bakri's second documentary, *Jenin Jenin / Jénine Jénine* (2002), is a sparse film, using only limited music to underline its horrifying images. Indeed, it relies exclusively on documentary footage of the devastated Jenin camp, filmed in the immediate aftermath, and on the direct testimony of those Palestinians involved. It contains neither commentary nor explanatory titles to locate even the immediate causes and outcomes of the conflict. Historian of modern Palestine Ivan Pappe explains the significance of Jenin: "After the deaths after [Ariel] Sharon's visit [to Haram al-Sharif], the Palestinian resentment took another form. . . . They took up suicide bombing as the sole way of ending the occupation. The Israeli retaliation was even more severe than in the past, culminating in the destruction of the Jenin refugee camp, with the massacre of scores of Palestinians in April 2000."[315]

The film opens with shots of the ruined Jenin, accompanied by plaintive music, and similar images recur throughout the film. At the time of the Israeli incursion, the Palestinians tried to fight back, but armed only with Kalashnikov rifles, they were self-evidently no match for the Israeli F16s, tanks, heavy artillery, and giant bulldozers, used, they claim, to assault them. When the film was shot, no clearance of the rubble had been possible, and there was no way of knowing how many bodies were buried there. No outside help had been allowed into Jenin, and Palestinians are shown still grappling by hand with the crushed remnants of their homes, schools, and hospitals. In these circumstances, at least one of those interviewed questions the purpose of the film: "Stop filming will you. What good is your filming when no Arab has been able to do anything?" But most of the victims wanted to be heard by the outside world.

A whole range of Palestinians, young and old, give their testimony direct to camera, all filmed amid the debris. The first old man to be interviewed is in despair, crying out, "Where is God!" and there are horrifying tales of Israelis driving their tanks over captured young men and making men and women strip naked in public, supposedly to check for hidden weapons, and of snipers deliberately targeting children and even a heavily pregnant woman. Perhaps the most poignant testimony comes from those prevented by the firing from helping a wounded child or those who held a dying victim in their arms when no medical aid was available. But most Palestinians show remarkable resilience, including one man who emerged from fifteen years in an Israeli prison and began his life again from scratch.

Small children show their resistance ("We will never give up"), and an old man of seventy-two pledges to rebuild his home and his life. Obviously, there is anger about the Israelis ("They want to treat us like animals"), but it is also directed toward "hypocritical" Arab governments ("Nobody defended us") and the United Nations, which does nothing to help. One of the most eloquent witnesses is a young girl who sends her message to the Israelis: "Proud as eagles will we live. Erect as lions we will die." One witness captures the general mood when he argues, "They wanted to terrorise us. Instead they strengthened our will." The film ends on a more lighthearted note with a man entertaining a crowd of bystanders with a mock call to George Bush and Kofi Annan, demanding an international investigation. In fact it was only two years later—"after the horrific events in Jenin became public knowledge"[316]—that the American administration embarked on the peace plan, which became known as the "Road Map."

Jenin Jenin is a controversial film. It presents only the evidence of Palestinian witnesses and allows no space for an Israeli response. At its first showing, it was violently attacked and within days had been banned by the Israeli authorities. The film's accuracy has been questioned by some outside critics, for example, by the Algerian-born French filmmaker Pierre Rehov, who made his own version of events in *Road to Jenin* a year later.[317] Certainly Bakri offers little factual information (such as the number of those killed), relying totally on the accounts given in the immediate aftermath of the assault by those he interviews from behind the camera.

Throughout *Jenin Jenin*, Bakri keeps himself totally in the background, never appearing in shots and offering no personal comments on the situation he is documenting, though, of course, it is his editing of the material that shapes our response. The stance adopted in Bakri's next documentary, *Since You Left / Depuis que tu n'es plus là / Min youm ma ruhat* (2006), is totally different. This is a very personal film, structured around Bakri's visit to the grave of his great friend and hero Emile Habibi, who died in 1996. Habibi, whom Bakri refers to by his nick-name, Abu Salaam, was a remarkable figure: poet, novelist, and one of the lead-ing figures in the Israeli Communist Party. As such, he was part of a group who were "periodically jailed, interrogated or tortured for their support for the right of return of the refugees or for their open call to abolish the military regime."[318] Habibi stayed behind in Haifa when the Israelis occupied it in 1948, and his writ-ing "is possibly unique in its focus on the Arab citizens of Israel rather than on the Palestinian refugees"[319]—hence its relevance to Bakri, himself an Arab Israeli. Habibi's best-known novel, to which the film makes several allusions, is the oddly named *The Pessoptimist*, which "mixes pessimism and optimism about the Israeli Arabs' situation. . . . So bizarre can this situation seem that Saeed, the novel's nar-rator and protagonist, scarcely knows whether to laugh or cry."[320]

Bakri's own life, as narrated in voice-over at the graveside, has a similar mix of surprises and shifting emotions, though in a largely tragic vein. Throughout, Bakri's account is illustrated by a range of material, such as home movies, inter-views with members of his own family, television footage, and film of his stage performances, as well as documentary footage of his public appearances. He begins his friendly "conversation" with Abu Salaam with generalities—artistic ones, such as his own touring in plays, including one based on *The Pessoptimist*, and political events, principally the Arab responses provoked by Sharon's ill-judged visit to Haram al-Sharif, as well as the Israeli reply at Jenin and elsewhere.

Then, as he tells Abu Salaam, two highly personal events coincided in the summer and autumn of 2002. First, his nephew was involved in a suicide bomb-ing at Meiron Junction in which nine Israelis were killed in an attack on a bus. As a result, the whole Bakri family were immediately branded as terrorists in the Israeli press. Mohamed Bakri's public position as one of Israel's best-known and most successful actors was made extremely difficult. Things got even worse when *Jenin Jenin* was screened for the first time at the Cinémathèque in Jerusa-lem. Israeli members of the audience protested noisily, shouting for this "Pales-tinazi propaganda"—as they called it—to be stopped. A member of parliament described the film as "constructed of tendentious lies that amount to a blood libel," and the censor banned all screenings in Israel. There were calls for a boy-cott of all Bakri's stage performances, and he and his son were forced to try to sell videos and DVDs of *Jenin Jenin* on the streets in order to get the film some visibility. The censorship was personally painful for Bakri, since he had intended his film for his fellow Israeli citizens, naïvely thinking he might influence pub-lic opinion. Meanwhile, the kind of destruction he had witnessed at Jenin was repeated, though on a lesser scale, as houses in his own village were bulldozed, with members of his family caught up in the violence. But the film does end on a positive note. The proceedings in the Supreme Court reverse the ban on the film, and Bakri acquires a new and supportive friend, in the person of his

Jewish defending lawyer, Avigdor Feldman, members of whose family had died in Auschwitz.

Bakri handles the complex interaction of public and personal and the shifting moods and tensions extremely well throughout the film. But the end credits have a fresh surprise that points to the ambiguities of the situation of an Arab Israeli filmmaker. While *Jenin Jenin*, an openly propagandist work telling the Palestinian side of the story of an Israeli military action, may or may not have received partial funding from the Palestinian Authority, *Since You Left* is an Israeli production backed by three organizations: the New Israeli Foundation for Film and Television, the Ministry of Education, Culture and Sport, and the Israeli Film Council.

Zahara / Zahra (2009) is another personal documentary and deals with the experiences of those Palestinians who have stayed put in Israel and become Israeli citizens. Bakri uses the life and experiences of Zahara, an elderly member of his own extended family, to relate the story of ordinary Palestinians from the period before 1948, through the upheavals of the founding of the Israeli state, and up to the present situation, where they find themselves an oppressed minority in their own land.

Samir Abdallah was born in Denmark in 1959 but has lived in France since the age of six and has French nationality. From his production base in France, Abdallah has made a diverse selection of documentaries, mostly looking at Palestine from an outside (and therefore less controversial) perspective, beginning with *We Shall Return Some Day / Nous retournerons un jour* (with Walid Charara, 1998).

In *Writers on the Borders / Ecrivains des frontières* (codirected with José Reynès, 2004), Abdallah follows eight writers from four different continents—including Breytan Breytenbach and Wole Soyinka—who arrive to support Mahmoud Darwish, at the time unable to leave Ramalah. Their collective reading session in the town is very well received, but three days later, the theater itself is destroyed by the Israeli army. They go on to experience what a Palestinian activist describes as the "banality" of Palestinian humiliation: the ruthless destruction of Palestinian-owned olive groves to make way for the building of the wall, the systematic division of the occupied territory by Israeli checkpoints and Israeli-only roads, and the "collective punishment" inflicted on the Palestinian people by the hindrances of access to Bir Zeit University. Some of the comments made by members of the group—references to Auschwitz and Israeli fascism—are in no way productive. The group meets with Yasser Arafat, and Breytenbach sends an open letter to Ariel Sharon. But basically they find themselves helpless in face of the overwhelming might of the Israeli occupying force. The film ends with them in Rafah, witnessing the "war of bulldozers" as the Israeli forces destroy Palestinian homes to create a so-called buffer zone.

After the War . . . / Après la guerre, c'est toujours la guerre (made in Lebanon, 2008) follows a similar pattern, tracing a group of (largely French) journalists as they are confronted with the ongoing devastation of Beirut in July 2006 and meet a range of victims in hospitals and newly set up shelters. Again there is no explanatory voice-over, and events are allowed to speak for themselves. The group encounters a number of Lebanese journalists setting out to establish a new newspaper, *Al-Akhbar*, under bombardment in the last days of the assault. On the first day of the ceasefire—August 14—they experience firsthand both the devastation and the rejoicing of ordinary people, who see this as a victory. But when the group moves to South Lebanon, the problem of removing rubble is replaced by that posed by the million or so cluster bombs dropped by the Israelis in the last days of the conflict, when the war ceased to be against Hezbollah and became a punishment of Lebanese citizens in general.

Gaza on Air / Gaza crève l'écran, also shown initially at festivals as *Gaza-Strophe: The Day After / GazaStrophe, le jour après* (2010), deals with the twenty-two-day Israeli bombardment of Gaza, which began on the December 27, 2008, in response to the election of a Hamas government. The election process appears to have been totally in order (no foreign government, not even Israel, queried its legality), but the totally unprotected citizens of Gaza were nonetheless submitted to collective punishment (there was no possibility for the Israelis, using airstrikes, tanks, and artillery fire, to single out Hamas militants embedded among the ordinary citizens). In the end, 1,300 Gazan citizens were killed. *Gaza on Air* is a full feature-length documentary with a classically simple structure. The opening titles set out the key facts: the date and the facts that Gaza is the most densely populated territory on earth and that no foreign reporters were allowed into the war zone. The film therefore records the views and experiences of the Palestinian cameramen and journalists resident in Gaza. Their testimony to camera, filmed in close-up in a studio and against a uniform black background, is alternated with the images they have recorded. The structure is basically chronological: the images become more horrific as the onslaught continues.

Initially the response was one of surprise—"Israel doesn't attack on Saturdays"—and panic. The attack was totally unexpected, and many children were still in school. As the death toll mounts, the reporters and cameramen have increasing fear for their own families, and they have to confront the problem of how to simply film suffering when other sorts of intervention—by EMTs and doctors—are what is needed. But in the absence of foreign witnesses, they all feel it is their duty to get images and coverage shown abroad. They struggle to find reasons for the unceasing bombardment, some concluding that they are the victims of the Israeli political process (elections there are imminent). Whatever the case, the devastation constantly rises, and more and more bodies have to be dug from the rubble. As the journalists themselves come under seemingly deliberate attack and chemical weapons are used against the few UN refuges, the cameramen and reporters talk of their own fears and nightmares. As abruptly as it started, the bombardment ends, but Gaza remains blockaded. *Gaza on Air* is the most deeply felt and personal of Abdallah's works, though it was put together from outside Gaza, using just the material the participants could transmit. It remains a powerful testament to Palestinian suffering.

*

The work of Khleifi, Bakri, and Aballah does not constitute the whole richness of Palestinian filmmaking in this period. One of the leading female documentary filmmakers in the Arab world of the 1980s, 1990s, and beyond is the Palestinian Maï Masri. But since almost all of her work, created in collaboration with her Lebanese husband, Jean Chamoun, deals with issues in Lebanon, it has already been dealt with in the appropriate section. Other 1950s-born Palestinian filmmakers who turned their attention to Palestinian issues are the documentary filmmakers Norma Marcos and Ali Nassar, who moved from documentary to fiction. There are also a number of precocious filmmakers born in or after 1960 who made their first features in the late 1990s. These include Rashid Masharawi and Elia Suleiman, whose careers have been considered elsewhere.[321]

Norma Marcos, journalist and filmmaker, was born in Nazareth in 1951 and has lived in Paris since 1977. She worked as an assistant on a number of productions and codirected a documentary, *Bethlehem Under Surveillance / Bethléem sous surveillance*, for Canal Plus in 1990. She has since made a number of solo documentaries, mostly on video: *Veiled Hope / L'espoir voilé / Al'amal al-ghamid* (1994); *Land Development* (1999); *Waiting for Ben Gurion / En attendant Ben Gourion* (2006), based on her experiences in an Israeli prison; and, more recently, *Fragments of a Lost Palestine / Fragments d'une Palestine perdue / Malameh filistinia dai'a* (2010), which combines the director's own memories of her birthplace with interviews made during a visit there.

Her best-known work, *Veiled Hope*, was shot on 16mm. At the beginning of the film, Marcos introduces us to her five principal protagonists: Yusra Barbari, who represented Palestine at the United Nations in 1963; Hanan Ashrawi, well-known for her role in negotiations with Israel; Joumana Odeh, a doctor; Rima Tarasi, a musician and teacher; and Hanan Arouri, a frustrated student. The focus of this wide-ranging and loosely constructed documentary is on the difficulties faced by women in Palestine. It gives the statistics of those women involved in the struggle against the Israeli occupation in the years 1967 to 1990: 250 exiled, 460 imprisoned (12 for life), 7,000 wounded, 129 killed, and over 1,000 a year arrested. But the film's main concern is with the difficulties and barriers imposed by the traditions of Arab society and the attitudes of men—brothers as well as fathers—within it. Though the struggle for women's status and education has a long history (which Marcos documents), there is little progress to be discerned in the present. Women are still blocked from positions of influence, many of them regard it as normal that their husbands beat them (though both Ashwari and Odeh have husbands who support and aid their careers), and too many women are complicit with male dominance. The film finds little hope for change. It begins with Arouri's lament that her family would not let her study medicine in the Soviet Union, though she had won a bursary, and ends with her complaint that though she has now achieved certain freedoms at home, she is still not regarded as capable of making the most important decisions in her own life.

Ali Nassar, who was born in the Galilean village of Arraba in 1954, studied film in Moscow, graduating in 1981. Returning to Haifa, he founded a theater group and worked as a newspaper photographer. He began his filmmaking in the mid-1980s, completing two short films, *The City on the Coast / Madina ʿala al-shati* (1985) and *The Source of the Gift / Naabq al-ata'* (1992). He has subsequently completed four feature films: *The Wet Nurse / La nourrice / al-Mardhaʾah* (1993), *The Milky Way / La voie lactée / Dar al-tabbanat* (1997), *In the Ninth Month / Au neuvième mois / Bahodesh hatshi'i* (2002), and *Whispering Embers / Jamr athikoya* (2008).

The Milky Way is set in 1964, the last year of Israeli military rule, but echoes of the 1948 *Nakba* resonate through the film. The milky way of the title refers to the name villagers have given to the path leading from the fields into the village, along which they used to carry in their harvest. It was on this road that Mabruq witnessed the massacre of his family, and the event has affected him mentally so that he is now, in effect, the "village idiot," who plays with the village children as an equal and has difficulty keeping track of the adult world. But, as is usual in Arab narrative, it is sometimes he who sees a truth hidden from the others. The other mentally damaged person in the village is the young girl Jamila, who saw her mother slaughtered before her eyes in a subsequent Israeli massacre in 1956. Not surprisingly, these two young people are drawn closer together as the narrative proceeds.

The film opens with a peaceful rural scene into which strides the *mukhtar*, who immediately makes presence unpleasantly. He has a crucial role in the community, acting as the crucial link between the villagers and the Israeli occupiers, who regard him as a friend and of whom he can ask occasional favors. The occupation is depicted as uncompromisingly violent. The villagers no longer work their own land but are hired laborers who travel out daily to work in the fields for the Israelis who have seized their land. Even to do this, they need a permit, and trouble arises when it is discovered that some of these permits have been forged. The Israeli response is aggressive and unforgiving. Initially, they decree that no one will be able to work and feed their families. The village schoolteacher, Ahmad, is the immediate suspect; he is brutally beaten, imprisoned without evidence, and given the threat that his wife will be thrown into jail if he does not cooperate. A demonstration by the villagers does not persuade the Israeli military governor to change his mind in the slightest.

But the film's main focus is on the villagers, and here the major source of contention is who, between the *mukhtar*'s spoiled son, Mohamed, and the upright village blacksmith, Mahmud, should marry the beautiful Suad, who loves and is engaged to Mahmud. The confrontation leads to a brawl in Mahmud's house in which Mohamed is killed. All looks lost as Mahmud is forced to flee for his life. As Gertz and Khleifi point out, the house which could function as a focus for the whole community in Khleifi's *Wedding in Galilee* can no longer serve that function here.[322] The *mukhtar*'s official residence is a place of corruption, injustice, and the humiliation of the hapless Mabruq. The teacher's house is ransacked by the Israelis, while Mahmud's is raided and burned down by Mohamed and his friends.

At the end, however, Nassar shies away from the logic of the narrative he has forcefully created. The *mokhtar* has an unexpected change of heart. In front of the governor, he accepts that his son was responsible for his own death (allowing Mahmud his freedom) and (though we know his daughter was the real culprit) puts the blame for the forged permits on his dead son (allowing the released of Ahmad from prison). The film ends with Mabruq and Jamilah standing together in silence looking not at the village milky way, which has such terrible memories, but the celestial constellation of the same name.

*

What all these filmmakers have in common is a concern with creating images documenting and dramatizing Palestinian life. As Gertz and Khleifi observe, "Palestinian cinema, in its attempt to invent, document, and crystallize Palestinian history, confronts the trauma."[323] The same point is made by Edward Said: "The whole history of the Palestinian struggle has to do with the desire to be visible."[324] Sixty years after the founding of Israel, the struggle continues: how do we find a way to counteract the old Zionist slogan that Palestine was "a land without people" seemingly designed for "a people without a land."[325] Palestinian cinema has a double role, aptly summed up by Said: "On the one hand, Palestinians stand against invisibility, which is the fate they have resisted since the beginning; and on the other hand, they stand against the stereotype in the media: the masked Arab, the *kufiyya*, the stone-throwing Palestinian—a visual identity associated with terrorism and violence."[326]

Palestinian filmmakers work under very difficult circumstances and often at great physical risk in a context that former president Jimmy Carter has likened to South African apartheid. They therefore have to take their funding where they can find it. Those who are Israeli citizens and have taken funding from Israeli government sources have on occasion been subjected to unjustified criticism. But all Palestinian filmmakers' commitment to the cause of their people—those within Israel itself, those in the Occupied Territories, and those living by necessity or choice in exile—is as unquestionable as are the many talents they have brought to their work.

Iraq

As the filmmaker and critic Qassim Hawal has noted, since the 1980s Iraqi cinema has become a "cinema of the diaspora, making the most of possibilities for experimental, documentary and short films, often working in difficult conditions with low budgets of around ten thousand dollars, and then being faced with great difficulty in obtaining screenings."[327] Iraqi documentary filmmakers are, indeed, scattered across Europe, and this type of Iraqi production is precisely the kind of diasporic filmmaking so ably analyzed by Hamid Naficy. The nature of the films produced reflects quite a new definition of what exile actually represents at the present time, as Naficy explains: "There was a time when exile implicitly or explicitly involved a present or absent home, or a homeland, as referent. However, the referent is now in ruins or in perpetual manipulation, and the concept of exile, once stabilized because of its link to the homeland, is now freed from the chains of its referent. This destabilization has forced a radical redefinition of what constitutes exile, from a strictly political expulsion and banishment to a more nuanced, culturally driven displacement."[328] Some of the key features in Naficy's definition of exilic filmmaking are particularly relevant to Iraq: "Fragmented, multilingual, epistolary, self-reflective, and critically juxtaposed narrative structure. . . . Subject matter and themes that involve journeying, historicity, identity and displacement . . . and inscription of the biographical, social and cinematic (dis)location of the filmmakers."[329]

Four makers of feature-length documentary works stand out: Kassim Abid, Maysoon Pachachi, Samir and Saad Salman. When working with a television audience in mind, these filmmakers keep to conventional formats, with a running time of around 90 minutes. But particularly when working on highly personal material, making films for themselves or for and about their families, they are much more expansive. Abid's study of his family runs to 155 minutes and Samir's to 164. Samir expresses a view held by many exilic directors when talking about *Iraqi Odyssey*: "The nice thing about cinema is that you can make time. Time that television doesn't allow. . . . A family story which spans over a century and the entire globe cannot be told in 90 minutes. My film is like a symphony to me. It consists of a number of movements and this takes time."[330]

Kassim Abid was born in 1950 in Baghdad and studied at the Academy of Arts there, before beginning his film training at the VGIK film institute in

Moscow. There he graduated as a director of photography (his graduation film, *Black Cross*, is available on the internet—with Russian dialogue). He has lived since 1982 in the United Kingdom, where he has been active as director of photography and documentary filmmaker, making short films since the 1990s. With Maysoon Pachachi, he cofounded the Independent Film and Television School in Baghdad in 2003, at the beginning of his long stay in Iraq, where he shot his first full-length film.

The first available example of Abid's documentary filmmaking is *Amid the Alien Corn / Dans les champs étranges de maïs* (1990), a conventionally structured, thirty-eight-minute documentary about Iraqi artists living in exile in Italy. It gives them the space to talk and explore their memories of Iraq, the effect of exile on their personal lives, and their struggles for survival. They also talk of the impact of exile on their artist concerns and on the development on their artistic style. There is space, too, after each major interview, for the director to explore their work with a sensitive camera and an appropriate musical score.

Naji al-Ali—An Artist with Vision / Naji al-Ali, un artiste visionnaire (1999) is a similarly sensitive, if conventionally structured, study of the radical Palestinian cartoonist Naji al-Ali's, whose works are perhaps better designated as satirical drawings, always attacking the rich and powerful of the Arab world in the name of the poor. The artist was shot in 1987 outside the London apartment where he was living after having been expelled from Kuwait. The circumstances of his death have never been resolved. It is known that he was in bitter conflict with Arafat and the PLO at the time, but the UK police made no arrests.

The film retraces al-Ali's life in chronological order, setting it against the contemporary Arab political events on which he commented. Throughout his career, al-Ali recalled his own childhood years at Ain al-Hilwah refugee camp in Lebanon through the figure of Handhalah, the barefoot, destitute, and deprived ten-year-old who is regularly depicted—always from behind—as the witness of a drawing's subject matter. As the anonymous reviewer of the film in *Al Jadid Magazine* writes, "The story is told using a variety of traditional documentary techniques, including a main narrator, a second narrator reading al-Ali's statements about himself, photographs of al-Ali, as well as a wide range of interviews with friends, colleagues and experts."[331] What is crucial to its success is the intervention of Widad al-Ali, his widow, whose "facility for anecdotal storytelling transforms what would have been an ordinary documentary into a warm and intimate meeting place."[332]

By contrast, *Surda Checkpoint* (2005), shot with an Arab crew, is an early example of Abid's preferred later style of observational documentary. The film has no commentary or musical accompaniment, just five intertitles to locate and explain the significance of the checkpoint. Surda is on the road to Ramallah and was the point at which concrete roadblocks were placed in 2001 to impede the passage of all vehicles. Travelers had to make a two-kilometer detour by foot over rough ground before they could reenter a vehicle. This restriction of movement within the Palestinian Territories served no known Israeli security need, but it did harass and humiliate Palestinians, violating one of their most basic freedoms. Accompanied by the extended searches inflicted on all pedestrians trying to pass through, the blockade caused endless queues and huge traffic jams. This situation continued up to 2003, when the physical blockage was lifted and replaced by a traveling checkpoint. Though the film lasts just under half an hour, the filmmaker's unrelentingly focused style, demanding that we look and work to make up our own minds, makes the viewer very conscious of the experiences of the frustrated travelers.

Abid released his first feature-length work, the two-and-a-half-hour-long *Life After the Fall / La vie après la chute / Hayat ma bood al-suqoot*, in 2008. The fall is, of course, that of Saddam Hussein. The film, which took four years to shoot and an additional year of editing to complete, opens with the director's return to Baghdad after thirty years of exile. The year is 2003, just after the fall of Saddam Hussein, and Abid, who serves as his own cameraman, welcomes us to Baghdad and introduces us to the members of his family—his brothers, his sister, their spouses, and their children. One of his first acts on returning to his birthplace after so many years must have been to explore the city, but any such exploration forms no part of the film. This points to the particular stance adopted by Abid. He is making an observational documentary about his family, no more no less, so his own role must be cut to the bone. Though he is the film's narrator, he does no more than simply name, where relevant, the people, places, and events. There is no comment from him about the situation he has encountered or about his own activities in Baghdad. The setting up of the film school goes unmentioned. There is no intervention from Abid to probe or question statements by his family, and no stimulation of discussion among family members when they express differing views. Abid simply films what he sees and hears, making himself as invisible as possible.

This is in total conformity with his aim in undertaking the film: "By filming ordinary Iraqis, we are able to show the outside world that we are just the same as anyone else. I wanted to make a film that concentrated on the human experience, one that showed the audience that Iraqis are real people."[333]

After the Fall is therefore narrated solely at the level of experience and insight of an ordinary Iraqi Shiite family. There are no outside expert witnesses or analysts, no inserts of newsreel footage. The images we see from outside—the capture and trial of Saddam, for example—are simply those viewed by the family on their own domestic television sets. Even here the coverage is limited—there is no mention, for example, of Saddam's execution.

The family seem not to have suffered greatly under the rule of Saddam (no arrests or executions), though they were subject to regular and intense questioning because of Abid's absence abroad. The bombings and explosions of the 2003 invasion did not directly affect any of them, though they were all, of course, intensely frightened. The US occupation, for which they have high hopes, has no immediate impact on their lives. It is reduced to a few tanks patrolling in the streets outside, manned by soldiers whom Ilhan, Abid's sister, describes as "young and handsome." They attend the Shiite festival of Ashura (allowed for the first time since 1991), but the event is observed from the sidewalk, not built into a powerfully dramatic moment. The dramatic curve of the film is supplied by their emotional response to events: "From jubilation and optimism to despair, anger and disappointment."

Their concerns and preoccupations are banal and domestic: cooking, getting petrol for the car, and, for the adolescent girls, worrying about their education and lamenting their lack of fashionable Western-style clothes. The family has no particular involvement with, or interest in, religious or political activities. They turn out twice to vote, but we are never told about issues or outcomes. To start with, they are not affected immediately by the new wave of sectarian violence, though the bombings and shootings get nearer and nearer.

Everything changes, however, when Abid's younger brother, Ali, who runs a store in the neighborhood, is taken away and shot. Ali has hardly figured in the narrative—all we have seen him do is cut his elder son's hair at home. No one has bothered to mention what was probably the cause of his abduction—his conversion from Shia to Sunni beliefs. That has been a matter of indifference within the family, though not, it seems, to his assailants. Now the family begins to split up: Ilhan goes to Syria, and her brother Sa'ad is transferred to Irbil in the North. This is observational documentary filmmaking at its most austere: there are no farewells for Abid when he departs, and no reflection by him on his four-year experience.

It must be remembered that Abid trained as a director of photography, and when, a few years later, he introduced *Whispers of the Cities* on his website, he made clear that the pared-down approach of *After the Fall* was only one step he was taking to distance himself from the conventional structures adopted in his 1990s documentaries:

> For many years I have wanted to create a film, which works only through its visual images and to liberate myself from spoken narration, voice-over or interviews. But I wondered how one could make such a film that would be as dramatic and emotionally involving as a fiction without words or script. It would be like a play without a playwright. . . . Film can be built on the elements of cinematic language: cinematography, composition, shot

design, dramatic lighting, the expressive use of colour, dynamic movement, time-lapse imagery. These elements of cinematic language are universal, and they can be used to provide an alternative way for documentary
films to explore the human condition on its many levels: emotional, spiritual, political, intellectual.[334]

Wings of the Soul (2011) is a small step toward this ideal. True, it contains a
long (written) opening statement, in which Abid presents himself as a nonprac-
ticing Muslim and explains that he was invited to this Sufi ritual in Omdur-
man by one of his students when he was teaching at a documentary workshop
in Khartoum. But the fifteen-minute ritual itself is presented without any verbal
explanation or intervention by a narrator. Instead, we simply see and hear the
male singing, chanting, and, above all, dancing, watched by an appreciative audience of women and children, along with the occasional passing tourist.

Whispers of the Cities / Murmures des villes / Hams al moodun (2013) is a
more ambitious use of the same technique. Abid has described the film, shot
intermittently over a period of ten years, as "a subjective, personal journey to
the world close to my heart." What it requires of its viewer is "to watch, see and
feel."[335] The film comprises three separate unlinked episodes, shot from behind
windows or on balconies, in three different Middle Eastern cities: Erbil in Iraqi
Kurdistan (2002), Ramallah in the West Bank (2003), and Baghdad (2004 to
2012). The director's aim was "to reveal the daily struggle of the human spirit in
this region, express a faith in their resilience and courage."[336] The response of
critics has been generally favorable. Charlotte Gerson notes that it "restores the
original of the cliché that the documentary is a window onto the world," while
for Nina Rotha, the film is "surreal, wonderful, enlightening, infuriating and
then once again, wonderfully surreal." But Sophie Chas draws attention to the
importance of one element that Abid (a cinematographer by training) does not
include among his list of cinematic elements—namely, editing: "He dictates what
is and is not significant through what he edits out and what he allows to remain,
through what he chooses to linger on or skim over, through his arrangement and
positioning of scenes."[337]

Maysoon Pachachi was born in 1947 in Washington, DC, the daughter of
the prominent Iraqi diplomat, Adnan Pachachi, who was the foreign minister of
Iraq during the Six Day War and was also twice Iraq's permanent representative
to the United Nations. She was educated first in the United States and then in
the United Kingdom, where she took a degree in philosophy at University College London and also followed the film courses run by Thorold Dickinson at the
Slade School of Fine Art. She has, for many years, been a resident in the UK, but
the major concern in her documentary film work has been the Muslim world.
She has filmed in Palestine, Lebanon, Egypt, and Iran, as well as Iraq. She set up

the Independent Film and TV College in Baghdad together with Kassim Abid in 2003 and has been involved in many training workshops across the Middle East.

Pachachi's first major contact with UK television came when she produced and edited Antonia Caccia's *Voices from Gaza / Voix du Gaza* (1989), in which "Palestinian men, women and children speak frankly about the effect of Israel's occupation on their lives. . . . They also reveal the work of 'popular committees' through which they provide each other with alternative education, health care, and welfare service, even under these most daunting situations."[338] Her own chance to direct for channel 4 came five years later with *Iraqi Women: Voices from Exile / Les Irakiennes . . . une voix de l'exil* (1994). This fifty-minute documentary features interviews with a doctor, a guerrilla fighter, a teacher, a theater director, an actress, a journalist, young mothers, civil servants, and students. The United States Institute of Peace says of the film that it "provides a fascinating and rare look at the recent history of Iraq through the eyes and experiences of Iraqi women living in Britain. . . . This documentary features moving interviews with women about life in Iraq before Saddam Hussein came to power, in the years of repression under his regime and through the Gulf War in 1991."[339]

In *Iranian Journey / La femme-chauffeur, une traversée en bus de l'Iran* (1999) Pachachi retains her concern with women's lives, but this time looks at the situation in Iran. The focus is on Masoumeh Soltan Bolghie, the only female bus driver in Iran (and probably in the Muslim world). Formerly a nurse, she took over driving the school bus when her husband had a heart attack. From there, she moved on to full-time professional bus driving, making the return trip from Tehran to Bandar Abbas, on the Persian Gulf, twice a week (a distance of over five thousand kilometers). Now that her husband has recovered, they often work together as a team.

Before setting out with Masoumeh, Pachachi explores the general situation of women in Iran after the 1979 Khomeini revolution, which many of them supported. This is a conservative, patriarchal society in which women have difficulty in playing an active public role. This is confirmed by interviews with a trio of women: a lawyer (who finds the judicial system out of date), a lute player (denied the possibility of playing to male audiences), and a painter (who has difficulty in exhibiting her work). But a magazine editor argues that things are changing, with more women in the workplace and female university students outnumbering their male contemporaries. Masoumeh, modestly dressed and unassertive, is not a feminist activist. She merely wants to show that she can cope in a male-dominated world, and she gets her support, not from a women's group, but from her husband and from her daughters, both of whom want their own careers (the elder wants to be a camerawoman; the younger, a judge).

The trip to Bandar Abbas, 1,300 kilometers from Tehran and twenty-two hours driving time, involves some comments from Masoumeh and a few (fairly inconsequential) conversations with passengers. But basically it is a travelogue, showing us Iranian landscapes and deserts and allowing glimpses of life in the old Iranian cities on the way—Qom, Kashan, Yazd, and Kerman—as well as a look at Bandar Abbas (and the island of Qeshm with its duty-free department stores). Most of these cities keep to traditional crafts, but there is one surprise, an all-female university medical school outside Qoms that has one thousand students and staff.

Pachachi's next film, the fifty-six-minute documentary *Living with the Past: People and Monuments in Medieval Cairo / Vivre avec le passé* (2001), does not seem to have received any real distribution. But *Bitter Water / Eau amère* (codirected with Noura Sakkaf, 2003) shows a return to form, with a powerful study of broken lives. It is set in the Bourj al-Barajneh refugee camp, established in Lebanon for Palestinians displaced by the foundation of Israel. Fifty-four years and four generations later, there are still twenty thousand refugees living there on one square kilometer of territory. They have no prospect of returning "home," emigrating, or assimilating into Lebanese society. The film's title comes from an unsourced quotation used toward the end of the film that sums up perfectly the refugees' situation: "The vial of patience has been exhausted but for a single drop of bitter water—and drink it I must."

The film's structure is simple. A series of a dozen or so titles, scattered unevenly throughout the film, set out the basic facts: there are 5 million Palestinian refugees, descendants of the 750,000 displaced from their homes (illegally in terms of international law) with the founding of Israel. Bourj al-Barajneh is only one of fifty-nine such camps, originally set up as a "temporary measure" and now spread across the West Bank and the Gaza Strip, Syria, Jordan, and Lebanon. There is a long list of the wars and massacres that have worsened their circumstances.

We meet dozens of the refugees, whose statements to camera (the interviewers are not shown) make up a consistent and horrifying picture. The living conditions in the camp, with its dilapidated housing and cramped sunless alleyways, are appalling. Cut off from the outside world, the refugees have maintained and in some ways reinforced traditional Arab patriarchal values so that women dancing, even among themselves, is deemed a "sin." Work outside the camp is virtually impossible for young men to obtain, discrimination against them being perfectly legal under Lebanese law. Those who have set up small businesses within the camp cannot thrive, as their customers have no money. As days go by, all are ground down by the circumstances. The fact is that most of them are not technically refugees. Only the great-grandparents remember living in rural Palestine. Even those in middle age, now themselves grandparents, have known nothing but life in this or other camps. One longs for signs of change, but there are none. Protest is vain, as is shown by the case of Abu Rabi (one of the few named refugees). After ten years in custody and two years in an asylum, he roams the streets outside the camp, venting his anger at everyone he meets. But his rage is futile. As the filmmakers, who spent five weeks filming in Bourj al-Barajneh, note, "The camp is permeated with a sense of loss, whether of a home in Palestine or of children and parents killed during the civil war in Lebanon."[340]

Return to the Land of Wonders / Retour au pays des merveilles (2004), which takes its title from an ironic comment by one of the filmmaker's drivers, was intended as an international statement, being coproduced by Pachachi's own company, Oxymoron Films, alongside the German companies ZDF and ARTE. It records a special moment. The year is 2004 and Pachachi is returning to Iraq after a thirty-six-year absence, accompanying her father, Adnan. He has been appointed by the United Nation's to join Iraq's Governing Council and to chair the committee drafting the new national constitution. Interviews with her father and coverage of these negotiations form one thread through the film. At first, Pachachi finds it difficult to get outside the house Adnan has rented as his head-quarters and as a base for the Iraqi Independent Democratic Party, to which he belongs. He himself travels out only in a four-vehicle cavalcade, accompanied by a dozen security guards. But eventually Pachachi does begin to venture forth—initially with friends, then on her own.

She visits places she knew as a child, but many of these are now totally trans-formed, rebuilt for new purposes or derelict because of the war and subsequent looting. She meets and interviews a wide range of Iraqis—the family's old chauf-feur, for example, and a colleague of her father's who had a sack containing $1 million thrown into his garden by an absconding thief (we are never told what happened to the money).

She also makes new acquaintances: a trader in the old gold and silver market; female activists; a translator who spent thirteen years in prison, five on death row; patients in the local hospital; economists; and journalists. A vivid picture of life under Saddam's arbitrary rule emerges: privation, random imprisonment, torture, and execution. But the more frightening image is that of Iraq under US occupation: prevalent theft and corruption, as well as arbitrary arrests and imprisonment. Above all, there is the universal sense of lost national identity. A silver trader puts it succinctly: "Living in Iraq is not like living in your own coun-try." The finalizing of discussion on the constitution coincides with the resump-tion of ceremonies to celebrate the Shiite festival of Ashura (the first allowed since 1991). But this is not just a night of festivity. Terrorists use the occasion for acts of sectarian violence, killing hundreds in Karbala and Kardhistan. The offi-cial signing is suspended (the gap bizarrely accompanied on the sound track by an unaccompanied Bach violin suite) but finally occurs on March 8, 2004.

Pachachi and her father can now leave Baghdad, but the film has a brief postscript, set in London in July 2004. Adnan has turned down the offer of the presidency (he did not want to be seen as a tool of the US government, which made the offer), but he does plan to return to Iraq to help prepare for the elections he has worked to ensure. The film is a thoroughly professional piece of work, with Pachachi keeping rigidly to her role as off-camera narrator-cum-director. Judging by a review by an American critic, Pamela Crossland, it is well designed to meet its target audience: "Maysoon Pachachi has produced a beautiful, thoughtful documentary about the homeland she loves that still holds wonders for its people. I would highly recommend this film be shown at gatherings for anyone concerned about the US presence in Iraq."[341] It is, however, possible to agree with Noel Murray,[342] that perhaps the director has been too professional by keeping her own personal feelings totally in check. She shows her grandmother's home movies from 1949 but makes no comment on them or on her life as a privileged child, and she treats her father stylistically as just another interviewee; there is no image of the two of them together in shot.

Our Feelings Took the Pictures: Open Shutters Iraq / Nos sentiments ont pris les images d'Irak (2008) was a project from which she could not distance herself in any way. The origins of the film lie in a call from the British photojournalist Eugenie Dolberg, who asked whether Pachachi would be interested in making a film about the *Open Shutters Iraq* project she was setting up. There was no money, so, for the very first time, Pachachi had to direct, shoot, and edit the film on her own, without a crew. The project involved a group of Iraqi women producing photo-essays about their own lives and experiences. The shooting lasted three and a half months: a month living in the house in Damascus, where the women trained; six weeks in Iraq, where they shot their photos; and a month back in Syria, where they edited their photos and wrote their accompanying autobiographical essays. As Pachachi has said, "For everyone participating, it was a transformative experience. When the women drew life maps and presented them to each other, they unearthed memories which had lain buried in the course of just trying to survive 30 years of wars, dictatorship, sanctions and military occupation. . . . As the shooting and editing went on, I realized that this was a film about the alchemy that can sometimes turn trauma and loss and grief into creative work."[343]

Using a script cowritten with the Iraqi novelist Irada al-Jabbouri, Pachachi spent months setting up funding for what would be her first fictional feature, *Nothing Doing in Baghdad / Kulshi makoo*. Set in Baghdad in the last week of 2006—when Saddam Hussein was executed—the film follows the intersecting lives of several characters from different regions living in the same neighborhood. Pachachi received initial funding from the European Media Fund, the Dubai International Film Festival and Abu Dhabi's funding body, Sanad. There was further support from Visions Sud Est and the Arab Fund for Arts and Culture (AFAC), and the coproduction arrangements involved companies from Kuwait, France, Germany, and Sweden, alongside Pachachi's own company, Oxymoron

Films. Shooting was scheduled to start in February 2014, but at the time of this writing, the film has still not been released.

Samir was born in Baghdad in 1955 to a Swiss mother and an Iraqi father. His full name is Samir Jamal al-Din. Asked why he uses only his first name, he replied that "Jamal al-Din" means "beauty of religion," while "Samir" is perfect, as it means "storyteller." The family moved to Switzerland when he was six, and he has lived there ever since. He studied design in Zurich and then trained as a cameraman. Since the mid-1980s, he has directed over forty short films and television pieces, as well as three feature-length documentaries. He has also been very active as a producer, through the company Dschoint Ventschr, which he runs with Werner Schweizer. In addition, he has directed stage plays and devised video installations.

Samir's films are all intensely personal, and his first feature, *Babylon 2* (1993), deals with the subject that will preoccupy him in all his feature film work: the experience of migration. Throughout Samir's lifetime, the number of immigrants in Switzerland has continued to grow, and *Babylon 2* explores the experiences and opinions of eight second-generation migrants who have come from across the globe. The eight are: Saida from Tunis, Luana from Italy, Carlos from Spain, Yegya from Turkey, Debbie from Jamaica, Ersan from Turkey, Miklos from Hungary, and Sergio from Italy. The first question they are asked as they are initially introduced to the audience concerns their nationality. Only Yegya, who has just received his new identity papers, describes himself as Swiss—all the others, even if they were born in Switzerland, refer back to their place of family origin.

Samir begins the main body of the film with an account of his own arrival in Switzerland and revisits the places he remembers from childhood. Then the interviewees talk vividly—in a variety of languages—about their own experiences, their emotional lives, and the careers they have begun (three are pop performers whom we see on stage). A vivid and diverse picture emerges, offering the audience a wide range of insights and surprises. We are captivated by their liveliness and spontaneity. The interviewing is deft, and it comes as a total surprise at the end of the film to discover that the person we have seen on screen as "Samir" is in fact a Jewish actor called Michel. Samir seems not to have considered how far this calls into question the account of his own personal experiences: is his own tale, as it purports to be, one of exploration and spontaneous discovery, or has it been devised beforehand and prescribed for the needs of the film?

Samir's second, and best known, feature-length documentary is *Forget Baghdad: Juifs et Arabes—la connection / Oublie Bagdad: Juifs et Arabes: la connection irakienne* (2002).[344] The film opens with Samir at the airport, announcing that he is traveling into enemy territory—that is to say, Israel. His late father had been a member if the Iraqi Communist Party in the heady years after the end of British rule and had talked of the Jews who had been his active comrades.

Samir's mission is to meet up with some of these Jews, now resident in Israel: "I wanted to know what it's like to change countries, to forget your culture and your language and to become the enemy of your own past." The four interviewees, none of whom knew his father personally, are Simon Ballas, a novelist and scholar; Moshe (Moussa) Houri, a now retired trader; Sami Michael a major Israeli novelist; and Samir Naqqash, another major writer, who has chosen to continue writing in Arabic. Their experiences are supplemented by those of a member of Samir's own generation, the film historian Ella Shohat, well known for her incisive and broad-ranging survey: *Israeli Cinema: East/West and the Politics of Representation.*[345]

The film's title, *Forget Baghdad* is a little enigmatic, since the one thing none of the male protagonists will ever be able to forget is the Iraqi capital. In any case, the film is not about fighting nostalgia but rather about the shock for Jews of dislocation from an Arab environment where Arabs, Jews, and Christians had lived side by side for thousands of years to a purely Jewish state. As communists and internationalists, they now found themselves in a nationalist state, where, as Oriental Jews (*Mizrahim*), they were under the domination of the newly arrived European Jews (*Ashkenazi*). Some were humiliated as soon as they arrived at the airport by being sprayed with DDT, as if they were carriers of vermin, and all were shocked to be located in a refugee camp (very different from their comfortable houses and apartments in Iraq). Some were expected to work as laborers in a kibbutz (a role for which their professional training had not prepared them). The four male interviewees are very different individuals, each with his own approach to issues of assimilation and language. The variety of their experiences adds to the richness of the film, but the technique of constantly intercutting their statements rather than allowing them to debate the issues collectively in some ways blurs the film's focus. Each seems to deserve a chapter of his own.

This is even more strongly the case with Ella Shohat, who was born in 1959 and so does not belong in this group. She merits a film of her own. Part of a different generation (Samir's own) and born in Israel of Iraqi descent, she has no direct memories of Baghdad—just memories of her parents' recollections. From her earliest years of childhood, she experienced life between two cultures, Arab and Jewish, but these memories have been supplemented by the new experience derived from living in New York, where she stayed after completing her master's and doctorate degrees. We see her routing the hostile presenter of a television talk show, but her input would have been more fascinating still if Samir had allowed her to elaborate her views on Israel with specific and substantial extracts from the films she discusses in her book. Long and rambling in structure, *Forget Baghdad* contains numerous insights and some illuminating stories.

Twelve years later, Samir made *Iraqi Odyssey* (2014), the story of his extended family, which has a full running time of 164 minutes but also exists in a television version that lasts 90 minutes and is, in his view, inadequate. The shooting alone took over a year and financing the project was complex: "Besides a large share invested by our own company we also received backing from the Swiss Cultural Funding body. Later, with the help of our co-producer Coin Film, we also received funding from Germany as our co-operation country. Additionally the Swiss Television company (SRF) and the West German Broadcasting (WDR) have given us their support. At an earlier stage we received funding from the Abu Dhabi film festival. We invested a lot of time seeking French funding, but to no avail." There were unexpected problems too with directing members of his own family: "In past documentary films I have not experienced any difficulties in dealing with the protagonists. However, it is not possible to direct family members in the same manner. Difficult and sensitive situations arose throughout due to the fact that old family ties were loaded with preconceptions."[346]

Samir, who has lived since childhood in Zurich, comes from a large, scattered and prosperous Iraqi family: five siblings, six aunts and uncles (plus their spouses), and twenty cousins. The precredit sequence introduces us to the five who have agreed to assist him, filmed in their present locations: Jamal in Moscow, Sabah in London, Souhair in Buffalo, Samira in Auckland, and Tanya in Lausanne. The film largely comprises family members giving their own personal stories and experiences, backed up by a wealth of family photographs tracing romances, weddings, and the children growing up. Samir's informants are of different ages—statements by an aunt or an uncle are intercut with those of a cousin or his half sister. They have had varied life experiences, and their current residences cover the globe. As a result, a very complex and, at times, rather confusing picture of Iraqi society emerges. Perhaps, for that very reason, what we are given is a true picture of Iraq. Certainly the family has lived through interesting times.

Samir's family is not a typical one. His grandfather's generation was accorded high status in Iraq because of the family's claim they descended from the Prophet, but there was the problem of Ottoman rule. Samir's grandfather was, by all accounts, a remarkable man, but Samir is not sure which of the stories about him to believe. What is certain is that he believed in women's rights—all Samir's aunts were university educated or professionally trained. Studying initially in Baghdad, they and their brothers chose socially concerned professions—such as teaching and medicine. Following up their studies abroad, they were opened up to modern Western values and often acquired a European spouse. For this generation, the great event was the end of British imperial rule, and several, like Samir's father, were tempted by the ideals of the Communist Party.

The film is loosely structured. We constantly shift from one witness to another or from the personal to the political, and though there is a succession of intertitles, the film is not divided into clearly separated parts or chapters. There is, however, a progression through the film. As Samir first explores the experience of previous generations, the emphasis is on the personal, with historical events providing just a background. But as Samir comes to deal with events he himself has experienced, the film's emphasis shifts to the flow of political events and shifts, with his own testimony and that of the family serving merely as illustrations of a stronger narrative. The film's final sequence shows Samir submitting the film to the scrutiny of the family whom he has invited to Zurich. Their response is favorable, though it does stimulate some debate and disagreement. The final wish is that their country could follow the family's example of successfully bringing together, though at times with some difficulty, Shiites and Sunnis, Kurds and Christians.

Iraqi Odyssey is a remarkable work, well summed up by Rasha Salti after the Toronto Festival Screening: "Weaving together the ironic, wistful, and witty testimonies of Samir's relatives with rare documents from private and state archives . . . *Iraqi Odyssey* is a riveting epic that creates a genuine people's history of Iraq, at once humble and majestic."[347]

Samir has a distinctive stylistic approach to filmmaking, combining the directly personal with technical innovation. Critics who have seen the films projected at festivals talk of success of the digitally enhanced imagery of *Forget Beirut* and the use of 3-D in *An Iraqi Odyssey*. But having been able to see only DVD versions of the films, I cannot confirm this. In the DVD versions, the imagery is often cluttered by the visual overlay, which serves to diminish rather than enhance the film's major quality—the direct-to-camera interviews. The texture of Samir's films is enlivened by the inclusion of amusing little clips from popular movies to enliven his commentary or to illustrate his interviewees' comments. He has clearly done extensive research to locate relevant archive materials. But he shows little interest in exploring analytically the major international political issues raised by his films: massively enhanced emigration, international involvement in the demise of the Communist Party in Iraq, and the actual circumstances of the departure of Iraqi Jews to Israel. These are clearly central issues in the lives of his interviewees and the members of his family, but he does not probe any of them about their statements, nor does he provoke dialogue and discussion among them. He accepts their assertions at face value, just as he does the newsreel footage on which he draws extensively. The lasting strength of his films lies in the personal testimony of individuals, whose illuminating views he brings expertly to the fore.

Saad Salman was born in 1950 in Baghdad and studied there at the Academy of Fine Arts. He worked for Iraqi television for several years before he left, clandestinely, for Paris, where he is now active as a film editor. In the 1990s, he made a number of video documentaries and moved on to feature-length works, beginning with *Because of Circumstances / En raison de circonstances* (1982).

Salman's best-known film is *Baghdad On/Off* (2002), which was shot during a return to Iraq in 2001 and released in Paris just a month after the US campaign that overthrew Saddam Hussein, a decision that Salman supported at the time, as there seemed to be no alternative. The result of Salman's earlier clandestine return in 1972 had been thirteen months in prison. This time, he kept strictly to the Kurdish area in the north of Iraq, working alone, without a film crew and without backing from any French television organization (he regarded them all as complicit with Saddam Hussein). The impact on him was immediate and full of contradictions: "I felt myself a foreigner, in so far as I was entering my country through a region where I didn't speak the language. . . . Secondly, I entered Iraq at a time when everyone wanted to leave. . . . [And] I found myself behaving as I did when I left the country, when I was twenty, as if nothing had happened and I'd been there for ever."[348]

Baghdad On/Off is the most basic of road movies. Salman, who has lived for twenty-five years in Paris, learns that his mother is seriously ill in Baghdad and sets out to visit her. This is before the invasion that brought the downfall of Saddam Hussein, so he has to enter via Kurdistan, far to the north of Baghdad, using a driver who admits that this is the first time he has smuggled anyone *into* Iraq: normally people are desperately trying to escape from the country. Ostensibly this is a simple record of Salman and his driver trying to reach Baghdad. Certainly it is shot and recorded with nonprofessional equipment. It feels like a home movie, but the film's end titles credit three cameramen in addition to Salman and attribute the "dialogue" to Salman and Salah al-Hamdamir. The film is therefore not quite what it purports to be—which explains Salman's equanimity, as he is constantly told, "Tomorrow, we'll be in Baghdad," and "I have given you my word of honor." In fact, very early in the film, we realize that this goal is not going to be reached.

This does not detract from the vivid image of Kurdistan that Salman offers us. We see real people struggling with a world that is quite beyond their control. Virtually all live in some kind of refugee camp, with the barest of facilities. The snatches of interview and fragmentary straight-to-camera statements give us a real sense of a society in crisis. There are Kurds displaced within their own country, and refugees from southern Iraq trying to find a way of reconstituting their lives. Over them all hovers the specter of Saddam Hussein and the violence he has wrought on his people. There are mothers who have waited twenty years for the release of their sons, abducted without reason or trial. We see people who cannot reconstruct their lives and a society in which roads quite literally lead to nowhere. Eventually, Salman abandons his quest to reach Baghdad. A final title tells us his mother died on the day the film was completed, without him having been able to reach her.

*

The 1980s and 1990s were years of war for Iraq: the eight-year war with Iran initiated by Saddam Hussein in 1980; the invasion of Kuwait in 1990, leading directly to the first Gulf War; and then, twelve years later, came the second invasion, with its continuing occupation. It is hardly surprising that there is no new generation of Iraqi filmmakers in the 1980s to match those in, say, Tunisia or Syria. The most important work of these years is that of the Iraqi documentary filmmakers, scattered in exile across Europe. Only two fictional feature filmmakers, Khairya al-Mansour and Hiner Saleem, have gained any kind of international recognition and, since Hiner Saleem was born after 1960, his work is outside the scope of this study. It has, however been discussed elsewhere.[349]

Khairya al-Mansour was born in 1958 in Baghdad, where she studied at the Academy of Arts. She subsequently trained at the Cairo Higher Film Institute and worked as an assistant to several leading Egyptian directors, including Salah Abou Seif, Tewfik Saleh, and Youssef Chahine. Returning to Iraq, she made a score of documentaries tackling women's issues and offering portraits of various Iraqi artistic figures. She was the only woman in Iraq to be given the opportunity to direct, and she completed two fictional features: *20/20 Vision / Sitta 'ala sitta* (1988), dealing with a couple who both have impaired vision and fear for their children if they marry, and *100 Percent / Miya 'ala miya* (1992), about a pair of identical twins who have very different lives but whose close resemblance causes humorous confusions. Neither film seems to be currently available.

Syria

The possibilities of exilic documentary production are exemplified in the career of Omar Amiralay (1944–2011). The filmmaker pioneered Syrian documentary but was rapidly driven into exile in Paris, where he lived for thirty-seven years, until his death at the age of sixty-seven. Amiralay studied at IDHEC in Paris before returning to Syria to make his first three documentaries. He began with a eulogy to the building of the Assad dam, *Film Essay about the Euphrates Dam / Essai sur un barrage de l'Euphrate / Muhawwalu sudd al-furat* (1970), a subject to which he returned in a more disillusioned mood over thirty years later in *A Flood in Ba'ath Country / Déluge au pays du Baas / Tufan fi balad el-ba'th* (2003). His other two early 1970s documentaries were critical studies of rural conditions in Syria: the feature-length *Everyday Life in a Syrian Village / La vie quotidienne dans un village syrien / Al-hayat al-yawmiya fi qaria Suriya* (1974) and the satirical short *The Hens / Les poules / Al-fara'ij* (1974).

When *Everyday Life* was banned by the Syrian government, Amiralay went into exile in Paris. There he began with a documentary on the socialist revolution in Yemen, *About a Revolution / Au sujet d'une révolution / An al-thawra* (1978), and a study of the civil war in Lebanon, *Some People's Misfortunes / Le malheur des uns / Maçaibu qawmin* (1982). From then on, Amiralay worked largely for French television on a dozen or so documentaries. Many of these are highly personal portraits, such as his tribute to Michel Seurat, a friend killed by Islamists in Lebanon; his conversation with the filmmaker Mohamed Malas about the Israeli seizure of Kuneitra; and his studies on Pakistani prime minister Benazir Bhutto and the Lebanese prime minister Rafiq Harari. He also collaborated with Malas and fellow feature filmmaker Ousama Mohamed on two video portraits, one of which deals with the pioneer Syrian filmmaker Nazir Shahbandar, *Shadows and Light / Ombres et lumière / Nouron wa thilal* (1991).

The distance traveled by Omar Amiralay is very apparent if you compare his first short, *Film Essay on the Euphrates Dam* (1970), with his return to the subject in 2003. The first film is a simple audio-visual exercise, with no commentary or speech to camera—except for one conversation with an old man working from dawn until dusk building a mud wall with his bare hands. The film starts with lots of activity, images of welding and crane work, virtually a hymn to steel construction, overlaid with a very positive-sounding music track of a traditional dance. After these virtually abstract stark images of steel against the sky, the film shows far less dynamic images of traditional, partially nomadic, life in what is essentially a desert landscape. The film ends with the massive waterwheels moving, intercut with images of traditional water-carrying figurines and the faces of children engrossed in learning. The final image is that of a child's celebratory drawing of the construction work. The film offers no documentary-style information on the how or why of the project—nothing explains why the Euphrates is to be diverted and the valley flooded.

A Flood in Ba'ath Country, by contrast, opens with footage from the 1970 film, this time accompanied by an explanation from Amiralay, thirty-three years later, that he was originally a firm advocate of the modernization of Syria and so dedicated his first film to the Baath Party. Now he regrets "this youthful error of judgement," as he returns to look at the failing structures of the whole dam-building project. The bulk of the film comprises three interviews to camera. The first is with an aged peasant who lived in a village now flooded by Lake Assad. He can sense where his house was located below the huge expanse of the lake and laments that the site of the first fixed settlement in human history (8–10,000 BC) is now lost forever. This sequence—like the subsequent interviews—ends with shots of the lake, accompanied by the sounds of thunder.

The focus now switches to the village of El Machi, "a microcosm of the country," where the Baath Party has ruled without opposition for over forty years. The following two interviews, with Diab El Machi, a local tribal sheikh and the local member of parliament for the past fifty years, and his nephew, the school principal and local head of the Baath Party, give a vivid picture of Syria at the turn of the century. For Diab El Machi, the rule of Hafez al-Assad—"the father of the people" and "a true Arab"—was "an era rich in real accomplishments and gifts . . . unparalleled in the glorious history of this country." The shots introduced by his nephew give a frightening insight into the Syrian education system, where the young pupils, automatically enrolled in the Baath Party, are endlessly drilled in chanting Baathist slogans and praise of the national leader. The film ends with Amiralay's reflection that the Euphrates is no longer a river but a sea and, enigmatically, with a Muslim call to prayer. Amiralay offers no overt comment on the views of either of these two latter interviewees, but the juxtaposition of probing close-ups and distancing, carefully framed, long shots of the action makes his views very clear.

One striking example of Amiralay's portrait films is *Rafiq Hariri: The Man with the Golden Soles* / *L'homme aux semelles d'or* / *Rajol al-hitha' al-thahabi* (2000), a remarkably self-reflective documentary that Amiralay openly presents as a failure to get fully to grips with its subject. When the film was shot in 2000, Hariri, a multibillionaire who had made his vast fortune in Saudi Arabia and who had full backing from the Saudi royal family, was in opposition after two terms as prime minister. Yet he was shortly to return to power and remained arguably the most powerful figure in Lebanon, as well as the driving force behind the rebuilding of Beirut, until his assassination in 2005.

The film has a symmetrical structure, opening and closing with the same sets of sequences (though in reverse order at the end). There are extracts from an English-language promotional documentary on the rebuilding of Beirut, "the ancient city of the future." Amiralay comments (in French-language voice-over) on both Lebanon and his own ambitions. His friends (including the novelist Elias Khoury and journalist Samir Kassir) initially warn him of the difficulties he will face and finally conclude that he has, predictably, failed to probe his subject adequately. Hariri himself is seen, at both beginning and end, as a silent, dominant figure, shot from below, more like a statue than an ordinary human being. Given that Hariri was assassinated in mysterious circumstances just five years after the film was shot, it contains numerous ironies, such as the concluding comments by one of Amiralay's friends that "anyone willing to govern Lebanon is condemned to failure" and "ten years from now Hariri might become a great tragic figure."

The core of the film comprises the filmmaker's encounters with Hariri, which the director describes as "a strange and subtle game." Amiralay reveals his reservations from the start, and the discussions between the two are characterized by hesitations and mutual suspicions. Hariri, in his responses to Amiralay, as well as in the television clips included of his meetings with world leaders, shows himself to be totally confident (or, as Amiralay's voice-over describes him, "ostentatious and self-important"). He continually refers to himself in the third person ("Rafiq Hariri is / does . . .") while always addressing the filmmaker, in their private interviews and in the public meetings he allows to be filmed, as "Omar." Oddly, the gulf between the men is expressed through their view of each other's shoes (hence the film's title). Amiralay, in his voice-over, comments on a detail he has noticed—Hariri's shoes are constantly resoled, suggesting that a man so concerned with getting close to people has an odd aversion to making physical contact with the soil. In turn, Hariri, who has most certainly not heard this comment, belittles Amiralay as a mere intellectual and tells him how he would have conducted the interviews, describing the filmmaker's reliance on his research notes as that of "a big man wearing tiny shoes." There is no real interpersonal communication and no revelation of the Rafik Hariri who must exist behind the public image. The key question of why the city of Beirut is being rebuilt by Hariri's private company, rather than by state funds, is never properly addressed, and Amiralay seems to admit his defeat by ending, without apparent irony, with the image of the new proposed Beirut offered by Hariri's own promotional video.

*

For the filmmakers who returned from study abroad to work in Syria in the 1980s, the difficulty was how to offer an individual voice in a context of state-organized production, strict censorship, and the absolute impossibility of making any direct political statement. Mohamed Malas speaks for them all when he said: "The prevailing mind set in that period played a significant role on the directors' refusal to be subsumed by the values and conventions of commercial production; they were invested in making a different cinema."[350] Three state-sponsored, Soviet-trained Syrian filmmakers in particular—Samir Zikra, Mohamed Malas, and Ousama Mohamed—rose to the challenge and achieved international recognition in the mid-1980s. This renewal of national filmmaking is comparable to that achieved, in a context of independent production structures, by Nouri Bouzid and his colleagues in Tunisia or to the French-financed "cinema of the intelligentsia" spearheaded by Maroun Bagdadi in post–civil war Lebanon. The films of these three constitute a highly distinctive body of work within the context of contemporary Arab filmmaking.

Cécile Boëx, who lived in Syria from 2002 to 2011, captures their particular achievement: "Denouncing various modes of domination, they call into question the legitimacy of the power in place. They do not sign up for a militant approach, which would deliver a clear message aimed at achieving a reawakening of conscience and sense of engagement on the part of the audience. The critical statements are instead directed through a shift in the passage of meaning: the recourse to parable, irony or satire allowing a reinterpretation of the shared political experience."[351] Boëx's analysis is backed up by Mohamed Malas: "The generation . . . that began working in the early 1980s had returned home to a society and a memory; it was less compelled by prevailing ideology and more in touch with the contemporary preoccupations of Syrian society. It could imagine a cinema without running the risk of censorship from the governmental institutions producing films. The return to memory, just like the desire to describe with sincerity the yearnings of society, was without doubt the appropriate reaction to the ugliness of the films produced by the public sector by the preceding generation."[352] Malas would no doubt exclude from these strictures the work of Nabil Maleh, with whom Samir Zikra collaborated in 1977.

The three Syrian filmmakers mentioned in this section—Zikra, Malas, and Mohamed—form a fairly tight-knit group, frequently collaborating on the writing of each other's films, with Zikra coscripting Malas's *City Dreams* and Mohamed collaborating similarly on *The Night*. Mohamed and Malas also worked with Omar Amiralay on two video documentaries in the 1990s, the first of which was a study of Nazir Shahbandar, the pioneer of Syrian filmmaking. But, working within the confines of the Syrian state organization, they have made only a handful of features apiece in some thirty years, often with gaps of ten years or more between productions.

Samir Zikra, who was born in Beirut in 1945 but brought up in Aleppo, graduated from the Moscow film school, VGIK, in 1974 and, on his return to Syria, began making documentary films. He joined the General Establishment for Cinema in 1976. Zikra's first feature was *The Half-Metre Incident / L'accident du demi-mètre / Hadithat al-nisf mitr* (1983), which, Rasha Salti notes, "is considered a watershed for a generation of new film makers in Syria, heralding the turn to auteur cinema while presenting an unapologetic social and political reading of Syrian society. The film received wide critical acclaim within the region and internationally."[353] Though set against the background of the second Arab-Israeli war, this is a story about individuals. The half meter of the title is the space that separates two people who travel daily on the same bus in Damascus. He is a repressed man in his thirties who still lives with his mother, while she is a university student. They are attracted to each other and overcome the half-meter barrier, but their romance fails to succeed. As Yves Thoraval says, this "minimalist story" is "a sarcastic story about the danger of trying to change your routine and about the faint-heartedness of Arab men!"[354]

Zikra went on to make three further features, *Chronicle of the Coming Year / Chronique de l'année prochaine / Waqai al'am al-muqil* (1986), "a scorching tale very critical of Syrian society in the 1990s, marked by sexual repression, bureaucracy, mafias in cahoots with the authorities, and the hollow speeches of petit-bourgeois bureaucrats proclaiming themselves *taqaddumi*, that is to say progressives."[355] This was followed, twelve years later, by *A Land for Strangers / La terre des étrangers / Turab al-ajaneb* (1998) and, more recently, *Public Relations / Relations publiques / Alaqat amah* (2005). Zikra set out his beliefs in an essay published in 2006: "The films we were able to make, no matter how humble their lot, remain the bridge between illusion and reality. We shouldered the responsibility of mediating narrative, meaning and representation in a society whose roots strike into the history of human civilisation. . . . And we were impelled to encapsulate all of this in a single film that signalled a new world, like a memory chip embedded in the cells of new-born babies. A world condensed in a film, a film summoning engagement with the world."[356]

Oussama Mohammad, the youngest of the group and the third to make his debut, was born in 1954 at Lattakiah, and, like Abdellatif Abdelhamid, a member of the Alouite sect that ruled Syria from the beginning of the 1970s. He graduated from VGIK, the Moscow Film School in 1979. On his return, he directed two short films, before making his feature debut with *Stars in Broad Daylight / Étoiles du jour / Nujum al-nahar* (1988). He has said of his own situation, "Our own image [does not] conform with our sounds-voice, we, the handful of Syrian filmmakers. We are quelled by the routine of everyday life. When questions press us in the media we are jolted into awakening and answer in our idiom of allegories and metaphors. In reality however, we are absent from the screen."[357] The official synopsis of the film reads: "A double wedding in a small village turns to high drama when one bride runs away and the other refuses to go on with her marriage. . . . Ultimately tragic, the film is rife with biting humour and sharp political critique as it exposes how the violence of arbitrary and absolute power in a patriarchal society seeps into the unit of the family."[358]

The film was banned after initial successful screenings, and Thoraval judges it to be "one of the most powerful and non-conventional Middle Eastern films ever made, whose aim is to shake patriarchal order."[359] Rasha Salti writes of the film that though it is "a jewel of contemporary Syrian cinema which has invariably earned critical acclaim, standing ovations and awards wherever it has screened, the film has never been shown to the Syrian public."[360]

Of the director himself, she writes: "It is arguably Oussama Mohammad's eye for striking imagery that distinguishes his work. The framing of every shot, the movement of his camera, his skill for visual composition all display a supreme talent. . . . Oussama Mohammad, a secular humanist, achieves a feat that postmodernity has long since denied to artistic practice: the ability to induce the spectator towards a transcendence, a dizzying upward lift."[361]

Mohammad had to wait thirteen years before he could make a second film, *Sacrifices / Sanduq al-dunya* (2001), which won similar praise. The official synopsis says it is "a fantastic and visually captivating cinematic fable, *Sacrifices* reflects on how violence and power legitimize themselves, producing rituals and a vocabulary to perpetuate themselves."[362] As Lawrence Wright notes, "*Sacrifices* was screened at Cannes in 2002. It received enthusiastic reviews although some audiences were put by its allegorical, highly compressed storytelling. Indeed, when I first saw *Sacrifices*, the references seemed so personal I wondered if this is what happens when a director no longer expects to have an audience; he makes a film entirely for himself."[363]

More recently Mohammad has completed a feature-length documentary, *Silvered Water, Syria Self-Portrait / Eau argentée, Syrie autoportrait* (2014), that documents the havoc wreaked by the civil war in Syria, with footage provided from the internet and by a school teacher in Homs, Wiam Simav Bedirxan, who asked him online what he would film if he were in Syria. The couple met for the first time face to face when she managed to reach France in time for the film's premiere. In addition to chronicling the war's horrors, the film also reflects the director's feelings of guilt at living in exile while his country is plunged into war.

The member of the group who has achieved the highest international acclaim is Mohamed Malas, who was born in Quneitra in 1945 and made his debut with *City Dreams* in 1984. Malas is unusual among filmmakers in that his original ambition was to be a writer, and he chose the Moscow film school because it was the only destination for which he could obtain a bursary for foreign study. For him, writing a film is always a literary endeavor, and he has always sought to have his scripts published: "The cinematographic texts from which my films were born . . . have a literary value in themselves, which I cherish. They hold within them preliminary sketches for ideas, events and characters and allow the reader to engage with a realm detached from theory or philosophizing, regardless of whether the films are familiar to her or him. It is also my conviction that the cinematic text, or the literary film script, ought to be regarded as a legitimate creative and literary expression in itself. The film is a distinctive creative endeavour that may or may not follow the text."[364] It is unsurprising that he has collaborated on the scripts of films by both Zikra and Mohammad.

Malas constantly mentions his tutor at VGIK, Igor Talankin, who, he says, "always told me 'The only thing I taught you is how to know yourself' . . . and that to me is what cinema is all about: knowing yourself and expressing it."[365] It was in Moscow that Malas discovered for the first time the potential of filmmaking and the wealth of achievement in cinema across the world. He has spoken of his discovery of the films of Kurosawa, Tarkovsky, and Bergman and, within Arab cinema, those of Salah Abou Seif and Chadi Abdel Salam. His 2013 film, *Ladder to Damascus*, contains homages to Omar Amiralay and to Theo Angelopoulos, who died shortly before the shooting began. On his return to Syria in 1974, Malas, who had made four short films during his studies in Moscow, joined Syrian television and went on to direct a number of short films, both documentaries and fictional works. As he has said: "I use fiction to express myself and make direct use of reality to articulate expression. . . . Both allow me to discover that cinema is cinema! I make no distinction between one genre and another in my compulsion for expression. The documentaries I made belong just as much to art house cinema; they are entrenched in my subjectivity as a director."[366]

He has continued his documentary filmmaking throughout his career. An example, recently given international distribution, is *Aleppo, Magams for*

Pleasure / Alep, maqam de plaisir / Nadi lekol el nas (1998), a fifty-two-minute documentary made for television.

For the start of his feature film career, Malas conceived a trilogy of which the first film actually produced, *City Dreams*, formed the second part. The first part of the trilogy, *The Night*, was made as Malas's second feature, while the third part, *Cinema al-Dunya / Sinama al-dunya*, was never realized. More recently, he has described *Ladder to Damascus* (2013), which is set during the Arab Spring of 2011, as the missing third part of the trilogy, though it is in no way an autobiographical work drawing its inspiration from his childhood.

City Dreams / Les rêves de la ville / Ahlam al-madina (1984) is to a considerable extent an autobiographical film (Malas himself arrived in Damascus as a young refugee in the early 1950s) and was coscripted by Samir Zikra. It is set in a popular neighborhood of Damascus in the 1950s, beginning in 1952 with one of the many military coups of the decade and ending with the merger of Syria and Egypt under President Nasser in 1958. These political events form a constant thread through the film and are constantly alluded to by the characters, but they are always in the background. The events are never stages for the camera, few of them are precisely located in time, and there is no use of newsreel footage. The film's focus is on individuals, and the stance is fundamentally bleak; the first three shots set the tone of the film: the image of a solid blank wall, then pigeons desperately trying to escape from the warehouse in which they are trapped, and finally a stark, empty road.

The film's action begins with the arrival of a young widow and her two children in Damascus. Their destination is her father's house, but he takes them in only grudgingly and constantly abuses them, both verbally and physically. The younger child, Omar, is taken into care, and the central focus is on the adolescent Adib, who grows to maturity during these turbulent years, trying desperately to combine his work with at least some schooling. The mother is, of course, unable to work, and Adib starts earning his living in a laundry close to where they are living. The nearby merchants and shopkeepers, constantly rivaling and feuding with each other, are of very different political persuasions. Collectively, they offer a vivid portrayal of the discordant lives of a Syrian population affected by the military and political events but unable to influence them (there is no question of a popular democracy). Adib's mother is tempted into a remarriage, even though this will mean abandoning her children. But the effort fails, leading to a painful, but tender, reunion with Adib. As spectators, we are drawn to Adib because of his openness, growing awareness, ambition to learn, and his basic optimism. But at the end of the film, he is a battered figure, bleeding from head wounds acquired when he tries to beat his way back into the family home. He is last seen looking up at a full moon, which may, or may not, herald a new era for Syria.

The Night / La nuit / Al-layl (1992) is a multilayered film that, on one level, covers the events of a decade or so of Syrian history (from fight against the British and the Jews in 1936 to the first military coup d'état after Syrian independence, in 1949). The events of these years are not narrated directly but from the standpoint of a later period that "wavers between a memory desired, yearned for and a memory imagined, between the occupation of the city in 1967, its destruction in 1974, and today.³⁶⁷ *The Night* is essentially a film about memory, not a piece of historical analysis. The setting is Quneitra, a village in the Golan Heights, which is also the place where Malas was born, and he is proud that, in this film, he "reconstructed it and recovered its life, cinematically."³⁶⁸ There is no way, however, that Quneitra is even slightly glorified. It is a backward, tradition-dominated place where women have no rights. Even the girl's mother is not allowed to see, let alone meet, the man who has been chosen by her husband, on impulse, to marry her daughter, Wissal, who is made to go through a marriage contract with a man she has never been allowed to see. *The Night* also reflects the external tortured politics of these years in a way that almost constitutes a caricature, as each successive opposed armed group (the Mujahadeen in 1936, the Black Brigades, the French, the English, the Syrians celebrating their coup d'état in 1949) pauses for a group photograph before moving on.

The Night relates the lives and dreams of its two central characters: a mother called Wissal, and her only son, Alall. Both figure as voice-over narrators and are at times placed visually in shots as observers as their lives unfold. But in one sense, the key figure of the film is the person absent from the point at which the narration occurs—the father, also called Alall. He links the external political events and the personal lives within the village. Alall the father is one of the group of freedom fighters passing through the village, on their way to defeat, in 1936. On his return, as a starving and broken man, he is chosen by the village innkeeper as a suitable husband for his daughter, Wissal. Alall does not really fit into village life; he is always an outsider—given to violent rages and twice arrested by the authorities—who grows more and more opposed to his father-in-law. He is a figure constantly on the move, edgy and difficult to pin down. As he he abandons his family, on impulse, to join a second battle against Syria's enemies, his message to his son is: "Tell your mother I've gone off to pick oranges for her in Jaffa." Even the cause of his death is left deliberately undefined.

The Night opens, as *City Dreams* ended, with two people—here Wissal and her son—looking up at the night sky. The narrative begins with her memories and dreams of her dead husband. The son Alall struggles to come to terms with his father's life, and the latter part of the film becomes his story and his memories, real or imaginary, as well as those of his mother.

Visually, the film is very formally composed, and the narrative, full of echoes and repetitions, constantly operates on a number of levels simultaneously. At certain points, we are unclear which time we are inhabiting; at others, we are in very real sense experiencing at once story lines occurring at different times. *The Night* is a complex interweaving of intense personal experiences within the family, set against the startling political transitions in the streets outside. It is clearly intensely autobiographical, and its complex structure is perhaps best defined in the director's own words: "The city [of Quneitra] is forever etched in my memory. . . . After my father's death and the city's demise, the etchings in my memory became mirrors, surfaces reflecting other images. My mother—the woman—shrouded in the black of mourning, framed the flow of images and imbued them with scents."[369]

It was thirteen years before Malas could make another feature. *Passion / Bab al-maqam* (2005), which was largely European-financed and coscripted by the great Tunisian producer Ahmed Attia, marks a shift away from the auto-biographical stance of the previous two films. It is based on an actual incident recorded on June 25, 2001, when a woman in Aleppo was killed by the male members of her family, who deemed that her love of singing and her passion for the music of Oum Kalsoum must indicate that she was in love and, therefore, potentially, if not actually, adulterous. This, they concluded, represented a threat to the family's honor. In *Passion*, the narrative is brutally direct and precisely located against the backdrop of the Bush invasion of Iraq, which the protagonist Imene's news-obsessed husband, Adnan, constantly follows on the radio. In the background, but shaping the unfolding narrative, is a character we never see, Imene's brother Rachid, a political dissident, whose imprisonment has brought to a halt the career his uncle Abu Sobhi. The latter now applies all his masculine energy to dominating his family: his wife, his own children, and those of his aging, bedridden brother. This is a society in which women have no say.

Imene has a loving relationship with her husband and her happiness is partially expressed through her singing, particularly with her own children and Rachid's daughter, Joumana, whom she is bringing up. Her love of Oum Kalsoum's music brings her into contact with Badia—the *khoujat*, or praise singer—who helped celebrate her own parents' wedding. But the slightest signs of an independent life, while her taxicab-driver husband works day and night to support his extended family, provoke the suspicions of her uncle, who turns her brother against her and even tries to enlist her children to spy on her. Imene's total innocence is no protection: she is stabbed by her brother and finished off by her uncle. All Malas's work is imbued with his love and respect for women, and *Passion* is a passionate indictment of the whole notion of "honor killing" and, implicitly, of the Bashar al-Assad regime in which it flourishes.

Eight years later, Malas was working on the script for a new feature when the uprisings of the Arab Spring occurred. This new film was to explore the director's characteristic thematic concern with the interactions between reality, memory, and imagination. The central figure Ghalia was "inhabited' by the spirit of Zeina, a young woman who died on the day she was born. This device was intended to allow Malas "to insert history into current events," since the two girls' lives cover the forty-year span of the al-Assad regime to that date. Malas did not abandon his half-completed project but merged it with an account of immediately current events to create the highly complex narrative of *Ladder to Damascus / Une échelle pour Damas* (2013). His aim was clear: "I wasn't really trying to politically analyse the situation or to predict how it would evolve. I merely wanted to reflect what was happening, to capture the hope and uncertainty it stirred and to convey its effect on the characters."[370]

Though the film does not draw directly on Malas's memories of his youth, he has an alter ego (a young filmmaker Fouad), giving the film a personal dimension. In addition, he has admitted that the reincarnation theme in Zeina and Ghalia's story "allowed me a playful re-creation of fiction and fantasy, dreams and imagination. The three main characters are in harmony with my own personal experience."[371] While these personal aspects are crucial, the bulk of the film examines the effect on young people of the events, outside their control, that occur within Damascus at the time of the film's shooting. The actors are largely nonprofessionals from various backgrounds and sects, and Malas encouraged them "to give birth to the characters inspired by their own lives." The figure of the sculptor is played by a real-life sculptor and that of the soldier by a man doing his military service. Only one of them, Hussein, had actually participated in the spring uprising. The immediate events occurring off the set obviously affected the actors—they faced the same constraints as the characters they play—but also Malas himself, who shot a large amount of footage: "The restrictions created a situation where every day that we used to shoot a scene, I had one main preoccupation: If I were to stop shooting tomorrow, would I have enough material to make out of the material I had. This was a decision that dictated my work."[372]

The tone of *Ladder to Damascus* is set in three short scenes and comments forming part of the credit titles. The first is the young filmmaker Fouad's statement to the camera (an echo of Malas's own beliefs), beginning, "I live in a country that gives me nothing, yet demands everything from me. It demands of me that I be afraid and that I be silent." The second is an homage to the great Syrian documentary filmmaker Omar Amiralay, who died two years before the shooting began. The third is a brief quote from the Syrian poet Ibn Hazm: "You are haunted by people who are like you." The action itself begins while Damascus is still calm with the meeting between Ghalia, a twenty-year-old actress, and Fouad, nicknamed "Cinema," at an audition, where she gives a startling enactment of her personal situation. Fouad immediately sees her double personality of Ghalia/Zeina as the perfect subject for the film he is hoping to make.

When Ghalia decides to move to Damascus, Fouad finds her a room in the shared house where he lives and that is home to a variety of young people: a sculptress, a writer, a designer, a boxer, a soldier, and so on. Fouad's passion for cinema means that he is constantly projecting videos in his room, most of which attract the attention of at least some of his neighbors. The house, originally a refuge, gradually becomes a prison for the inhabitants, who are increasingly hesitant on go out onto the streets, which are now progressively filled with ever more violence. Malas's camera barely leaves the house, where tensions rise, but no linear narrative involving the group develops. Instead we get a succession of unconnected scenes of their anxieties, hopes, dreams, and couplings. There is no attempt at narrative continuity, and much of the action is filmed in semi-darkness or through screens and curtains. As the end credits reveal, the film is also full of almost indiscernible filmic allusions, with clips from a couple of Malas's own shorts, as well as from features by Theo Angelopoulos and Abbas Kiarostami, combined with briefly glimpsed stills from Amiralay, Ingmar Bergman and René Clément.

The power of the film comes from its ambiguities—often we are initially unable to discern whether we are seeing Ghalia or her double, Zeina, whether we are in the past or the present. The film moves effortlessly between the actual and the reenacted, between reality and imagination. The film concludes with the group's only joint sortie from their cramped interior. After a violent outburst, Hussein, who had been tortured when he ventured from safety, leads them out, but only onto the roof, where Rana's statue is already located. Supported by his fellow tenants, Hussein climbs a ladder to shout his defiant nickname, "Freedom."

For most filmmakers, to show what is happening on the streets by filming largely indoors, in a space where the forces outside never intrude, would seem impossible. But in interviews concerning the making of *Ladder to Damascus*, Malas has pointed out his own particular situation. His whole filmmaking career has occurred during the al-Assad regime. He and his contemporaries "have so far made films without provoking Syrian authorities. We gained the ability to infiltrate our thoughts, to embed them between the lines, and get past Syrian censorship. . . . A director must speak honestly, but in a language that is indirect, so they can craft the message they wish to send."[373] Immediacy remains, however. The explosions we hear throughout the film are real explosions, recorded inadvertently as they interrupted the shooting of specific scenes. Malas then isolated these sounds and reinserted them at appropriate moments elsewhere in the unfolding narrative. The desire to reflect the national situation while continuing to pursue his own personal concerns reflects his deep attachment to Damascus: "If I leave the country now I will be doing it as a refugee, and I refuse to live the few remaining years of my life as one. I want to stay in my city, even if it is no longer safe."[374]

*

Abdellatif Abdelhamid, the fourth Soviet-trained Syian filmmaker, was born, like Oussama Mohammad, in Lattakiah in 1954. But though he is close to his contemporary colleagues (appearing as an actor in films by both Malas and

Mohammad), his career has been very different. His course was set by his first feature, *The Nights of the Jackal / Les nuits du chacal / Layali ibn awa* (1989), after which he was able to make an unbroken series of seven features up to 2008: *Verbal Messages / Lettres orales / Rasa'il al shafahyya* (1991), *The Rising Rain / La montée de la pluie / Su'ud al-matar* (1996), *Breeze of the Soul / Le souffle de l'âme / Nassim ar-ruh* (1998), *Two Moons and an Olive Tree* aka *Qamaran and Zeltouna / Deux lunes et un olivier / Qamarn wa zyrunah* (2001), *At Our Listeners' Request / Au plaisir des auditeurs* aka *Ma chanson préférée / Ma yatlubuhu al-mustami'un* (2003), *Out of Coverage / Hors réseau / Kahref al-taghtiya* (2007), and *Days of Boredom / Jours d'ennui / Ayyam al-dajar* (2008). Unlike some of the work of his colleagues, his films are immediately accessible to a wide public, and he is one of the most popular filmmakers with Syrian audiences. He is, as Thoraval notes, a very resourceful filmmaker whose work is to be followed.

The Nights of the Jackal is currently the only one of his films available internationally. The film is a basically realistic tragi-comedy, set in 1967 in the arid countryside near the port of Lattakiah, where the director was born. But the film also has a touch of pure fantasy. At night, the farm is surrounded by jackals, whose howling cannot be silenced except by extremely high-pitched whistling, which only the hero's wife, Um Kamel, can manage. Kamel himself cannot whistle, though his wife makes it clear that she regards this as a man's responsibility. By day, Kamel's apparent authority is restored, as he leads his family out to the fields, pompously riding a donkey. But the daytime world, too, is full of unseen dangers, and gradually the basis of Kamel's authority is destroyed, as he loses the members of his family, one by one. His older daughter gets married, but the second one gets pregnant, elopes, and is later slaughtered in an "honor killing." His Westernized elder son abandons his university studies, while the reliable second son is conscripted and killed, resulting in the death of Um Kamel, too. When Kamel grows tomatoes, they fall in price in the state-controlled market; when he volunteers for military service, he is promptly dismissed.

Kamel's one recognized skill is repairing radios. He carries his own with him at all times, enjoying the stirring music and believing the patriotic propaganda. But toward the end of the film, the radio also lets him down, bringing only news of the Arabs' humiliating defeat at the hands of the Israelis. When his final child, his youngest son, Bassam, leaves him, Kamel is totally alone. He had tried buying a whistle on a trip to Lattakia, but the jackals were not deceived. Now, still unable to whistle, he succumbs to the night and the jackals. Beneath the surface farce, *The Night of the Jackal* has a serious message about the place of the traditional Arab male, and of Syria, in the modern world.

There have also been further debuts in the 1990s by directors trained in the former Soviet Union. Riyad Shayya (born 1951 in Souwayda) returned from the VGIK in Moscow to make *Al-lajat / Al-leja* (1995), but he has not been able to establish himself and complete a second feature. Two other filmmakers returned from the Kiev film school. Raymond Boutros (born in 1950 in Hama) made a number of short documentaries and then three features: *The Greedy Ones* / *Les gourmands* a.k.a. *Les algues d'eau douce* / *Al-tahalib* (1991), *The Displacement* / *Le déplacement* / *Al-tarhaj* (1997), and *Hasiba* (2008). Ghassan Shmeit (born in 1956 in Quneitra), who graduated from Kiev in 1982, also completed a number of documentaries and three features in the course of a decade and a half: *Something Is Burning* / *Quelque chose brûle* / *Shay'ma yahtariq* (1993), *Black Flour* / *La farine noire* / *Tahin al-aswad* (2001), and *I.D.* / *Vos papiers* (2007). A fourth filmmaker, Maher Kaddo (born in 1949 in Deir-Ezzar), studied film directing at the Academy of Art, Film and Theatre in Bucharest. His feature films are *Noises from All Sides* / *Le hénissement des directions* aka *Le périple* / *Sahil al-jibat* (1993, 97', 35mm) and *Gate of Heaven* / *La porte du ciel* / *Bawabet al-janna* (2009).

Despite the small number of films produced, critics are united in their praise for the work of the Syrian directors. According to Diana Jabbour, "Syrian cinema experienced a visible renaissance, manifested in innovative treatment of ordinary subjects combined with sophisticated cinematic styles. The camera moved closer to reality, and each director had a unique style of approaching this reality."[375] Richard Pena notes that for their narratives, "Syrian filmmakers often rely on allegory, the microcosm of a single family serving as stand-in for the nation." At the same time, "the films also don't shy away from making big statements. Historical events are never far off screen, and they often permeate even the most intimate personal relations."[376]

As with Mali, many of whose filmmakers were similarly trained in Moscow, Syrian cinema has a very distinctive quality when compared with its neighbors. Livia Alexander excellently locates its place in the spectrum of national cinemas: "Syrian filmmaking is rather distinct. With its strong emphasis on formalism, aesthetic composition and symbolism, it is unlike any other cinema produced in the region. A cinema strongly influenced by the training of a whole generation of filmmakers in the former Soviet Union in the 1970s, it stands apart from contemporaneous Egyptian film's realism with its gritty on-location shooting in the streets of Cairo or, alternatively, the national mobilizing force propelling Palestinian film production."[377]

Notes

1. Albert Memmi, *The Colonizer and the Colonized* (New York: Souvenir Press, 1974), 114.

2. Edward Said, *Culture and Imperialism* (London: Vintage, 1994), 64.

3. Nouri Bouzid, inverview in *Actes du Onzième Festival International de Montpellier*, 1989, 181.

4. Moumen Smihi, "Moroccan Society as Mythology," in *Film and Politics in the Third World*, ed. John D. H. Downing (New York: Praeger, 1987), 80.

5. See Hamid Miduni, *Ahmed Baha Eddine Attia—Une vie comme au cinéma* (Tunis: Editions Roives Productions, 2008).

6. David Murphy and Patrick Williams, *Postcolonial African Cinema: Ten Directors* (Manchester: Manchester University Press, 2007), 30.

7. Nouri Bouzid, "New Realism in Arab Cinema: The Defeat-Conscious Cinema," *Alif* no. 15 (special issue, 1995), 244.

8. Ibid., 245.

9. Full-length studies of Chahine in English and French include Christian Bosséno, ed., *Yossef Chahine l'Alexandrin* (Paris: CinémAction 34, 1985); Tahar Chikaoui, ed., *Spécial: Le Moineau de Y Chahine* & *Chahine, l'enfant prodiguedu cinéma arabe* (Tunis: Cinécrits, 2004); Alberto Elena, *Youssef Chahine: el fuego y la palabra / Youssef Chahine: Fire and Word* (bilingual) (Cordoba: Junta de Andalucia, 2007); Ibraham Fawal, *Youssef Chahine* (London: BFI, 2001); Jean Jonassaint, ed., *Chahine et le cinema égyptien* (Montreal: Dérives 43, 1984); and Thierry Jousse, *Spécial Chahine* (Paris: Cahiers du cinema, 1996).

10. Bouzid, "New Realism in Arab Cinema," 242.

11. Nouri Bouzid, "Sources of Inspiration Lecture," *Sources* (1994), 46.

12. Hamid Dabashi in *Insights into Syrian Cinema: Essays and Conversations with Contemporary Filmmakers*, ed. Rasha Salti (New York: Rattapallax Press / Arte East, 2006), 18.

13. Of particular interest is the 1990 survey, edited by Guy Hennebelle and Roland Schneider, *Cinénas metis* (Paris: CinémAction, 1990); Carrie Tarr's critical analysis, *Reframing Difference* (Manchester: Manchester University Press, 2005); and Sylvie Durmelat and Vinay Swamy, *Screening Integration* (Lincoln: University of Nebraska Press, 2011).

14. Armes "African Filmmaking North and South of the Sahara" (2006), 147.

15. Rithy Panh, preface to Jean-Michel Frodon, ed., *Au sud du cinéma* (Paris: Chiers du Cinéma / Arte, 2004), 7.

16. For a full analysis of *Miss Mona*, see Armes "Postcolonial Images" (2005), 123–131.

17. For a brief discussion of *Number One*, see Roy Armes, *New Voices in Arab Cinema* (Bloomington: Indiana University Press, 2015), 134–35.

18. Will Higbee, *Post-Beur Cinema* (Edinburgh: Edinburgh University Press, 2013), 204. See also Armes, *New Voices in Arab Cinema*, 91–95, 165–66.

19. Wassyla Tamzali, *En attendant* Omar Gatlato (Algiers: Éditions EnAp, 1979), 87.

20. Mohamed Zinet, quoted in Khelfa Ben Aissa, *Tu Vivras, Zinet* (Paris: Éditions L'Harmattan, 1990), 59.

21. Lizbeth Malkmus, in *Arab & African Film Making*, ed. Lizbeth Malkmus and Roy Armes (London: Zed Books, 1991), 149–150.

22. Bruno Muel, quoted in Ben Aissa, *Tu Vivras, Zinet*, 86–87.

23. Nacer Khemir, quoted in Ben Aissa, *Tu Vivras, Zinet*, 94.

24. Mireille Calle-Gruber, *Assia Djebar, ou la résistance de la littérature* (Paris: Maisonneuve & Larose, 2001), 9.

25. For a full analysis of *La nouba*, see Armes (2005), 114–22.

26. Farouk Beloufa and Merzak Allouache, "Farouk Beloufa & Merzak Allouache: Nous pratiquions un cinema vivant!," joint interview by Samir Ardjoum, *El Watan2*, August 31, 2012, elwatanlafabrique.wordpress.com.

27. Farouk Beloufa, "Interview exclusive de Farouk Beloufa, cinéaste, par Samir Ardjoum," *Africine*, June 14, 2010, www.africine.org.

28. Brahim Tsaki, interview by M. Kali, Algiers, *El Watan*, January 19, 1997.

29. Brahim Tsaki, interview by Mohamed Balhi, in *Cinémas du Maghreb*, ed. Mouny Berrah, Victor Bachy, Mohand Ben Salama, and Ferid Boughedir (Paris: CinémAction 14, 1981), 112.

30. Brahim Tsaki, "Statement of Intent," Affricultures, cited in www.africultures.com.

31. Mahmound Zemmouri, l'Humanité, undated, www.humanite.fr.

32. Alexandra Guellil, review in toukimonréal.com/ actualités, August 31, 2014.

33. Merzak Allouache, interview in Berrah et al., *Cinémas du Maghreb*, 104.

34. For a full analysis of *Omar Gatlato*, see Roy Armes, *Omar Gatlato* (Trowbridge: Flicks Books, 1998).

35. Allouache, interview in Berrah et al., *Cinémas du Maghreb*, 104.

36. Ibid., 102–3.

37. Abdou B., "Le dernier tabou," in *L'Algérie vue par son cinema*, ed. Jean-Pierre Brossard (Locarno: Festival International de Locarno, 1981), 106.

38. Merzak Allouache, interview, www.mondomix.com, February 23, 2010.

39. Merzak Allouache, interview by Said Khatabi, www.english.al-akbar.com, November 23, 2011.

40. Merzak Allouache, interview in the pressbook of *Le repemti*.

41. Amira Soltane, www.lexpressiondz.com, June 16, 2012.

42. Allouche, interview in www.huffpostmahgreb.com, October 6, 2014.

43. Armes, *New Voices in Arab Cinema*.

44. Jean-Pierre Lledo, cited in the presentation of the DVD.

45. Saïd Bakiri, interview by Samuel Lelièvre, in *Cinémas africains, Une oasis dans le désert?*, ed. Samuel Lelièvre (Paris: Corlet / Télérama, 2003), 211.

46. Belkacem Hadjadj, interview by Mustapha Laribi, *Djazaîr Magazine*, April 1996, 52–53.

47. All quotations in this paragraph are from Abderrahmane Bouguermouh, interview by Denise Brahimi, "À propos de *La colline oubliée*: le roman et le film," *Awal* no. 15 (1997), 3–8.

48. Azzedine Meddour, interview in the pressbook of *La montagne de Baya*.

49. Ibid.

50. Zinaï-Koudil, interview by, in *Encyclopedia of Arab Women Filmmakers*, by Rebecca Hillauer, trans. by Allison Brown, Deborah Cohen, and Nancy Joyce (Cairo: American University in Cairo Press, 2005), originally published as *Freiräume—Lebensträume, Arabische Filmemacherinnen* (Unkel am Rhein: Arte-Edition, 2001), 320.

51. Mohamed Chouikh, interview by, in *Le cinéma métaphorique de Mohamed Chouikh*, by Camille Taboulay (Paris: K Films Éditions, 1997), 66.

52. Ibid., 13.

53. Denise Brahimi, "Images, symbols et paraboles dans le cinéma de Mohamed Chouikh," in *Cinémas du Maghreb*, ed. Michel Serceau (Paris: Corlet / Télérama, 2004), 154.

54. Camille Taboulay, *Mohamed Chouikh*, long interview plus script of *L'Arche du desert* (Paris: K Films Éditions, 1997), 66.

55. For a full account, see Denise Brahimi, "*Hamlet of Women*: Village Chronicles from a Time of Terror," in *Film in the Middle East and North America: Creative Dissidence*, ed. Josef Gugler (Austin: University of Texas Press, 2011), 315–24.

56. Richard Porton, "Mambety's *Hyenas*: Between Anti-Colonialism and the Critique of Modernity," *Iris* 18 (1995): 97.

57. Smihi, "Moroccan Society as Mythology," 81.

58. Ibid., 82.

59. Ibid., 83.

60. Hamid Benani, writing in *Lamalif*, no. 45, cited in the London Film Festival program notes, 1972.

61. Fouad Souiba and Fatima Zahra El Alaoui, *Un siècle de cinema au Maroc* (Rabat: World Design Communication, 1995), 80.

62. Benani, London Film Festival program notes, 1972.

63. Smihi, interview in Downing, *Film and Politics in the Third World*, 80.

64. Ibid., 79.

65. For a full analysis of *El Chergui*, see Armes "Postcolonial Images" (2005), 87–95.

66. Nourredine Ghali, "*El Chergui ou le silence violent*: Une interrogation sur la société," *Cinéma* 76, no. 205 (1976): 131.

67. Moulay Driss Jaïdi, *Vision(s) de la société marocaine à travers le court métrage* (Rabat: Collection al majal, 1994), 108.

68. Souiba and el Aloui, *Un siècle de cinema au Maroc*, 83.

69. Ahmed Araib and Eric de Hullesen, *Il était une fois . . . Le cinéma au Maroc* (Rabat: EDH, 1999), 56.

70. Moumen Smihi, declaration of intent on the cover of the film's VHS tape.

71. Smihi, cited in the booklet accompanying a season of Moumen Smihi's films, "Moumen Smihi: Moroccan Mythologies," curated by Peter Limbrick and presented at the Tate Modern in London in 2014.

72. Moumen Smihi, *Écrire sur le cinéma, idées claandestines 1* (Tangier: Slaiiki Frères, 2006).

73. Azzedine Mabrouk, "Moumen Smihi sur le chemin poétique," www.africine.org, February 4, 2008.

74. Sandra Gayle Carter, *What Moroccan Cinema? A Historical and Critical Study, 1945–2006* (Lanham: Lexington Books, 2009), 139.

75. Ahmed Bouanani, cited in fr.wikipedia.org, August 23, 2015.

76. Souiba and El Alaoui, *Un siècle de cinema au Maroc*, 86.

77. Araib & Hullessen (1999), 46.

78. Noureddine Mkakkak, "Adieu Ahmed Bouanani (1938–2011): The Poet of Film who Loved Light," Africine, February 24, 2011, www.africine.org.

79. "Ahmed Bouananai: Après sa mort, son oeuvre ressuscitée," HuffPost Magreb, April 5, 2015, www.huffpostmaghreb.com.

80. Ibid.

81. All information in this paragraph is derived from Souiba and El Alaoui, *Un siècle de cinema au Maroc*, 80–81.

82. Mustafa Derkaoui, cited in Carter, *What Moroccan Cinema?*, 159.

83. Ibid.

84. Armed Ferhat, "Le Cinéma marocain aujord'hui: Les atouts et constraintes d'une émergence annoncée," in Serceau, *Cinémas du Maghreb*, 57.

85. Carter, *What Moroccan Cinema?*, 115–116.

86. Mohamed Reggab, cited in Souiba and El Alaoui (1995), 96.

87. Souiba and El Alaoui, *Un siècle de cinema au Maroc*, 95.

88. Ibid., 54.

89. Ahmed Fertat, "Le Cinéma marocain aujourd'hui," in Serceau, *Cinémas du Maghreb*, 55.

90. Michel Webb, cited in bampfa.berrkeley.edu, 2014.

91. Valery K. Orlando, *Screening Morocco: Contemporary Film in a Changing Society* (Athens: Ohio University Press, 2011), 148–49.

92. Unsigned review, in menarama/fr, February 9, 2014.

93. Farida Benlyazid, "Image and Experience: Why Cinema?" in *Images of Enchantment*, ed. Sherifa Zuhur (Cairo: American University in Cairo Press, 1998), 206–7.

94. For a detailed analysis of this film, see Florence Martin, "*Bab al-sama maftouh / A Door to the Sky*," in *The Cinema of North Africa and the Middle East*, ed. Gönül Dönmez-Colin (London: Wallflower Press, 2007), 123–32.

95. Farida Benlyazid, cited in Hillauer, *Encyclopedia of Arab Women Filmmakers*, 339.

96. Ibid., 340.

97. Ibid., 342–43.

98. Olivier Barlet, africultures.com, September 2, 2003.

99. "Synopsis," in africultures.com, May 19, 2006.

100. Ibid., 339.

101. www.simonebitton.com.

102. Ibid.

103. Ibid.

104. Ibid.

105. Ami Elad-Bouskila, *Modern Palestinian Literature and Culture* (London: Frank Cass, 1999), 7.

106. Olivier Barlet, "*Mémoire en detention*," www.africultures.com, April 18, 2006.

107. Jillali Ferhati, interview, in Serceau, *Cinémas du Maghreb*, 175.

108. M'barek Housni, "Jillali Ferhati, un auteur de cinema," www.africine.org, August 5, 2007.

109. Hakim Noury, cited in Kevin Dwyer,"Un pays, une décénnie, deux comedies," in Serceau, *Cinémas du Maghreb*, 89.

110. Dwyer, ibid.

111. Mohamed Abderrahman Tazi, interview by Kevin Dwyer, in *Beyond Casablanca*, by Kevin Dwyer (Bloomington: Indiana University Press, 2004), 110.

112. Ibid., 175. "A feminine sensibility" are Tazi's words.

113. Ibid., 154.

114. Mernissa, cited, ibid., 190.

115. Tazi, cited ibid., 191.

116. Ibid., 197.

117. Fatima Mernissi, *Beyond the Veil: Male-Female Dynamics in Muslim Society* (London: Al Saqi Books, 1985), 144.

118. Mohamed Abderrahman Tazi, cited in www.diplomatie.gouv.fr.

119. Mohamed Abderrahman Tazi, unpublished interview by Kevin Dwyer, Rabat, 1999–2000.

120. Abdelkaader Lagtaâ, cited in Kevin Dwyer, "'Hidden, Unsaid, Taboo' in Moroccan Cinema: Adelkader Lagtaâ's Challenge to Authority," *Framework* 43, no. 2 (2002), 117–133.

121. Ahmed Ferhat, "Le cinema marocain aujourd'hui: Les atouts et les constrainrts d'une emergence annoncée," in Serceau, *Cinémas du Maghreb*, 52.

122. Abdelkader Lagtaâ, interview by Olivier Barlet, africultures.com, September 2, 2002.

123. Ibid.

124. Abdelkader Lagtaâ, interview by Olivier Barlet, www.africultures.com, December 5, 2003.

125. Ibid.

126. Mouna Mekouar, *Daoud Alouad-Syad* (Paris: Filigranes Éditions, 2015).

127. Review in www.yabiladi.com.

128. Gian Maria Annovi, "Oedipus at Ouarzazate," www.etudesitaliennes.hypsthesis.org, 2015.

129. Daoud Alouad-Syad, interview by Olivier Barlet, www.africultures.com, November 2010.

130. This, and all references to the making of *The Mosque* in the precceeding paragraphs, come from Alouad-Syad, interview by Barlet.

131. Ibid.

132. Omar Khlifi, *L'histoire du cinéma en Tunisie* (Tunis: Société Tunisienne de Diffusion, 1970).

133. Touti Moumen, *Films Tunisiens—Longs Métrages 1967–1998* (Tunis: Touti Moumen, 1998), 11.

134. Victor Bachy, *Le Cinéma de Tunisie* (Tunis: Société Tunisienne de Diffusion, 1978), 166.

135. Khélifa Chater, quoted in Moumen, *Films Tunisiens*, 16.

136. Bachy, *Le Cinéma de Tunisie*, 124.

137. Omar Khlifi, cited in Moumen, *Films Tunisiens*, 39.

138. Khlifi, cited in Moumen, *Films Tunisiens*, 47.

139. All quotes from Moumen, *Films Tunisiens*, 48–51.

140. Khlifi, cited in Moumen, *Films Tunisiens*, 110–11.

141. Taïeb Louhichi, interviews in *Réalités*, March 17, 1998, cited in Moumen, *Films Tunisiens*, 221.

142. Mahmoud Ben Mahmoud, "Leçon de cinéma de Mahmoud Ben Mahmoud," www.her galcinema.org, August 2014.

143. For a full analysis of the film see Roy Armes, "*Traversées / Crossing Over*," in Dönmez-Colin, *Cinemas of North Africa and the Middle East*, 70–78.

144. Moumen, *Films Tunisiens*, 161.

145. Ben Mahmoud, "Leçon de cinéma de Mahmoud Ben Mahmoud."

146. Mahmoud Ben Mahmoud, statement at the film's presentation at the Ciné-Club de Tunis, June 1, 2013.

147. Stephen Dalton, www.hollywoodreporter.com, November 24, 2012.

148. Ben Mahmoud, "Leçon de cinéma de Mahmoud Ben Mahmoud."

149. Cited in Berrah et al., *Cinémas du Maghreb*, 188.

150. Ibid., 190.

151. Fadhel Jaïbi and Fadhel Jaziri, cited in Moumen, *Films Tunisiens*, 126.

152. Ibid., 127.

153. For Attia's contribution, see Hamid Miduni, *Ahmed Baha Eddine Attia: Une vie comme au cinéma* (Tunis: Editions Rives Productions, 2008).

154. Nouri Bouzid, interview in Hédi Khelil, *Le parcours et la trace* (Salambo: MediaCom, 2002), 105.

155. Bouzid, "New Realism in Arab Cinema," 243.

156. For a detailed analysis of the film, see Roy Armes, "The Body in Maghrebian Cinema: Nouri Bouzid's *Man of Ashes*," *Le corps dans tous ses états*, Celaan 4, nos. 1–2 (2005), 20–30.

157. Nouri Bouzid, "Mission Unaccomplished," *Index on Censorship* 6 (1995), 102.

158. Ibid., 103.

159. Ibid., 102.

160. For a fuller reading of *Bezness*, see Robert Lang, "Sexual Alegories of National Identity in Nouri Bouzid's *Bezness*," in *North African Cinema in a Global Context: Through the Lens of the Diasopora*, ed. Andrea Khalil (New York: Routledge, 2008), 33–52.

161. Bouzid, interview, Khelil, *Le parcours et la trace*, 122.

162. Nouri Bouzid, interview in the press book of *Tunisiennes*.

163. Bouzid, interview, Khelil, *Le parcours et la trace*, 123.

164. Amira Ben Youssef, quoted in Moumen, *Films Tunisiens*, 211.

165. Nouri Bouzid, "Note d'intention," in the press book of *Poupées d'argile*.

166. Ibid.

167. Nouri Bouzid, interview by Henda Haoula Hamzaoui, in www.euromediaaudiovisuel.net, October 22, 2012.

168. Ibid.

169. Bouzid, interview, Khelil, *Le parcours et la trace*, 107.

170. Ibid.

171. Nouri Bouzid, interview, in the pressbook for *Bent familia*.

172. Ferid Boughedir, "Un été à la Goulette," in *Une saison tunisienne*, ed. Frédéric Mitterand and Soraya Elses-Ferchichi (Arles: Actes Sud / AFAA, 1995), 121.

173. Bouzid, "Sources of Inspiration Lecture," 59.

174. Mernissi, *Beyond the Veil*, 140.

175. For a full analysis of Dhouib's first three short films, see Andrea Flores Khalil, "Images That Come Out at Night: A Film Trilogy by Moncef Dhouib," *Celaan* 1, nos. 1–2 (2002): 71–80.

176. Robert Lang, *The New Tunisian Cinema: Allegories of Resistance* (New York: Columbia University Press, 2014), 23–224.

177. Mernissi, *Beyond the Veil*, 137.

178. See Hélé Béji, *Désenchantement national* (Paris: François Maspero, 1982).

179. Zakia Smail Salhi, "Maghrebi Women Filmmakers and the Challenge of Modernity: Breaking Women's Silence," in *Women and Media in the Middle East: Power through Self-Expression*, ed. Naomi Sakr (London: I. B. Tauris, 2004), 71.

180. Sonia Chamkhi, *Le cinéma tunisien 1996–2006 à la lumière sw la modernité* (Tunis: Centre de Publication Universitaire, 2009), 54–55.

181. Mohamed Zran, pressbook for *Being Here*.

182. Ibid.

183. Ibid.

184. Ibid.

185. Selma Baccar, interview, in Tamzali, *En attandant* Omar Gatlato, 204. Baccar is referred to here as Selma Bedjaoui, presumably her unmarried name.

186. Florence Martin, *Screens and Veils: Maghrebi Women's Cinema* (Bloomington: Indiana University Press, 2011), 186.

187. Selma Baccar, interview, cited in Hillauer, *Encyclopedia of Arab Women Filmmakers*, 378–79.

188. Ibid.

189. Selma Baccar, interview, in Martin, *Screens and Veils*, 188.

190. Ibid.

191. Martin, *Screens and Veils*, 183–202.

192. Néjia Ben Mabrouk, interview by Werner Kobe, in Hillauer, *Encyclopedia of Arab Women Filmmakers*, 380.

193. Néjia Ben Mabrouk, interview by Sarra Daldoul, in Abdelkrim Gabbous, *Silence, elles tournent!: Les femmes et le cinéma en Tunisie* (Tunis: Cérès Éditions / CREDIF, 1998), 91–98.

194. Kalthoum Bornaz, statement of intent in the pressbook of the film.

195. Ibid.

196. Kalthoum Bornaz, interview cited in Hillauer, *Encyclopedia of Arab Women Filmmakers*, 386.

197. Kalthoum Bornaz, synopsis given with the film's publicity.

198. Sonia Chamkhi, "*L'autre moitié du ciel* de Kalthoum Bornaz," moutaches.wordpress.com, October 19, 2008.

199. Nacer Khemir, interview by Khemais Khayati, 1995, 255.

200. Nacer Khemir, *Le livre des djinns* (Paris: Syros Jeunesse, 2002), 2.

201. Interestingly, Viola Shafik ends her synopsis of the film at this point, see Viola Shafik, *Arab Cinema: History and Cultural Identity* (Cairo: American University in Cairo Press, 1998), 195–96.

202. Nacer Khemir, quoted in Moumen, *Films Tunisiens*, 108.

203. Denise Brahimi, *Cinémas d'Afrique francophone et du Maghreb* (Paris: Editions Natham, 1997), 102.

204. Ferid Boughedir, "Les nouveaux films maghébins d'aujourd'hui," in Berrah et al. (1981), 66.

205. Nacer Khemir, interview with the editors, in Jaeggi & Ruggle, ed. (1992), 98.

206. Ibn Hazm, *The Ring of the Dove*, cited in *The Penguin Anthology of Classical Arabic Literature*, ed. Robert Irwin (London: Penguin Books, 1999).

207. Khemir, interview by Khayati, 259.

208. Nacer Khemir, interview in the pressbook for *Bab' Aziz*.

209. Ibid.

210. Ibid. (for all quotations in this paragraph).

211. Nacer Khemir, *Conteur / Story-teller* (Paris: Éditions de l'Oeil, 2005), 16.

212. Ibid., 21.

213. Khemir, interview by Khayati, 257.

214. Ibid.

215. Benjamin Geer, "Yousry Nasrallah," in *Ten Arab Filmmakers*, ed. Josef Gugler (Bloomington: Indiana University Press, 2015), 146.

216. Yousry Nasrallah, cited Gugler, *Ten Arab Filmmakers*, 147.

217. Ibid., 151.

218. Ibid., 154.

219. Elias Khoury, interview by Franck Garbarz, in the booklet accompanying the DVD.

220. Ibid.

221. Yousry Nasrallah, "Director's Statement," in the pressbook for the film.

222. Elias Khoury, interview by Franck Garbarz, in the pressbook for the film.

223. Nasrallah, cited in the pressbook for the film

224. Phippe Royer, cited in Hillauer, *Encyclopedia of Arab Women Filmmakers*, 58.

225. Asma El Bakry, interview by Serge Henry, cited in Hillauer, *Encyclopedia of Arab Women Filmmakers*, 57.

226. See Armes, *New Voices in Arab Cinema*, 191–99.

227. Ken Seigneure, *Standing by the Ruins: Elegiac Humanism in Wartime and Postwar Lebanon* (New York: Fordham University Press, 2011), 99.

228. Ibrahim al-Ariss, "An attempt at reading the history of cinema in Lebanon: From cinema to society and vice versa," in Arasoughly (1996), 32.

229. Heiny Srour, "Hindrance and Gender Representation in Documentary Filmmaking," paper presented at the AUC Symposium on Visual Anthropology, in Cairo, April 19, 2010.

230. Heiny Srour, "Straddling Three Stools," in Hillauer, *Encyclopedia of Arab Women Filmmakers*, 194.

231. Ibid., 188.

232. Srour, "Hindrance and Gender Representation."

233. Ibid.

234. Hillauer, *Encyclopedia of Arab Women Filmmakers*, 183.

235. Heiny Srour, interview by Edward Mortimer, cited in Hillauer, *Encyclopedia of Arab Women Filmmakers*, 183.

236. Claude Michel Cluny, *Dictionnaire des nouveaux cinémas arabes* (Paris: Sindbad, 1978), 107.

237. Ibid., 108.

238. Borhan Alawiya, "Sculpteur du temps," interview by Michèle Driguez and Françoise Haffner, in *Cinéma et Méditerranée: Actes du 11e Festival International de Montpellier* (Montpellier: Climats, 1989), 204.

239. Hamid Naficy, *An Accented Cinema: Exilic and Diasporic Filmmaking* (Princeton: Princeton University Press, 2001), 5.

240. Alawiya, "Sculpteur du temps," 205.

241. Lina Khatib, *Lebanese Cinema: Imagining the Civil War and Beyond* (London: I. B. Tauris, 2008), 74.

242. Jocelyne Saab, interview in Hillhauer, *Encyclopedia of Arab Women Filmmakers*, 173.

243. For a full listing, see Hillauer, *Encyclopedia of Arab Women Filmmakers*, 177–78.

244. For a full analysis of Wagdi's film, see Kay Dickinson, "*Ghazal al-banat / Candy Floss*," in Dönmez-Colin, *Cinema of North Africa and the Middle East*, 12–21.

245. Saab, interview in Hillhauer, *Encyclopedia of Arab Women Filmmakers*, 174–75.

246. Ibid., 175.

247. Ibid., 180.

248. Ibid., 175.

249. For a detailed analysis of the film, see Lina Khatib, *"Kan ya ma kan Beirut / Once Upon a Time in Beirut,"* in Dönmez-Colin, *Cinema of North Africa and the Middle East,* 157–66.

250. Anny Gaul, "From Dance to Tanscendence," www. Jadilyya.com, June 13, 2011.

251. Saab, interview in Hillauer, *Encyclopedia of Arab Women Filmmakers,* 181.

252. Publicity material on their various DVDs.

253. Olga Nakkas, interview cited in Hillauer *Encyclopedia of Arab Women Filmmakers,* 169.

254. Al-Ariss, "Attempt at reading the history of cinema in Lebanon," 36–37.

255. Mohamed Souheid, statement accompanying the DVD of *Tango of Yearning.*

256. Laura U. Marks, "Mohamed Soueid's Cinema of Immanence," *Jump Cut* 49 (Spring 2007), www.ejumpcut.org.

257. Ibid.

258. Al-Ariss, "Attempt at reading the history of cinema in Lebanon," 32.

259. Khatib, *Lebanese Cinema,* 39.

260. Ibid., 41.

261. Ibid., 172.

262. Hady Zaccak, *Le cinéma libanais* (Beirut: Dar el-Marchreq, 1997), 125.

263. Ibid., 126.

264. Maroun Bagdadi, quoted in Zaccak, *Le cinéma libanais,* 126.

265. Khatib, *Lebanese Cinema,* 61–62.

266. Maroun Bagdadi, quoed in Zaccak, *Le cinéma libanais,* 160.

267. Zaccak, *Le cinéma libanais,* 158.

268. Nidal El Achkar, quoted in Zaccak, *Le cinéma libanais,* 160.

269. Ibid.

270. Khatib, *Lebanese Cinema,* 107.

271. All quotations in his paragraph from Jean-Claude Codsi in the pressbook for *A Man of Honour.*

272. Zakkak, *Le cinéma libanais,* 170.

273. Lynn Maalouf, in *al-Ra'ida* (1999), cited in Hillauer, *Encyclopedia of Arab Women Filmmakers,* 153.

274. Deborah Young, in *Variety* (1992), cited in Hillauer *Encyclopedia of Arab Women Filmmakers,* 151.

275. Hillauer, *Encyclopedia of Arab Women Filmmakers,* 154.

276. Marina Da Silva, Paris: *Le monde diplomatique,* May 2000.

277. Ibid.

278. Khatib, *Lebanese Cinema,* 35.

279. Ibid., 158 (citing Assaf).

280. Ghassan Salhab, interview, www. diplomatie.gouv.fr, undated.

281. Ibid.

282. Ghassan Salhab, in Khatib, *Lebanese Cinema,* 163.

283. Ghassan Salhab, pressbook for *The Mountain.*

284. Ibid.

285. Jacques Mandelbaum, preface to *Fragments du Livre du naufrage,* ed. Ghassan Salhab (Beirut: Amers Éditions, 2011), 9.

286. Maï Masri, "Transcending Boundaries," mai masri.webarchive, undated.

287. Ella Shohat, *Israeli Cinema: East/West and the Politics of Representation* (London: I. B. Tauris, 2010), 271.

288. Ibid., 273.

289. Michel Khleifi, "From Reality to Fiction—From Poverty to Expression," in Dabashi (2006), 51.

290. Nurith Gertz and George Khleifi, *Palestinian Cinema: Landscape, Trauma and Memory* (Edinburgh: Edinburgh University Press, 2008), 49.

291. Mohamed Bakri, quoted in www.camera.orq.

292. Hany Abu-Assad, quoted in Gertz and Khleifi, *Palestinian Cinema*, 49.

293. Michel Khleifi, statement of intention, in the pressbook for *Fertile Memory*.

294. Gertz and Khleifi, *Palestinian Cinema*, 74.

295. Khleifi, statement of intention, in the pressbook for *Fertile Memory*.

296. Michel Khleifi, in *Dreams of a Nation: On Palestinian Cinema*, ed. Hamid Dabashi (London: Verso, 2006), 51.

297. Ibid.

298. Bashir Abu-Manneh, "Towards Liberation: Michel Khleifi's *Ma'loul* and *Canticle*," in Dabashi, *Dreams of a Nation*, 61.

299. Gertz and Khleifi, *Palestinian Cinema*, 80.

300. Michel Khleifi, interview by Philippe Elhem, in the film's pressbook, Brussels, May 1987.

301. Michel Khleifi, interview by Miriam Rosen, *Black Film Review*, Spring 1989, 4.

302. Michel Khleifi in Dabashi, *Dreams of a Nation*, 57.

303. Michel Khleifi, statement of intention, in the film's pressbook.

304. Michel Khleifi in Dabashi, *Dreams of a Nation*, 57.

305. Gertz and Khleifi, *Palestinian Cinema*, 93.

306. Abu-Manneh, in Dabashi, *Dreams of a Nation*, 67.

307. Michel Khleifi in Dabashi, *Dreams of a Nation*, 55.

308. "Michel Khleifi—Palestine's Film Poet" in www.thisweekinpalestine.com, January 2008.

309. Khleifi, "From Reality to Fiction—From Poverty to Expression," 57–58.

310. Khleifi, interview by Elhem.

311. Michel Khleifi, interview by Yousseh Hijazi, "Film as a Eork of Political Art," www .en.qantara.de, March 22, 2005.

312. Sousan Hammad, "Eyal Sivan Speaks to Al Jazeera," *Al Jazeera*, May 2011, www .aljazeera.com.

313. Eman Morsi, "*Zindeeq*: Film Review," www.jadaliyya.com, November 3, 2010.

314. Gertz and Khleifi, *Palestinian Cinema*, 139.

315. Ilan Pappe, *A History of Modern Palestine* (Cambridge: Cambridge University Press, 2006), 277.

316. Ibid.

317. See the review by Tamar Sternthal, "Film Review: Jenin, Jenin Road to Jenin," http:// www.camera.org/index.asp?x_context=46&x_review=10, January 18, 2005.

318. Pappe, *History of Modern Palestine*, 180.

319. David Trsilian, *A Brief Introduction to Modern Arabic Literature* (London: Saqi, 2008), 96–97.

320. Ibid., 97.

321. See Armes, *New Voices in Arab Cinema*.

322. See the chapter, "The House and Is Destruction: The Films of Ali Nassar," in Gertz and Khleifi, *Palestinian Cinema*, 119–33.

323. Gertz and Khleifi, *Palestinian Cinema*, 3.

324. Edward Said, preface to Dabashi, *Dreams of a Nation*, 2.

325. Ibid.

326. Ibid. 3.

327. Kassem [Qassim] Hawal, "Regard sur le cinéma irakien," in *Septième Biennale des Cinémas Arabes* (Paris: Institut du Monde Arabe, 2004), 101.

328. Hamid Naficy, ed., *Home, Exile, Homeland* (New York: Routledge, 1999), 9.

329. Naficy, *Accented Cinema*, 4.

330. Samir, "Director's Note," in the pressbook of *Iraqi Odyssey*, 2015.

331. Review in www.aljadid.com. 2016.

332. Ibid.

333. Kasim Abid, interview by Jerome Taylor, www.independent.co.uk, July 27, 2008.

334. Kasim Abid, Director's Statement, www.kasimarbid.com, 2013.

335. Ibid.

336. Kasim Abid, www.en.menarfeat.com, 2015.

337. Cited in www.kasimabid.com, 2015.

338. Publicity material, www.icarusfilms.com.

339. Review, www.peacemedia.usip.org.

340. The filmmakers' statement on the producers' website, www.oxymoron.com.

341. Pamela Crossland, "Return to the Land of Wonders," www.elevateddifference.com, March 16, 2007.

342. Noel Murray, "Return to the Land of Wonders," July 12, 2005.

343. Maysoon Pachachi, interview by Tessa Moran, www.washingtoncitypaper.com, October 7, 2004.

344. For a detailed analysis of the film see Ruth Tsoffar, "*Forget Baghdad: Jews and Arabs— The Iraqi Connection*," in Dönmez-Colin, *Cinemas of North Africa and the Middle East*, 257–65.

345. Shohat, *Israeli Cinema*.

346. Samir, "Director's Note."

347. Rasha Salti, quoted in Samir, "Director's Note."

348. Saad Salman, interview, www.avoir-alire.com, April 30, 2003.

349. See Armes, *New Voices in Arab Cinema*, 289–90.

350. Mohamed Malas, interview by Tahar Chikhaoui, in Salti, *Insights into Syrian Cinema*, 143.

351. Cécile Boëx, *Cinéma et politique en Syrie* (Paris: L'Harmattan, 2014), 201.

352. Malas, interview by Chikhaoui, in Salti, *Insights into Syrian Cinema*, 143.

353. Ibid., 188–89.

354. Yves Thoraval, *Les écrans du croissant fertile: Irak, Liban, Palestine, Syrie* (Paris: Séguier, 2002), 95.

355. Ibid.

356. Samir Zikra, "A Cinema of Dreams and . . . Bequest," in Salti, *Insights into Syrian Cinema*, 146.

357. Oussama Mohammad, "Tea Is Coffee, Coffee Is Tea: Freedom in a Closed Room," in Salti, *Insights into Syrian Cinema*, 155.

358. Synopsis: www.arteeast.org, 2008.

359. Ibid., 98.

360. Rasha Salti, "'Nujum al-nahar / Stars in Broad Daylight," in Dönmez-Colin, *Cinemas of North Africa and the Middle East*, 101.

361. Ibid., 110.

362. Synopsis in pressbook.

363. Lawrence Wright, "Disillusioned," in Salti, *Insights into Syrian Cinema*, 56.

364. Mohamed Malas, "Between Imaging and Imagining, Women in Film," in Salti, *Insights into Syrian Cinema*, 119.

365. Yasmine Zahdi, "The Cinema of Mohamed Malas: Recreating a Nation's History," ahram.org, May 12, 2014.

366. Mohamed Malas, interview in Salti, *Insights into Syrian Cinema*, 141.

367. Ibid., 119.

368. Ibid.
369. Ibid., 120.
370. Mohamed Malas, interview by Yasmine Zohdi, english.ahram.org.eg, May 12, 2014.
371. Mohamed Malas, interview by Tamara Qibawi, in the film's pressbook.
372. Ibid.
373. Ibid.
374. Malas, interview by Zohdi.
375. Jabbour in Arasoughly (1996), 46.
376. Richard Pena, preface to Salti, *Insights into Syrian Cinema*, 15–16.
377. Livia Alexander, preface to Salti, *Insights into Syrian Cinema*, 13.

Bibliography

World Cinema, Colonialism, Immigration

Ager, Dennis. *"Francophonie" in the 1990s: Problems and Opportunities*. Clevedon: Multilingual Matters, 1996.

Armes, Roy. *Third World Film Making and the West*. Berkeley: University of California Press, 1987.

Awed, Ibrahim, ed. *First Mogadishu Pan African Film Symposium*. Mogadishu: Mogpafis Management Committee, 1983.

Bachy, Victor. *To Have a History of African Cinema*. Brussels: OCIC, 1987.

Bataille, Maurice-Robert, and Claude Veillot. *Caméras sous le soleil: Le Cinéma en Afrique du nord*. Algiers, 1956.

Beaugé, Gilbert, and Jean-François Clément, ed. *L'image dans le monde arabe*. Paris: CNRS Éditions, 1995.

Benali, Abdelkader. *Le Cinéma colonial au Maghreb*. Paris: Editions du Cerf, 1998.

Benguigui, Yamina, *Mémoires d'immigrés: l'héritage maghrébin*. Paris: Albin Michel, 1997.

Bernstein, Matthew, and Gaylyn Studlar. *Visions of the East: Orientalism in Film*. London: I. B. Tauris, 1997.

Boëx, Cécile. *Cinéma et politique en Syrie: Écritures cinématographiques de la contestation en regime autoritaire (1970–2010)*. Paris: Éditions L'Harmattan, 2014.

Bossaerts, Marc, and Catherine Van Geel, eds. *Cinéma d'en Francophonie*. Brussels: Solibel Edition, 1995.

Bosséno, Christian, ed. *Cinémas de l'Emigration 3*. Paris: Éditions L'Harmattan, 1983.

Boulanger, Pierre. *Le Cinéma colonial*. Paris: Seghers, 1975.

Cameron, Kenneth M. *Africa on Film: Beyond Black and White*. New York: Continuum, 1994.

Chaudhuri, Shohini. *Contemporary World Cinema*. Edinburgh: Edinburgh University Press, 2005.

Codell, Julie F., ed. *Genre, Gender, Race and World Cinema*. Malden: Blackwell Publishing, 2007.

Convents, Guido. *A la recherche des images oubliés: Préhistoire du cinéma en Afrique, 1897–1918*. Brussels: OCIC, 1986.

Dale, Martin. *The Movie Game: The Film Business in Britain, Europe and America*. London: Cassell, 1997.

Dönmez-Colin, Gönül. *Women, Islam and Cinema*. London: Reaktion Books, 2004.

Downing, John D. H., ed. *Film and Politics in the Third World*. New York: Praeger, 1987.

Durmelat, Sylvie, and Vinay Swamy, eds. *Screening Integration: Recasting Maghrebi Immigration in Contemporary France*. Lincoln: University of Nebraska Press, 2011.

Elad-Bouskila, Ami. *Modern Palestinian Literature and Culture*. London: Frank Cass, 1999.

Elena, Alberto. *El cine del tercer mundo: diccionario de realizadores*. Madrid: Ediciones Turfan, 1993.

———. *"Romancero marroquí": el cine africanista durante la guerra civil*. Madrid: Filmoteca Española, 2005.

État et culture: le cinéma. Paris: La Documentation Française, 1992.

Ezra, Elisabeth, and Terry Rowden, eds. *Transnational Cinema: The Film Reader*. London: Routledge, 2006.

Fina, Luciana, Cristina Fina, and António Loja Neves. *Cinemas de África*. Lisbon: Cinemateca Portugesa and Culturgest, 1995.

Frodon, Jean-Pierre, ed. *Au Sud du Cinéma*. Paris: Cahiers du Cinéma, 2004.

Garcia, Jean-Pierre, ed. *Sous l'arbre à palabres: Guide pratique à l'usage des cinéastes africains*. Amiens: Festival International du Film d'Amiens, 1996.

Guneratne, Anthony R., and Wimal Disanayake. *Rethinking Third Cinema*. New York: Routledge, 2003.

Gutmann, Marie-Pierre, ed. *Le Partenariat euro-méditerranéen dans le domaine de l'image*. Morocco: Service de coopération de d'action culturelle de l'Ambassade de France au Maroc, 1999.

Hafez, Kai. *The Myth of Media Globalization*. Cambridge: Polity Press, 2007.

Hayward, Susan. "State, Culture and the Cinema: Jack Lang's Strategies from the French Film Industry 1981–93." *Screen* 34, no. 4 (1993): 380–91.

Hennebelle, Guy. *Les cinémas nationaux contre Hollywood*. Paris: Corlet, 2004.

———. *Quinze ans de cinéma mondial*. Paris: Éditions du Cerf, 1975.

Hennebelle, Guy, ed. *Cinémas de l'émigration*. Paris: CinémAction, 1979.

———. *Le Tiers monde en films*. Paris: CinémAction, 1982.

Hennebelle, Guy, and Chantal Soyer, eds. *Cinéma contre racisme*. Paris: CinémAction (hors série), 1980.

———. *Cinémas métis: De Hollywood aux films beurs*. Paris: Corlet, 1990.

Higbee, Will. *Post-Beur Cinema: North African Émigré and Maghrebi French Filmmaking in France since 2000*. Edinburgh: Edinburgh University Press, 2014.

Hjort, Mette, and Scott Mackenzie, eds. *Cinema and Nation*. New York: Routledge, 2000.

Ibnifassi, Laïla, and Nicki Hitchcott. *African Francophone Writing: A Critical Framework*. Oxford: Berg, 1996.

Iorndanova, Dina, David Martin-Jones, and Belén Vidal, eds. *Cinema at the Periphery*. Detroit: Wayne State University Press, 2010.

Judge, Anne. "The Institutional Framework of *la Francophonie*." In *African Francophone Writing: A Critical Introduction*, edited by Laïla Ibnlfassi and Nicki Hitchcott, 11–30. Oxford: Berg, 1996.

Kassir, Samir. *Being Arab*. London: Verso, 2006.

Khalaf, Samir, and Roseanne Saad, eds. *Arab Society and Culture: An Essential Reader*. London: Saqi, 2009.

L'Afrique noire. Perpignan: *Confrontation Cinématographique*, 1983.

Landau, Jacob M. *Studies in the Arab Theater and* Cinema. Philadelphia: University of Pennsylvania Press, 1958. Translated into French as *Etudes sur le théâtre et le cinéma arabes*. Paris: G-P Maisonneuve et Larosé, 1965.

Lang, Robert. *New Tunisian Cinema: Allegories of Resistance*. New York: Columbia University Press, 2014.

Lazare, Pascal, and Jean-Daniel Simon, eds. *Guide du cinéma africain (1989–1999)*. Paris: Écrans Nord-Sud, 2000.

Leaman, Oliver, ed. *Companion Encyclopedia of Middle Eastern and North African Film*. New York: Routledge, 2001.

Maillet, Raphaël. "(In)dépendence des cinémas du Sud &/vs France: L'exception culturelledes cinémas du Sud est-elle française?" In *Théorème: Cinéma & (in) dépendence—une économie politique*, 141–77. Paris: Presses de la Sorbonne Nouvelle, 1998.

Mirzoeff, Nicholas, ed. *Visual Culture Reader*. London: Routledge, 1998.

Moran, Albert, ed. *Film Policy: International, National, and Regional Perspectives*. New York: Routledge, 1996.

Mowitt, John. *Re-takes: Postcoloniality and Foreign Film Languages*. Minneapolis: University of Minnesota Press, 2005.

Naficy, Hamid. *An Accented Cinema: Exilic and Diasporic Filmmaking*. Princeton: Princeton University Press, 2001.

Naficy, Hamid, ed. *Home, Exile, Homeland: Film, Media, and the Politics of Place*. New York: Routledge, 1999.

Naudillon, Françoise, and Jean Ouédraogo, eds. *Images et mirages des migrations dans les littéraures et les cinémas d'Afrique francophone*, Montreal: Mémoire d'encrier, 2011.

Nicollier, Valéri. *Der Offene Bruch: Das Kino der Pieds Noirs*. Munich: *Cinim*, 1991.

Nowell-Smith, Geoffrey, ed. *The Oxford History of World Cinema*. Oxford: Oxford University Press, 1996.

N'Zelomona, Berthin. *La Francophonie*. Paris: L'Harmattan, 2001.

Prédal, René. *Le cinéma d'auteur, une vielle lune*? Paris: Éditions du Cerf, 2001.

Sherzer, Dina. *Cinema, Colonialism, Postcolonialism: Perspectives from the French and Francophone Worlds*. Austin: University of Texas Press, 1996.

Shohat, Ella, and Robert Stamm. *Unthinking Eurocentrism: Multiculturalism and the Media*. New York: Routledge, 1994.

Slavin, David Henry. *Colonial Cinema and Imperial France, 1919–1939*. Baltimore: Johns Hopkins University Press, 2001.

Spagnoletti, Giovanni, ed. *Il cinema europeo del métissage*. Millan: Editrice Il Castoro, 2000.

Spass, Lieve. *The Francophone Film: A Struggle for Identity*. Manchester: Manchester University Press, 2000.

Steven, Peter, ed. *Jump Cut: Hollywood, Politics and Counter-Cinema*. Toronto: Between the Lines, 1975.

Tarr, Carrie. *Reframing Difference: Beur and Banlieue Filmmaking in France*. Manchester: Manchester University Press, 2005.

Vitali, Valentina, and Paul Willemen, ed. *Theorising National Cinema*. London: BFI Publishing, 2006.

Wayne, Mike. *Political Film: The Dialectics of Third Cinema*. London: Pluyo Press, 2001.

Zuhur, Sherifa, ed. *Colors of Enchantment: Theater, Dance, Music, and the Visual Arts of the Middle East*. Cairo: American University in Cairo Press, 2001.

———. *Images of Enchantment: Visual and Performing Arts of the Middle East*. Cairo: American University in Cairo Press, 1998.

Studies of Arab Cinema

"African Cinema." *Sight and Sound*, February 2007: 26–35.

Abdel Wahed, Mahmud. "Syrian Cinema: History and Evolution." In *Il cinema dei paesi arabi/Arab Film Festival*, 4th ed., edited by Anna Di Martino, Andrea Morini, and Michele Capasso, 127–182. Naples: Fondazione Labatorio Mediterraneo, 1997.

Abdelhamid, Abdellatif. "Comme un fil de soie dans les cœurs" (interview). In *Cinéma et Mediterranée (Actes du 11e Festival International de Montpellier)*, 195–202. Montpellier: Festival de Montpellier, 1989.

———. "La pluie est porteuse de fertilité." Interview by Henri Talvat. In *Actes du 18e Festival International*, 55–56. Montpellier: Festival de Montpellier, 1996.

Abdel-Malek, Kamal. *The Rhetoric of Violence: Arab-Jewish Encounters in Contemporary Palestinian Literature and Film*. New York: Palgrave Macmillan, 2005.

Africa on Africa. London: Channel 4, 1984.

Ahmed, Ali Nobil, ed. "Cinema in Muslim Countries." *Third Text* 102 (24–31), 2010.

Al-Ariss, Ibrahim. "An Attempt at Reading the History of Cinema in Lebanon: From Cinema to Society and Vice Versa." In *Il cinema dei paesi arabi/Arab Film Festival*, 4th ed., edited by Anna Di Martino, Andrea Morini, and Michele Capasso, 34–70. Naples: Fondazione Labatorio Mediterraneo, 1997. Reprinted in *Screens of Life: Critical Film Writing from the Arab World*, edited by Alia Arasoughly, 19–39. Quebec: World Heritage Press, 1998.

———. "Hommage à Maroun Bagdadi." In *Deuxième Biennale des Cinémas Arabes*, 181–98. Paris: Institut du Monde Arabe, 1994.

Alawiya, Borhan. Interview by Anna Albertano. In *Il cinema dei paesi arabi/Arab Film Festival*, 4th ed., edited by Anna Di Martino, Andrea Morini, and Michele Capasso, 88–97. Naples: Fondazione Labatorio Mediterraneo, 1997.

———. "Sculpteur du temps" (interview). In *Cinéma et Méditerranée (Actes du 11e Festival International de Montpellier)*, 203–214. Montpellier: Festival de Montpellier, 1989.

Allouache, Merzak. *Omar Gatlato* (script). Algiers: Cinémathèque Algérienne/Éditions LAPHOMIC, 1987.

———. *Salut cousin!*. Paris: L'Avant-scène Cinéma, 1996.

Al-Mafraji, Ahmed Fayadh. *The Cinema in Iraq*. Baghdad: Research and Studies Centre, General Establishment for Cinema and Theatre, Ministry of Culture and Information.

Al-Roumi, Mayyar [Meyar], and Dorothée Schmid. "Le cinéma syrien: du militantisme au mutisme." *Cinéma et Monde musulman, cultures et interdits, EuOrient* 10 (2001): 4–25.

Amar Rodriguez, Victor Manuel, ed. *El Cine marroqui: secuencias para su conocimiento*. Cadiz: Servicio de Publicaciones de la Universidad de Cadiz, 2006.

Amiralay, Omar. "A Conversation." Interview by Luisa Ceretto and Andrea Morini. In *Il cinema dei paesi arabi*, edited by Andrea Morini, Anna Di Morini, and Adriano Aprà, 156–60. Venice: Marsilio Editori, 1993.

Arab Cinema and Culture (Three Round Table Conferences). Beirut: Arab Film and Television Centre, 1962, 1963, 1964.

Araib, Ahmed, and Eric de Hullessen. *Il était une fois . . . Le cinéma au Maroc*. Rabat: EDH, 1999.

Arasoughly, Alia, ed. *Screens of Life: Critical Film Writing from the Arab World.* Quebec: World Heritage Press, 1998.

Armbrust, Walter. *Mass Culture and Modernism in Egypt.* Cambridge: Cambridge University Press, 1996.

Armbrust, Walter, ed. *Mass Mediations: New Approaches to Popular Culture in the Middle East and Beyond.* Berkeley: University of California Press, 2000.

Armes, Roy. *African Filmmaking: North and South of the Sahara.* Bloomington: Indiana University Press, 2006.

———. *Arab Filmmakers of the Middle East: A Dictionary.* Bloomington: Indiana University Press, 2010.

———. "The Body in Maghrebian Cinema: Nouri Bouzid's *Man of Ashes.*" *Le Corps dans tous ses états. Celaan* 4, nos. 1–2 (2005): 20–30.

———. "Cinema." In *The Oxford Encyclopedia of the Modern Islamic World,* edited by John Esposito, 286–90. New York: Oxford University Press, 1995.

———. "Cinemas of the Maghreb." In *Black Camera* 1—1 (2009): 5–29.

———. *Dictionary of African Filmmakers.* Bloomington: Indiana University Press, 2008.

———. *Dictionary of North African Film Makers/Dictionnaire des cinéastes du Maghreb.* Paris: Éditions ATM, 1996.

———. "History or Myth: *Chronique des années de braise.*" *Cinéma Maghrébin,* special issue of *Celaan* 1, nos. 1–2 (2002): 7–17.

———. "Imag(in)ing Europe: The Theme of Emigration in North African Cinema." In *Mediating the Other: Jews, Christians, Muslims and the Media,* edited by Tudor Parfitt and Yulia Egorova. London: RoutledgeCurzon, 2004.

———. *New Voices in Arab Cinema.* Bloomington: Indiana Press, 2015.

———. *Omar Gatlato.* Trowbridge: Flicks Books, 1998.

———. "The Poetic Vision of Nacer Khemir." *Third Text* 102, no. 24-1 (2010): 69–82.

———. *Postcolonial Images: Studies in North African Film.* Bloomington: Indiana University Press, 2005.

———. "Reinterpreting the Tunisian Past: *Les Silences du palais.*" In *The Arab-African and Islamic Worlds: Interdisciplinary Studies,* edited by Kevin R. Lacey and Ralph M. Coury, 203–14. New York: Peter Lang, 2000.

———. "Taïeb Louhichi's *Shadow of the Earth* and the Role of the Rural in Mahgrebian Film Narrative." In *Representing the Rural: Space, Place and Identity in Films about the Land,* edited by Catherine Fowler and Gillian Helfield. Detroit: Wayne State University Press, 2006.

Austin, Guy. "Against Amnesia: Representation of Memory in Algerian Cinema." *Journal of African Cinemas* 2, no. 1,210i: 27–35.

Bachy, Victor. *Le Cinéma de Tunisie.* Tunis: Société Tunisienne de Diffusion, 1978.

Bagdadi, Maroun. *Hors la vie* (script). Paris: L'Avant-scène Cinéma, 1994.

———. "L'éternelle jeunesse du cinema." Interview by Thierry Lenouvel and Henri Talvat. In *Actes des 15e rencontres,* 3–7. Montpellier: Festival de Montpellier, 1993.

Bakrim, Mohammed. *Le Désir permanent, chroniques cinématographiques.* Rabat: Nourlil Éditeur, 2006.

Barlet, Olivier. *Les cinémas d'Afrique des années 2000: Perspectives critiques.* Paris: L'Harmattan, 2012.

Behna, Marie-Claude. "Gros plan sur le nouveau cinéma libanais." In *Troisième Festival des Cinémas Arabes,* 60–75. Paris: Institut du Monde Arabe, 1996.

Belfquih, Mohamed. *C'est mon écran après tout!: Réflexions sur la situation de l'audiovisuel au Maroc.* Rabat: Infolive, 1995.

Ben Aissa, Anouar, ed. *Tunisie: Trente ans de cinéma.* Tunis: EDICOP, 1996.

Ben Aissa, Khelfa. *Tu vivras, Zinet!: Tahia ya Zinet!*, Paris: Éditions L'Harmattan, 1990.

Bensalah, Mohamed. *Cinéma en Méditerranée, une passerelle entre les cultures.* Aix-en-Provence: Édisud, 2005.

Bergmann, Kristina. *Filmkultur und Filmindustrie in Ägypten.* Darmstadt: Wissenschaftliche Buchgesellschaft, 1993.

Berrah, Mouny. "Algerian Cinema and National Identity." In *Screens of Life: Critical Film Writing from the Arab World*, edited by Alia Arasoughly, 63–83. Quebec: World Heritage Press, 1998.

Berrah, Mouny, Jacques Lévy, and Claude-Michel Cluny, eds. *Les Cinémas arabes.* Paris: CinémAction, 1987.

Berrah, Mouny, Victor Bachy, Mohand Ben Salama, and Ferid Boughedir, eds. *Cinémas du Maghreb.* Paris: CinémAction, 1981.

Boëx, Cécile. *Cineema et politique en Syrie (1970–2010).* Paris: l'Harmattan, 2014.

Bosséno, Christian. "Des maquis d'hier aux luttes d'aujourd'hui: Thématique du cinéma algérien." *La Revue du Cinéma–Image et Son* 340 (1979): 27–52.

———. "Le Cinéma tunisien." *La Revue du Cinéma* 382 (1983): 49–62.

Boudjedra, Rachid. *Naissance du cinéma algérien.* Paris: François Maspéro, 1971.

Boughedir, Ferid. *Halfaouine, l'enfant des terrasses.* Paris: L'Avant-scène Cinéma, 1999.

———. *Le Cinéma en Afrique et dans le monde.* Paris: Jeune Afrique Plus, 1984.

Bouzid, Nouri. *"Sources of Inspiration" Lecture: 22 June 1994, Villepreux.* Amsterdam: Sources, 1994.

Brahimi, Denise. *Cinémas d'Afrique francophone et du Maghreb.* Paris: Nathan, 1997.

Bresheeth, Haim. "The Continuity of Trauma and Struggle: Recent Cinematic Representations of the Nakba." In *Nakba: Palestine, 1948, and the Claims of Memory*, edited by Ahmed H. Sa'di and Lila Abu-Lugod, 161–87. New York: Columbia University Press, 2007.

Brossard, Jean-Pierre, ed. *L'Algérie vue par son cinéma.* Locarno: Festival International du Film de Locarno, 1981.

Calle-Gruber, Mireille. *Assia Djebar.* Paris: ADPF & Ministère des Affaires Étrangères, 2006.

———. *Assia Djebar, ou la résistance de l'écriture.* Paris: Maisonneuve & Larose, 2001.

Canetta, Carlo, and Fiorano Rancati, eds. *Il cinema maghrebino.* Milan: Arci Nova, 1991.

Carter, Sandra Gayle. *What Moroccan Cinema? A Historical and Critical Study, 1956–2006.* Lanham: Lexington Books, 2009.

Cent ans de cinéma: Cinéma arabe (Bibliographie de la bibliothèque de l'IMA). Paris: Institut du Monde Arabe, 1995.

Challouf, Mohamed, Giuseppe Gariazzo, and Alessandra Speciale, eds. *Un posto sulla terra: Cinema per (r)esistere.* Milan: Editrice il Castoro, 2002.

Chamoun, Jean, and Maï Masri. "Contre la guerre-spectacle." Interview by Hubert Corbin and Michèle Driguez. In *Actes des 10e rencontres*, 91–97. Montpellier: Festival de Montpellier, 1998.

Chebli, Hakki. "The Cinema and Theater in Iraq." In *Arab Cinema and Culture*, vol. 3, 28–34. Beirut: Arab Film and Television Centre, 1964.

———. "History of the Iraqi Cinema." In *The Cinema in the Arab Countries*, edited by Georges Sadoul, 117–19. Beirut: Interarab Centre for Cinema and Television, 1966.

Cheriaa, Tahar. *Cinéma et culture en Tunisie*. Beirut: UNESCO, 1964.

———. *Ecrans d'abondance . . . ou cinémas de libération en Afrique?* Tunis: STD, 1979.

———. "Le Cinéma tunisien de la maladroite euphorie au juste désarroi." In *Aspects de la civilisation tunisienne*, edited by Abdelmajid Cherfi, 5–33. Tunis: Faculté de Lettres de Manouba, 1998.

———. "Le Cinéma tunisien des années 90: permanences et spécifités." *Horizons Maghrébins* 46 (2002): 113–19.

Chikhaoui, Tahar, ed. *Spécial: La nuit de Mohamed Malas*. Tunis: Edition Sahar, 1995.

Chmayt, Waid. "Images de la guerre du Liban." In *Les cinémas arabes*, edited by Mouny Berrah, Jacques Lévy, and Claude-Michel Cluny, 84–89. Paris: Institut du Monde Arabe CinémAction, 1987.

Choukroun, Jacques, and François de La Bretèche, eds. *Algérie d'hier et d'aujourd'hui*. Perpignan: Institut Jean Vigo, 2004.

Cinéma et libertés: Contribution au thème du Fespaco 93. Paris: Présence Africaine, 1993.

Cinéma marocain, filmographie générale longs métrages, 1958–2005. Rabat: Centre Cinématographique Marocain, 2006.

Cinéma: production cinématographique 1957–1973. Algiers: Ministère de l'Information et de la Culture, 1974.

Cinquante ans de courts métrages marocains 1947–1997. Rabat: Centre Cinématographique Marocain, 1998.

Clerc, Jeanne-Marie. *Assia Djebar, écrire, transgresser, résister*. Paris: Éditions L'Harmattan, 1997.

Cluny, Claude Michel. *Dictionnaire des nouveaux cinémas arabes*. Paris: Sindbad, 1978.

———. "Le cinéma syrien: une dizaine de bons films." In *Les Cinémas arabes*, edited by Mouny Berrah, Jacques Lévy, and Claude-Michel Cluny, 75. Paris: Institut du Monde Arabe, 1987.

———. "Syrie—un très proche orient." *Cinéma 75* 197 (1975): 100–101.

Coletti, Maria. *Di diaspro e di corallo: L'immagine della donna nel cinema dell'Africa francofono*. Rome: Fondazione Scuola Nazionale di Cinema, 2001.

Colla, Elliott. "Shadi Abdal-Salam's *al-Mumiya*: Ambivalence and the Egyptian Nation-State." In *Beyond Colonialism and Nationalism in the Maghrib: History, Culture and Politics*, edited byAli Abdullatif Ahmida, 109–43. New York: Palgrave Macmillan, 2000.

Corbin, Hubert. "Etat du cinéma syrien." Round table discussion with Omar Amiralay, Mohamed Malas, and Samir Zikra in *Actes des 19e Rencontres Cinématographiques*, 101–9. Montpellier: Festival de Montpellier, 1987.

Costandi, Nicholas. "The Cinema in Jordan." In *The Cinema in the Arab Countries*, edited by Georges Sadoul, 182–84. Beirut: Interarab Centre of Cinema and Television, 1966.

Dabashi, Hamid, ed. *Dreams of a Nation: On Palestinian Cinema*. London: Verso, 2006.

Dadci, Younès. *Dialogues Algérie-Cinéma: première histoire du cinéma algérien*. Paris: Éditions Dadci, 1970.

———. *Première histoire du cinéma algérien, 1896–1979*. Paris: Editions Dadci, 1980.

Darwish, Mustafa. *Dream Makers on the Nile: A Portrait of Egyptian Cinema*. Cairo: American University in Cairo Press, 1998.

De Arabische Film. Amsterdam: Cinemathema, 1979.

Deeley, Mona. *"Beyrouth al-Gharbiyya/West Beirut."* In *The Cinema of North Africa and the Middle East,* edited by Gönül Dönmez-Colin, 190–98. London: Wallflower Press, 2007.

De Franceschi, Leonardo. *Hudud! Un viaggio nel cinema maghrebino.* Rome: Bulzoni Editore, 2005.

Dehni, Salah. "History of the Syrian Cinema." In *The Cinema in the Arab Countries,* 98–107. Beirut: Interarab Centre of Cinema and Television, 1966.

———. "The Syrian Cinema in 1963." In *The Cinema in the Arab Countries,* 179–81. Beirut: Interarab Centre of Cinema and Television, 1966.

———. "Quand cinéma et télévision se regardent en chiens de faïence." In *Les Cinémas arabes,* edited by Mouny Berrah, Jacques Lévy, and Claude-Michel Cluny, 72–75. Paris: Institut du Monde Arabe, 1987.

———. "Une évolution difficile au service du cinéma arabe." *Cinéma 75* 197 (1975): 102–15.

De Hullessen, Eric. *Guide du cinéma et de l'audiovisuel marocain/Guide of Moroccan Cinema and Audiovisual.* Rabat: Éditions EDH, 1998.

Di Giorgi, Sergio, and Joan Rundo. *Una terra promessa dal cinema: Appunti sul nuovo cinema palestinese.* Palermo: Edizioni della Battaglia and La Luna nel Pozzo, 1998.

Di Martino, Anna. "The Representation of Woman in Contemporary Arab Cinema." In *Il cinema dei paesi arabi/Arab Film Festival,* 4th ed., edited by Anna Di Martino, Andrea Morini, and Michele Capasso, 80–87. Naples: Fondazione Labatorio Mediterraneo, 1997.

Di Martino, Anna, Andrea Morini, and Michele Capasso, eds. *Il cinema dei paesi arabi/ Arab Film Festival.* 4th ed. Naples: Edizioni Magma, 1997.

Dine, Philip. "Thinking the Unthinkable: The Generation of Meaning in French Literary and Cinema Images of the Algerian War." *Maghreb Review* 19, no. 1–2 (1994): 123–32.

Djebar, Assia. *Ces voix qui m'assiègent* (essays). Paris: Albin Michel, 1999.

Dossier: Spécial Cinémas d'Afrique. Paris: CNC (*Info* 237), 1991.

Du fonds d'aide . . . à l'avance sur recettes. Rabat: Centre Cinématographique Marocain, 2006.

Durmelat, Sylvie, and Vinay Swamy, eds. *Screening Integration: Recasting Maghrebi Immigration in Contemporary France.* Lincoln: University of Nebraska Press, 2011.

Dwyer, Kevin. *Beyond Casablanca: M. A. Tazi and the Adventure of Moroccan Cinema.* Bloomington: Indiana University Press, 2004.

———. "'Hidden, Unsaid, Taboo' in Moroccan Cinema: Adelkader Lagtaa's Challenge to Authority." *Framework* 43, no. 2 (2002): 117–33.

———. "Moroccan Filmmaking: A Long Voyage Through the Straits of Paradox." In *Everyday Life in the Muslim Middle East,* edited by Donna Lee Bowen and Evelyn A. Early, Bloomington: Indiana University Press, 2002.

El Khodari, Khalid. *Guide des réalisateurs marocains.* Rabat: El Maarif Al Jadida, 2000.

Elena, Alberto, ed. *Las mil y una imágenes de cine marroqui.* Las Palmas: Festival Internacional de Cine de las Palmas de Gran Canaria, 2007.

Farid, Samir. *Arab Film Guide.* Cairo: Samir Farid, 1979.

———. "Periodisation of Egyptian Cinem." In *Screens of Life: Critical Film Writing from the Arab World,* edited by Alia Arasoughly, 1–18. Quebec: World Heritage Press, 1998.

FEPACI. *L'Afrique et le centenaire du cinéma/Africa and the Centenary of Cinema*. Paris: Présence Africaine, 1995.

Fertat, Ahmed. *Une passion nommée cinéma: vie et oeuvres de Mohamed Osfour*. Tangier: Altopress, 2000.

Festival: Images du monde arabe. Paris: Institut du Monde Arabe, 1993.

Film in Algerien ab 1970. Berlin: *Kinemathek* 57, 1978.

Friedman, Yael. "Palestinian Filmmaking in Israel: Negotiating Conflicting Discourses." PhD diss., Westminster University, London, 2010.

Gabous, Abdelkrim. *Silence, elles tournent!: Les femmes et le cinéma en Tunisie*. Tunis: Cérès Editions/CREDIF, 1998.

Garcia, Jean-Pierre. *Itinéraires: les cinéastes africains au festival de Cannes*. Paris: Ministère de la Coopération, 1997.

Gariazzo, Giuseppe. *Breve storia del cinema africano*. Turin: Lindau, 2001.

———. *Poetiche del cinema africano*. Turin: Lindau, 1998.

Gertz, Nurith, and George Khleifi. *Palestinian Cinema: Landscape, Trauma and Memory*. Edinburgh: Edinburgh University Press, 2008.

Ghazoul, Ferial J., ed. *Arab Cinematics: Toward the New and the Alternative*. Cairo: American University in Cairo, 1995.

Givanni, June, ed. *Symbolic Narratives/African Cinema: Audiences, Theory and the Moving Image*. London: British Film Institute, 2000.

Gugler, Josef. *African Film: Re-Imagining a Continent*. London: James Currey, 2003.

Gugler, Josef, ed. *Film in the Middle East and North America: Creative Dissidence*. Austin: University of Texas Press, 2011.

———. *Ten Arab Filmmakers: Political Dissent and Social Critique*. Bloomington: Indiana University Press, 2015.

Gutberlet, Marie-Hélène, and Hans-Peter Metzler, eds. *Afrikanisches Kino*. Bad Honnef: Horlemann/ARTE, 1997.

Hadj-Moussa, Rahiba. *Le Corps, l'histoire, le territoire: les rapports de genre dans le cinéma algérien*. Paris: Publisud and Edition Balzac, 1994.

———. "The Locus of Tension: Gender in Algerian Cinema." In *African Cinema: Post-Colonial and Feminist Readings*, edited by Kenneth W. Harrow, 255–76. Trenton, NJ: Africa World Press, 1999.

Hafez, Sabry. "The Quest for/Obsession with the National in Arabic Cinema." In *Theorising National Cinema*, edited by Valentina Vitali and Paul Willemen, 226–53. London: BFI Publishing, 2006.

Hakki, Haytham. "Regard sur le documentaire syrien." In *Festival: Images du monde arabe*, 80–111. Paris: Institut du Monde Arabe, 1993.

Hamzaoui, Hamid. *Histoire du cinéma égyptien*. Marseilles: Editions Autres Temps, 1997.

Haustrate, Gaston. "Irak: Mutation prometteuse du secteur cinéma." *Cinema 78* 233 (1978): 64–65.

Hawal, Kassem. "Regard sur le cinéma irakien." *Septième biennale des cinémas arabes*, 99–113. Paris: Institut du Monde Arabe, 2004.

Hennebelle, Guy, and Janine Euvrard, eds. *Israel Palestine: Que peut le cinéma*. Paris: Société Africaine d'Edition, 1978.

Hennebelle, Guy, and Khémais Khayati, eds. *La Palestine et le cinéma*. Paris: E. 100, 1977.

Hennebelle, Guy, Mouny Berrah, and Benjamin Stora, eds. *La Guerre d'Algérie à l'écran*. Paris: Corlet, 1997.

Higbee, Will. *Post Beur Cinema: North African Émigré and Maghrebi Filmmaking in France since 2000*. Edinburgh: Edinburgh University Press, 2014.

Hillauer, Rebecca. *Encyclopedia of Arab Women Filmmakers*. Translated by Allison Brown, Deborah Cohen, and Nancy Joyce. Cairo: American University in Cairo Press, 2005. Originally published as *Freiräume—Lebensträume, Arabische Filmemacherinnen* (Unkel am Rhein: Arte-Edition, 2001).

Hotait, Laila. "Itinéraire des cinéastes libanais de l'après-guerre: le parcours d'une reconstruction." In *Itinéraires esthétiques et scènes culturelles au Proche Orient*, edited by Nicolas Puig and Franck Mermier, 204–19. Beirut: Presses de l'Ifpo, 2007.

Ibrahim, Abbas Fadhil. "Le cinéma irakien: un accouchement de quarante ans." In *Les Cinémas arabes*, edited by Mouny Berrah, Jacques Lévy, and Claude-Michel Cluny, 76–83. Paris: Institut du Monde Arabe, 1987.

Image(s) du Maghrébin dans le cinéma français. Paris: *Grand Maghreb*, 1989.

Images et représentations des Maghrébins dans le cinéma en France. Paris: *Migrance*, 2011.

Images et visages du cinéma algérien. Algiers: ONCIC, Ministère de la Culture et du Tourisme, 1984.

"The Iraqi Cinema in 1964." In *The Cinema in the Arab Countries*, ed. Georges Sadoul, 185–86. Beirut: Interarab Centre of Cinema and Television, 1966.

Ismaël. *Cinéma en Tunisie*. Tunis: Arts Distribution, 2008.

Jabbour, Diana. "Syrian Cinema: Culture and Ideology." In *Screens of Life: Critical Film Writing from the Arab World*, edited by Alia Arasoughly, 40–62. Quebec: World Heritage Press, 1998.

Jabre, Farid. "The Industry in the Lebanon." In *The Cinema in the Arab Countries*, edited by Georges Sadoul, 172–78. Beirut: Interarab Center for Cinema and Television, 1966.

Jaïdi, Moulay Driss. *Cinégraphiques*. Rabat: Collection al majal, 1995.

———. *Cinéma et société*. Rabat: Almajal, 2010.

———. *Diffusion et audience des 11rabes audioivisuels*. Rabat: Collection al majal, 2000.

———. *Histoire du 11rabes au Maroc, le 11rabes colonial*. Rabat: Collection al majal, 2001.

———. *Public(s) et 11rabes*. Rabat: Collection al majal, 1992.

———. *Vision(s) de la société marocaine à travers le court métrage*. Rabat: Collection al majal, 1994.

Jemni, Mahmoud. *Quarante ans de 11rabes tunisien*. Tunis: Jemni, 2007.

Jibril, Mohamed. "Cinéma marocain, l'improbable image de soi." In *Le Maroc en mouvement: créations contemporaines*, edited by Nicole de Pontcharra and Maati Kabbal, 179–84. Paris: Maisonneuve & Larose, 2000.

Joyard, Olivier. "La Palestine dans l'œil d'Elia Suleiman le niomade." *Cahiers du Cinéma* 572 (2002): 12–19.

Karmy, Boulos. "Le rabes palestinien: en attendant la fiction." In *Les Cinémas 11rabes*, edited by Mouny Berrah, Jacques Lévy, and Claude-Michel Cluny, 90–93. Paris: Institut du Monde, 1987.

Kchir-Bendana, Kmar. "Ideologies of the Nation in Tunisian Cinema." In *Nation, Society and Culture in North Africa*, edited by James McDougall, 35–42. London: Frank Cass, 2003.

Kennedy-Day, Kiki. "Cinema in Lebanon, Syria, Iraq and Kuwait." In *Companion Encyclopedia of Middle Eastern and North African Film*, edited by Oliver Leaman, 364–419. London: Routledge, 2001.

Khalil, Andrea, ed. *North African Cinema in a Global Context: Through the Lens of the Diasopora*. New York: Routledge, 2008.

Khalil, Andrea Flores. "Images That Come Out at Night: A Film Trilogy by Moncef Dhouib." *Celaan* 1, nos. 1–2 (2002): 71–80.

Khamarou, Samir. "Le cinéma documentaire en Irak de 1940 à 1980." In *La Semaine du Cinéma Arabe*, 55–60. Paris: Institut du Monde Arabe, 1987.

Khatib, Lina. *Filming the Modern Middle East: Politics in the Cinemas of Hollywood and the Arab World*. London: I. B. Tauris, 2006.

———. *"Kan ya ma kan Beirut/Once upon a Time in Beirut."* In *The Cinema of North Africa and the Middle East*, edited by Gönül Dönmez-Colin, 156–66. London: Wallflower Press, 2007.

———. *Lebanese Cinema: Imagining the Civil War and Beyond*. London: I. B. Tauris, 2008.

Khayati, Khémais. "Cinéma arabe, cinéma dans le tiers monde, cinéma militant . . ." Interview by Jean Jonassaint. *Dérives* 3–4 (1976): 3–16.

———. *Cinémas arabes, topographie d'une image éclaté*. Paris: Editions L'Harmattan, 1996.

———. *En désespoir d'image: Chroniques de cinéma et de television*. Tunis: Editions Sahar, 2000.

———. "The Palestinian Cinema." In *Il cinema dei paesi arabi/Arab Film Festival*, 4th ed., edited by Anna Di Martino, Andrea Morini, and Michele Capasso, 71–79. Naples: Fondazione Labatorio Mediterraneo, 1997.

———. "La Problématique de la liberté individuelle dans le cinéma arabe." In *L'image dans le monde arabe*, edited by Gilbert Beaugé and Jean-François Clément, 305–10. Paris: CNRS Éditions, 1995.

———. *Salah Abou Seif: cinéaste égyptien*. Paris: Sindbad, 1993.

Khélil, Hédi. *Abécédaire du cinéma tunisien*. Tunis, Hédi Khélil, 2007.

———. *Le Parcours et la trace, témoignages et documents sur le cinéma tunisien*. Salammbô: MediaCon, 2002.

———. "Representations de la femme dans le cinéma tunisien." In *L'Image de la femme au Maghreb*, edited by Khadija Mohsen-Finan, 47–70. Le Méjan: Actes Sud & Algiers: Editions Barzakh, 2008.

———. *Résistances et utopies, essais sur le cinéma arabe et africain*. Tunis: Édition Sahar, 1994.

Khemir, Nacer. *Das Verlorene Halsband der Taube*. Baden: Lars Müller, 1992.

Khleifi, Michel. *Noce en Galilée*. Paris: L'Avant-scène Cinéma, 1988.

Khlifi, Omar. *L'Histoire du cinéma en Tunisie*. Tunis: Société de Diffusion, 1970.

Khoury, Lucienne. "History of the Lebanese Cinema." In *The Cinema in the Arab Countries*, edited by Georges Sadoul, 120–24. Beirut: Interarab Cinter for Cinema and Television, 1966.

Kilani, Dr. Ibrahim, and Salah Dehni. "The Cinema and Television in Syria, Their History and Future.' In *Arab Cinema and Culture*, vol. 3, 52–113. Beirut: Arab Film and Television Centre, 1964.

Krifat, Michel. "Gros plan sur le cinéma palestinien." In *6e Biennale des cinémas arabes à Paris*, 93–127. Paris: Institut du Monde Arabe, 2002.

Kummer, Ida, ed. *Cinéma Maghrébin*. Saratoga Springs: *Celaan* 1, nos. 1–2 (2002).

La semaine du cinéma arabe. Paris: Institut du Monde Arabe, 1987.

La Tunisie: Annuaire 1995 (Etats des lieux du cinéma en Afrique). Paris: Association des Trois Mondes/FEPACI, 1995.

Lang, Robert. *New Tunisian Cinema: Allegories of Resistance*. New York: Columbia University Press, 2014.

Lanza, Federica. *La donna nel cinema maghrebino*. Rome: Bulzoni Editore, 1999.

Leaman, Oliver, ed. *Companion Encyclopedia of Middle Eastern and North African Film*. London: Routledge, 2001.

Léon, Marys, and Magda Wassef, ed. "L'image de la femme dans le cinéma arabe." *CinémArabe*, nos. 10–11 (1978): 55–73.

Lequeret, Elisabeth. *Le Cinéma africain: un continent à la recherche de son propre regard*. Paris: Scérén, 2003.

Les cinémas d'Afrique: dictionnaire. Paris: Éditions Karthala and Éditions ATM, 2000.

Lledo, Jean-Pierre. "Le cinéma documentaire et la revolution." In *Art et engagement: Actes du colloque en hommage à Abdelhamid Benzine*. Algiers, 2008.

Mahajar, Jaffar. "The Transformation of the Act of Narration: Strategies of Adaptation of *Al-Qamar w'al-Aswar*." *Alif: Journal of Comparative Politics* 28 (2008): 165–87.

Maherzi, Lotfi. *Le Cinéma algérien: institutions, imaginaire, idéologie*. Algiers: SNED, 1980.

Malas, Mohamed. "*The Dream*: Extracts from a Film Diary." In *Arab Cinematics: Toward the New and the Alternative*, edited Ferial J. Ghazoul, 208–28. Cairo: American University in Cairo, 1999.

———. "Le cauchemar palestinien." Interview by Hubert Corbin. In *Actes des 9e Rencontres*, 115–16. Montpellier: Festival de Montpellier, 1987.

———. "The State of Things." In *Il cinema dei paesi arabi*, edited by Andrea Morini, Anna Di Morini, and Adriano Aprà, 150–155. Venice: Marsilio Editori, 1993.

Malkmus, Lizbeth. "A Desk between Two Borders" and "Merzak Allouache: An Interview." *Framework* 29 (1985): 16–41.

Malkmus, Lizbeth, and Roy Armes. *Arab and African Film Making*. London: Zed Books, 1991.

Mandelbaum, Jacques. "Au Moyen-Orient, tous les cinéastes sont des Palestiniens." In *Au sud du cinéma*, edited by Jean-Michel Frodon, 60–73. Paris: Cahiers du Cinéma, 2004.

Mansour, Guillemette. *Samama Chikly, un tunisien à la rencontre du XXième siècle*. Tunis: Simpact Editions, 2000.

Mansouri, Hassouna. *De l'identité ou Pour une certaine tendance du cinéma africain*. Tunis: Editions Sahar, 2000.

Marei, Salah, and Magda Wassef, eds. *Chadi Abdel Salam: le pharaon du cinéma égyptien*, Paris: Institut du Monde Arabe, 1996.

Martin, Florence. "Tunisia." In *The Cinema of Small Nations*, edited by Mette Hjort and Duncan Petrie, 213–28. Edinburgh: Edinburgh University Press, 2007.

Martin, Florence. *Screens and Veils: Maghrebi Women's Cinema*. Bloomington: Indiana University Press, 2011.

Masri, Maï, and Jean Chamoun. "Contre la guerre-spectacle." Interview by Hubert Corbin and Michèle Driguez in *Actes des 10e Rencontres Cinématographiques*, 91–97. Montpellier: Festival de Montpellier, 1998.

Megherbi, Abdelghani. *Le Miroir aux alouettes*. Algiers: ENAL, UPU, GAM, 1985.

———. *Les Algériens au miroir du cinéma colonial*. Algiers: SNED, 1982.

Mekouar, Mouna. *Daoud Aoulad-Syad*. Paris: Filigranes Éditions, 2015.

Miduni, Hamid. *Ahmed Baha Eddine Attia: Une vie comme au cinema*. Tunis: Editions Rives Productions, 2008.

Millet, Raphaël. *Cinémas de la Méditerranée, cinémas de la mélancolie*. Paris: Éditions L'Harmattan, 2002.

Milò, Giuliva. *Lecture et pratique de l'Histoire dans l'œuvre d'Assia Djebar*. Brussels: Peter Lang, 2007.

Mimoun, Mouloud, ed. *France-Algérie, images d'une guerre*. Paris: Institut du Monde Arabe, 1992.

Mohammad, Oussama. "A Conversation." Interview with Luisa Ceretto and Andrea Morini. *Il cinema dei paesi arabi/Arab Film Festival*, 4th ed., edited by Anna Di Martino, Andrea Morini, and Michele Capasso, 161–64. Venice: Marsilio Editori, 1993.

———. "Quand les gens sont sinceres, ils se ressemblent." Interview by Henri Talvat in *Actes des 10e Rencontres Cinématographiques*, 98–100. Montpellier: Festival de Montpellier, 1998.

Mondolini, Dominique, ed. *Cinémas d'Afrique*. Paris: ADPF (*Notre Librairie* 149), 2002.

Moumen, Touti. *Films tunisiens: longs métrages 1967–98*. Tunis: Touti Moumen, 1998.

Mounir, Zamni. "Le cinéma syrien au passé et au présent." In *La Semaine du Cinéma Arabe*, 67–71. Paris: Institut du Monde Arabe, 1987.

Murphy, David, and Patrick Williams. "Youssef Chahine." In *Postcolonial African Cinema: Ten Directors*, 30–49. Manchester: Manchester University Press, 2007.

N'Zelomona, Berthin. *La Francophonie*. Paris: L'Harmattan, 2001.

Naudillon, Françoise, Janusz Przychodzen, and Sathya Rao, eds. *L'Afrique fait son cinéma: Regards et perspectives sur le cinéma africain francophone*. Montreal: Mémoire d'Encrier, 2006.

Nicholas, Kostandi. "The Cinema and Television in the Hashemite Kingdom of Jordan." In *Arab Cinema and Culture*, vol. 3, 22–25. Beirut: Arab Film and Television Centre, 1964.

Nouri, Shakir. *A la recherche du cinéma irakien, 1945–1985*. Paris: Editions L'Harmattan, 1986.

Orlando, Valérie K. *Francophone Voices of the "New" Morocco in Film and Print: (Re) presenting a Society in Transition*. New York: Palgrave Macmillan, 2009.

Où va le cinéma algérien?. Paris: *Cahiers du Cinéma*, hors-série, February–March 2003.

Paquet, André. *Cinéma en Tunisie*. Montreal: Bibliothèque Nationale de Québec, 1974.

Petiot, Benoîte, and Pierre Petiot. "Syrie, métaphores et réalités historiques." Round table discussion with Mohamed Malas and Nabil al-Maleh in *Actes des 21e Rencontres*, 30–34. Montpellier: Festival de Montpellier, 1999.

Petiot, Pierre. *Méditerranée. Le génie du cinéma*. Montpellier: Indigène Éditions, 2009.

Pour une promotion du cinéma national. Rabat: Centre Cinématographique Marocain, 1993.

Quarante Ans de Cinéma Algérien. Algiers: Dar Raïs Hamidou, 2002.

Ramahi, Suyan. "Cinéma palestinien." In *La Semaine du Cinéma Arabe*, 61–66. Paris: Institut du monde Arabe, 1987.

Regard sur le cinéma au Maroc. Rabat: Centre Cinématographique Marocain, 1995.

Rocca, Anna. *Assia Djebar, le corps invisible—Voir sans être vue*. Paris: Éditions L'Harmattan, 2004.

Russell, Sharon A. *Guide to African Cinema*. Westport: Greenwood Press, 1998.

Sakr, Naomi, ed. *Women and Media in the Middle East: Power through Self-Expression*. London: I. B. Tauris, 2004.

Salah, Rassa Mohamed. *35 ans de cinéma tunisien*. Tunis: Éditions Sahar, 1992.

Salhab, Sabine, ed. *Cinéma: Le Moyen Orient sous les projecteurs*. Paris: Les Cahiers de l'Orient, 2012.

Salmane, Hala, Simon Hartog, and David Wilson, eds. *Algerian Cinema*. London: British Film Institute, 1976.

Salti, Rasha, ed. *Insights into Syrian Cinema: Essays and Conversations with Contemporary Filmmakers*. New York: Rattapallax Press, 2006.

Salti, Rasha. "*Nujum al-Nahar/Stars in Broad Daylight*." In *The Cinema of North Africa and the Middle East*, edited by Gönül Dönmez-Colin, 101–10. London: Wallflower Press, 2007.

Salti, Rasha. "From Resistance and Bearing Witness to the Power of the Fantastical: Icons and Symbols in Palestinian Poetry and Cinema." In *Third Text* 102 (24) (2010): 39–52.

Sandrini, Luca, ed. *Luminescenze: Panoramiche sui cinema d'Africa*. Verona: Cierre Edizoni, 1998.

Serceau, Michel, ed. *Cinémas du Maghreb*. Paris: Corlet, 2004.

Shafik, Viola. *Arab Cinema: History and Cultural Identity*. Cairo: American University in Cairo Press, 1998. Originally published in German as *Der arabische Film: Geschichte und kulturelle Identität* (Bielefeld: Aisthesis Verlag, 1996).

———. "Egyptian Cinema." In *Companion Encyclopedia of Middle Eastern and North African Film*, edited by Oliver Leaman, 3–129. New York: Routledge, 2001.

Shiri, Keith, ed. *Directory of African Film-Makers and Films*. London: Flicks Books, 1992.

Shohat, Ella. *Israeli Cinema: East/West and the Politics of Representation*. 2nd rev. ed. London: I. B. Tauris, 2010.

Smihi, Moumen. *Écrire sur le cinéma: Idées clandestines 1*. Tangiers: Slaïki Frères, 2006.

Soil, Daniel, ed. *Parcours de cinema*. Tunis: Ceres Éditions, 2010.

Souiba, Fouad, and Fatima Zahra el Alaoui. *Un siècle de cinéma au Maroc*. Rabat: World Design Communication, 1995.

Srour, Heiny. "Femme, Arabe . . . et Cinéaste." *CinemArabe* 4–5 (1976): 34–42.

Stollery, Martin. "Masculinities, Generations, and Cultural Transformation in Contemporary Tunisian Cinema." *Screen* 42, no. 1 (2001): 9–63.

Taboulay, Camille. *Mohamed Chouikh* (long interview plus script of *L'Arche du désert*). Paris: K Films Éditions, 1997.

Tarr, Carrie. "Questions of Identity in Beur Cinema: From *Tea in the Harem* to *Cheb*." *Screen* 34, no. 4 (1993): 321–42.

Thoraval, Yves. "Égypte, de la littérature au réalisme cinématographique." *Mésogeios* 15 (2002): 107–23.

———. *Les cinémas du Moyen-Orient: Iran, Égypte, Turquie*. Paris: Séguier, 2000.

———. *Les écrans du croissant fertile: Irak, Liban, Palestine, Syrie*. Paris: Séguier, 2002.

———. *Regards sur le cinéma égyptien*. Beirut: Dar El-Machreq, 1975.

Thouard, Sylvie, ed. "Palestine-Israel—territoires cinématographiques." *La Revue Documentaire* 19–29 (2005): 5–124.

Tlatli, Moufida. *Les silences du palais* (script). Paris: L'Avant-scène, 2004.

Tsoffar, Ruth. *"Forget Baghdad: Jews and Arabs—The Iraqi Connection."* In *The Cinema of North Africa and the Middle East,* edited by Gönül Dönmez-Colin, 256–65. London: Wallflower Press, 2007.

Venturini, Fabrice. *Mehdi Charef, conscience esthétique de la génération "beur."* Biarritz: Séguier, 2005.

Vieyra, Paulin Soumanou. *Le Cinéma africain des origines à 1973.* Paris: Présence Africaine, 1975.

———. *Le Cinéma et l'Afrique.* Paris: Présence Africaine, 1969.

Wazen, Abdo. "War as Subject for Cinema." In *Arab Cinematics: Towards the New and the Alternative,* edited by Ferial J. Ghazoul, 229–234. Cairo: American University in Cairo Press, 1995.

Westmoreland, Mark. "Cinematic Dreaming: On Phantom Poetics and the Longing for a Lebanese National Cinema." *Text, Practice, Performance* 4 (2002): 33–50.

White, Jerry. "Children, Narrative and Third Cinema in Iran and Syria." *Canadian Journal of Film Studies* 11, no. 1 (2002): 78–97.

Zaccak, Hady. *Le cinéma libanais: itinéraire d'un cinéma vers l'inconnu (1929–1996).* Beirut: Dar el-Machreq, 1997.

Zikra, Samir. "A Conversation." Interview by Luisa Ceretto and Andrea Morini. In *Il cinema dei paesi arabi/Arab Film Festival,* 4th ed., edited by Anna Di Martino, Andrea Morini, and Michele Capasso, 165–69. Venice: Marsilio Editori, 1993.

———. "A force de mentir, on finit par se croire." Interview by Hubert Corbin in *Actes des 9e Rencontres,* 110–14. Montpellier: Festival de Montpellier, 1987.

A Selection of Other Creative Works by Arab Filmmakers

Allouache, Merzak. *Bab el-Oued.* Casablanca: Éditions le Fennec, 1995.

Aoulad-Syad, Daoud. *Boujaâd, Espace et mémoire* (photographs). Paris: Datapress, 1996.

———. *Marocains* (photographs). Paris: Contrejour/Belvisi, 1989.

Aoulad-Syad, Daoud (photographs), and Ahmed Bouanani (poems). *Territoires de l'instant.* Paris: Éditions de l'Oeil, 2000.

Bouanani, Ahmed. *L'hôpital.* Lagrasse: Editions Verdier, 2012.

Charef, Mehdi. *À bras-le-cœur.* Paris: Mercure de France, 2006.

———. *Le harki de Meriem.* Paris: Mercure de France, 1989.

———. *La maison d'Alexina.* Paris: Mercure de France, 1999.

———. *Le thé au harem d'Archi Ahmed.* Paris: Mercure de France, 1983. Translated as *Tea in the Harem.* London: Serpent's Tail, 1996.

Djebar, Assia. *Ces voix qui m'assiègent.* Paris: Albin Michel, 1999.

———. *Femmes d'Alger dans leur appartement.* Paris: Editions des Femmes, 2001. Translated as *Women of Algiers in Their Appartment.* Charlottesville: University of Virginia Press, 1992.

———. *La Disparition de la langue française.* Paris: Albin Michel, 2003.

———. *La Femme sans sépulcre.* Paris: Albin Michel, 2002.

———. *L'amour, la fantasia.* Paris: Albin Michel, 1985. Translated in English as *Fantasia: An Algerian Cavalcade* (London: Quartet Books, 1985).

———. *Le Blanc de l'Algérie.* Paris: Albin Michel, 1996. Translated in English as *Algerian White* (New York: Seven Stories Press, 2001).

———. *Les enfants du nouveau monde.* Paris: Union Générale d'Editions, 1983.

———. *Les nuits de Strasbourg.* Le Méjan: Actes Sud, 1997.

———. *Loin de Médine.* Paris: Albin Michel, 1991. Translated in English as *Far from Madina* (London: Quartet Books, 1994).

———. *Nulle part dans la maison de mon père.* Paris: Fayard, 2007.

———. *Ombre sultane.* Paris: Lattès, 1987. Translated in English as *A Sister to Scheherazade* (Portsmouth, NJ: Heineman, 1993).

———. *Oran, langue morte.* Le Méjan: Actes Sud, 1997. Translated in English as *The Tongue's Blood Does Not Run Dry: Algerian Stories* (New York: Seven Stories Press, 2009).

———. *Vaste est la prison.* Paris: Albin Michel, 1995. Translated in English as *So Vast the Prison* (New York: Seven Stories Press, 1999).

Genini, Izza, and Jean du Boisberranger. *Maroc* (photographs). Paris: Richer/Hoa Qui, 1995.

Genini, Izza, Jacques Bravo, and Xavier Richer. *Maroc—Royaume des mille et une fêtes.* Paris: Editions Plume, 1998.

Ghalem, Ali. *Une femme pour mon fils.* Paris: Syros, 1979.

Hellal, Abderrezak. *Place de la Régence.* Paris: L'Harmattan, 1989.

Khemir, Nacer. *Gran-père est né.* Bordeaux: Le Mascaret, 1985.

———. *J'avale le bébé du voisin.* Paris: Editions La Découverte & Syros, 2000.

———. *L'alphabet des sables.* Paris: Syros, 1998.

———. *La quête d'Hassan de Samarkand.* Arles: Actes Sud Junior, 2003.

———. *Le chant des génies.* Arles: Actres Sud Junior, 2001.

———. *Le conte des conteurs.* Paris: Editions La Découverte, 1984. Reissued as *Le conte des conteurs* (Paris: Syros Jeunesse, 2001).

———. *Le juge, la mouche et la grand-mère.* Paris: Editions La Découverte & Syros, 2000.

———. *Le livre des djinns.* Paris: Syros Jeunesse, 2002.

———. *L'ogresse.* Paris: Éditions La Découverte, 1991. Reissued *L'ogresse* (Paris: La Découverte & Syros, 2001).

———. *Paroles d'Islam.* Paris: Albin Michel, 1994.

Khémir, Nacer, and Oum el Khir. *Chahrazade.* Bordeaux: Le Mascaret, 1988.

Lagtaâ, Abdelkader. *Éloge d'errance.* Paris: Edilivre, 2014.

———. *Perte d'équilibre.* Paris: Edilivre, 2015.

———. *Québec je me souviens.* Paris: Edilivre, 2014.

Meddour, Azzedine. *La montagne de Baya.* Algiers: Editions Marinoor, 1997.

Saddiki, Tayeb. *Le dîner de gala.* Casablanca: EDDIF, 1990.

———. *Les sept grains de beauté.* Casablanca: EDDIF, 1994.

———. *Molière, ou Pour l'amour de l'humanité.* Casablanca: EDDIF, 1994.

Salhab, Ghassan. *Fragments du livre du naufrage.* Beirut: Amers Éditions, 2011.

Zinaï-Koudil, Hafsa. *La fin d'un rêve.* Algiers: ENAL, 1984.

———. *Le papillon ne volera pas.* Algiers: ENAP, 1990.

———. *Le pari perdu.* Algiers: ENAL, 1986.

———. *Le passé d'composé.* Algiers: ENAl, 1993.

———. *Sans voix.* Paris: Plon, 1997.

Index

ROY ARMES is professor emeritus of film at Middlesex University. He has published widely on world cinema for the past fifty years, with over twenty books, contributions to sixty collectively authored volumes, and some two hundred journal articles and shorter pieces. His initial concern was with European film history (France, Italy, and the United Kingdom) and aspects of cinematic modernism. More recently, his research—beginning with the widely distributed *Third World Film Making and the West* in 1987—has focused on third-world issues and, especially, on African and Arab cinemas: *Arab and African Film Making* (with Lizbeth Malkmus, 1991), *Dictionary of North African Film Makers/Dictionnaire des Cinéastes du Maghreb* (1996), *Omar Gatlato* (1998), *Postcolonial Images: Studies in North African Film* (2005), *African Filmmaking: North and South of the Sahara* (2006), *Dictionary of African Filmmakers* (2008), *Arab Filmmakers of the Middle East: A Dictionary* (2010), and *New Voices in Arab Cinema* (2015). His work has been translated into fourteen languages, with books in French, Spanish, (Brazilian) Portuguese, Turkish, Hebrew, Arabic, Japanese, and Chinese.

0 1341 1717892 8

CPSIA information can be obtained
at www.ICGtesting.com
Printed in the USA
FFHW02n1432100818
47740852-51412FF

9 780253 031723